The Cathedral

William R. Cook, Ph.D.

THE
GREAT
COURSES™

PUBLISHED BY:

THE GREAT COURSES
Corporate Headquarters
4840 Westfields Boulevard, Suite 500
Chantilly, Virginia 20151-2299
Phone: 1-800-832-2412
Fax: 703-378-3819
www.thegreatcourses.com

William R. Cook, Ph.D.

Distinguished Teaching Professor of History
State University of New York at Geneseo

Professor William R. Cook was born and raised in Indianapolis, Indiana, and attended public schools there. He is a 1966 graduate of Wabash College in Crawfordsville, Indiana (cum laude, Phi Beta Kappa). He received Woodrow Wilson and Herbert Lehman fellowships to study Medieval History at Cornell University, where he received his Ph.D. in 1971.

In 1970, Professor Cook was appointed Assistant Professor of History at the State University of New York (SUNY) at Genesco, the honors college of SUNY. He has taught there for 40 years, teaching courses in medieval and ancient history, the Renaissance and Reformation periods, and the Bible and Christian thought, and currently holds the rank of Distinguished Teaching Professor of History. He recently taught a course on Alexis de Tocqueville and freshman seminars that focus on several aspects of African American history and American politics. For two years (2008–2010), Professor Cook returned to teach at Wabash College, his alma mater, as Visiting Professor of Religion and History. In 2010, Wabash conferred on him the honorary degree of Doctor of Humane Letters.

In 1992, Professor Cook was named CASE Professor of the Year for New York State. He received the first-ever CARA Award for Excellence in the Teaching of Medieval Studies from the Medieval Academy of America in 2003. He was recently named the alternate for the Robert Foster Cherry Award for Great Teaching, receiving a prize of $15,000 plus a substantial award to his department.

After publishing several articles on Hussite theology and monastic thought during his early career, Professor Cook has, for the past 30 years, focused much of his research on Saint Francis of Assisi. Since 1989, Professor Cook has published three books about Saint Francis and how he is represented in paintings in Italy. Professor Cook has also contributed to the *Cambridge Companion to Giotto* and is the editor of and a contributor to *The Art of the Franciscan Order in Italy*.

Professor Cook spends part of each year doing research and teaching in Italy. From his base in Siena, he works frequently in Florence, as well as Assisi. He has taken students from SUNY Geneseo to Italy on eight occasions and conducts study tours for the public. In recent years, Professor Cook has been a lecturer and site-visit leader for the Young Presidents' Organization and Chief Executives Organization, groups of corporate leaders from around the world. He has participated in their programs in Florence, Prague, Istanbul, Dublin, Kyoto, and Paris. In 2005, he was invited by the Friends of Florence, a group of philanthropists dedicated to preserving works of art in Tuscany, to make presentations for the group's fall meeting in Florence; he now presents programs for the group in Florence each February.

Professor Cook has directed 11 Summer Seminars for School Teachers for the National Endowment for the Humanities (NEH) since 1983; 7 have had Saint Francis as their subject and were conducted in Siena and Assisi. In 2003, 2006, and 2008, he directed NEH seminars for college teachers in Italy titled Saint Francis and the 13th Century.

In addition to his research in Italy, Professor Cook has studied the writings of Alexis de Tocqueville. This interest came about primarily after Professor Cook's unsuccessful run in 1998 for a seat in the U.S. House of Representatives. He has written three volumes of western New York history and writes a weekly column for his local newspaper, *The Livingston County News*. He was also a frequent contributor to the editorial pages of the Rochester *Democrat and Chronicle* in 2004–2005. ∎

Table of Contents

Table of Contents

Table of Contents

The Cathedral

Scope:

The modern mind cannot comprehend the symbolic—and real—power that the cathedral has held for much of the past 2,000 years of Western civilization. Rising to the heavens, a three-dimensional manifestation of art, science, and religious fervor, a cathedral was the local seat of power, community, worship, and often economics.

To understand the deep historical, religious, social, and architectural context that makes a serious study of the cathedral possible, we start at the beginning with the development of cathedrals: Why did they come about and when? Why did they take on a particular shape? Who designed and built them, and for what purpose?

After exploring cathedrals from the earliest eras, we will become familiar with the monumental style of church architecture and decoration that we call Romanesque. We will then turn our attention to the Gothic style, developed in the area around Paris in the second half of the 12th century. It became the predominant form of church architecture for the next 300 years and beyond and is the main focus of our course.

Many of Europe's most famous Gothic cathedrals will be featured, starting with the church recognized as the first Gothic structure: Saint-Denis in Paris. From there, many of the lectures will examine the most famous Gothic cathedrals of northern France, including Notre Dame, Chartres, Amiens, Laon, and Reims. Although that region is considered the birthplace of Gothic, we will follow the spread of the style to other parts of Europe, including England, Germany, Spain, Italy, the Czech Republic, and even the New World.

Although Gothic architecture is usually associated with pointed arches and flying buttresses, in fact it contains a wide range of forms, and we will see that no two Gothic churches are alike. So as we progress, we will look carefully at the "story" of each cathedral: geographic orientation, local influences, individual stylistic innovations, and unique features, including architectural design, detailed exterior sculpture, exquisite stained-glass windows, and precious relics.

Although the Gothic era is in some senses long past, we will finish with a look at the Gothic revival in modern times and the extraordinary array of neo-Gothic buildings found on every continent and probably in the town or city where you live.

This course is profusely illustrated by 3-D animations and photographs, many of which are from your professor's own lens, for his photography work rivals that of any professional. Once you have studied these extraordinary structures, you may very well feel the need to see them in person, whether you are a first-time visitor or a frequent traveler. ■

What Is a Cathedral?

Lecture 1

There are many styles of Christian buildings—St. Paul's in London is very different than St. Peter's in Rome, not to mention Notre Dame in Paris or a modern cathedral. ... But for many people, the Gothic cathedral is, in fact, what a Christian building is supposed to look like.

Many of you have no doubt entered a Gothic building, whether an original in Europe or a modern version in New York City or Washington DC. If you have, likely your first response is awe: These are enormous buildings, full of detail and imagery, shadows and light. Many believe that— artistically and theologically—the Gothic church is one of the great expressions of the truths and values of Christianity. But one need not be a Christian to enjoy, understand, and experience the Gothic cathedral.

© iStockphoto/Thinkstock.

The Gothic style of architecture and decoration offers endless variety and detail for us to explore.

The title of this course is *The Cathedral*, but we will examine other types of Gothic buildings, as well as some of their Romanesque predecessors. For example, what most people regard as the very first Gothic building—Saint-Denis, on the outskirts of Paris—was a Benedictine monastery. We will glimpse some so-called Cistercian Half-Gothic or Transitional Gothic buildings, built in an architectural style that, today, seems not quite Romanesque and not quite Gothic. We will also look at Franciscan and Dominican churches, college chapels, and royal chapels from the later Middle Ages to see how the Gothic style was used in many kinds of ecclesiastical—and non-ecclesiastical—buildings. Please note that "Gothic" is not a term that was used in the Middle Ages when these buildings were built; it came into wider use in the 18th century, when many looked on these churches as primitive, superstitious, and Catholic. It was not meant kindly; referring to the Germanic Goths, the word meant "barbaric" in a real sense.

Entering a cathedral today is not at all like entering a museum. Virtually all of the buildings we will visit are still in use for worship. Therefore, many have undergone constant updating and remodeling over the centuries. Some have changed because they were damaged during Reformation, revolution, and war or were ravaged by natural disaster, pollution, time, and neglect. Thus we find cathedrals built in the Middle Ages that contain Renaissance, Baroque, Neoclassical, and even modern elements, added as the needs of the building, the community, or the liturgy changed. Many original details, even whole structures, have simply been lost; it is vital—and very expensive—to protect and preserve what is left.

One of the very first buildings we can legitimately call a cathedral is the cathedral of Rome, called St. John Lateran. Originally built in the 4th century on land granted to the church by the Roman emperor Constantine I, this building has been rebuilt many, many times; today, its features are largely Renaissance and Baroque. But it still contains the chair of the **bishop** of Rome—in Latin, a **cathedra**. Hence, in the most literal sense, a cathedral is a building with a cathedra—that is to say, it is the seat of a bishop.

The earliest big churches were built in Rome, but as Christianity spread throughout the Roman Empire, cathedrals followed. Then, as the empire collapsed in the West, the roles of bishops changed. They had apostolic jurisdiction over the Christians (virtually the entire population) in their regions, called **dioceses**; many cathedral cities survived into the Middle Ages primarily as ecclesiastical centers after their other functions essentially disappeared. The traditional duties of Roman administrators more and more fell to bishops. The church developed a body of law, called canon law, administered by bishops, and many secular legal issues in our day were the jurisdiction of the ecclesiastical courts in the Middle Ages. Bishops became wealthy; many people gave the church land, gold, silver, jewels, all kinds of things—perhaps out of piety, perhaps hoping for ecclesiastical or divine favors. It's been estimated that a third of the land in medieval Europe was controlled in some way by the church. Therefore, bishops had significantly more power and played a number of roles in medieval society that they do not play today. In many ways, a city's cathedral came to symbolize the city as a whole—its grandeur, its power, its wealth, and its holiness.

In many ways, a city's cathedral came to symbolize the city as a whole—its grandeur, its power, its wealth, and its holiness.

Cathedrals also often housed the relics of saints, and therefore almost every cathedral in Europe was a place of pilgrimage during the Middle Ages. Cathedrals needed to be big because they were used for large gatherings of people; they weren't so much where you went to mass on Sunday as where people flocked for the great feast days of the church, both universal feasts like Christmas and Easter and local feasts like the feast of San Cerbone in Massa Marittima in Tuscany. Baptisms took place in cathedrals in the early Middle Ages, because there were so few parish churches; in fact, some Italian cathedrals had separate buildings, called baptisteries, on the cathedral grounds for this purpose. Very often, collective baptisms were performed on the feast of a patron saint or on the feast of John the Baptist, so again, cathedrals needed to be big.

Gothic architecture was invented in France, so our focus will lie there. But we will also see the same stylistic elements all around Europe, from Salisbury Cathedral in England to Prague Cathedral in the Czech Republic, and in the New World as well. Each cathedral looks different because each was built in a different time and place to serve a different community, yet we can recognize common elements within all this variety. Ultimately, we will come to understand how all these buildings were built, what they mean, and what they were and are. ■

Important Terms

bishop: The chief ecclesiastical official of a diocese, believed to have the authority in his diocese that Christ gave to his apostles. *See also* **apostolic succession**.

cathedra: The seat or chair of a bishop in a cathedral.

diocese: A territory, usually a city and surrounding countryside, under the ecclesiastical jurisdiction of a bishop.

Suggested Reading

Erlande-Brandenburg, *The Social and Architectural Dynamics of Construction*, introduction, chap. 1.

Wilson, *The Gothic Cathedral*, introduction.

Questions to Consider

1.   What is the necessity for and what are the functions of a cathedral?

2.   Why is a cathedral so different in function from other sorts of churches, such as parish churches?

3.   Which forms of Christianity today have bishops and hence cathedrals?

What Is a Cathedral?

Lecture 1—Transcript

Welcome to this course that's going to deal with cathedrals. I think you're going to enjoy it, not only because the cathedrals are so interesting, but because we have such wonderful visuals for you including some animations, a lot of photographs, and a few diagrams. I think you're going to be able to take a look at the medieval cathedrals that we're going to examine in Europe and even briefly in America and find that it's an extraordinary experience. The experience, though, is something that many of you have no doubt directly had: going into a Gothic building; whether it by a building in New York or Washington, or one of the original, if you will, Gothic cathedrals in Europe. Let's talk about what that's all about.

If you've ever walked into one of these extraordinary buildings, I think our first sense is awe; these are very big buildings. I think also, although there are many styles of Christian buildings—Saint Paul's in London is very different than Saint Peter's in Rome, not to mention Notre Dame in Paris or a modern cathedral like the one in Los Angeles that was just dedicated—but for many people, the Gothic cathedral is, in fact, what a Christian building is supposed to look like; so that if somebody says to you, "I was someplace the other day," doesn't matter where, "and I walked into this great big beautiful church," chances are you're envisioning a Gothic cathedral with some statues, with some stained glass windows, and with a lot of other things that we identify with buildings of this period. Many people also believe that not just artistically but even theologically the Gothic church is one of the great expressions of the truths and values of Christianity: It makes us look up to God; the sculpture on the outside often explains basic truths; and, of course, the most important and essential functions of the Christian church take place inside these buildings (although, of course, not only these buildings, for they also take place in parish churches and even occasionally outdoors).

Let me say that although these buildings are special for Christians, one doesn't need to be a Christian to enjoy, understand, and experience the Gothic cathedral. After all, I'm sure that many of you have been, let's say, to Athens and you have been in the Parthenon, or you've been to Rome and have been in the Pantheon. You don't worship all the gods of the Pantheon or Athena of the Parthenon, and yet we can, I think, in our own minds recreate the experience of those who did come to worship those gods who are no longer worshiped there or just about anywhere in the world. This is an experience for everybody. It's an intellectual experience; and without being confessional, it's a spiritual experience to understand these buildings and how they function and how they operate, and also to have enough historical and artistic context to understand how they came to be and what specific ways they expressed the values, meanings, hopes, aspirations, and sometimes even worldly desires of the people who actually built them.

I had the extraordinary experience of going to Europe for the first time when I was 17, and the first cathedral I visited was the cathedral of Amiens, about 100 kilometers north of Paris. It's an extraordinary building, and certainly the first thing I experienced was awe; it is simply—and I don't like my students overusing this word, but I'm going to use it here—an awesome experience to stand before this building. Look at the image of the cathedral of Amiens: If you look real closely by the left door, you'll see there's a person standing there, and the person's almost invisible in that blue shirt because the building is so enormous. That enormity carries forward into the interior of the cathedral. This is what you see when you walk into Amiens Cathedral: a vault that's about 140 feet above the ground; the light coming in, as you can see; and again, if you look just to the right of center, you'll see a little bitty person—who's really, of course, an average-sized person—standing there, once again giving us a sense of the awesome size and complexity of this structure that was built in the 13th century. We're going to come back to Amiens and look at it in great detail later on; but this was my introduction to Gothic, and therefore I wanted it to be yours. I did that in 1961 when I was 17; but I was just back in Amiens a couple months ago to do some photography for this course, in fact, and I had with me two students from where I'm teaching now, Wabash College in Indiana. To watch them have something of that experience that I had when I was 17 was literally thrilling to me: to have them stand in front of that church and see the facade, and to just sort of watch the breath come out of them as they walk in and look at the interior, which, after all, looked pretty much like it did in 1961 when I walked into Amiens.

Let me make a few general statements about the kinds of buildings we're going to be looking at in this course. Overwhelmingly, we're going to be looking at cathedrals, which are basically the topic of this lecture—what a cathedral is—to define it; but before I do that, let me point out that there are other kinds of Gothic buildings and some of their Romanesque predecessors that we're also going to be looking at.

For example, what most people regard as the very first Gothic building—Saint-Denis, on the outskirts of Paris—is, in fact, not a cathedral but it was a Benedictine monastery; and some of the Romanesque and a little bit of the Gothic that we're going to look at is, in fact, monastic buildings. One particular group of monks, Cistercian monks, an order founded at the end of the 11th century, established in a sense their own kind of architectural style that at least for us today—remember, these are modern categories—are not quite Romanesque and not quite Gothic, and so we sometimes actually call it Cistercian Half Gothic or Transitional Gothic. That's another kind of monastic building we'll be taking some glimpses at. But also, especially as we move on to the later Middle Ages, we're going to be looking at churches of new religious orders—Franciscans and Dominicans, the so-called Mendicant orders—even parish churches, a college chapel in Cambridge, England, and royal chapels; so although the focus is primarily cathedrals, Gothic is a style that, in fact, was used in the building of many kinds of ecclesiastical buildings and, I might add, some non-ecclesiastical buildings: There are Gothic city halls; there are even Gothic homes, although we're not going really to dwell on them.

Let me suggest also that the term "Gothic" is not a term that was used in the Middle Ages when these buildings were built, it is a term that was largely invented and put into use in the 18th century; and in the Enlightenment, where many people looked upon these churches as primitive and representing the superstitious medieval Catholic church, "Gothic" was not a kind term. "Gothic" refers to the Germanic tribe of the Goths, and therefore "Gothic" meant "barbaric" in a real sense. Even though we use the term today as a kind of value neutral term, it was, in fact, a term that was designed to critique, to criticize, and to downgrade these buildings that we're going to be studying.

When one walks into a cathedral today, one does not walk into a completely medieval setup. It's not like, at all, going into a museum; for, after all, virtually all the buildings we're going to look at are still in use as cathedrals and other kinds of churches. That means that they have constantly been remodeled and even redesigned. Remodeled because somebody says, "I want to put a new chapel in this," or "I think we should have a new altar," or whatever it might be; there is a lot of remodeling in newer styles, so you will find cathedrals that are medieval but they have Renaissance, Baroque, Neoclassical, and even modern elements to them; and also, we need to remember that to do the same things, buildings need to change because the liturgy of the church has changed. Most cathedrals have altars that are at the east end of the church, either at the very back end or against a series of columns. Those altars are no longer in use because of the fact that now the priest must face people when he says mass and therefore, in fact, what we find is the new altars—which are usually just simple tables—are put closer to the middle of the church rather than against a wall at the east end of the church. There's this constant rearrangement of things because these are living ecclesiastical buildings that have been functioning by and large, in most cases, for 800 years; they are not museums. They are not meant to look like they did inside the day that the cathedral was built. Of course, we also realize they are remodeled because they now have electric lights, and they now have heating systems and other things, not to mention security, for example.

In addition to the remodeling that takes place, a lot of churches have been changed because of bad things that have happened to them. That began in the Protestant Reformation when in some places churches were not so much torn down but much of the decoration was destroyed; especially in France, a lot of churches were badly damaged during the French Revolution; in Eastern Europe, communist governments destroyed or at least abandoned some churches, and that abandonment and that disuse is costly to old buildings, of course; and, alas, too, we need to remember war. We look here at a photograph of the cathedral of Soissons after World War I, because Soissons was, like many cathedrals especially in the eastern part of France, bombed during World War I, and if you look closely you can see the right half of the roof—that is to say, just to the left of the tower—that's just a skeleton roof; in fact, most of the roof is gone and the vaulting had collapsed at Soissons Cathedral. The good news is, it's all been rebuilt now; but war and all these other things are very bad for cathedrals as it turns out.

We also need to remember that there are other ways in which the churches are damaged. They're damaged by natural causes—fire, earthquakes—but also by modern problems such as industrial pollution. Sometimes one goes to a church and sees that some of the stone, 800 years old, sculpted into figures has been eroded in recent years—you can compare with old photographs from the 19th century—by a lot of industrial pollution. That means a lot of cleaning, a lot of preservation, but it also means that certain things simply are lost; certain kinds of details of sculptures are lost, for example. We must realize a) that the buildings we see are not exactly the buildings that were built in the Middle Ages; and b) it is vital—and by the way, very expensive— to keep these buildings protected. In fact, in many parts of Europe—England in particular—almost all the cathedrals charge fees to go in, although there's always a way to go in free if you go in to pray or for a service. Whatever one thinks of that policy, we at least need to appreciate the fact that these are buildings that take a tremendous amount of upkeep, because I have a house built in 1895 and I know how many things go wrong and when you need the furnace guy, the plumber, and all the rest; you have a building some enormous number of times the size of my house made out of stone, wood, glass, and other things, and we can simply imagine what the upkeep of these buildings must be.

But before we study cathedrals per se, we need to understand how the church is organized so we understand not just physically but in other ways the centrality of these buildings to the medieval church. To do that, we need to focus on the role of the bishop. If we ask ourselves what a bishop is, the answer basically is, "The chief ecclesiastical figure in each region." The idea developed after the apostles died in the first century, those who had followed Jesus around and who were clearly sources of authority when they were alive. But where does that authority go, or does it simply disappear, when the apostles die? The church and various individual congregations wrestled with this for a while, but what ultimately developed was the idea that in every Christian community, an urban-based community, there would be a kind of chief priest—we use the word in Greek *episkopos*; in English we call him a bishop—and that this bishop had the authority in his region that the apostles had. In other words, even today I live near Rochester, New York, and so my bishop, the bishop of Rochester, has apostolic authority in Rochester and the region around it, which we call the Diocese of Rochester. This idea of the apostolic succession of bishops was essentially beginning to be in place by around the year 100. Today, many forms of Christianity reject this idea of what's called apostolic succession. Today, apostolic succession—having bishops with apostolic authority—is accepted by Catholics, by Orthodox, and by Anglicans; but almost all other forms of Christianity—let's say Presbyterians or Baptists—reject the idea of apostolic succession, and, of course, those denominations have no one with the title of bishop.

These Christian communities operated locally, and people met in homes primarily, perhaps sometimes outdoors; we really don't know a lot about all the practices of the early church because a lot of it was done not so much in secret, but in quiet. But in the fourth century, at the beginning, the conversion of the empire Constantine to Christianity changed the church forever. Now, first of all, the number of Christians is going to be much, much larger; the government favors Christianity, as opposed to persecuting Christians; and the church, as we see, is going to accumulate wealth and so there is a need for big buildings for the church to function properly. One of the very first of those big buildings, although it's been remodeled many times, is still standing; it is the cathedral of Rome, named Saint John Lateran. The land and a palace next to where the church is now built was given to the Bishop of Rome—whom we call the Pope—by the emperor Constantine when he moved to Constantinople, and as a result a large church was built there to be the seat of the Bishop of Rome. Until this time, there really had not been churches because, again, Christians met if not in secret at least in quiet, and in small groups and in small numbers. This building has been rebuilt many, many times; but nevertheless, what we have here is the cathedral of Rome. Note that Saint Peter's is not the cathedral of Rome, but rather this church, Saint John Lateran, which is also older.

If we go inside—and the building looks nothing like it did in the fourth century; it's largely Renaissance and Baroque today—we see at the east end of that church there is, right in the center, a chair, and that's the chair of the Bishop of the Rome. The word for chair of a bishop is *cathedra*, and hence, in the most literal sense of the term, a cathedral is a building with a *cathedra*; that is to say, it is the building that also is the seat of a bishop. In this case, it is the Bishop of Rome.

The earliest big churches were built in Rome, but pretty soon, as Christianity became the primary religion all over the Roman Empire—parts of Europe, Africa, and Asia, after all, were part of the Roman Empire at that time—so too were cathedrals, most of them more modest than the cathedral of Rome, built; and therefore, we had bishops on their *cathedras* in their cathedrals all over. This is a 13th century piece of sculpture from Amiens, but it shows a bishop of Amiens in northern France sitting on his *cathedra* and, as you can see there, reading or speaking or making a pronouncement. This is a very good illustration of a bishop. He has his hat on, which we call a "mitre," and he is sitting on his *cathedra*; this is a position of authority, and a cathedral is first and foremost the seat of a bishop.

As the Roman Empire collapsed, at least in the West in the fifth century—although not everywhere in the fifth century, as we know—it's important to understand that the role of bishops changed and bishops became more and more prominent—bigger and bigger players, if you will—in European society. As we already established, they had apostolic jurisdiction over the Christians in their regions or territories that we call dioceses, and eventually that was virtually the entire population. We need to appreciate that even though cities declined with the collapse of the Roman Empire, which was an urban-based empire, cathedrals remained urban buildings. Almost all cathedrals are and were in cities; and, in fact, many cities survived into the Middle Ages primarily as ecclesiastical centers after their other functions essentially disappeared. Bishops became wealthy: not just the emperor, but many people gave the church land, gold, silver, jewels, all kinds of things, perhaps out of piety, perhaps in part hoping for ecclesiastical or divine favors; but nevertheless, bishops grew to be wealthy in land and in other things.

Furthermore, the church developed a body of law we call a canon law and canon law, the law of the church, was administered by bishops sitting on their *cathedras*, just as we see in this image that we have here from Amiens. This bishop that we see sitting on his throne here may be speaking about a theological or doctrinal issue, but may also be adjudicating a case. It's important to understand the role of the church; and many things that we think of taking place in secular courts in our day—for example, the probation of wills—was done in ecclesiastical courts, and the rules of the game were canon law rather than civil law. Needless to say, with wealth, jurisdiction, and influence, bishops grew in power; that bishops became important people in Western Europe in the Middle Ages; and, in fact, they often had political roles. Think of it this way: Traditionally, the things that had been done by a Roman administrator in a city, there are no Roman administrators after the collapse of the Roman Empire, so who does those things? Who provisions the city? Who makes sure that the walls are intact in case there's an invasion? Who does all those "secular" things? More and more, that power fell to bishops. There's a story from the sixth century of a plague coming to France; it's the bishops who provided aid to the plague victims because there was no Roman civil authority to do that as there would have been a couple hundred years earlier. The bishops become important political figures; and therefore bishops played a number of roles in medieval society that they don't play today. They still have today apostolic jurisdiction, and there still is canon law, although what it does is much more restricted than what it was in the Middle Ages; bishops have lost virtually all of their political power, and certainly a great deal of their wealth. It's been estimated that a third of the land in Europe in the Middle Ages was controlled in some way by the church; obviously that is no longer true.

But when all is said and done, bishops had other things, too. Bishops, in their cathedrals, very often had the relics, the bones of great saints—martyrs, and founding bishops, and so on— and these relics were seen as powerful and therefore to some extent almost every cathedral in Europe was a place of pilgrimage. One of the most "pilgrimaged" places in Europe in the later Middle Ages was Canterbury, and here we see pilgrims on the way to Canterbury Cathedral. Why are they going to Canterbury Cathedral? Because, you may recall from the Prologue of Geoffrey Chaucer's *Canterbury Tales*—which is about these pilgrims going to Canterbury—that's where the relics are of the holy blissful martyr, Thomas a Becket, who was murdered in Canterbury Cathedral in 1170. Let me give you another example: This is the tomb of a founding bishop in a small city in Tuscany, named Massa Marittima. You've probably never heard of San Cerbone; he was an important bishop in this city and the cathedral is named for him, and this is his tomb. The tomb was made later in the Middle Ages, but it illustrates the fact that these cathedrals were not just the seat of bishops; they were also the places of important relics.

Cathedrals also were places that needed to be big because they were for large gatherings of people. Cathedrals weren't so much where you went to mass on Sunday; it's where people flocked for the great feast days of the church whether those are universal feast days like Christmas and Easter, or whether they are local feast days like the feast of San Cerbone, for example, whose tomb, again, we're looking at for Massa Marittima in Tuscany. One thing that happened in cathedrals was the baptism of children; only later on did that take place in parish churches, because in the early Middle Ages there really are very few parish churches. But what we find is that therefore the cathedral needed to be a place for these great ceremonies like baptism. Interestingly, in Italy, baptism often took place in a separate building adjacent to the cathedral. That's what we see here: This is the cathedral of Parma in northern Italy, and that building to the right, that sort of octagonal building is, in fact, the baptistery of Parma; many of you have seen perhaps the baptistery in Florence, which sits right in front of the cathedral of Florence as well. But in France, for example, there are no separate baptisteries, and so baptism took place inside these churches. We need to remember that baptisms could be of famous, important families; but also very often there was collective baptism on the feast of a patron saint or on the feast of John the Baptist, and that meant that there needed to be places for a lot of people, if you will. Cathedrals needed to be big.

I want to show you a couple pictures that help us to place cathedrals in later medieval society. This is an image of the city of Siena in Tuscany, and as you'll be able to see there are two great big chunks of things that stand out in this famous medieval hill town. The big white building with the dome is the cathedral, it's the center of ecclesiastical power; and the building with the tall tower and the piazza in front of it is the civic center of the city, it's where the city government was located. As cities grew and developed all over Europe—in Italy, cities are more independent of larger political entities than they are in the north—we have these sometimes agreeing and sometimes competing centers of power, and they, as you can see, both build big: The city government builds big, the bishop builds big, because in many ways these buildings demonstrate the power. Even today in rather large cities, for example the city of Rennes in northeastern France: This is a city of over 100,000 people, and yet when you look at the skyline of this city you can see in this image that the cathedral of Rennes, built just after 1200, dominates the skyline of this modern city; that it still stands out, surrounded by the urban buildings that are much more modern than it. In many ways, a cathedral also comes to symbolize a city; to represent its grandeur, its power, its wealth, its holiness to any who would come and be awed by it.

To sum up very quickly: A cathedral is the seat of a bishop. It is economically important, politically important, legally important, ritually important, a center of pilgrimage, and a source of pride for the community. In this course, we are largely going to focus on France; Gothic architecture was invented in France, so we should expect that's where our focus is going to lie. But let me just for the last couple minutes give you a kind of quick tour around Europe to see that the style that we see here represented at Rennes is also a style we're going to see many other places. For example, this is the cathedral of Salisbury. It doesn't look just like the cathedral of Rennes—you can see its central tower is so tall, its facade a little bit more, perhaps we should say, laid back than the cathedral of Rennes—because there are going to be a lot of different Gothic styles, both geographically determined but also the style will evolve at any one place over time. Here's an example of English Gothic; by the way, this building was going up at exactly the same time the one we just saw, the cathedral of Rennes, was being built.

This is the cathedral of Prague. It dominates the hill, the Hradčany it's called in Czech. This is taken from across the Moldau, or Vltava River, and you can see this extraordinary dominating cathedral that, in this case, is surrounded by the royal palace that is now, by the way, the presidential palace of the presidents of the Czech Republic. Here, we look at the facade of this massive cathedral of Cologne in Germany; in fact, this part of it was actually completed only in the 19th century, although it was begun in the 13th century and the plans were drawn up in the 13th century that were used for this modern completion of this building. Here we have a very different-looking Gothic cathedral because we're in a very different place: This is the piazza in front of the cathedral of Milan in northern Italy. This is later than the ones that we've looked at, and it is also in a somewhat different style as you can see. Finally, this is the cathedral of Burgos in Spain, another great 13th century cathedral.

We're going to see a style that we can recognize, although in many varieties, all over Europe and even coming into the New World when Columbus opened up the New World to European exploration and settlement. This is going to be at trip into what these buildings are, how they're built, what they mean; we're going to be looking a lot at decoration; and although, again, we're going to focus in France, we're going to do a lot of exploring not just of Western Europe but farther beyond, both to the West in the New World and to the East when we go into the Czech Republic. Put on your seatbelts, it's going to be a great trip through Gothic Europe.

Early Christian Architecture
Lecture 2

> Why not use those shapes and forms of buildings that are already religious? … What the Christians wanted to do is not join as another cult in Rome, but rather to distinguish themselves from these cults; that would be difficult to do if you use the very same kinds of building that these various religious traditions used in Rome, Athens, or anyplace else in the Roman Empire.

Until the 4th century, Christians were a small and occasionally persecuted minority in the Roman Empire. They worshiped privately, if not secretly, in houses or sometimes outdoors. Constantine's conversion to Christianity changed everything. Christianity could have a role in public life, and Christians had the resources to build large buildings for worshiping.

So what kind of building did they build? We might think that Christians would model their churches on existing religious buildings, such as Roman temples. But there were two problems with this form: first, Christians wanted to distinguish themselves from their pagan neighbors, and second, in these buildings, the public was meant to gather outside, while the priest or priestess was inside carrying out the rituals. That doesn't work for Christianity; the very word "church" means "assembly." So Christians turned to another form of building, the **basilica**.

The Roman basilica was a secular building used for economic and judicial business. These were rectangular buildings with roofs supported by two rows of columns, essentially dividing the interior into three aisles. The far end from the entrance was slightly rounded; this area was used as a sort of judge's bench. Many basilicas, like other Roman buildings, had floor mosaics.

Several Roman-era Christian basilicas have survived, although like St. John Lateran, they have been rebuilt so many times it is hard to imagine their original forms. In the great church of Santa Sabina, off the beaten tourist track in the city of Rome, you can see the three-aisled structure and the rounded end opposite the entrance, where the altar is. Generally, these churches were oriented from west to east; and that's true of almost all the cathedrals we will see. Jesus is called the Light of the World, and in the morning, when the Mass is traditionally celebrated, light enters the eastern windows, flooding the altar with light.

We have virtually no remains of churches from the 6th, 7th, and 8th centuries; no cathedrals were built in Europe in those centuries.

To decorate their basilicas, Christians adapted the Roman floor mosaics into wall decorations representing Christian stories and figures. In the 6th century Sant'Apollinare Nuovo in Ravenna, Italy, for example, a parade of saints travels west to east, toward the altar and toward Jesus, in the same direction the congregation would travel to take communion. The 5th-century church of Santa Maria Maggiore in Rome portrays Old Testament stories and an image of Christ Triumphant in the half dome above the altar, a shape similar to a Roman triumphal arch.

Changes were made over time to the basic shape of the basilica. Most significantly, **transepts** were added, bisecting the structure about two-thirds of the way toward the east end of the rectangle, creating a cross-shaped footprint. In addition to its symbolic function, the transept makes the cathedral even bigger. (However, not all Gothic churches adopted this cruciform structure, as we will see later in the course.)

Despite this expansion of church size, as the Roman Empire in the west collapsed, there was a decline in urban life and thus in large-scale building. We have virtually no remains of churches from the 6th, 7th, and 8th centuries; no cathedrals were built in Europe in those centuries. We can't look at the development of cathedrals as an unbroken streak because the ones that were built were smaller, many of them were probably made of wood, and none of them survives. We have some pictures of them in manuscripts; but, of course, manuscripts are hardly photographs. We have some written descriptions, but it's hard to turn that into a visual representation. However, in the eastern half of the empire, centered on the new capital of Constantinople, there were extraordinary cathedrals being built. The most famous of them is the

6ᵗʰ-century Hagia Sophia—which means "holy wisdom." It has minarets because it was converted into a mosque after the conquest of the Turks in 1453, although today it is neither a mosque nor a church but a museum. It is one of the greatest cathedrals, one of the greatest buildings, ever constructed. It looks very different from the basilicas of the West.

In the year 800, on Christmas day, the Frankish king **Charlemagne** was crowned Roman Emperor over all of modern France, plus much of Italy and Germany. Like his predecessors in that office, he was a great builder. At his capital at Aachen, in western Germany, he constructed an octagonal chapel that is the earliest surviving large stone building constructed in Western Europe north of the Alps following the collapse of the Western Roman Empire. Charlemagne was inspired by the 6ᵗʰ century Church of San Vitale in Ravenna, which was Roman as far as Charlemagne was concerned. This is a departure from the basilical rectangle footprint.

Almost no parts of the large stone buildings from 9ᵗʰ-century Western Europe remain beyond a few remnants like the *Westwerk*, or facade, of Corvey

© iStockphoto/Thinkstock.

Istanbul's Hagia Sophia, one of the greatest cathedrals ever constructed, looks very different from Western European cathedrals.

Abbey in Höxter, Germany. Vikings and Hungarians raided, looted, and destroyed these structures in the 9th and 10th centuries, and there was little money or labor to rebuild them. In the late 10th century, building began again in Germany and Italy under Emperor **Otto I** and his successors, based on but not copying the basilical plan. A period of relative peace began in A.D. 1000 after the conversion of the Vikings and Hungarians, which led to a rise in population and a boom in church building that lasted for the rest of the Middle Ages. ■

Important Terms

basilica: A rectangular building with aisles and an apse. The basilica was originally a Roman building used for various secular functions such as law courts. Most Christian churches are in shape an adaptation of the basilica, and the term is sometimes used to describe such Christian churches.

transept: The "wings" of a basilica, usually about two-thirds of the way from west to east, that make the building into the shape of a cross.

Names to Know

Charlemagne (r. 768–814): King of the Franks and, from 800–814, (Holy) Roman Emperor. There was a cultural revival under Charlemagne, which included building large churches. His chapel in Aachen, still standing, was modeled on the 6th-century church of San Vitale in Ravenna.

Otto I (r. 936–973): Holy Roman Emperor. During the reign of Otto and his son and grandson, a cultural revival occurred in Germany sometimes rather exaggeratedly called the Ottonian Renaissance. The cathedral of Hildesheim is an important Ottonian/Romanesque building.

Suggested Reading

Krautheimer, *Early Christian and Byzantine Architecture*.

Wilson, *The Gothic Cathedral*, chap. 1.

1. What were the principal reasons Christians adopted the Roman basilica as the form for their churches rather than other available types of buildings?

2. Why are there more large churches in Europe today from the 4th and 5th centuries than from the subsequent five centuries?

3. Are the buildings of the early Middle Ages primitive, as we might expect them to be, coming from what are commonly referred to as the Dark Ages?

Early Christian Architecture
Lecture 2—Transcript

Let's go back to the fourth century. Up to that time, Christians had been a small and off-and-on persecuted minority in the Roman Empire. As I pointed out, by and large they met in private spaces for worship, primarily—certainly we see this in some of the epistles of the New Testament—in houses, perhaps sometimes outdoors, generally not so much secretly but privately. But with Constantine's conversion to Christianity and support of Christianity, it changed everything. Now the number of Christians increases; Christianity can, in fact, come out of the houses and the private places and have a public role that it never had before; and there are resources to build large buildings for Christians to gather and worship in and for bishops to use as the seats of their authority.

Question: What kind of building do you build? Perhaps for us, we would think that what Christians would do is look at religious buildings that already existed and model churches on that. Here we have a photograph of two pagan temples, very small ones, still standing in Rome; one round and one, as you can see, with a pediment on the right side. It's actually a more or less rectangular building with a porch; we're looking at the back of it in that photograph. Why not use those shapes and forms of buildings that are already religious? Good question; and, in fact, we do find there are a few round churches, although they don't look much like that temple. But basically, there were two problems with this form of building: Number one, we need to remember, paganism doesn't appear; that pagan cults remain legal for a while and are practiced even after they were no longer legal in the Roman Empire. What the Christians wanted to do is not join as another cult in Rome, but rather to distinguish themselves from these cults; that would be difficult to do if you use the very same kinds of building that these various religious traditions used in Rome, Athens, or anyplace else in the Roman Empire. The second problem is this: If you think about these buildings, or think about a big one like the Parthenon in Athens, what you discover is the public gathers outside and the inside is for the priest of priestess to carry out certain ritual acts, but the people didn't go inside. Of course, that doesn't work for Christianity; Christians need to gather in an assembly—the very word "church" means "assembly," after all; it doesn't mean a "building"—

and therefore this kind of building, even a big one like the Parthenon, was not appropriate for the kind of worship that Christians did. For those two reasons—not wanting to be identified as another cult and therefore differentiating themselves from those cults, and the fact that these buildings really wouldn't work very well, we might say, liturgically—the Christians turned to another form of building, a form called the basilica.

What we're looking at here is an aerial image taken of Pompeii; and if you look at the building in the lower center—the one that sort of angles slightly downward and to the left—that is what's called the Basilica in Pompeii. The basilica is a secular building; that is to say, it's not a religious place, it's a place where business took place: economic business, judicial business. If you look at this aerial shot—of course, this building has no roof, it's a ruin—you can see that it's a rectangular building. You entered it from that main plaza or square or forum that is on the right, and you can see there that there are two rows of columns; so there was sort of a main center aisle if you will and a smaller aisle on either side. You can see at the far end of this basilica—that is to say, far end from the entrance—that the shape of the building is different; it's sort of rounded at that end a little bit. Therefore, when this was used, let's say, as a courtroom, that would be where the judge would sit. This building as it turns out—this style of building—was much better suited to Christian worship than these ancient pagan temples, and there are no sort of, shall we say, religious leftovers associated with this building. Here are pieces of a fourth century basilica still standing in Ancient Rome, the Basilica of Maxentius; and if you look at the Basilica of Maxentius, you can see that the rounded part—and we're looking from both the inside and the outside in this particular set of photographs—is on one of the long sides. Sometimes the rounded part was on one of the short sides of this rectangle, sometimes on one of the long sides. This is the shape of a building that Christians chose when they decided how to build their large assembly buildings, their large churches.

I want to say one thing about the decoration of basilicas. Many of them had—and many other buildings in Rome did, too—floor mosaics. We see here in this photograph just one of literally thousands of surviving Roman floor mosaics. Some of these are in villas, some are in public buildings, some are outdoors; whenever you go to a Roman site anywhere in the old Roman

Empire, I can almost promise you either still in situ or in a museum you will see mosaics, and they very often had images of gods and goddesses, they had various stories of the *Odyssey* or the *Iliad*, they had sometimes purely decorative motifs. This is the building that Christians started with: A rectangular building with some rounded piece and some floor decoration in little pieces of stone called mosaics.

The Christians began to build their own basilicas. Luckily, especially in Rome, several of these basilicas survived. We looked in the last lecture at the Basilica of Saint John Lateran; however, it's been rebuilt so many times it's sort of hard to imagine what it might have looked like at the time it was built. Here we have another basilica in Rome—one, alas, not very often visited because it's not right in the main tourist area of Rome—this is the great church of Santa Sabina. If you take a look at it carefully, we're looking at it from the back, you can see that there's a main center part of the church and then there's an aisle on either side—we can see the lower roof of the aisle on the left here—and then the entrance is at the opposite end from where we're looking and that the rounded part of the basilica here, as you can see, is at the far end; that is to say, the end farthest away from the entrance. Christians put the round part opposite the entrance on one of the short sides of the basilica; and therefore, when you see this from the inside as we do here, you can see that as you walk into the church, where your eyes focus—you can see the aisle on either side and the roof—is on that rounded part right there in the center in front of you and that's where the altar is, because after all, that's the focus of a Christian church: where the altar is, where the mass sacrifice takes place; the bread and the wine are consecrated. This works pretty well, as it turns out, as a form of Christian building.

Let me suggest that generally these churches were oriented from west to east; and that's true of almost all the cathedrals we will see, although there are some exceptions, usually for geographical reasons (where they'll fit in a city). We walk in the west entrance and we move toward the rising sun; because, after all, Jesus is the light of the world. It also means that in morning, when the mass is traditionally celebrated, the light is coming in to the east so that one experiences the presence of Christ in word (in sermons and the reading of the Gospel), one experiences God in the form of bread and wine, and one experiences God in the form of light. This orientation of the building takes an already well-adapted Roman form and makes it by its orientation even more useful for Christian worship and for the inspiration and the teaching that take place in this particular space.

Now what we want to talk about is: How do you decorate this thing? Let's take a look. If you think about the mosaic as an important kind of decoration, then you have to say, "Christians could take those little bits of stone and instead of having pagan gods and goddesses or Odysseus doing this or Achilles doing that, they could have Christian figures and stories." Indeed you can; but you can't put them on the floor. You're not going to walk on an image of the saints; you're not going to walk on an image of Jesus. Ultimately, what the Christians did was to use the art form of the mosaic but they put it in different places in their churches, so that we have not only a building that teaches, but the walls teach; and as we'll see in a minute, the apse, the east end of the church, teaches because in addition to the light coming into the east end, there are also stories. We're looking here at a sixth century basilica in the city of Ravenna—this is called Sant'Apollinare Nuovo, a very long name, right inside the walls of the city of Ravenna—and what we see in this mosaic is a long parade, if you will, of saints. They're coming from the right to the left—and you can see in the purple robe to the left in the center, that's Jesus sitting among the angels—so what we really have is the saints coming to Jesus.

Think about that, because if you're in this basilica and you move forward in the church to take communion, you are journeying with those saints toward Jesus; that they and you—to use Saint Augustine's language—the Church Triumphant (that is to say, those who have died and are in heaven) and the Church Militant (its members on earth) are journeying together to the same goal, they're both journeying to Christ. Once again, we can see how the decorative art helps to expand the meaning of the experience of being there for a mass, and this is something we will see developing in somewhat different forms, although we will see one Gothic mosaic: We will see other art forms taking the place of the mosaic but doing much of the same thing.

In addition to this sort of parade, if you will, we also have a lot of stories in this same church in mosaic, and I've simply chosen one to show you here: This is the story of the betrayal of Jesus by Judas. In addition to that parade of saints with whom we can sort of join, we also have the story of Christ. We start with the birth of Christ and even before with the Annunciation, and, of course, this goes on from here to the Crucifixion, the Resurrection, and so on; so we also have narrative as well as symbolic or abstract images, again, to help us remember where we are. After all, Christianity is a historical religion; that is to say, its basic premise is that at a moment in time, God entered history in a new way by becoming human. We need to know that story; and we're going to celebrate that by having the bread and wine that, of course, Christ commanded at the Last Supper just before this event took place. You can see Judas here on the left embracing Christ, and you can see all the folks around observing this. This is one of the decorative schemes that we find.

Let me show you another one, even earlier actually, from the fifth century. This is from Santa Maria Maggiore, the largest church in Rome other than Saint Peter's, and what we see is we're looking toward the east end of the church. That great big thing in the center below is the top of the altar and that's much, much more modern, so we're going to try to pretend that isn't there. There actually is a mosaic behind that in the half dome, although we can't see it very well; but you can see there are all sorts of figures and stories on the arch as we prepare to enter into that rounded apse, or space in the east end of the church. These tell, in fact, Old Testament stories; and that's interesting, because, of course, we prepare for Jesus through Old Testament, and then the Old Testament is filled according to the Christians in the New, and, in fact, we have Christ in Heaven, although in a later mosaic, in the rounded part (the half dome) that we see behind that baldacchino as it's called, that sort of baroque altar that is there. Once again, this almost is like a Roman triumphal arch—which we find used by Roman emperors to celebrate their military victories—because all of this leads to the celebration of Christianity; after all, Christ triumphed over death and broke down the gates of Hell. How's that for a triumph worth celebrating? I want us to see here how this art is used, how this mosaic decoration is used.

There are some changes that are made gradually over time to the basic shape of the basilica. Let me show you one: This is part of our animation of the cathedral of Laon in northern France, and we're looking down on it. What you notice is, indeed, it is generally basilical in shape—it is a long, rectangular building—but as you can see, about two-thirds of the way from the west to the east ends there is, in fact, a piece on either side. We call that the transept and that essentially makes the church into the shape of a cross; so that when you enter the cathedral of Laon, and almost all of the cathedrals we're going to look at, you are entering into the cross of Christ. You enter at the base of the cross, and as you move toward the east end where the light is, you move toward—if you think about the cross—where the head of Christ would be. It's there that the bread and wine are consecrated; it's there that Christ is reproduced in material form here on earth at the mass. I might add, the transept has a secondary function: It makes the cathedral still bigger; it provides for more space for people to come in. I'm going to talk a little bit later about why these things needed to be so very big.

Although the cruciform—simply the adjective for "cross-shaped"—church such as we see here in this animation of Laon is cross-shaped, nevertheless there are some exceptions to that among the cathedrals we're going to look at. Chief among them is the cathedral of Bourges, build in the 13th century. We're looking at it from the rear end, from the back end. You can see the towers on the front and the rounded east end here with all the flying buttresses—again, we'll talk about all that stuff a lot later, obviously—but what I want you to notice is it has no transept; it is really the basilical shape of the older form rather than with this added cruciform shape with the transept.

Let me suggest that although we have big buildings like the ones we've seen in Rome (Saint John Lateran, Santa Sabina, and Santa Maria Maggiore) and we looked at a large sixth-century church in Ravenna (Sant'Apollinare Nuovo) we need to remember that generally when the Roman Empire collapses, which is the century after Constantine, what tends to happen is that there's a decline in urban life; there's a decline in trade; Germanic tribesmen and their chieftains come in to rule, replacing the Roman administration (bishops fill in some of the gap but not all of it); but there is very little large-scale building after the collapse of Roman authority in the West. In fact, we have virtually no remains of churches from the sixth, seventh, and eighth centuries and there are no cathedrals in Europe that were built in those periods; so we have a gap in following the history of Christian architecture, although there are some foundations and fragments that we can date to those times after the fall of Rome. We can't really look at the development of cathedrals as an unbroken streak because the ones that were built were smaller, many of them were probably made of wood, and none of them survives. We have some pictures of them in manuscripts; but, of course, manuscripts are hardly photographs and it's really hard to know from those manuscripts what these buildings looked like. We have some written descriptions; but again, it's hard to turn that into a visual idea.

We need to remember, however, that the eastern half of the Roman Empire, focused in its new capital of Constantinople beginning in the 4th century, did not collapse like the Western Roman Empire did; and while there is no major building in the West for several centuries, there are extraordinary Christian buildings, cathedrals, being built. The most famous of them is the cathedral of Hagia Sophia—which means "holy wisdom"; it doesn't mean "Saint Sophie"—the cathedral of Holy Wisdom, in what's now Istanbul in Constantinople. You see in this photograph it has minarets because in the 15th century it was converted into a mosque with the conquest of the Turks in 1453. Today, by the way, it is neither a mosque nor a church, it is a museum. This is one of the great cathedrals, one of the great buildings, ever built anywhere in the world. It's certainly on my top-five list of great buildings to be in. it is a cathedral built in the 6th century; obviously it looks very different than the basilicas we saw in the West. We have somewhat different sets of traditions operating in the East than in the West; but we do at least need to be aware of the building of some very large-scale churches, even in what some people call—I wouldn't, by the way—the Dark Ages in Western Europe.

But in the 8th century, along comes Charlemagne who, as king of the Franks, also conquers much of Italy—and remember, being king of the Franks also meant ruling a good chunk of what's now Germany—and in 800 on Christmas Day, Charlemagne is crowned Roman Emperor. Today, we say "Holy Roman Emperor," but they didn't say that; they just said "Roman Emperor." The Roman Empire was theoretically renewed in the West in 800. That meant a lot of things to Charlemagne, but one of the things we know: Charlemagne saw himself as the heir of all the Roman emperors; and one thing you can say about Roman emperors, both pagan (like Augustus) and Christian (like Constantine) is that they were buildings, and so Constantine, too, reinitiated building of stone buildings in the northern parts of Europe. Here is an image of Charlemagne; this is actually a 12th-century reliquary that we're looking at that contains some of his physical remains. He was an extraordinary figure and ruled from 768–814; and again, after 800 is not just king of the Franks but also Holy Roman Emperor.

This is the cathedral of Aachen in the western part of Germany. The left part with the pointed tower and the right part are many, many centuries after Charlemagne, but the central part with the dome was the chapel of Charlemagne in Aachen; Aachen became more or less Charlemagne's capital after his coronation as Holy Roman Emperor. This basically octagonal building, which has now been incorporated into a larger complex of ecclesiastical buildings, is the first remaining large stone building built in Western Europe north of the Alps following the collapse of the Roman Empire. Where did Charlemagne get an idea of how to build a building that shape? He, of course, knew Italy; and he looked to Italy, and in particular to this church, the Church of San Vitale in Ravenna, which was built in the sixth century, commissioned at the time of the Emperor Justinian, a Byzantine emperor who also controlled much of Italy. This church in Ravenna, built in the sixth century, was Roman to Charlemagne and therefore became the model. Notice that, as an octagon, it is sort of round rather than basilical, obviously; again, I talked about the fact there are some round or roundish churches. Notice though, unlike that temple we saw in Ancient Rome at the beginning of this lecture, the columns don't go outside; notice the outside is a series of walls so there's more interior space because, again, even if you use an old shape it has to be converted to a new function.

Later on, in the ninth century, we have some other large stone building taking place in the Holy Roman Empire, the empire that Charlemagne had; but almost none of it remains. This is one of the very few, and by far the most magnificent example: This is the facade—it's usually called by its German name, the *Westwerk*—of a church in Corvey in what's now Germany, and you can see it's this large, imposing facade with two towers. That's all that's left of the building from the time of Charlemagne and his successors—the adjective for that is the Carolingian Empire, the Carolingian world—so it's a very rare ninth-century structure. The rest of the church today is, in fact, baroque, so that's why I'm not showing you the rest of it. But this is one of those very rare pieces that survive from the time of Charlemagne and his immediate successors. Another example, a little bit more modest perhaps, is this building: This is part of the modern cathedral of Beauvais in Northern France; and it, too, is Carolingian, although it's been rebuilt more than once. What's interesting about this is the choir, the east end of the cathedral of Beauvais, is this enormous Gothic structure where the nave is just dwarfed by what was built several centuries later. But at least we have standing here a Carolingian building, a somewhat modest one to say the least, in Beauvais.

Why aren't there more of these? The main answer is that the empire of Charlemagne breaks down in the 9th century and the early 10th century. Why? A lot of reasons, family disputes and so on; but the main reason is that Europe came under attack: Vikings and Hungarians in particular attacked Western Europe. Neither of these groups was Christian; one of the things that means is you go after the best loot, and the best loot was in churches, monastic churches and cathedrals. Why? Because somebody gave this church a gold chalice or a jeweled this or whatever it might be; and so you go for where the loot is. There was massive destruction, even of many modest monastic and cathedral buildings, in Western Europe. Of course, when the attacks continue, you have neither the time nor the resources to rebuild them, because whatever building you're going to do is going to be defense; you need to keep the Vikings out, you need to keep the Hungarians out. So once again, we have very little large-scale ecclesiastical architecture from the 9th and the 10th centuries.

However, late in the 10th century, things began to change. The Holy Roman Empire was somewhat reconstituted by an emperor named Otto the Great, who was crowned Holy Roman Emperor in 962. By this time, the Holy Roman Empire no longer consists of what we would call France, but rather Germany and Italy; and Otto the Great, and in particular his successors—his son and grandson, Otto's II and III, if you will—were important builders, once again, because that's what Roman emperors do: they build buildings, among other things. As it turns out, Otto II married a Byzantine princess, and, of course, she came from a place where there was this continuous tradition of large ecclesiastical buildings being built in the Byzantine Empire. We find some buildings from the late 10th/beginning of the 11th century in Germany that, once again, mark beginnings of new kinds of building of large-scale stone structures.

Here, for example, we have an important church in Hildesheim. You can see that it's basically basilical in structure, but you can also see there are some oddities about it; that is to say, there is a different take here on the basilical form. For one thing, as you can see, there are sort of large walls at either end; and, in fact, either end is rounded, both the entrance end and the altar end are rounded, making this a particular form of architecture based on but not copying the basilical plan. Here is the interior of Hildesheim: It's a wooden roof; it looks very basilical from the inside, but its outside has some peculiarities that we would not find, for example, in Rome. Another example is the church in Genrode. Again, here we can see that there is sort of a massive end facing us and you can just see on the left side there's a massive end at the other end, too, and there really is no front door; this is the front of the building, but there really is no front door because, again, both east and west short ends of the basilica are rounded. These are, we would call them, Ottonian—based on the name Otto, the three Otto emperors in a row—and therefore a kind of prelude to what's going to happen in Europe beginning around the year 1,000.

By the year 1,000, some things have changed: First of all, the Vikings have sort of stopped raiding; many of them have settled in France and become Christians. The Hungarians? The first Christian king of Hungary was crowned around the year 1,000. So there is, for the first time in a long time, relative—and I want to point out the word "relative"—peace and, for a variety of reasons including the development of agricultural technique, there was a rise in population; there were a lot of destroyed buildings, leftovers from the Vikings and the Hungarians, that need to be replaced; there is an opportunity for monks to settle in again, after sometimes literally being chased around Europe by Vikings and Hungarians out to get their goods, and they need places to live; and therefore, for a number of reasons, around the year 1,000 we begin an extraordinary expansion of the building of churches. That expansion, and growth of this industry and this movement to build large churches, will last for the rest of the Middle Ages.

Romanesque—A New Monumental Style
Lecture 3

One of the great misnomers that we have to deal with is there's this word "Romanesque," and it makes it sound like Romanesque is a style of architecture and decoration. Nothing could be further from the truth. ... It's more useful to think of it as a period of building in which there are borrowings from Roman style to make buildings that fit into a variety of cultures.

The architects of the **Romanesque** period, beginning around A.D. 1000, borrowed much less consistently and much more episodically from ancient Roman buildings in creating a new architectural style. There were still many Roman ruins all over Western Europe in this period, certainly more than there are today, along with a few Carolingian and Ottonian buildings that survived the Viking and Hungarian raids. Although we distinguish these into distinct architectural periods, we should remember that medieval Europeans did not do the same. So while it may sound odd, the Romanesque is a Roman period of architecture—an early medieval Roman period.

What the Romanesque is not, however, is an architectural style. Building and rebuilding was going on all over Western Europe in this period using a variety of surviving Roman buildings as models; therefore, Romanesque encompasses wide variety of styles. Buildings that we call Romanesque may look radically different from one another. To take just one example, a Romanesque church might have a central tower, as does the abbey church of Saint-Martin-de-Boscherville, in Normandy, France; it might have several towers, as does Speyer Cathedral in Germany; or it might have a completely detached bell tower, such as the famous Leaning Tower of the cathedral of Pisa in Italy. Romanesque churches vary not just from nation to nation but within national or ethnic regions; compare Pisa's cathedral and its Byzantine and Muslim influences to Sant'Antimo in Siena, Italy, which is more French in style.

There are a few things, however, that we will find that many Romanesque churches have in common. They're almost all basilical in form, and most are cruciform basilicas. They are usually built of stone and have very thick walls. Often, but not always, the roofs are made of stone; that's one of the reasons the walls are so thick. Finally, most Romanesque churches are quite dark inside—or were, as today many have been updated with electrical lighting. This was in part an engineering matter: windows might weaken the walls. But there was also a sense, which some still hold today, that darkness is more conducive to prayer and contemplation than light.

Most surviving Romanesque churches in Europe are found in small towns and in the countryside, many of them part of monastic communities. Most urban Romanesque churches have been destroyed by accidents such as fire and war or through deliberate urban planning. Three interesting examples survive in Paris, however: Saint-Germain-des-Prés (just a few blocks from Notre Dame); Saint-Pierre, next to Sacré-Coeur en Montmartre; and Saint-Martin-des-Champs, which is part of the Musée des Arts et Métiers. (Saint-Martin-des-Champs is home to Foucault's original pendulum.) Another interesting exception is the city of Lucca, in Tuscany, which holds a dozen Romanesque churches inside its walls.

Very often, we think of Romanesque churches being relatively small, but there are extraordinarily large Romanesque churches. The largest of them all was at the monastery of Cluny in Burgundy—we call it the third abbey church. Almost none of the church survives; most of it was torn down during the French Revolution. We can get some idea of what Cluny would have looked like by examining a church in the nearby little town of Paray-le-Monial, which is pretty large itself but much, much smaller than Cluny. Cluny had more towers and had two transepts, rather than one.

There are several French churches that demonstrate the transition from the Romanesque to the Gothic. Mont-Saint-Michel in Normandy is divided into Gothic and Romanesque halves. The Gothic section is much taller and more elaborately decorated than the Romanesque nave. The facade of the Abbaye aux Hommes in Caen, Normandy, has two enormous towers, a common feature in Gothic churches, yet it is a Romanesque church. Saint-Trophime

The abbey church at the monastery of Cluny was once the largest Romanesque cathedral in the world, but little of it survived the French Revolution.

in Arles, Provence, although small, is beautifully decorated on the outside. This will become common, in fact almost universal, in French Gothic.

In Germany, the best-preserved Romanesque church is the monastery of Maria Laach. The cathedral of Mainz is unusual for being made of red stone that resembles brick and having a large number of soaring towers. In Quedlinburg, we find a grand church with more familiar Romanesque elements. Spain's great pilgrimage church, Santiago de Compostela, has a wildly decorated interior. In Italy, San Miniato in Florence is built from many colors of marble and has a mosaic over its major door. Durham Cathedral, in the north of England, is a rare surviving example of Anglo-Saxon Romanesque. Among this great variety, certain aspects will become more directly influential on the building of Gothic churches than others. ■

Important Term

Romanesque: A term used for a wide variety of styles of architecture of the 11th and 12th centuries, when many large stone buildings were constructed. The English Romanesque style is known as Norman.

Barral i Altet, *The Romanesque: Towns, Cathedrals and Monasteries*.

Erlande-Brandenburg, *The Social and Architectural Dynamics of Construction*, chap. 1.

Stoddard, *Art and Architecture in Medieval France*, chaps. 1–7.

Wilson, *The Gothic Cathedral*, introduction, chap. 1.

Questions to Consider

1. Why do we have to be careful when we label a church as Romanesque?

2. To what extent is the diversity of Romanesque styles a product of poor communications and lack of large centralized states?

3. Is the word "Romanesque," derived from "Roman," an apt term to describe buildings that do not look much like any Roman buildings we know of?

Romanesque—A New Monumental Style
Lecture 3—Transcript

Let's go back 1,000 years, around the year 1000. As I pointed out in the last lecture, by about that time, we have a changing situation in Western Europe. The Vikings and the Hungarians, or Magyars, have been tamed to some extent and incorporated into the culture by their conversion to Christianity. We have, perhaps primarily due to agricultural advancements, a real rise in population; if you change from leaving half your land fallow to a third of your land fallow a year by having a three-rotation rather than a two, you obviously increase food production by 17%. There are a lot of important things happening that are not directly part of our interest in architecture and art, but are nevertheless important for understanding new conditions in Europe.

As I mentioned last time, given the destruction of the end of the Carolingian world from the Vikings and the Hungarians, there is a lot to rebuild— monasteries, cathedrals, and so on—and so the style that begins to develop around 1000 is a style we call Romanesque. We want to listen to that word carefully; that is to say, it is Roman-esque, it is Roman-like. In fact, this style in French is called *Romain*, and in Italian *Romano*; it's simply the word for "Roman." What that suggests is that what builders are going to do is look at ancient Roman buildings and use the knowledge they can gain from them to build new buildings. These new buildings are not going to look very much like Roman buildings; in fact, sometimes they will look as un-Classical as we can imagine. But yet, if we look closely—we'll see there's a Corinthian column as a decorative motif or whatever—the architects in this Romanesque Period beginning around 1000 are going to borrow much less consistently and much more, perhaps we might want to say, episodically from Ancient Roman building to create a new architectural style.

Let's remember, there are a lot of Roman ruins in Western Europe around 1000, more than there are today, and let's remember that they're not all in Italy. What we're looking at here is a Roman temple called the Maison Carrée ("Square House") and it is in the city of Nîmes in southern France. But let's remember, there are also Roman ruins in Trier in Germany, in York in England, all over Spain and Italy, all the places where the Roman Empire was; so there are plenty of examples still standing today, and obviously many more 1,000 years ago. That's an important thing to remember.

As we've also seen, there are a few buildings from the Carolingian and Ottonian Period, the time of Charlemagne in the 9th century and the time of the Ottonian emperors in the 10th; and remember that we distinguish them from Roman buildings. But we shouldn't assume that in the Middle Ages that same distinction would have been made, because after all, buildings like the Maison Carrée were built during the time of Roman emperors and so were Carolingian and Ottonian building because they were the revived Roman Empire; so where we tend to draw lines historically into periods, we should not assume that other people draw those lines the same way. The Romanesque style is going to borrow from ancient Roman building, but also, if you will—it's sort of an odd way of saying it—early medieval Roman building; things like those we saw in the last lecture from Corvey and Hildesheim and whatever.

One of the great misnomers that we have to deal with is there's this word "Romanesque," and it makes it sound like Romanesque is a style of architecture and decoration. Nothing could be further from the truth. We have the same kind of phenomenon going on in many parts of Western Europe, rebuilding or building new buildings and using various elements of Roman building as models; but if we take a look, let's say from England to Italy, or even within Italy or England or France or one piece of those places, we'll see that Romanesque really is a wide variety of styles. In many ways, Romanesque is a collective term, so that I can show you—and will show you—buildings that we call "Romanesque" that look radically different from one another. Instead of thinking of it as a style, perhaps it's more useful to think of it as a period of building in which there are borrowings from Roman style to make buildings that fit into a variety of cultures, some more influenced by Germanic culture than others, some more urban—there are more cities in Italy than there are in England, for example—so the variety of cultural and physical settings are going to mean that many different things come under that rubric of "Romanesque."

Having said that, let me just give you one quick way of seeing some of the varieties. Here is a Romanesque church in Normandy. This is Saint Martin de Boscherville, and it's a beautiful building as you can see with a large centralized tower. You can see the church is built in the shape of a cross; it's one of those picturesque buildings that we see when we drive through Normandy. Here is another Romanesque building, very different looking. First of all, notice this is urban; this is a cathedral rather than a monastery, and we'll see that it has towers on both ends and we'll see that it has a lot of features that make it different from what we just saw. This is the cathedral of Speyer in Germany; in fact, it's the burial place for some Holy Roman Emperors. Although Speyer's a small city today, this was an extraordinarily important place. This is a monumental building—again, we would call it Romanesque—but it sure doesn't look like the first building we saw. Now, let's jump across the Alps—no mean feat—this is another Romanesque cathedral. This is certainly recognizable to most people, for this is the cathedral of Pisa; and the cathedral of Pisa's bell tower is not attached to the building as bell towers are in many churches, but it stands separately and, of course, we know it as the Leaning Tower of Pisa. We're looking here from the rear, so we see the rounded east end and we can see that this is built in the shape of a cross, and we can see that instead of a tower at the crossing of the main part of the church and the transept—that is to say, where the cross pieces come together—we see there's a dome; we didn't see that in the earlier churches we've looked at.

Just by looking at these three churches in different parts of Europe—one now in France, one now in Germany, one now in Italy—we can really see how "Romanesque" is a catch-all term and not a way of talking about a style. In fact, let's talk about not just how these styles might vary from what we would call nation to nation: Pisa is in Tuscany, so is this church. It is a Romanesque church in the province of Siena, south of the city of Siena, named Sant'Antimo. It was consecrated in the year 1018, so this is an early Romanesque church. You can see how different this is from the cathedral of Pisa, which is actually not all that far away; and we might ask why? One reason is that we know there were some French involved in building this building; that is, people who came from France. With regard to Pisa, what we have is influence from the fact that the Pisans were great traders in the Mediterranean, and there are elements of Byzantine and even more so elements of Muslim style of architecture in this building that is lacking in the monastery of Sant'Antimo, which is inland and away from that direct influence from the international trade being conducted at the port of Pisa.

Even just looking at two Tuscan churches, we're struck by how different they are: the building materials are different, the shape is different. Yet, there are some similarities: They're both basilical, although Sant'Antimo doesn't have a transept; they both have bell towers standing separate from the church toward the rear. We'll see some patterns, we'll see some repetitions, but we have to look carefully at two things at the same time: What are the distinct elements of these churches, and what is it, despite so many surface differences, they have in common? Let me suggest, if you will, a little list of things that we will find in many Romanesque churches that on the surface look quite different from one another. First of all, they're almost all basilical in form and most of them are going to be cruciform basilicas, basilicas in the shape of the cross; again, that's not true with the church of Sant'Antimo that we looked at, but it will be true the great majority. Generally speaking, they are built of stone and have very thick stone walls. There are some exceptions; we're going to see in a little while a brick Romanesque church of monumental size in southern France because of the paucity of good building stone around the city of Toulouse. Normally, though, we're going to find they're stone and the walls are quite thick. Often, but not always, the roofs are made of stone; that's one of the reasons the walls are so thick, because the walls have to hold up that roof made of stone. We're going to see there are, more in Italy than other places, roofs made of wood; and so once again, it is not a rule of Romanesque that a church has a stone roof, but as you can imagine, for those that do have stone roofs—again, especially those—the walls are very thick.

Another factor that sometimes surprises us—and for people who are used to Gothic, sometimes depresses them a little bit—is when you walk into most Romanesque churches, they are pretty dark inside. Obviously that's somewhat changed today because of the fact you have electric lights, but they're pretty dark. Let me suggest two reasons: One is the fact that if you're going to build a great big church with a stone roof, you can't just punch big holes in the wall to put in windows; you need the strength of those walls to hold up that roof. Part of it is technical; part of it is an engineering matter. But also, we need to remember that many of these churches, like Sant'Antimo, are monastic churches; and monks live a prayerful, contemplative life. Let me tell you a story: I live a few miles away, in Upstate New York, from a Trappist monastery, and in the mid-70s they decided to build a new church, so they got to design things from scratch. The abbot specifically said, "I want a dark church." Of course, with the technology today you can have virtually glass walls; but he wanted a dark church because he thought that was more monastic, that was more conducive to the kind of contemplative, prayerful life of the monk than something that lit up, either from the inside or from the outside. I think in some ways we need to remember that when we look at many of these dark Romanesque churches, it's a combination of engineering matters but also a kind of aesthetic and spiritual preference that we find.

Today, most Romanesque churches in Europe are in small towns and in the countryside. They're in the countryside largely because so many of them that survive are monastic, and therefore for many visitors to Europe, especially those who don't have their own cars, they aren't visited very much; and so in many ways, there are a lot more Romanesque churches than people would suspect, even if they're fairly widely traveled from city to city in Europe. I once wanted to visit a Romanesque church in France, for example, that was 67 kilometers from the nearest train station. We think of France being honeycombed with train tracks, and yet I had to find a way to get 67 kilometers from where I got off the train to get to the monastic church at Conques, which we'll be looking at later in Lecture 5. The reason we don't have many Romanesque churches in cities is not because they weren't built, but because they've either been destroyed by fire or something else, or they've been torn down or radically remodeled because as cities continued to grow and get richer, they wanted more and more grand buildings; and therefore a Romanesque church built in, let's say, the 11th century is much less likely to survive in the city than it was in the countryside.

Let me give you an example of a great city where Romanesque is hard to find: that city is Paris. Of course, we think of churches in Paris we think of the cathedral of Notre Dame, with which we'll be spending a good deal of time. But we need to be aware that there are some Romanesque churches. There is this one, for example, Saint Germain des Prés, a very beautiful church just a few blocks, in fact, from the cathedral of Notre Dame. It's very dark inside; it's not terribly well preserved inside; and it's one of the buildings that people walk by because it's on a fashionable shopping street and very rarely look at the building let alone go in, and yet it's a large Romanesque church in Paris. There are also two small Romanesque churches in Paris: One sits right next to Sacré-Coeur en Montmartre called Saint-Pierre; and the other one is actually incorporated into a museum today, the Museum of Arts and Meters (Arts et Métiers) and this is the church of Saint-Martin-des-Champs, Saint Martin in the Fields (of course, there aren't any fields these days, it's right in the middle of Paris). This is a beautiful church to visit. To do so, you must buy a ticket to the Museum of Arts and Métiers; and by the way, it's worth doing, it's a very interesting museum, and inside Saint-Martin-des-Champs is the original pendulum of Foucault just swinging away. You get two for one when you go to the museum, even this little piece of the museum: You get a beautiful 12th-century church that's usually ignored by the tour guides and in the tour books and you also get an interesting piece of modern history as well.

There are some exceptions to what I've just said about Romanesque churches not really being much in cities anymore. Let me, for example, show you this one: This is the cathedral of the city of Lucca in Italy. Lucca is in Tuscany, not very far from Pisa; and, in fact, the facade of it suggests, like the cathedral in Pisa, it is influenced by the trading of this part of Tuscany with both the Byzantine and the Muslim worlds. You can see here the bell tower's in the front rather than the back. But Lucca's an interesting city because there must be a dozen Romanesque churches inside the city walls—which still stand— of Lucca. If you want to do a quick visit to see the world of Romanesque architecture and decoration, Lucca's probably the single best place to go simply because of the number of Romanesque churches that survive there. San Martino, the Church of Saint Martin, is, in fact, the cathedral of the city of Lucca. There are places in France, too, that have Romanesque cathedrals, although not very many. We will visit the Romanesque cathedral of Autun in Lecture 5.

Very often when we think about Romanesque—especially if we think about what's coming, the Gothic—we think of Romanesque churches being sort of small. Many of them are, many of them were a place where few monks worshipped; but there are extraordinarily large Romanesque churches, and the largest of them all was the monastery of Cluny in Burgundy, south and east of Paris. This is a tower of the abbey church—we call it the third abbey church because there were two previous ones there—the third abbey church of Cluny, and what's interesting is almost none of the church survives; most of it was torn down during the French Revolution, so this is just one tiny fragment of the third abbey church at Cluny. You can see it is an extraordinary and large monument. Luckily for us, even though we don't have Cluny, we have a sort of "mini Cluny," if you will; that is to say, a church attached to Cluny with its own monastic community that built a kind of a miniature Cluny as its own church. This is the church in the little town of Paray-le-Monial; and as you can see here from this beautiful picture—because it sits right on a riverbank and we get this nice reflection here; it looks like an Impressionist painting of some sort almost—that this is a pretty big building and it really is much, much, much smaller than Cluny. But at least we get some idea of what Cluny would have looked like, although it had more towers; it was so large it actually had two transepts, two crossbars of the main part of the cross, rather than one.

What I want to do for the rest of this lecture, really, is to survey Europe and just get a sense of some of the Romanesque styles that prevail. We've obviously looked a good deal already at France, but we can't leave France without looking at a couple more famous monastic churches of the Romanesque style. This is, if course, the famous Mont Saint Michel in Normandy. If we look at this from a distance, as we are here, you'll see that really the church, with a steeple in the middle, is divided into two very different halves. On our left it is Gothic and it is much taller than the Romanesque, and you can even from this angle and from this distance see some of the flying buttresses. On the right is the older front part, or nave, of the church and it's in the Romanesque style. It is somewhat simpler, and as you can see it is not vaulted as high, it's sort of "squishier down," if you will—that's not a very good phrase, is it?—but that's what it is: It seems like a "squished down" version. Here we see a half-Romanesque, half-Gothic church and we're reminded of some of the differences, even though we're also going to talk about continuity.

This is the facade of the Abbaye aux Hommes in the city of Caen in Normandy, with these two enormous towers in the front. By the way, this is going to be a common pattern in Gothic for there to be two large, tall bell towers in the front of the church. We'll see this at Chartres and Notre

Dame in Paris, and Amiens, and many other places. We can see that it's not a Gothic invention; this is a Romanesque church. It is an elaborate building and we're going to come back to it a little bit later on, but let me point out among other things it is the resting place of one of the dukes of Normandy; not just any old duke, by the way: William, Duke of Normandy, who became William I; that is to say, William the Conqueror, King of England. He had this built, and his wife is buried across town in another wonderful Romanesque church called the Abbaye aux Dames, a female monastery. This is a male monastery here.

Let's go to Southern France: This is the church of Saint Sernin in Toulouse. Here you see there are no front towers, but there's this enormous tower at the crossing where the large and short bars of the cross come together. Furthermore, you can see in this photograph and from the color in this photograph that the building is largely, not entirely but largely, made of brick. I mentioned before that usually we have stone but there are places where stone is hard to get or the right kind of stone is not easily available or closely available, and so we do have a few brick buildings although most of the great Romanesque and Gothic churches are made of stone. This is the church of Saint Trophime in Arles. Arles is in the southeastern part of France in the area we call Provence; and you can see although this is a fairly small church, one of the things that strikes us about this church is its beautiful decorative scheme on the outside. You can see there is sculpture above the door and there are figures on either side of the doors of large holy men and women. Once again, with some adaptation, this kind of way of decorating a door is going to become common, in fact almost universal, in French Gothic; so once again, the idea of putting certain kinds of sculpture around the portal doesn't have to be invented in the Gothic area, it's already been in vented in a church that we call Romanesque.

If we move to Germany, we see, again, very different styles than what we've just looked at. This is the monastery of Maria Laach, one of the best-preserved Romanesque churches in Germany; an extraordinary building with this western part that is on the right with the towers, but again the rounded front part. We're used to a flat front part; but in Germany, as we've seen in the earlier Ottonian architecture, we get rounded parts on both short ends of the basilica. This is, again, one of the really finest, best-preserved, and purest examples of Romanesque in Germany. Here we have the cathedral of Mainz. Mainz is an important town; it was an important town in the Middle Ages. it's made of a reddish stone—this is not brick even though the color may look that way from a distance, but rather this is made of a kind of reddish local stone—and what we're struck by is this great number of towers, it just sort of soars up with these extraordinary and wonderful towers. Here's a smaller, more modest Romanesque church in the German city of Quedlinburg, and as you take a look at it you can see that it has towers on the front (we're looking from the back), you can see that it's in the shape of a cross, you can see it has the rounded east end; this is more familiar shape for a Romanesque or Gothic church than we have seen in the last few. Again, it reminds us there are varieties, and certain varieties become more directly influential on the building of Gothic churches than others.

Let's stop very briefly in Spain. I show you the interior here only because the exterior is wildly decorated in other periods. But this is the great pilgrimage church—and I'll talk more about the pilgrimage church later—of Santiago de Compostela, which had the body of one of the apostles; Saint James the Apostle is buried here, Santiago. This is the subject of great pilgrimage, and we're looking in this large, powerful—it's actually darker than this photograph makes it look because you can see that you have an aisle on the right side and above that a kind of balcony or gallery, but there are no big windows letting in light here; there is at the far east end because that was redone in a different style—but this is an example, probably the most famous example, of Spanish Romanesque.

We'll take a look in Italy: This is the beautiful 11th century Romanesque church of San Miniato al Monte that overlooks the city of Florence. You can see here the different colors of marble in the decoration; there's actually a small mosaic above the major door there, you wouldn't find that in any other part of Europe than Italy, which has more mosaics preserved and mosaics used in early Roman churches as we have seen in the first lecture. We have here this beautiful facade, and it is a wonderful building; we'll actually take a look at the interior a little bit later in another context. A very different Romanesque church in Italy is this one of San Nicola, Bari in the southeastern part of Italy. The body of Saint Nicholas—that is to say, Santa Klaus—was stolen by the Italians in the 11th century and they built this elaborate Romanesque church to house the body; he's still there. This is the interior, and as you can see it's a very large space and it doesn't look very much like the very large space of Santiago de Compostela that we looked at just a minute ago. By the way, many churches including this one in southern Italy and Sicily are not only influenced by their proximity to the Muslim world just across the Mediterranean—and, in fact, these areas were controlled by Muslims for a while in the early Middle Ages—but also influenced by Byzantium and, oddly enough, by the Normans (from Normandy), because by the end of the 11th century a dynasty of Norman kings is ruling southern Italy and Sicily. The style in that area is really an extraordinary mixture of different pieces and makes it a wonderful place to go to take a look at the various kinds of Romanesque that can develop.

Let's finally take a brief glimpse at England, and I'm only going to show you one church because we're going to spend more time with England later on in the course. But what we're looking at now is the facade of the cathedral of Durham. In England, there is sort of an indigenous pre-Romanesque architecture that we call Anglo-Saxon of which very little remains; but when the Normans—and we've seen that they built very large Romanesque churches in Normandy—conquered England in 1066, in a sense they brought that style with them and, of course, it was adapted into the English style. In fact, if you read books written in England about the Romanesque architecture of England, it will simply be called the Norman style to remind us how much this is influenced by the Normans. What we see here is the facade of Durham Cathedral. It is the best-preserved and sort of purest of the Romanesque churches. Others survive in part and then have been rebuilt in part, but the cathedral of Durham really is a fine example of this Norman or English Romanesque architecture. You can also see from this photograph that Durham is beautifully set up on a hill and this is taken from the next hill over.

I wanted to make sure we have this sense of the breadth of Romanesque styles; the variations of the Romanesque styles. Now, what we want to do in the next lecture is to talk about one particular problem in Romanesque: How do you build a big roof made of stones? How do you get it to stay up there, and how do you get any light in the church if you have to build walls to hold up a stone roof? That's, again, the topic of our next lecture.

Vaulting—A Look at Roofs

Lecture 4

In various churches ... there was a need to figure out how to vault odd spaces. ... If you can build a rib, then it's much easier to fill in because you're filling in four smaller sections, and therefore you don't need so much scaffolding. ... You can build those ribs in such a way that all of the vaults line up in an aisle and eventually even in the main part of a church.

How did cathedral architects go from building flat wooden roofs to the soaring vaults characteristic of Gothic churches? The essential innovations in roofing took place in the Romanesque period. In Italy, wooden roofs predominated even in the 13th and 14th centuries, but in the rest of Europe, stone roofs were being developed in a variety of Romanesque styles.

Although lighter and easier to build, there are several problems with wooden roofs, most obviously that they are in constant need of repair and can be destroyed very quickly by fire, weather, and insects. They do not last; the wooden roofs that we see today on medieval churches are replacements. The appeal of stone is thus obvious, but it presents construction challenges, namely, weight.

The monastery of Saint-Martin du Canigou in the Pyrenees is a relatively small church with several remarkable features, including a **barrel-vaulted** roof. It's one continuous running piece of stone roofing. There are serious practical problems with barrel vaults, however. First of all, they need to be built in a continuing campaign; you can't delay if there are budget or supply or labor problems. Once constructed, they are also very hard to repair, and damage in one area can affect the entire vault. So, while sturdier than wood, barrel vaults are still expensive and difficult to build, as well as hard to maintain.

An interesting early variation on the barrel vault is found at the church of Saint-Philibert, in Tournus, Burgundy. The architects built a series of barrel vaults at 90-degree angles to the main line of the church. This design allows for more windows, and thus more light, and can be built or repaired one section at a time. The primary problem with this style is aesthetic; the church, of course, runs from west to east, but the lines of the roof run north to south, breaking up the unity of the design and, most importantly, leading the eye away from the altar.

The cathedral of Durham is the earliest surviving example of a church whose principal vaulting is ribbed vaulting.

At Saint-Sernin in Toulouse, the architect built a series of arches and placed short barrel vaults, one after the other after the other, between each of the arches. These are called **transverse arches**. This has similar advantages to the perpendicular vaults above, plus, the arches lead your eyes toward the altar. From this design developed the **groin vault**, which is the intersection of two barrel vaults. Groin vaults both lead you in the right direction and allow for some openness and light. Soon, architects began using groin vaults as the principal vaulting of churches, as at the church of Mary Magdalene at Vézelay.

Yet problems remained. Groin vaults are very hard to center and align along the length of the church. They are very difficult to build because, since there's no structure to them within the individual segment, you need a lot of scaffolding underneath. So architects looked to further refine this vaulting, and they found the key in churches that had odd spaces to vault, like rounded **apses** (or eastern ends). They found the solution by building ribs within the groin vault. Filling in smaller sections within the fault was easier and required less scaffolding and

© iStockphoto/Thinkstock.

At the time of its construction, Durham Cathedral's vaulting was new and innovative.

helped the builders align the vaults more evenly. The cathedral of Durham is the earliest surviving example of a church whose principal vaulting is ribbed vaulting. The church of the Abbaye aux Hommes in Caen, France, has a variation on the kind of rib vaulting found in Durham. Consisting of three ribs within two **bays**, this form will be used in several of the great early Gothic cathedrals.

Note that all of the arches we have looked at so far have been rounded, and this type of arch is usually classified as Romanesque. But it's not quite that simple. The Cistercian Order created great churches with a certain austerity to the architecture. But they were incredibly inventive, and since this was a highly centralized order, they shared their plans and building ideas with other Cistercians across Europe, so that Cistercian churches in Germany, Italy, France, or England look very similar. At the Romanesque Cistercian abbey at Pontigny, we find pointed arches. (Remember from Lecture 1 that the Cistercian style is sometimes called Half-Gothic or Transitional Gothic.) It's important to realize that two of the most important elements of Gothic, the ribbed vault and the pointed arch, are in fact Romanesque inventions.

Despite these innovations, the issue of weight was still a problem—heavy stone roofs lying atop heavy stone walls, which have now been weakened by windows. The solution that would eventually arise is the other key feature we associate with Gothic architecture: the flying buttress. But first, the architects of the Romanesque experimented with other techniques. We turn again to Abbaye aux Hommes, looking at the gallery between the upper and lower windows. The roof of that gallery contains arches as well, an incorporated buttress. Instead of the weight of the roof coming straight down into the aisle pillars, it also some weight into those gallery arches. As far as we know, this was the first buttressing cathedral scheme. ■

Important Terms

apse: The rounded east end of a cathedral or other church.

barrel vault: Sometimes called a tunnel vault, a rounded stone roof and the earliest form of stone roofing for a church.

bay: One section of a nave, transept, or choir of a Romanesque or Gothic church. Sets of pillars mark a bay.

groin vault: A vault created where two barrel vaults meet at right angles. These vaults were easier to build than barrel vaults because small areas could be vaulted independently of one another. The groin vault was an important step in the developing technology of roofing a large stone church.

transverse arch: An arch of a vault that runs perpendicular to the nave that divides one bay from another.

Suggested Reading

Courtenay, *The Engineering of Medieval Cathedrals.*

Fitchen, *The Construction of Gothic Cathedral.*

Frankl, *Gothic Architecture*, introduction, chap. 1.

Stephenson, *Heavenly Vaults.*

Questions to Consider

1. Why was the roof the central problem for builders of large buildings in the Middle Ages?

2. How does the experimentation with roofs call into question some of the stereotypes about the Middle Ages—e.g. that it was a dull and uninventive age?

3. What were the reasons that such experiments as ribbed vaults and pointed arches and buttresses won out over other forms of roofs?

Vaulting—A Look at Roofs
Lecture 4—Transcript

When we think of Gothic cathedrals, one of the things we think of is those great hovering stone roofs with those fabulous roofs so far up. But very often we fail to wonder how that kind of roofing system evolved, because if we think back to where we began to look at large Christian churches beginning in the fourth and fifth centuries in Rome, those churches, despite their grand size, had, in fact, flat wooden roofs. How are we going to get from a flat wooden roof—such as we see in Santa Sabina in Rome, a basilica we looked at in the first lecture—how are we going to get from that kind of roofing system to what we think of as those soaring, Gothic vaults that need to be propped up by flying buttresses? We're going to focus still in the Romanesque period today, but we're going to see that the essential innovations in roofing took place in the Romanesque period, and that later on what Gothic architects are going to do is borrow and develop certain ideas that develop in the Romanesque period; so we need to get from this flat, wooden roof at Santa Sabina and other basilicas in Rome to those soaring vaults of Amiens, Chartres, Notre Dame in Paris, and the other great Gothic cathedrals.

Let me suggest first of all that in Italy more than in northern Europe we continue to see wooden-roofed buildings in the Romanesque and even in the Gothic periods. For example, one of the famous and beautiful Romanesque churches in all of Italy, San Miniato al Monte overlooking the city of Florence, as you can see here has a wooden roof. You'll notice it's not quite like the roof of the basilica we just saw of Santa Sabina because instead of it being flat, you can see that there are beams that go in parallel to the floor, and then there are those that also rise upward to make a pointed roof. But this is a good example of an 11th century Romanesque church in Italy with a wooden roof.

But while in France, as we will see in most of this lecture, there developed different forms of stone roof we still find in Italy even in the 13th and 14th centuries: wooden-roofed Gothic building. For example, this is the enormously large church of the Franciscan order Santa Croce in Florence. I'm sure that many of you have been there or read about it because among other things it contains famous paintings by Giotto. Here, as we can see, despite the soaring walls and aisles, and just the overall size of this building, it has a wooden roof very much like that one at San Miniato that we just saw a minute ago, which is basically a mile away sitting on top of a hill overlooking Florence. So keep in mind that Italy is sort of an exception to what I'm going to say about the way that roofs developed in the Romanesque and Gothic periods.

We do find, in early Romanesque churches in France, that there are indeed wooden-roofed buildings. Here, for example, we have a small Romanesque church in the town of Vignory in France, and you can see here with these walls, these large stone walls with windows toward the top, that there is this wooden roof. There is a problem with wooden roofs—actually, there are several problems—and I suppose they are obvious: One, they are in constant need of repair; they, of course, can be just destroyed very quickly by fire and, let's not forget, also by weather and by insects. Although wooden roofs are relatively easy to build and relatively lightweight, they are not going to last you a long time; these wooden roofs that we see of medieval churches, for example, are wooden replacements. We just don't find wooden roofs lasting many, many hundreds of years and, of course, these churches are quite old. So we find developing in the 11th century with the development of various Romanesque styles all over Europe attempts to build with roofs of stone.

Let's start with this church; it's almost exactly 1,000 years old. This is the monastery in the Pyrenees named Saint Martin du Canigou. You can see what a beautiful place it is; you can see the cloister is an irregular shape because it's perched up there on that mountain where you just can't lay things out the way you might. The building that we see in front of the tower there is the church; you can see it is relatively small, but when we look inside we discover something extraordinarily interesting: It has a stone roof. It isn't a very big church, as we can see; but if you look carefully, because there's no plaster over the stones, you can see that the columns have resting on them arches of cut stone, and then the roof is rounded and made of cut stone. We call this very simple form of roofing a barrel vault, because it's one continuous running piece of stone roofing.

There's one obvious thing to say about this church: It is very dark inside. I want to suggest, as I mentioned in an earlier lecture, that's not necessarily a huge problem because, again, monks might somewhat like dark, contemplative spaces. But as you can see, this is very dark; there is very little light coming in. This is a flash photograph, and when you walk in it really takes a while for your eyes to adjust before you can see what's going on. Nevertheless, I want to show you a bigger barrel vaulted church, and also a barrel vaulted church with plaster on it. This is the beautiful church of Saint Savin sur Gartempe in France, and as you can see its principle aisle—we're looking right from the west to the east here; you can see the seats in the middle—is one long barrel vault. In fact, not only is it plastered over but almost uniquely surviving among Romanesque churches in France, the vault is painted; that is to say, there are frescoes telling various stories of the Bible, and saints, and so on. The roof actually becomes, in this case, another place to put pictures.

This is not going to be, I guess what we could say, the final solution to the problem, because there are serious problems with barrel vaults, and they are really practical ones. First of all, if you're going to build a church like this—or like Saint Martin, a much smaller one—this needs to be built in a continuing campaign. You can't build, take a few years off because you're out of money or whatever it might be, and then build some more; you really need to build this in one continuous campaign, because everything is connected obviously, there's no stopping point other than the beginning and the end of the vault. The other thing to say about it is if part of it is damaged, it is very hard to repair and that damage can affect the entire vault. Again, this is expensive and hard to build, and hard to maintain.

How do we find, therefore, a more efficient way of building the roofs of churches now that we've started this process of making roofs out of stone? One really interesting, and as far as we know unique, example is in the city of Tournus in Burgundy. It's a very interesting church, take a look at it here; this is the church of San Philibert, Saint Philibert. We're looking from the east end to the west in this photograph, and if you look you can see that what the architects have done is build a series of barrel vaults at 90 degree angles to the main line of the church. What you have is a series of barrel vaults crossing we would say across the nave, the western part of the church. You can see this series of barrel vaults; let me let you look straight up into that and you can see how this works. This is pretty neat in a couple ways: First of all, as you can see, at the end of each of these barrel vaults there are windows because that's where they open up to, and therefore that allows more light in; and gain, you can build this in segments, as you can see, because you can build one piece at a time.

However, there is a problem, perhaps primarily an aesthetic problem—I want to go back and take a look at the photograph we just looked at—and that is the church, of course, runs from west to east (again, we're looking from east to west but it runs from west to east), and with the main pieces of architecture perpendicular, if you will, to the church, it sort of breaks up the unity of the church; it leads your eyes away from focusing on the altar, which is where I'm standing when I took this picture, and therefore focusing on where the body and blood of Christ are consecrated.

How else can you use this concept of the barrel vault? How's this one? This is the church of Saint Sernin in Toulouse, an enormously large church as you can see; and what the architect has done here is basically to build a series of arches and then basically make a short barrel vault, one after the other after the other, between each of these arches. Of course, this has several advantages: You can build a piece of it at a time; you can repair a piece of it at a time; and you can see—I'm standing here on the west end looking toward the altar—all those arches lead you toward the altar, so the aesthetics work very well. By the way, let's just look up and see what one of these individual vaults looks like: You can see the two arches, and you can see that there's a simple, short barrel vault essentially. These are called "transverse arches"; so this is a barrel vault with transverse arches.

This is all pretty neat; but something interesting happens: an idea for building a stronger kind of vault. This is an aisle from the church of Tournus; and if you look at it, you'll see what happens is that these vaults look different. They're called "groin vaults," and basically a groin vault is the intersection of two barrel vaults because when you are building a church with aisles and a transept, you're going to have a place where the two pieces come together. They created, as you can see here in the aisle, this notion of two intersecting vaults being one vault; and, of course, what's nice about this is first of all you have room for a window—in this case, since it's an aisle, on the left side—but, unlike having the barrel vaults at right angles to the main line of the church like the main part of Tournus did as you can see, what goes on here is you also have this way of looking back and forward; you aren't taken by these rough angles. It both leads you in the right direction and also allows for some openness, and therefore for some light. This groin vault is now going to be used not just in these places where there were intersections or for a small aisle like this, we're going to be able to see the groin vault being employed to be the principle vaulting of the church.

This is the church of Mary Magdalene at Vézelay, and you can see here it's a very elegant church—you can see those beautiful alternating pieces of stone that make up the transverse arches—but when we look up, you will see here that these are, in fact, groin vaults; that is to say, each one of these pieces of an arch is actually two intersecting arches. You can see the lines, because obviously this vault has a shape to it; it's not just barrel-shaped, it's not just semicircular, but rather it has a kind of shape to it that is the intersection of these two vaults. The design of the groin vault is a major move forward in the way that these churches are, in fact, constructed.

But—there are always a lot of "buts" in these things, as you know—there are some problems in constructing groin vaults. They are very hard to center; that is to say, you can see here that there is a place where what looks like the kind of x-shaped design you can see where they meet in the middle; but, if you will, in any two groin vaults they will meet in slightly different places, there will not be a straight line of meeting points up and down the church. These are very difficult to build because, since there's no structure to them within the individual segment, you need a lot of scaffolding underneath; in other words, this takes a lot of construction in order to build these vaults and because you have to construct them and then fill them in and plaster them over, again, they're hard to center and they're hard to build.

So there was a way of looking around and asking this question: Are there other kinds of vaulting systems that can develop? Just as we saw the groin vault probably develop as a small kind of vault, not the principle vault of the church, so we find also in various churches that there was a need to figure out how to vault odd spaces. For example, we know that a lot of these churches have rounded east ends, rounded apses—that's the term for the east end of the church—and therefore if you start vaulting that rounded apse, you're going to get some fairly strange shapes; and so as we do that, we find maybe it's easier instead of doing what we see in the left part of this diagram, simply having this groin vault, to build a kind of skeleton. You can see the skeleton here on the right side. These are called "ribs," these pieces that kind of connect the parts, the corners of the vault; and if you can build a rib, then it's much easier to fill in because you're filling in four smaller sections, and therefore you don't need so much scaffolding—you can actually fill in from above, by the way—and the fact that you can build those ribs in such a way that all of the vaults line up in an aisle and eventually even in the main part of a church.

Let's take a look at how we imagine this kind of vault being created. This is a small French church in the town of Morienval in the eastern part of France. You can see here we have two columns on either side and an odd shape, an odd space, that we're looking into, and that what the architect has done here is to build ribs because you can see that it's not a square that's being vaulted but a very odd shape; so the vault on the right side has more stones in it than the little piece on the left side. So perhaps . . . we don't know, because this is not the first one, we don't know where this was invented. But the fact that we find them here—this is from the 1130s—shows us that perhaps it was in struggling with the problem of vaulting odd places that a new kind of solution was developed, and perhaps at some point somebody said, "Gosh (well, probably didn't say 'gosh'), if this helps us to solve the problem in this little, weird, odd space that we have, maybe we could transfer this to a bigger stage and maybe this would help us in making better vaults in aisles or even eventually the main part of a church." Here's probably an experiment that was done—again, not first here, but this is an example of it—to try to solve a particular problem, and what it ends up doing is developing a new technique that has new possibilities.

Let's take a look at how this plays itself out. This is the cathedral of Durham in northern England, and as far as we know this is the earliest church that's principle vaulting is, in fact, ribbed vaulting. This is actually older than the church I just showed you in Morienval; that is to say, the one I just showed you dates from around the 1130s. What we're looking at is not an original but sort of a second generation vault there, or perhaps—again, we don't know— this might have been invented in England and then invented separately in

France; we just don't have the answer to these things. But at any rate, this is the earliest example we have, and it's a rare sort of complete Romanesque church, in England that we have this wonderful set of vaults. Let's look up in those vaults, and you can see that we have these ribs. This is a unique example of how the ribs are used. You'll see there are actually two sets of ribs within one set of arches. Pretty soon there are going to be other ways of doing that, so this pattern is not going to become common. But this is the principle vault where we have the rib vault rather than the groin vault; and, as you can see, there are windows on either side because of the way the groin vault and now the rib vault open up, both up and down the church and also from side to side, where we see the light coming in. Durham is a particular and interesting example of how this vaulting occurs.

Where do we go from here? This is the church of the Abbaye aux Hommes in Caen in France. It is in Normandy; it is, in fact, where King William the Conqueror is buried. If we look here, we can see a variation on the kind of rib vaulting that we found in Durham. Take a look at this a little bit more carefully here: We're now looking up straight into the vault, and what we see is really a six part vault. We have the big transverse arches at the top and the bottom, the arches that cross over; then we have sort of a middle arch as well; and then we have the "x" shape. We have three ribs within two bays—each of those arches of the aisle is called a "bay"—each two-bay set marked off by a set of arches; that is to say, the transverse arches. Now we're looking up: These are rounded vaults, but we're looking up here to recognize that we have a sort of new solution, a sort of two-bay-at-a-time solution; and as we're going to see, this is going to be used in several of the great early Gothic cathedrals such as, for example, the cathedral of Laon, to which we'll be dedicating a lecture a little bit later on. those will be pointed arches and these are round; but nevertheless, we see here the evolution from the barrel vault to the groin vault to the ribbed vault, and we see that both of those innovations started out probably as experiments in small parts of churches and then were used as the principle vaulting structure, such as we see here in the Abbaye aux Hommes in Caen.

Therefore, we've gotten to the ribbed vault, which is so dominant in Gothic; again, except for some places in Italy, if you will. But, of course, I mentioned specifically that these are rounded arches, and if there's anything we think of—you probably learned this in grade school or high school—how do you tell a Romanesque church from a Gothic church? One has rounded arches; the other has pointed arches. Let me suggest—and we're going to look at this more in just a minute—"sort of," is the way I would respond to that. Yes, there are round; yes, Chartres and Amiens and Reims and Laon have pointed arches; but it's not quite that simple, because I want to suggest that in particular within the Cistercian Order, remember I mentioned them at the very beginning of the course, and talked about the fact that this particular monastic order is going to play an interesting role in the development of architecture in France and places other than France.

This is an interesting religious order for a lot of reasons; this is one of the great churches of the order in Pontigny in Burgundy. As you can see, compared to many of the churches we've seen, it doesn't have big bell towers; and if we were to go all the way around this church you would find nary a statue. There was a kind of austerity to the Cistercian architecture; but one of the things we know about Cistercians in general is they were incredibly inventive, and that means in building their churches, it means in designing the way they make a living. For example, sheep raising as a major industry in England was essentially invented by Cistercian monks in England; and Cistercian monks in France invented a lot of, well my term is "gizmos," to help make water power more efficient, because they were given sort of crummy land that nobody else wanted to use and they had to build their churches and develop their industries on that sort of crummy, out in the middle of nowhere land that they asked for as part of their monastic austerity. So they developed their own form of architecture; and since this was a really highly centralized order, various kinds of plans and building ideas were provided for monks wherever they were, so that Cistercian churches in Germany, Italy, France, or England look a lot more like each other than we find generally the buildings of those countries do.

This is the interior of the church of Pontigny, one of the great Cistercian abbeys. It is a Romanesque church—everyone would call it that—but you see what you have: First of all, you notice you have a series of transverse arches, and they are not rib vaults here, bu the arches are pointed. Again, if we say, "Aha, rounded arches means Romanesque and pointed arches means Gothic," is this Gothic then? I mentioned in Lecture One that we sometimes refer to the Cistercian style as Half Gothic and sometimes refer to it as Transitional Gothic because it really isn't quite Romanesque and it really isn't quite Gothic; and so the idea of this pointed arch, just like the idea of the ribbed vault, comes from the Romanesque period. Now, Gothic architects of the later 12th and 13th centuries are going to do extraordinary things with those inventions, if you will, that the Romanesque architects themselves never dreamt of presumably; but nevertheless, it's important to realize that two of the most important elements of Gothic, the ribbed vault and the pointed arch, are in fact Romanesque inventions.

Let's turn to one final problem: If there's anything we can say about stone roofs, no matter what kind of design they have, they are heavy. I mean, it's important to think about that. We're looking at building here—and most of the other ones we've looked at today, except for the wooden-roofed ones—that are these enormous buildings with enormous roofs made out of rocks, and rocks are heavy; and we've seen problems with trying to find places for light. We saw that in that very first barrel-vaulted church; we've seen some ways in which light has come in—there's light here in the church of Pontigny, for example, that we've been looking at for a while—but nevertheless, how do you keep those roofs up, just keep them from falling down, and how do you allow there to be holes in the walls that hold up those roofs so that light can come in, some sufficient amount of light? Again, the characteristic Gothic answer—we all learned this in grade school, too—is: the flying buttress.

The flying buttress was, indeed, invented in the Gothic period, probably at Notre Dame in Paris; and we will note that when we look at Notre Dame a little bit later on. But let me take a look at one more Romanesque experiment, if you will—in this case, holding up the roof—that's going to play out as very fruitful. We're back now in the Abbaye aux Hommes in Caen; again, this is where King William the Conqueror is buried because he was the Duke of Normandy, and this is in Normandy. See those vaults that we've already examined up there; now I want you to look: We have the aisle where that lowest level of windows is; then we have a gallery; then we have an upper row of windows before the vault. I want you to focus for a minute on that gallery; galleries are important parts of monastic churches. For one thing, they were probably places—since this was a monastery, after all—that if there were women in the church, that's where they would be; but also we believe that since many of these churches were pilgrimage churches, a gallery was a place where pilgrims went and perhaps even where pilgrims slept. Look at the gallery: I want you to look inside one of those arches of the gallery and you'll see that there's a stone arch in the roof there. That really is a structure that buttresses—hence the word—the roof. It's not flying; it's incorporated into the roof of the aisle of the church that is at the gallery level. But you can see those arches in there, and they are essentially incorporated buttresses; in other words, instead of all the weight of the roof coming straight down into those pillars, we also have some of the weight of the roof going off in those arches over the gallery and then being held up, in a sense, by the wall of the aisle of the church so that the weight is somewhat more distributed then simply all coming down through those pillars to the floor.

This is an incorporated buttress; but as far as we know, this is about the earliest of a buttressing scheme that allows the shifting of some of the weight of this stone roof somewhere other than in the pillars that are right below the base of the vault. There's a transfer of some of the weight; and, of course, if not all of the weight of the roof is dependent on those pillars it means that the walls can be a little bit thinner or perhaps can have more of a hole in them for light, that is to say, for windows. Here we have a really interesting example of a kind of buttressing system that would later on become separate from the building, not incorporated into the roof of the aisle but rather separate and outside what we'll call the flying buttress.

So a scheme that's going to lead to the flying buttress is a Romanesque invention. Again, to review, the ribbed arch and the pointed arch are Romanesque inventions. One of the things we're going to do in this course is to see how those ideas are, again, expanded in extraordinary ways; possibility played out in extraordinary ways in the Gothic period. But before we do that—because we're talked about Romanesque by looking around Europe; we've talked about Romanesque by looking at the particular problem of roofs—what I want to do in the next lecture is to take a look at three Romanesque churches, buildings and decorations, and then we'll be ready to move on to the first of all the Gothic churches.

Romanesque at Its Best
Lecture 5

Over the door we have this extraordinary sculpture [of the] Last
Judgment. ... You can see that our left side, Christ's right, is a bit more
orderly and organized than the right side; Heaven's a more organized
place, if you will, than Hell. This is an idea, I think, that has particular
Benedictine resonances, but an idea that's carried over also into the
Gothic period.

Gothic is not only an architectural style; it is also a decorative style,
and the decorative elements are both meaningful and useful. In this
lecture, we look at the decoration in three Romanesque churches
in France—the abbey church of Sainte-Foi, Conques; the abbey church of
Mary Magdalene, Vézelay; and the cathedral of Autun—that are largely
intact and foreshadow the decoration in Gothic churches. Two of the three
will be pilgrimage churches along the route to Santiago de Compostela.

Sainte-Foi is a very well-articulated church. It has a facade with two towers
with a sculpture in between, a pattern we will see over and over in the Gothic.
It also has a central tower where nave and transept meet. The three towers
are visible for a great distance, so that pilgrims could navigate by them. The
roof consists of transverse barrel vaults. The aisle is very, very high, with a
second gallery level and a row of upper windows. This three-level elevation
will be standard, if not universal, in Gothic cathedrals.

The sculpture over the door is a scene of the Last Judgment. Christ is in the
center; on Christ's right are the saved, and on his left are the damned. One of
the most obvious details is that the group of the saved is more organized, as
befits a Benedictine view of salvation. Another important but more obscure
detail to note is that remnants of paint can be found on this sculpture. Many
statues during both the Romanesque and Gothic periods were painted, which
is surprising to many of us viewing them today. The sculpture also depicts
heaven and hell. The image of heaven comes from the Gospel of Luke,
describing souls as children on the lap of Abraham. It also features Sainte-Foi
before the hand of God. The image of hell shows Satan and souls in torment,

including a poacher being roasted on a spit (like one of the locals who may once have poached on the monks' lands). Thus the sculpture combines the universal and the local.

The church of Mary Magdalene in Vézelay is built in the shape of a cross, with a Gothic period east end, complete with flying buttresses and pointed arches. On the western, Romanesque end, there is a **narthex**. In early Christian times, a narthex was where the unbaptized or the unforgiven could view the services before they were fully admitted to the church. By the 12th century, it had no particular function. Here, the sculpture inside the narthex serves as an introduction to the church itself, a sculpture of Christ sending the apostles out to preach. Around Christ's head are several pockets of individual, detailed groups of people to whom the apostles are to be sent—some of them quite fanciful. The top of Christ's body is still, and the bottom is in motion, perhaps in reference to his dual nature as human and divine. Inside we find alternating colors of marble illuminated by two rows of windows. The roof comprises a series of transverse arches and groin vaults. The carvings at the top and bottom of each column tell stories from the Bible and from monastic lore; we call these **historiated capitals**. They are rarely found in Gothic churches.

The cathedral of Autun is one of the few Romanesque cathedrals left in France. It has been rebuilt several times; its tower,

Some of the sculpture at Autun Cathedral is signed "*Gislebertus hoc fecit*"—"Gislebertus made this."

for example, was added in the 16th century. The interior, with its aisle, gallery, and windows, seems inspired by a nearby Roman gate. Autun, like Conques, has a Last Judgment over the door. Here Christ is weighing souls, and Satan is cheating by tipping the scales. An angel blows the trumpet, and the dead are rising. One soul is dramatically yanked from his grave, straight off to hell—a pretty serious warning. Some of the sculpture in Autun was carved by the same sculptor whose work we saw in Vézelay. His name is Gislebertus; he wrote "Gislebertus made this," "*Gislebertus hoc fecit*" on the sculpture itself.

Some of the sculpture in Autun was carved by the same sculptor whose work we saw in Vézelay.

Autun also has historiated capitals. The medieval story of Simon Magus is depicted across two capitals. It's interesting that his story, from which we derive the term simony—that is, the selling of church offices—was placed here at a time in the 12th century when there was a great deal of interest in reforming the church and getting rid of simony. Other sculptures depict stories from the Old Testament, the New Testament, and the lives of saints.

So the Romanesque, in sum, is a style of great breadth as well as great architectural elegance and complexity. Many of the basic elements that we think of as Gothic we find in Romanesque churches: cross shapes, towers, galleries, portal sculpture, pointed arches, ribbed vaults, and so on. It is also a form of art and architecture worthy of being enjoyed and appreciated on its own merits, not only as a prelude to the Gothic. ∎

Important Terms

historiated capital: The top part of a column containing sculpted figures, as opposed to those capitals derived from the Doric, Ionic, and Corinthian capitals of antiquity.

narthex: The entrance area of a church between the facade and the nave. Eventually, the narthex was reduced or disappeared completely in Gothic cathedrals.

Suggested Reading

Barral i Altet, *The Romanesque: Towns, Cathedrals and Monasteries*.

Stoddard, *Art and Architecture in Medieval France*, chaps. 1–7.

Wilson, *The Gothic Cathedral*, introduction, chap. 1.

Questions to Consider

1. How do our examples of Romanesque buildings and decorations give us a different understanding than we may have had about the "invention" of Gothic?

2. What are the qualities of Romanesque architecture and sculpture that you find most attractive and why?

3. How can we appreciate Romanesque for its own sake and not only as an overture to the coming Gothic symphony?

Lecture 5: Romanesque at Its Best

Romanesque at Its Best

Lecture 5—Transcript

In our last look at the Romanesque style before we move on to Gothic, what I want to do now is focus on three churches so we get a sense not just of a building or even a piece of a building like the last lecture, but rather that we get a sense of the whole; and I'm especially going to emphasize here something we really haven't looked at before: the decoration of Romanesque churches, because later on when we look at the Gothic churches, Gothic churches are not just buildings, they also have spectacular sculpture and other forms of decoration that are integral to the meaning and the usefulness to Christians of those buildings. We're going to look at three churches that are largely intact, largely unmodified from the Romanesque period. Obviously there is no such thing as one that's not been touched since; but nevertheless, we're going to look at ones relatively intact so we really can have a sense of how they worked.

Many churches in the Romanesque and the Gothic periods were pilgrimage churches; they were either places that pilgrims went to in droves—the best example of that is Santiago de Compostela in Spain, something I've mentioned before—but also there were other, lesser pilgrimage sites; and there were, if you will, a series of pilgrimage churches along the route to Santiago de Compostela. Two of the churches we're going to look at in this lecture, in fact, fit that definition. The first one is the church of Sainte Foi, a minor female saint, in the little village of Conques in the Rouergue, more or less in the middle of France, and the church of Mary Magdalene—it had her relics; they were thrown out during the French Revolution—in Vézelay in Burgundy. The third church we're going to look at—although urban and a cathedral, rather than monastic like Conques and Vézelay—the cathedral of Autun, was also a pilgrimage church because it claimed to have relics of Saint Lazarus, the biblical figure, or actually a combination (as we'll see) of two biblical figures. With that, let's turn to the church at Conques.

We look at it here from the rear, and you can see it's a very well-articulated church. You can see in the lowest part we have a chapel; and then the round part that goes around the altar; and then the higher round part where the altar is; and then the tower; and then you can see in the front of the church in this photograph, way in the distance, there's also, in fact, not just one that you see there but two towers. If we look here as we approach the church of Sainte Foi in Conques, you see this enormous facade with two large towers; and you might also be able to see—we'll look at it in more detail in a minute—there is sculpture over the main portal there and that notion of two towers in the front and sculpture over the door is, of course, a pattern we will see over and over in the Gothic.

Let's go inside and look at the church of Sainte Foi in Conques: You can see that there is a tower in the center. This photograph is taken at the crossing, where the nave (the western part of the church) crosses the crossbar of the cross called the "transept," and I'm standing just inside the apse of the church, the east end. So we're looking up at the tower and we're looking toward the west entrance, and we see these large transverse arches that are round as you can see, and, in fact, we have transverse barrel vaults in this church. You can see here the elevation, you can see the aisle where there are windows; you can see that there's a gallery, but there are no windows above the gallery, something that will be common later on in Gothic. Here is the vault itself; again, we saw this kind of vaulting in the last lecture: the transverse arches, the windows, we see the gallery. Then, this is the east end of the church: There is the altar as you can see, it is rounded; but if you look here, the aisle is very, very high and then there is a smaller gallery and then a row of windows, and that kind of three-level elevation that we see here in the east end of Conques is going to become not universal but standard in Gothic cathedrals.

Let's go back outside: Here we have the facade, this powerful facade; and, by the way, these towers are visible for a great long distance, as is the tower over the crossing, so that pilgrims coming could spot this and know that they have come to one of the points along the way of their pilgrimage to Santiago, but also a point where in and of itself it's important because of the relics of Sainte Foi. Over the door we have this extraordinary sculpture that is, as you can see here, a last judgment. We have Christ in the center—we're going to look at a lot of details of this in just a minute—and then on Christ's right, our left, are the good guys (the saved) and on the other side are the damned. We're going to look at some details, but I think even if you just sort of dim your eyes out of focus a little bit you can see that our left side, Christ's right, is a bit more orderly and organized than the right side; Heaven's a more organized place, if you will, then Hell. It's worth pointing out that in addition to being a pilgrimage church, it's a Benedictine monastery. Saint Benedict says in the Rule that you should always keep the judgment before you; always remember that you are going to face the judgment. Literally, that's what we see here; and we will see in places like Amiens we will also have a Last Judgment over the center portal of the door. This is an idea, I think, that has particular Benedictine resonances, but an idea that's carried over also into the Gothic period.

I want you to look at this—this is just one detail and I'm not going to focus on who the figures are here—but you will notice if you look very closely and squint a little bit, you'll be able to see that in a couple places, in the robe on the right and on the angel up above, there is some paint; there is some color. This is remaining paint; it tells us that a lot of statues—and this is true in the Gothic period, too—were either fully or partly painted. It may be that there were full-color ones; it may be there were some where perhaps just the robe is painted, where the skin is the color of the stone; but we're so used to this stone as the color of stone being the way sculpture is to us, whether it is Ancient Greek sculpture—much of which was painted—or whether it is medieval sculpture. But here, probably because we're in such an unpolluted place out in the boondocks in Conques, we're able to see some paint; and that's an important thing for us to remember, even though the sculpture we're going to look at in the cathedrals of these cities by and large has none left. There are one or two exceptions to that, but not very many.

Here is Christ in the center, and you can see Christ is the judge. His right arm is being raised—because, after all, that is the saving side—and as you can see his left arm is pointing down. You can see he's surrounded by angels, and he's in this almond-shaped thing called a mandorla; it simply comes from the Italian word that means "almond," by the way. There in the center is Christ the judge, and we must all face the judgment.

Now which way do you go? This is the entrance to Heaven; and if you look carefully here, you'll see that the door is open—it has a lot of locks on it, but it's open—and there is Saint Peter welcoming the faithful souls into Heaven. This, of course, is our goal; this is what we want; because ultimately we are either saved or damned, and here we see the saved. Opposite them—so this works symmetrically, if you will—is the entrance into Hell, and you can see that Hell is a mouth; you have to go through the Hell-mouth. You can see the mouth is open and somebody's feet are in there being swallowed up— literally swallowed up—by Hell, and you can see that demon with that big club there about ready to whack the next damned souls to sort of force them into the mouth, too. You have a choice to make: How are you going to live on earth, what are you going to believe? If you do it well, you'll go through the gate of Heaven and be welcomed by Saint Peter; if you don't do it, or do it badly, this is your final destination.

On one side we have an image of Heaven; it's an image of Heaven that actually comes from one of the parables of Jesus in Luke's Gospel: The souls are depicted as children on the lap, or to use the African-American folk song in the bosom, of Abraham. So these are the souls in the bosom of Abraham that are saved. Let's see what's opposite Abraham: Satan; and you see Satan there in place of Abraham, and you see that there is, for example, on our right a man being hanged. We know from the symbol that he has with him why he's being hanged: He is a miser, because he has a money bag around his neck. Do you want to be around where you can be hanged or where Satan is giving commands to the little devils to torture, or do you want to be in the bosom of Abraham?

There's an interesting local touch, because here we see the hand of God reaching out to Sainte Foi, the saint whose relics are in this church, to whom this church is dedicated; and opposite her, we see a guy being roasted on a spit by a rabbit. Perhaps, we think, it may even suggest some local people who poached on the land that belongs to the monks. So, if you will, we have these sorts of local touches here: the local touch of Heaven; Sainte Foi before the hand of God; and the local touch of Hell, perhaps suggesting to people, "Keep off our property," sort of an interesting notion. All this is important, but why would people want to come and stop in Conques? Because there were the relics of Sainte Foi; and this is the reliquary that contained her earthly remains. It's this beautiful wooden statue covered in gold and jewels; and although now it's in a museum rather than in the church, nevertheless this would have been an object of great veneration.

Let's move on to the Church of Mary Magdalene in Vézelay. Originally, the monastery was down below in the valley of the Yonne River, but not after those Hungarians kept raiding; they moved up on the safer hill. You can see that the church is built in the shape of a cross; I'm standing on one of the front towers and looking toward the rear end, and you can see again that we are up on a hill here. The buttressing that you see is not original, it was added later. Here we see the church from the east end, and I wanted to show you this primarily to show you that the east end—that is to say, on the left—has flying buttresses and pointed arches; that's because it was added in the Gothic period, so we're going to focus on the front part of the church rather than the back end.

Unusually, there's a separate room before you actually enter the main part of the church called the narthex. In early Christian times, the narthex was used as the place for the unbaptized or the unforgiven to be able to be outside the church and yet to look in at the services until they are fully admitted. By the 12th century, the narthex essentially has no particular function that way anymore because of infant baptism. Nevertheless, many churches kept the narthex, and we'll see even in the Gothic period there are little differences between the very back part of the church where you walk in and the rest of it; sort of an homage, if you will, to this narthex that really had no particular function anymore. You can see there is sculpture inside the narthex that serves as an introduction to the church itself.

Let's look at that sculpture: It's an extraordinary piece of Romanesque sculpture as you can see here, because in the center it's Christ, and you might say, "Ah, a judgment," but it's not a Last Judgment as it turns out, it's a different scene: It's Christ sending out the apostles to preach and teach to the ends of the earth; so those are the apostles on either side, and then you can see down below in the part that runs underneath Christ's feet, and in the part that runs right around his head we have several pockets of individual, detailed groups of people to whom the apostles are to be sent. What's so interesting is if you think about that notion that you should preach and teach to the ends of the earth, who is at the ends of the earth? Of course, we would say people in Europe didn't know; but they thought they knew, because they had ancient Roman sources that, in fact, had then been included in medieval texts, in particular a medieval encyclopedia by a sixth-century Spaniard named Isidore of Seville. Therefore, either real or imagined people at the ends of the earth are the subject of the call of Christ to go to the ends of the earth.

Here is Christ, an extraordinary figure, because the top half of Christ looks very calm, if you will; look at the folds of the drapery. But if you look at the bottom half, you can see his legs are bent and the movement of the draperies is much more active. Most scholars think this suggests that this is a way of showing that Jesus is both human, the bottom part (after all, humans move around) and divine, the upper part, and therefore unchanging; so it probably tells us something we would say—this is a very fancy word—Christological, something about the nature of Christ as fully human and fully divine. Let's take a look at who some of those people are at the ends of the earth: This is wonderful; if you look carefully, you'll see there's a little guy on the left and he's about to climb a ladder onto a horse. Who needs to climb a ladder to get on a horse? The answer is: pygmies; so these are meant to represent pygmies. Pygmies were known about through the ancient Romans because they traded with sub-Saharan Africa, and so this is a rendition, if you will, of the pygmies. It was also believed at the ends of the earth there were people with dog heads, and you can see them here; in fact, one of the great theological debates was if they have dog heads are they human or not? Because if they aren't human they don't have souls and you can't convert them, but if they're human, even though they have dog heads, then they have souls and they need to be converted or they'll be damned. Here, we seem to have a sculptor—or whoever designed this and decided what would be depicted—that the dog-heads are indeed humans. Maybe the most interesting, perhaps the most bizarre, is the belief in the big-eared people. If you look down below slightly to the right of center, you'll see that there's somebody who, almost turtle-like, is completely covered by sort of folding in his ears, while the person on the right has these great big flapping ears. In fact, let's zoom in on that person; now those are ears.

Here we have this wonderful set of depictions of Christ going to the ends of the earth and converting these people. By the way, Saint Bernard of Clairvaux preached the Second Crusade; the first great call of the Second Crusade was preached at this church in Vézelay. You can imagine him thinking about, and perhaps using in his preaching either in words or in gestures, "Look where the Crusaders need to go; we need to go to the ends of the earth and bring everybody to God."

If we look inside the church, we see this is one of the most beautiful and elegant of all churches of any style. You can see the alternating colors of marble; the east end looked brighter than where we are because, remember, the east end is Gothic while we're in the Romanesque part of the church. But look here at the elevation: You can see here that there are windows in two levels, in the aisle and up above, just below the vault; you can also see that at every column, both the upper and lower columns, they are all, in fact, carved with stories or allegories. We call those historiated capitals. They're not used much in Gothic, at least not in France—they are a little bit more in Italy, for example—but nevertheless, they are an important part of the decorative scheme, and we'll look at some in a minute. Here is a vault, and we saw this before in our discussion of roofs because here you can see we have a series of transverse arches and then we have groin vaults.

I want to look at some of the capitals; they are extraordinarily interesting and beautiful and they tell stories, and I want to use them in some ways also to talk about the differences in style and, if you will, in psychology between Romanesque and the Gothic sculpture we're going to see. This is a capital that tells the story of the parable of Lazarus in Luke's gospel. Remember there's a rich man who has this table and poor man Lazarus—you see him there on the left coming with his stick, he's walking with a stick—that he comes and he's willing to eat the crumbs but the rich man, of course, will give him nothing; so the banquet is contrasted with poor man Lazarus. On the other side, you can see a servant coming in with more food and more food; this guy is really being gorged, but poor man Lazarus is on the other side, a clear moral lesson. Or here we have the Old Testament story of David and Goliath. Notice that David is dressed like a medieval knight; and this will be true also in the Gothic period. There's really no interest in trying to say, "How did people dress in David's time?" That's our question; it was a not a question that was asked much in the Middle Ages as far as we can tell. So there's David the knight on the left, and then you can see in the center that David is in the process of hacking off the head of Goliath.

This is a story from monastic lore: When the first monk, Paul—who's a little bit older than Saint Anthony, whom we usually consider the first monk—died, Anthony wanted to bury him but the ground was too hard, so lions came along and dug his grave. You see Anthony at the top, then you see the embalmed body of the hermit Paul, and then you see those two wonderful lions doing God's work and digging the grave. Here we have—and this really demonstrates a side of Romanesque sculpture I want to talk about—the story of Moses and the Golden Calf. There's Moses on the left with the tablets of the Ten Commandments; there's the Golden Calf right in the center. How do you know that's not just a nice old cow? That's a good question; the answer is: Look what's sitting on its back. You have this really ugly, violent devil sitting on the back of the Golden Calf; so we don't have to sort of work it out—now who's a good guy, where's the bad stuff here?—it's all very well laid out for us; we know that the calf represents some sort of evil because of what's sitting on its back.

In addition to stories, there are also some allegorical figures. This is the allegorical figure of Despair. Look at the distorted face and the wild hair, and this man is stabbing himself; and notice how his back is all twisted, and that twisting of the body—which clearly, I think, represents a sinful body, the twisting of the soul if you will—leads to this act of self-destruction. Finally, I want to show you the capital that is really interesting: This is called the Mystic Mill; and you see there's a guy putting grain in a mill, the mill is being ground, and another guy is getting the flour out in a bag on the right side. We call this the Mystic Mill because we know that the figure at the top is Moses, he's putting in the rough grain of the Old Testament; and that's Paul down below receiving the finely ground and useful flour of the New Testament, a really wonderful allegory.

Finally, let's turn to the cathedral of Autun. Here we see it from a distance; again, one of the few Romanesque cathedrals left in France, although the tower that we see there was added in the 16th century. Again, this church has been built and rebuilt. I want to look first inside, and I want you to notice what we have here. This is the elevation with the aisle, gallery, and windows. This is an interesting pattern that we've seen before; but in Autun, we can say that there's a particular source for this pattern because at the edge of town stands a Roman gate to the city. What we see here is this pattern that really is echoed in the first two levels of the cathedral of Autun. Here is one of those places where we can talk about a Roman ruin seems to provide not something to copy, but something to guide and inspire perhaps the architect of Autun cathedral.

Autun, like Conques, has in the center of the front door a Last Judgment; and let's look at it. Here is the great judging Christ, here is the weighing of souls; that is to say, on the left is the archangel Michael (part of the scale is broken) and on the right you can see there's a devil that's trying to pull down on the crossbar of the scale and cheat in the weighing of souls. In fact, let's zoom in on that: You can see the devil's not only cheating, he's loaded another devil in the pan to try to make it weigh so that the soul on the other side will be found wanting and therefore will go to Hell. "Devils cheat" is the message there; and the kind of grotesqueness of all of this we'll see in a somewhat different way will be carried on in the Gothic period. On the other hand, we see here the angel blowing the trumpet, because at the Last Judgment the trumpets shall sound and the dead shall be raised. Speaking of the dead being raised, here we see them—below, in the lowest part of the sculpture— coming out of their graves. You can see by some of the expressions here, these folks are not happy about the Last Judgment because they're going to be found wanting. On the other hand, here are ones coming out of their graves and being welcomed by an angel. There's one particular detail that's so famous in this particular Last Judgment: You have this one soul where these hands—the devil's right up above—seem to come out of nowhere and just sort of yank this soul up and presumably yank him straight off to Hell. It really is dramatic and kind of scary to think that even at the Last Judgment this violence could be done to you even as you're coming out of the grave and getting your body back; it's a pretty serious warning.

There's another part of the exterior sculpture that no longer exists in its totality today, but one piece of it has survived. Here we have the image of Eve; you see her plucking the fruit with her left hand. You can see her nakedness there; but sometimes we look at those grotesque devils and whatever, and maybe they don't do much for us other than entertainment. Isn't that one of the most seductive people you've ever seen? This is early 12th century; it's a figure of Eve, the Temptress; and it's such an extraordinary figure to me: beautiful; and again, quite seductive and sensuous I think, even though it's a piece of rock carved in 12th century style from the front of a cathedral. Some of the capitals in Autun were done by the same sculptor that did some of them in Vézelay; in fact, we have the sculptor's name who did the Last Judgment and presumably some of the capitals as well because he actually wrote his name on the Last Judgment sculpture. His name is Gislebertus; he wrote "Gislebertus made this," *"Gislebertus hoc fecit"* on the sculpture itself. It's engraved there so we know.

I want to show you a two-capital story: It's a story of a guy named Simon the magician who's mentioned, but only mentioned, in Acts of the Apostles. This is a story that developed later on. He goes to Rome and he competes with Peter; and he sprouts wings and flies over the city. You can see him flying there, and Peter prays to God, "God, if you allow this guy to fly over the city, people are going to believe him rather than us telling them about you." All of a sudden, Simon the Magician, sometimes called Simon Magus, crashes to the ground and dies. You can see Peter and Paul on the left—Peter has great big keys so we recognize him—and we see Simon crashing, you can see his neck just sort of snapping as he hits the ground; there's the detail of it. It's an extraordinary piece of sculpture. By the way, it is from Simon the Magician that the sin of selling and buying church offices, "simony," comes; and therefore, he's the first simoniac, we would say, and it's interesting that his story is here at a time in the 12th century when there was a great deal of interest in reforming the church and getting rid of simony.

Here is one of the most beautiful of the capitals; this one's actually been removed and put in a museum now. This shows the angel coming to sort of tell the Magi what they need to do. You can see they're all sleeping—one of them has his eyes open—but you can see the angel pointing to the star saying, "You have to follow that star." Here we have another capital where we see, in a later part of this story, the Virgin Mary and Jesus being led by Joseph on the way to Egypt; this is the so-called "flight into Egypt." Here we have the story of Noah and the Ark. That's the Ark up there on the top of Mount Ararat, and you can see some of the animals inside. Here we have an interesting story, because Jesus is tempted. Remember the Devil comes and says, "Turn these rocks into bread," and Jesus says, "Man does not live by bread alone"; and we see that story being depicted here.

So in these sculptural programs on the outside and on the inside of the buildings, we find a lot of interesting kinds of stories from the Old Testament, the New Testament, the lives of saints; we find allegorical images and certainly we're haunted by those images of judgment. We are going to see that although the sculpture will not always be in the same place or of the same style, we will find lots of Last Judgments, lots of other stories depicted, and that will be part of the way the Gothic cathedrals mean.

Let me just sum up now what we've learned about the Romanesque. First of all, it is a style of great breadth and within individual buildings there's great architectural elegance and complexity. Many of the basic elements that we think of as Gothic we find in Romanesque churches: cross shapes, towers, galleries, portal sculpture, pointed arches, ribbed vaults, so many of these things. What I would want to point out, since for us this has been prelude to the Gothic, that as much as Romanesque is an important prelude to Gothic— without which we just can't understand Gothic—I want to suggest that Romanesque is not just a prelude to Gothic, it's a form of art and architecture that needs to be enjoyed and appreciated, even if it means getting out of the big cities when you travel and going out in the countryside.

But our task is Gothic, and now it's on to Gothic.

Saint-Denis and the Beginning of Gothic Style
Lecture 6

Scholars are a fairly contentious lot—the old academic joke, "You put 10 academics in a room, you have at least 11 opinions"—but just about everybody agrees that we know where Gothic begins. ... The answer is: It's at Saint-Denis.

Saint-Denis is a Benedictine monastery that was built near Paris in the 12th century; today, it is accessible via the Paris Metro. It is a problematic church to study. The parts that were built around 1140—our beginning date for Gothic—are the front and the very back, and the section between wasn't built until about a century later. Here we look at the early Gothic parts of Saint-Denis; we will come back to the middle section in Lecture 17. The abbot of Saint-Denis who supervised and provided the inspiration for this building was named **Suger**, and it is Suger's church we look at now.

Who was Saint-Denis? The Saint-Denis whose relics are at this church was, in fact, three different people whose stories merged over the centuries. The first man was a 3rd- or early-4th-century bishop of Paris. He was martyred on the hill in Paris we call Montmartre, but then he did something quite unusual: He decided he wanted to be buried somewhere else, so he picked up his head and took it to where the abbey of Saint-Denis now stands. His story merged with that of a character in the Acts of the Apostles, Dionysius the Areopagite, whom Paul converts to Christianity in Athens. The third man was a 5th-century Syrian monk who attained anonymity by using the pen name "Dionysius"—today called Pseudo-Dionysius—whose writings are among the most important mystical texts in the entire history of Christianity. So for people in the 12th century, those three discrete human beings from the 1st through 5th centuries are all the same person. Dating back to the 7th century, the kings of France were buried at Saint-Denis. It became a place of great royal patronage. The church also housed the Oriflamme, which was said to be the banner carried by Charlemagne to Saint-Denis as commemorated in a stained-glass window at Chartres Cathedral.

Abbot Suger was the abbot of Saint-Denis between 1122 and 1151. He was a man of humble origins, but he attended school at Saint-Denis, and one of his schoolmates was the future King Louis VI, to whom he became both friend and advisor; he even governed France as regent when the next king, Louis VII, went on crusade. In a sense, this association made Saint-Denis the center of a lot of French ideology and a place of pilgrimage. When Suger became abbot, he set about replacing the dilapidated Carolingian abbey church with a structure more befitting the site's importance. Writing about his vision for the church, he said he hoped it would rival Hagia Sophia and the Temple of Solomon itself.

As it turns out, unlike in other parts of France, there was relatively little Romanesque architecture in the Ile de France, the area around Paris. In some ways, the church is anti-Romanesque; that is to say, it really offers a new kind of vision. Built between 1137 and 1140, the facade has three decorated doorways. There is also a small **rose window**, one of Suger's innovations. The towers were recessed a bit from the facade, making the latter more prominent.

Only the center door's decoration is original. It is, of course, the Last Judgment, and as we're going to see, Suger's idea was that when one enters Saint-Denis, one is entering paradise, and we enter through the Last Judgment. In this sculpture, a crucified Christ is surrounded by apostles (and a tiny Suger praying at his feet). Souls are rising from graves

The abbey church of Saint-Denis is the undisputed birthplace of Gothic.

below, and above are a series of ascending figures that end with an image of the Trinity. Above all this is that rose window; we know from Dante's poetry that, a century and a half later, the rose is an image of heaven itself. Perhaps this was already the case when Saint-Denis was built. Or the window may be based on Ezekiel's vision of the wheel. Just behind this wall is the narthex, which contains ribbed and pointed vaults, two Romanesque features combined for the first time here.

The apse (or **choir**, as it is also called) is actually built on top of a 9th-century Carolingian crypt, which itself contains remnants of an even older church. Architecturally, the most important part of Saint-Denis is the **ambulatory**, or aisle and chapels radiating around the apse. Suger built a double ambulatory; although there are double ambulatories in Romanesque churches, they tend to be very heavy and dark, whereas this one is very light, and the vaulting is ingenious. Although the upper level of windows is a 13th-century addition, the lower windows are huge, with slender columns. Also, in Romanesque churches, very often the chapels around the ambulatory were almost little churches within a church. Here they are integrated, shallow spaces with wide entrances. The windows here are huge, as large as the arches into which they are set, so much of the east wall disappears. All of this creates a wide-open, light-filled atmosphere in the apse.

The apse windows have theological as well as architectural implications. Pseudo-Dionysus (who was available to Suger in Latin translation) wrote that we come to know God indirectly through signs and symbols and then must transcend them. Here in the apse, the windows tell Old Testament stories. They are just the sort of indirect, symbolic images Pseudo-Dionysus referred to, the first stage on the journey to God. Pseudo-Dionysus also spoke of supernatural light: Jesus says, "I am the light of the world." A new aesthetic of light, in such contrast to the monastic darkness of the Romanesque church, is fully on display here. ∎

Important Terms

ambulatory: The rounded aisle or aisles surrounding the apse of a cathedral.

choir: The part of a church east of the transept and containing the altar.

rose window: A round window in a facade or transept with stained glass in various patterns containing figures and designs.

Name to Know

Suger (r. 1122–1151): Abbot of Saint-Denis and the man generally believed to have created the first Gothic structures—namely, the narthex and choir of the abbey church.

Suggested Reading

Panofsky-Soergel, *Abbot Suger on the Abbey Church of St.-Denis and Its Art Treasures*.

Pseudo-Dionysius: The Complete Works.

Scott, *The Gothic Enterprise*, chap. 5.

Sumner Crosby, *The Royal Abbey of Saint-Denis*.

Questions to Consider

1. To what extent is Saint-Denis the creation of a single individual, Suger?

2. How does the architecture of Saint-Denis concretely express abstract and mystical ideas such as those found in the writings of Pseudo-Dionysius?

3. Why would it be vital to begin a trip to the Gothic cathedrals of France with a visit to Saint-Denis?

Saint-Denis and the Beginning of Gothic Style
Lecture 6—Transcript

As I'm sure all of you know, scholars are a fairly contentious lot—the old academic joke, "You put 10 academics in a room, you have at least 11 opinions"—but just about everybody agrees that we know where Gothic begins; we know where that label that we put on, although it's not a term from the 12th century, really means some significant change. The answer is: It's at Saint-Denis.

I have to tell you a story before we continue looking at Saint-Denis in some detail. Last night, I was reading a research paper done by a student of mine on Saint-Denis. We were there, in fact, two months ago; and the picture you see of the facade of Saint-Denis, that's my very cold student—because it was cold when we were there—standing in front of it. This was a really brilliant paper, as I would have expected nothing less from this student of mine named Seth from Zionsville, Indiana. But what was great is that I'm going to be using some of the insights that I got from his paper in this lecture. He didn't change my mind on a lot of things, but he certainly augmented some things I thought and understood about this church. This is why, by the way, being a college professor is being the greatest job in the world: It's all about teaching and learning for both students and faculty.

At any rate, as I said, everybody agrees that Saint-Denis is where gothic starts. Saint-Denis was near Paris in the 12th century, and it was a famous Benedictine monastery. It is now a suburb of Paris and, in fact, it's at the end of one of the metro lines. But very few people ever get out there; they are churched out, if you will, after Notre Dame, perhaps Saint Chapelle, which we'll also see in this course, and maybe another church or two along the way—Saint Eustache is now popular because of all the Dan Brown stuff—but at any rate, everybody ought to take that little metro pilgrimage to Saint-Denis because there is where Gothic begins.

Having said that, let me point out that this is a problematic church to study. You'll notice, for example, that it looks sort of lopsided. There actually was a second tower until the 19th century; sometimes towers don't all get built, this is one where actually one had to be removed because it was dangerous. But the main problem with looking at Saint-Denis is the fact that the parts that were built around 1140—which is sort of our beginning date for Gothic—are the front and the very back, and the in-between part wasn't built until about a century later. We are going to be looking at the early Gothic parts of the Saint-Denis, the front and the back, and, in fact, only much later, in Lecture 17, are we going to come back and look at the middle of Saint-Denis, because for a very different reason it, too, is important in the history of Gothic.

Let me take you around to the back, where I had to beg the owner of this property to let me come in and photograph the lower part of the apse, or east end of Saint-Denis; and you'll see it's a series of chapels. The part on top of this was, again, rebuilt in the 13th century; so all that's left of Suger's church—Suger was the abbot of Saint-Denis who supervised and provided the inspiration for this building—is the front part and the lower part of the back part; that's what it looks like from the outside, and that's what it looks like from the inside. Those windows at the very top of the photograph, you can forget about them; they were put in much, much later, about a century later. We're looking at the rounded east end here, and those windows, which we're going to look at in some detail because they're very important to understand Saint-Denis and they're very important in the history of stained glass.

Still, I have to show you the middle part; we're going to come back and study this later, I just wanted you to be aware of now what we have is this magnificent, 13th-century Western part or nave of the church, but in Suger's time you would have had that great big facade, a sort of creaky old middle part that actually dated from Carolingian times—the time of and just after Charlemagne—and then the east end. Suger built the top of the east end, but again, it was removed later on and was replaced.

What is Saint-Denis? Simply, as I said before, it is a Benedictine monastery; but it is so much more. First of all, we need to ask the very important question: Who is Saint-Denis? It turns out, that's a very difficult question to ask, because the Saint-Denis whose relics were at Saint-Denis was, in fact, three different people. That is to say, over the course of centuries, stories of three different people merged into the story of one person. All three of those people are going to be important to our story. First of all, there is the story of Saint-Denis, Saint Dennis. He was, by tradition, a third or early fourth century bishop of Paris, and he was martyred; in fact, the story is his head was cut off on a hill in Paris—we call that hill today Montmartre, "the mount of the martyr"—but then Saint-Denis did something if not unique at least I think we'd have to say unusual: He decided he wanted to be buried somewhere else so he picked up his head and took it to where the abbey of Saint-Denis is.

So Saint-Denis, number one, is, in fact, this martyred bishop of Paris; so he's a good, genuine martyr. Secondly, there is a character in the Acts of the Apostles whom Paul converts to Christianity in Athens—by and large, Paul wasn't very successful in Athens—and he's known in the Acts of the Apostles as Dionysius the Areopagite. He was, therefore, a disciple of Paul and goes back to the beginning of Christianity. That figure, who's mentioned once in the Acts of the Apostles and that's it—he doesn't even have 15 minutes of fame in the Bible—but he, in the eyes of people at Saint-Denis, merge with this bishop so that the bishop who was martyred and carried his head to Saint-Denis was a follower of Saint Paul. We sort of forget about those three intervening centuries. That's two people who are Saint-Denis. The third is there is a 5th century, we think, Syrian monk, anonymous—we don't know his name—who wrote works using the name "Dionysius." Therefore, those writings were associated with Dionysius/Denis, and these writings are among the most important mystical texts in the entire history of Christianity; and so martyr bishop of Paris, follower of Saint Paul, also becomes the writer of these great treatises. We today call those writings the works of Pseudo-Dionysius, but for people in the 12th century, those three discrete human beings from the first, third or fourth, and fifth centuries are all the same person. You can see there are many reasons why Saint-Denis himself is a superstar, and we're going to see how important all that is in the conception of this building.

But Saint-Denis is more than that; it is more than the place of the burial of this man, Saint-Denis, three rolled into one, because at least dating back to the seventh century, we know that the kings of France came traditionally to be buried there. Here we see a photograph of some of the tombs. These tombs are not as old as the bodies inside them and, of course, most of the bodies that were originally there are not there at all anymore because of the

French Revolution; I mean, if you're a French Revolutionary what a great place to go, you can toss out a thousand years of royalty just by looting one church. But at any rate, many of the tombs are still there; and so actually probably more French come to visit Saint-Denis to see the tombs of some of the famous kings than they do to look at the architecture of Saint-Denis. This becomes a place of great royal patronage and the royal burial ground; and, if having Saint-Denis and the French kings isn't enough, Saint-Denis had something else: It had a banner called the oriflamme, which was said to be the banner carried by Charlemagne and given by Charlemagne to Saint-Denis. Here we have an image: This is a stained glass window from Chartres cathedral, but we see Charlemagne—in fact, you can read his name just to the left of his shield, it says "Carolus"—and you can see he's carrying that banner; so that banner was believed to be at Saint-Denis.

Saint-Denis connects to the Bible, connects to martyrdom, connects to great theology, connects to the king, and connects especially to Charlemagne. What a special place, and the person who more than anyone else recognized and wanted to make even more important and special that place was Abbot Suger, the abbot of Saint-Denis, between 1122 and 1151. By the way, he left us some images of himself: This is a stained glass window in Saint-Denis, and this is Suger giving the stained glass window; he's actually holding the stained glass window there and you can see his name in Latin above. He's in his priestly garb here; we'll see him in his monastic habit a little bit later on in another one of the windows. Suger was a man of humble origin; he was a monk and he went to school at Saint-Denis, a famous place to go to school. One of his schoolmates was the future king of France, Louis VI, and therefore Suger was acquainted with royalty. Eventually he became the Abbot of Saint-Denis, and a friend and advisor both of Louis VI and of his son, Louis VII. In fact, when Louis VII and his wife, Eleanor of Aquitaine, went on the Second Crusade, Suger was left to be the regent of France; he governed France in the absence of the king while the king was away on crusade. Therefore, the abbey of Saint-Denis was to become this place associated with all the holiness that I've described, but also in a particular way with royal power; and this would make Saint-Denis in a sense—not literally, obviously—kind of the capital of France, the center of France, the center of a lot of French ideology, what we might call "patriotism," because of its connection with royalty and the martyred bishop of Paris. Saint-Denis was to be a place of pilgrimage.

There was a kind of dilapidated Carolingian church when Suger became the Abbot of Saint-Denis, and you can't do what Suger wants to do with that building. Suger decided to have it replaced; again, we know he only replaced a couple chunks and not the whole thing. Suger writes about this; so we don't have to speculate or rely on later sources because Suger tells us about the building of the abbey church of Saint-Denis. He says he hopes to rival two other buildings: Hagia Sophia in Constantinople, and the Temple of Solomon itself. I think it's fair to say that Suger does not lack ambition and vision. We don't know who actually did the architecture or the day-to-day supervision of the work at Saint-Denis—clearly Suger wasn't an engineer in any sense of the word—but this is clearly his building, his inspiration. In fact, Suger explains to us that the kind of timber needed for the roof couldn't be found; he actually went and found the forest. He also found the quarry from which the stone would come to build Saint-Denis. Whether that is all literally true or whether part of that is propaganda and sort of explaining how this building is really in some way a reflection of Suger is hard to say; but nevertheless, it is fair to say it's his.

What about the style? As it turns out, as opposed to Normandy or Burgundy or other parts of France, there was actually relatively little Romanesque architecture in the Ile de France, the area right around Paris that was under the direct control of the king; because it's important to remember that beginning in 987, the French dynasty had come out of the job of Count of Paris, so Paris was the center. The Ile de France did not have much Romanesque, and it did not have a distinguishable style or styles like Burgundy and Normandy that we've looked at so much. There are art historians who see what Suger builds as a kind of new collection of ideas into a building, as Ile de France Romanesque. In other words, he's adding another Romanesque style. On the other hand, some scholars see that although of course he borrowed from Romanesque predecessors in various parts of France, this church is not only not Romanesque, in some ways it's anti-Romanesque; that is to say, it really offers a new kind of vision, a new kind of building.

Let's take a look at that building: Here again is the facade, and there's my intrepid cold student still standing in front of it as you can see. This facade was built between 1137 and 1140. You can see that there are three doorways, and all the doorways are, in fact, decorated. The ones on either side are not original; the one in the center, although parts of it have been redone—and we don't quite know how much they've been redone—nevertheless, the sculpture in the center is largely original and, as we will focus in on in just a minute, it is of the Last Judgment. You'll notice that there is a rather small round or rose window in the facade; that is also, at least for a facade, the invention of the Suger, and we might want to talk about in a minute what it has to do with the building.

I want to show you a building we've looked at before; this is the Abbaye aux Hommes in Caen. You can see, if you look at the facade, it has a certain resemblance to the facade of Saint-Denis; of course, it has both of its towers still. However, you'll notice a couple differences: One is there is no sculpture on this facade; but in addition to that, the towers are sort of flat with the front, while at Saint-Denis the towers are receded just a little bit, which means that the facade becomes more prominent. Why shouldn't it be more prominent? After all, as we're going to see in the idea of Suger, when one enters into Saint-Denis one is entering paradise; it's going to be nothing less than a model of paradise, and we enter through the judgment.

It's an interesting piece of sculpture, because if you again sort of fuzz over your eyes a little bit, you can see that this seems to be a fairly calm piece of sculpture compared to some of those wild flailing arms of demons and all that sort of stuff that we saw in, let's say, Autun. We have Christ in the center, his arms stretched out on the cross—an innovation in and of itself—but those figures to either side are the apostles; the souls are coming out of the graves from down below, and then up above we actually have a series of ascending figures above the head of the Christ as judge that end with the image of the Trinity (God the Father, God the Son, God the Holy Spirit). We go from judgment to Trinity in the arches, called archivolts, up above, and then finally we get to that rose window way up at the top, and at least in Dante's time a century and a half later the idea of the rose is an image of Heaven itself. Think about judgment, Trinity, and Heaven itself as all being portrayed here.

Let's look at a few details: There is the Christ in the center; and by the way, notice down by Christ's right foot there's a little bitty guy kneeling and praying. That would be Suger. Here we have a detail of the figure of Christ. Again, some of this has been re-carved and we don't quite know exactly what was there at the time of Suger. Here we see the dead coming out of their graves, and on either side we have a biblical allegory that also suggests judgment. Here we have a wise virgin; remember we have virgins waiting for the king to come; some run out of oil, when the king comes they have to get more oil and while that happens the gates are locked and they're left outside. This is one of the wise virgins—you can see her lamp is right side up, and therefore she represents the saved—and there's one of the foolish virgins; you can see her lamp as at an angle, she's out of oil and she represents the damned. There is an interesting allegory that surrounds the door itself of the Last Judgment.

As I said, ultimately we look up toward this rose window, which might be based on the idea of the image of the vision of Ezekiel, which was Ezekiel saw the wheel. You'll see there are the symbols of the four evangelists in each of the four corners; those were added in the 19th century and whether there were ones there originally we alas just don't know. Just behind this wall we have what we call the "narthex" of the church—remember we talked about the narthex at Vézelay; this sort of lobby, if you will, of the church—as you can see in this photograph, it is marked by arches that are ribbed and pointed. We've seen pointed arches in Romanesque, we've seen ribs in Romanesque; here, they come together: These are pointed ribbed vaults, and we see two of them here. Then I give you a little bit larger picture of the narthex, this sort of confusing space that, again, was a kind of lobby, probably used more for liturgical purposes than for its original reason, which was a place for the unbaptized and the serious sinners.

The east end, where we're going to focus for a little while, is actually built on top of a Carolingian crypt, a crypt that goes back to the 9th century. One can go down there, and you can see it's kind of dark and things seem to be sort of scattered and even a little bit spooky, I suppose—although there are some windows because the crypt actually is not totally below ground—but at any rate, here you see some old sarcophagi and as it turns out there are actually remnants down there of a church that goes back even farther than the Carolingian church; so there was a church before that, then a Carolingian church, then there's Suger's church, and then we know that Suger's church was added to significantly in the 13th century; we can really explore several layers of history by investigating literally from bottom to top the abbey church of Saint-Denis.

The most important part of this church architecturally for the Gothic is the aisle around the apse. The apse is the east end of the church and, as we know, sometimes there is an aisle around it with little chapels radiating off; this, by the way, is called the "ambulatory," a term we will use a lot. Suger has constructed a double ambulatory; that is to say, as you can see, there's the inside where the main part of the church is (over on the left), then you have this column that is right in the center, then you have more ambulatory beyond that row of columns. It's a double ambulatory, which makes it very wide and although there are examples of double ambulatories in Romanesque churches, they tend to be very heavy and very dark. Look at this: It is very light, and the vaulting is ingenious. When you have an ambulatory, you have all kinds of odd spaces. As we saw in a church we looked at a couple lectures ago, in fact, probably the rib vault was invented dealing with odd spaces. But here we see some of the beautiful inventive vaults in these odd spaces that are created in this double ambulatory. Here's another set of these vaults.

But what I want you to notice is how light all of this is. First of all, you have big windows; but look at those columns. They are very slender, and therefore you have this opening and this widening out. Also in Romanesque churches, very often the individual chapels that were around the ambulatory were almost little churches within a church. In other words, they had three discrete walls and then opened as a fourth wall into the church; and if you looked at it from the outside, they very often seemed just to be sort of afterthoughts or attachments. But look what Suger has done: First of all, he's integrated those chapels into the building by making them very shallow and giving them wide entrances; so they kind of scallop around the ambulatory, and they are so close to the main part of the ambulatory—not far away in these little churches that are attached—that they, of course, provide a great deal of light into the east end of the church. This is really a sort of extraordinary invention that we have of Suger at Saint-Denis.

Again, let's look here at the choir. We're looking through that double ambulatory. "Choir" is another name for the east end of the church; I'll sort of use it more or less along with the word "apse," and then the ambulatory is the part behind all those columns (we get some terminology straight here). But look how light it is because look how big the windows are. In fact, I've talked about sort of punching holes in walls to make windows, and that's what a lot of Romanesque windows look like, a hole that's sort of been carved out. But look here: The windows are as big as the arches in which they're set; it almost looks like the arches are frames for the windows so that really much of the wall of the east end of the church disappears, and these chapels become staging areas for the light that comes through. That's what so different about Saint-Denis: It really is about that light and that airiness, whether the lightness comes from the small columns, whether it comes literally from those windows—which are stained glass here; of course, you can't really see the stained glass very well—but before we come back to looking a little bit at what the ideas are, the theological not the architectural ideas behind all this light, let's look at a few of the windows to see the kind of stories they tell, because I think they also will help us to understand, in a sense, what's old and new at Saint-Denis.

There are a lot of Moses stories, because one of the things that Pseudo-Dionysus writes about is that we come to know God indirectly; we come through signs and symbols, and then we must transcend them. Here's a story of Moses: Moses is on the left with a halo, and in the center is a column with a bronze statue on top of it, sometimes called the Brazen Serpent. The story is that the Hebrews in the desert were being attacked by scorpions and snakes and dying. Moses prays and God says, "Take a bronze serpent, put it up on the column, and those who look at it will be cured," so you can see the ones on the right looking up and being cured. Here's another Moses story: This is the story of Moses encountering God in the burning bush. Notice here that we have, in fact, in all these windows more Old Testament stories than New Testament stories, and that seems odd to us; but again, it's this idea of going through this indirection and we move in stages systematically from the sort of more difficult symbols to unpack to Christ to Heaven itself, and that the architecture of light and the stories in the windows help to take us there.

By the way, here's the Annunciation where the angel Gabriel comes to the Virgin Mary, and look who's down at the feet: that is Suger, this time in his monastic habit rather than in his priestly vestments. Here we have the story of the ancestry of Christ—by the way, it's interrupted by the fact there's a modern altar in this chapel, it sort of annoys me as an art guy—but this is the Tree of Jesse. Jesse has a dream and out of him comes this tree that includes his son David and then all the kings and ultimately the Virgin Mary and Jesus; and there is, in fact, Jesse sleeping and you can see the tree coming out of Jesse. Finally, because we saw this in sculpture in Vézelay, this is somewhat differently conceived: the Mystic Mill. This is Moses with the grain of the old, Paul with the flour of the new, and, of course, you can see how that fits with that aesthetic of all those Moses stories that I talked about a minute ago. This is a place of light. This is one of those windows; I took this in the morning so you have a lot of direct light coming in where sometimes it's even hard to see the stories because even coming through the colors the light is so bright.

Pseudo-Dionysus translated into Latin—he wrote in Greek—in the ninth century, available to Suger, who believed, of course, that the relics of the author of those books is in his own church. Suger talks about in the building, because Pseudo-Dionysus talks about it, supernatural light: We are being led by natural light to supernatural light; Jesus says, "I am the light of the world." The meditation of the things in the church, whether it's the Last Judgment on the front that takes us up all the way to the rose window, or whether it's looking at these stories in the windows, or whether it's simply being overwhelmed by the lightness of the place itself—which is, after all, where the body and blood of Christ are consecrated—it's the light; it's the aesthetic of light. We talked about monastic churches being dark, and even sometimes being deliberately dark; not the abbey church of Saint-Denis, this very special church as we have seen. Another writer who wrote in Greek, Maximus the Confessor—this work was also translated into Latin and almost certainly available to Suger—talks about the fact that the church itself can be an image of the cosmos as the cosmos is an image of Heaven. We really are entering from time to eternity in some real way when we walk into this church.

That's the aesthetic of Saint-Denis; that's the aesthetic of the Gothic. Both in terms of structure and aesthetics, Gothic begins at Saint-Denis.

The Urban Context of Cathedrals
Lecture 7

It is worthwhile remembering that Christianity, like the Roman Empire itself, was essentially urban. ... There's some urban rivalry, there's some ecclesiastical posturing, there's some royal intervention, and in some ways, all of these are important for understanding why there are so many of these cathedrals.

Most of our Romanesque churches have been rural; most of the Gothic ones we will see are urban. Thus we should look at the context of the urban revival in the West in the 11th and 12th centuries. Note that in Italy and Germany there are more functioning Romanesque cathedrals, and in England, many cathedrals are Gothic renovations on a Romanesque frame. But in France, these buildings were replaced almost entirely in the 12th, 13th and occasionally later in the 14th century. Why is this, and how did the urban revival in these centuries affect the development of Christianity?

Between about 1000 and about 1300, we find a growing number of people, whom we would probably call peddlers, reviving long-distance trade. As trade became a little bit more sophisticated, merchants wanted a place to settle in the winter. They had two obvious choices: a city, which has been reduced largely to an ecclesiastical center, or outside a castle, where they have the protection of a noble. Either way, they would be putting themselves under someone else's law: canon law or feudal law. But the kinds of disputes these budding merchants had were not well addressed by either. Eventually, some merchants sought autonomy. These centuries were also the great age of pilgrimage, including the Crusades, and cities were these pilgrims' destinations.

This new urban world required new urban ecclesiastical centers to meet the growing population's needs. Therefore, in the second half of the 12th and 13th centuries, there was a drive in many cities to replace rickety or too-small cathedrals. Bishops wanted more prestigious, dramatic, powerful, large, imposing statements of their authority at a time when that authority was being challenged. Kings and merchants favored building new cathedrals to increase the city's stature among its peers (and rivals). The merchants also wanted places to celebrate their patron saints. Remember, too, that a lot of things happened in cathedrals other than Mass and sacraments. Cathedrals expressed the values not only of the bishop but of the entire citizenry.

Now we turn to three **early Gothic** cathedrals. The first is the cathedral of Sens, the first complete Gothic cathedral. It was begun almost at the same time as Saint-Denis and was a very important ecclesiastical center; the archbishop of Sens had jurisdiction over the bishop of Paris. The church is in three vertical parts: an aisle, a gallery, and windows. It has a six-part vault, like in the Abbaye aux Hommes, but now the arches are pointed. The vault is supported by alternating major pillars and pairs of Corinthian columns, a solution unique to this cathedral. Sens has a single ambulatory and, originally, only one chapel coming off of it. The rest are later additions. The upper choir, scholars believe, shows us what the upper choir at Saint-Denis must have looked like in Suger's time.

Notice that, although the aisle and gallery arches are pointed, the window arches are round. Round-arched windows would linger in Gothic architecture

An Urban Rivalry

Sometimes, the competition between cities over their cathedrals reached extremes. In 1215, Siena built a wonderful new cathedral, which still stands. In 1296, the Florentines said, "We're going to build a new cathedral, and it's going to be a lot bigger than Siena's." In fact, they left their old cathedral up and they built the new cathedral around it; then, just before they finished the new cathedral, they dismantled the old cathedral and took the parts away. The Sienese then wanted to build an even bigger cathedral, but they didn't want to start from scratch, so they came up with a wild idea: to rotate the axis of the cathedral 90 degrees. The old nave and apse would become the transept. They began construction on the facade, but the Black Death swept through the city, and the new cathedral was never built. Only the skeleton remains.

for roughly a half century after Saint-Denis. We are looking at a transitional, experimental phase; the period from Sens to Chartres—begun in 1194—is called **early Gothic**.

Now we turn to another cathedral in the Ile de France, Senlis. The main entrance contains a sculpture of the end of the life of the Virgin: death, Assumption, and Coronation. The Coronation image becomes a very common theme in the Gothic because many French cathedrals are dedicated to the Virgin. On either side of that sculpture are structures called jamb statues. These have been used in Romanesque churches, but Senlis's are particularly beautiful and influential, being less about motion and more straightforward figures.

> **Cathedrals expressed the values not only of the bishop but of the entire citizenry.**

Finally, we look at the fortress-like cathedral of Noyon. Unfortunately, all of its sculpture is gone. This cathedral is where John Calvin was baptized, and these statues were, in fact, destroyed in the wars of religion. Both ends of the transept are rounded, which is highly unusual. The nave has not three but four elevation levels. The smaller, false gallery is called a **triforium**, and this will eventually expand as the main gallery disappears in Gothic churches. This four-level elevation is clearly an experiment to make these buildings taller. ∎

Important Terms

early Gothic: A term specifically employed to describe the beginning of the Gothic style in England. It is also sometimes used for French Gothic from the building of Saint-Denis to the building of Chartres Cathedral.

triforium: A false gallery that is part of the elevation of Gothic cathedrals. By about 1250, the triforia of Gothic churches in France were glazed (i.e., they contained windows).

Suggested Reading

Cook and Herzman, *The Medieval World View*.

Scott, *The Gothic Enterprise*, chaps. 4, 14, 15.

Wilson, *The Gothic Cathedral*, chap. 1.

Questions to Consider

1. What is the relationship between the growth of cities and the creation of Gothic cathedrals?

2. What were some of the more worldly reasons that cities undertook the construction of these enormous stone buildings?

3. Why can we consider the first half century of Gothic building in France the experimental age of Gothic?

The Urban Context of Cathedrals
Lecture 7—Transcript

This lecture is in some ways actually two smaller lectures. First, I thought before we looked at so many of these wonderful urban Gothic cathedrals it is wise for me to talk a little bit about the urban context since, after all, most of the Romanesque stuff that we've seen has been in small towns and countrysides; so the first part really is going to be about the revival of cities after the cities' decline following the destruction of the Roman Empire in the West. Then I'm going to turn three very significant cathedrals, each of which deserves a lecture, to talk about them as examples of varieties of early Gothic architecture. Then we're going to look at a couple early Gothic churches, different ones, in more detail: Notre Dame and Laon. Those are the two halves: The three early Gothic cathedrals as sort of a mini-lecture there, and looking at the urban context. Let me suggest also that this urban context piece fits with Lecture 16, where again we're going to step back for a while—in that case a whole lecture—from looking at buildings and decorations and so on to talk about context; in that case, I'll talk about who paid for these things and how they got built. We wanted to have at either end of the look at some of the classical Gothic cathedrals some other context for understanding and appreciating them.

It is worthwhile remembering that Christianity, like the Roman Empire itself, was essentially urban. Most people in the Roman Empire farmed; that's true anywhere in the world really until modern times. But Rome really was an empire of cities. Cities were seats of learning, of government, of commerce, and so on and so forth; and Christianity, after all, arose in the Roman Empire. To put it a simple way: When Paul traveled around as a missionary, he visited cities and created Christian communities in cities. That's reflected in his Letters: Paul wrote to Thessalonians and Corinthians and Ephesians; he didn't write to "that group of peasants I ran into one day." The very nature of Paul's Letters reminds us of the "urban-ness," if you will, of early Christianity. If we needed another reminder of that, let me point out that the word "pagan"—meaning, of course, somebody who's not a Christian—actually comes from the word that means "people who live in the countryside"; in other words, the countryside was converted long after the city, and that's reflected in that use of the word "pagan."

Christianity was an urban religion; and then just as Christianity triumphed in the West, urban places declined precipitously with the collapse of Roman authority. Cities survived better in Italy than most of the rest of the Western Roman Empire, but even there they precipitously declined. Just to give one example: In the 11th century, Rome had about 1% of the population it had at its height in ancient times. Think about that; 1%. We need to examine a little bit how Christianity functioned without many cities; and then, with the revival of cities in the 11th and 12th centuries how Christianity again became at least in part an urban religion. That really is what I want to follow through and look at. We're going to look primarily at France, because of course, that's where Gothic was invented as we saw in the last lecture; and that's where we're going to focus most, although not all, of the rest of our time looking at Gothic in Europe.

I pointed out in an earlier lecture that between about 1000 and about 1300, the population of Europe increased. There are a lot of reasons for that; I mentioned agricultural changes (technological changes), and of Viking and Hungarian raids, and so on. one of the things that meant is there were people living on the land who weren't needed; that is to say, you don't need all that extra population cultivating the land. We began to find a series of people that we would probably call "peddlers." They figured out that something they have a lot of where they live there isn't a lot of someplace else, and if they carried it from here to there they could make a profit; they could get some things that perhaps are not very well-known or grown very well in their own home areas. We begin to get very, very slowly the growth of some sort of trade, short distance or long distance. Eventually, as this became a little bit more sophisticated, merchants found themselves wanting to find a place in the winter where they could settle down in security and plan out more and more complicated routes for the next year. Two obvious places to settle: In a city, which remember has been reduced largely to an ecclesiastical center; or outside a castle, where they have the protection of a noble. Very often, in fact, what you find is sometimes with those people settling outside castles, they would eventually get so prosperous they would say to the guy who owned the castle, "Tell you what, let us move in the castle, you go build another one." That's why there are so many places named "Newcastle" in different languages all around Europe.

But there's a problem with all this, and the main problem for the merchants is if they're in a city, they're under the law of the church, canon law. If they're outside or inside a castle, they're under feudal law. But the kinds of disputes and problems that these budding merchants have are really not problems that the law of the church or feudal law are set to deal with. Law of the church doesn't handle commerce very well; feudal law is not about commercial things. So there was eventually a perceived need by some of these merchants to find some autonomy, perhaps in particular judicial autonomy, from these folks administering what was seen as inadequate law for them; not being able to settle their disputes very well. There are a lot of ways to try to obtain that autonomy: Sometimes it was simply declared. Sometimes it was no doubt paid off a little bit. Sometimes it was gained through violence. The subject of one of our future lectures, the cathedral of Laon, was built in a town where, in fact, in 1122 this band of merchants that had formed an association—we call it a "commune"—found that the way to violence was the way to establish some autonomy; it actually took the form of killing the Bishop of Laon. This could be violent. By and large, by the way, this is documented better in Italy than it is in the rest of Europe; but luckily a monk who lived near Laon wrote about this in great detail, his name is Guilbert de Nogent, and as a result we know that story in Laon in 1122.

The cities get bigger and they get more complex, legally, socially, and in other ways. They become more cosmopolitan: Goods go in and out, people go in and out. Remember, in addition to all this mercantile stuff, this is the great age of pilgrimage, including those pilgrimages to Jerusalem that we call the Crusades. In this new urban world, we're going to find the need for new urban ecclesiastical centers; that is to say, cathedrals. Why? First of all, the population is growing; second, of course a lot of these cathedrals, some of them are Romanesque, a lot of them are Carolingian. We saw, for example, in the 1130s, until Suger comes along, in his abbey you have a sort of rickety Carolingian building that was serving as the abbey church of Saint-Denis; the same thing happened in cities. So we find in the second half of the 12th and the 13th century, there's this enormous drive in many cities to replace cathedrals. Some were replaced by necessity; we know a lot about fires, for example, that destroyed cathedrals, especially those that had wooden roofs. But nevertheless, even without that, we know there was a great deal of replacement.

One question would be: So what, and who's for it? Everybody's for replacing the cathedral. First of all, the bishop's for it; he wants a more prestigious, dramatic, powerful, large, imposing statement of his authority at a time that his authority is being challenged. Kings very often helped to sponsor cathedrals because kings actually very often favor the merchants over the traditional powers of bishops and feudal lords. But the merchants, too, favored building new cathedrals, and in some places—in Italy more than others—actually tried to take over the building of the cathedral. Why? Because it gives stature to them; it gives places to celebrate their patron saints and the feasts of their patron saints of their various guilds; and it says, "Our city is more magnificent and therefore more prosperous and loved by God than the city next to it, our rival city." There's some urban rivalry, there's some ecclesiastical posturing, there's some royal intervention; and in some ways, all of these are important for understanding why there are so many of these cathedrals. If there were one or two Gothic cathedrals this wouldn't be an issue, but if you drive around France—especially northern France—every city seems to have this enormous medieval stone building in the Gothic style.

We have to try to understand why it is that there was this need for these new buildings. In Italy, there are more Romanesque cathedrals still functioning; in Germany, there are more Romanesque cathedrals still functioning than there are in France. In England, there are more pieces of Romanesque buildings that are still standing as cathedrals that were then added on to and remodeled in the Gothic style; but in France, again partly through fires and so on but partly through desire, these buildings were replaced almost entirely in the 12th, 13th and occasionally later in the 14th century. We have to appreciate how these cathedrals not only express the values of the bishop and state his authority, but how in many ways everybody involved—whether it's a king at a distance (except, of course, in Paris); whether it's the merchants; or whether it's the bishop—all found some reason to want big, new, beautiful statements of the relationship of this city to God, and that's what we're going to be looking at.

We need to remember, too, that a lot of things happen in cathedrals other than mass, other than baptisms. For example, if there is an army going off to war, they'll be blessed in the cathedral. The feast day of the patron saint of a city becomes as much a civic holiday as it does a religious holiday; that is to say, it doesn't just celebrate Saint So-and-So, it celebrates who we are. This is our day; this is our day of a special connection to God because we have the day that the saint died—that's almost always the feast day, the death day; there are very few exceptions to that—and today's that day and therefore we celebrate his or her going up to Heaven to be our intercessor and to be our protector and to be our intermediary with God. To do that, you can't do that well or convincingly in a rickety old building. You can't do that very well if your building is inferior to the people next door. I mean, sometimes it got perhaps even a little bit crazy where you want to have a higher tower, as if somehow God really is up there; you want to have a higher tower than the town down the road that you despise and dislike. We need to recognize how everything in these cities comes together to make these cities once again the splendid ecclesiastical center they were in that fairly short period of time between the time that Western Europe became Christian after Constantine and now we have it again with the revival of cities and the possibility of cities being able to undertake enterprises of this magnitude.

I do want to tell you one story before we turn to those three other cathedrals I want to look at briefly, and that is I want to tell you one particular story of competition. In 1215, the city of Siena in Italy—now much smaller than Florence, then much more Florence's rival; Florence about 40 miles to the north of Siena—built a new cathedral, and a wonderful cathedral that still stands. Then, in 1296, the Florentine's said, "We're going to build a new cathedral and it's going to be a lot bigger than Siena's." In fact, they did it in an interesting way: They left the old cathedral up and they built the new cathedral around it, and then before they finished the new cathedral they sort of took the old cathedral away.

The Sienese were not going to deal with this very well, and so the Sienese took their cathedral, which you see here in this aerial shot—the front of it, you can see the facade, is to the right and it goes from sort of slightly upper right toward lower left, and you can see that it's built in the shape of the cross and there's a dome in the center—the Sienese wanted to build a bigger cathedral but they didn't want to start from scratch so they came up with this wild idea: Let's rotate the axis of the cathedral 90 degrees. In other words, let's develop one piece of the transept—the crossing bar of the cathedral—way, way out and make the old nave and apse into the crossbar. What you see is their attempt to do that. You see that white arch in the upper left part? That was the facade of their new cathedral, and it was going to be built from there up to the building you see; the wall—the far wall, we can't see beyond the dome—of the old cathedral was going to be torn down and this was going to be made one enormous building. Isn't that cool? The Sienese might have been able to do it—they were well underway, as you can see, building it—but the Black Death came and decimated the population, and it just wasn't economically feasible. But they've left the sort of skeleton of the cathedral that never was. This is one particular story of a particular competition between these two cities; a competition, by the way, that goes on today: When Florence and Siena play in soccer, one side is deliriously happy, one side is deliriously sad.

I want to now turn to these three cathedrals and look briefly at them, because they're all important. The first one is the cathedral of Sens; we're going to look at the interior of it. This is the earliest Gothic cathedral. First of all, it's a whole building, not parts like Saint-Denis; and second, it's a cathedral, not an abbey like Saint-Denis. It was begun almost at the same time as Saint-Denis, and although Sens today is a fairly small town—although not very far from Paris—it was a very important ecclesiastical center; in fact, the Archbishop of Sens had jurisdiction over the Bishop of Paris. Paris didn't get an archbishop until after the Middle Ages. This is an important place that we want to look at.

We look here at the elevation, and we can see that it's in three parts: We have an aisle, and then we have a gallery, and then we have windows; and this becomes a standard, although there will be deviations, way of building cathedrals. Here we look up at the vault, and you can see it is a six-part vault. We saw six-part vaults, if you recall, at the church in Caen, the Abbaye aux Hommes. They were rounded, of course; here, you can see, they are pointed arches. But you can see, therefore, that we have sort of main pillars where those big transverse arches are and then smaller pillars where, in fact, we have the arch that divides the middle of this great enterprise of this vault. Again, I want you to look up here and see how this is all laid out, because you'll see that where the big arches are there are these huge piers and they soar all the way up to the base of the windows, but then they alternate with a double set of Corinthian columns. It's really interesting; in fact, it's a unique solution in the cathedral of Sens. We have major and minor; so there's this alternation of major piers, and then the double columns, and so on and so forth. Again, the alternation's not unique, but the particular way of alternating piers with double Corinthian columns is, in fact, unique.

I want you to see what this looks like standing right at those pillars. This is looking up one of those great piers or pillars. You can see with the little smaller piers attached to it, it just soars up and you can see how it goes right into the major arch. Now compare that with standing at the base of that double column set; in other words, another column right behind this one. You can see that we now look up, we pass the windows again and you can see we come to the minor division of this sexpartite vault. By the way, you can see the four-part vault in the aisle—that's what you see right in the center there—and you can see the windows in the aisle. It gives us an idea of how this alternation works. It's really quite beautiful. Again, it's not duplicated anywhere else; there will be alternation, but not between piers or pillars and columns. It's an extraordinarily interesting and unique device here at Sens.

Sens has, unlike Saint-Denis, a single ambulatory and, in fact, originally there was only one chapel in all the ambulatories; so it was a fairly modest structure. Later on, some chapels have been built; you can see one here. I'm standing just as the ambulatory turns to go right behind the high altar; so I am looking at part of the ambulatory and then looking all the way down that aisle broken by the transept and all the way to the west side door. That's the angle we're looking at here at Sens Cathedral.

I want you to look at this elevation; we've seen this before. Again, aisle, gallery, and windows; but I want you to notice something: You see the arches of the aisle are pointed; the arches, the two little ones, in each part of the gallery, they're pointed, although just barely; and then with the windows at the top are pointed arches. But look at the windows in the aisle: they're round. In fact, all of the early Gothic cathedrals for roughly a half-century after Saint-Denis have some round arches; the sort of final triumph of the pointed arch as the unique and only kind of arch used in a Gothic cathedral is going to take about a half a century to evolve. We again see a lot of Romanesque borrowing and we see that we are looking at a transitional phase; we usually call the period from Sens to Chartres—Chartres begun in 1194—Early Gothic for obvious reasons, and there are I guess what we could call a lot of experimentations, like the double columns, like using round and pointed arches together in the same building. It's good to see this particular structure here to get an idea that nobody sat down one day and just came up with Chartres out of nothing. Chartres, Amiens, and Reims, these great we call them High Gothic cathedrals are, in fact, evolved from some of these early more, we might say, experimental Gothic enterprises of roughly the half-century that is the second half of the 12th century.

I want to look at one more picture: This is the elevation in the choir in the east end, in the apse, of Sens Cathedral; it's a little bit different than the elevation I just showed you, you can see the arches are a little bit more pointed, for example, in the aisle. But at any rate, I show you this because some scholars speculate this is more or less the way that Saint-Denis would have looked in Suger's time. Remember, he built an upper choir, except it was later on torn down and replaced by something different. This might, in fact, resemble more what Suger did and this might be our best way of reconstructing in our minds what that east end of Suger's church had. It had a double ambulatory, it had a lot more windows than we see here, but it might have been something like this elevation; sort of an interesting notion.

I want to turn now briefly to another cathedral in the Ile de France and that is the cathedral of Senlis. Here, I only want to look at a little bit of the sculpture on the exterior, because it's particularly important. By the way, this is a beautiful building inside, and we could spend a lecture on Senlis and I think you would be happy and interested and say, "Boy, let me find that on a map so the next time I go to France I'll drive there"; but we only have so much time, even in a 24-lecture course. This is the main entrance to the cathedral of Senlis, and it contains sculpture of the end of the life of the Virgin. It is the death of the Virgin in the lower left part, it is the Assumption of the Virgin in the lower right part, and it is the Coronation of the Virgin—the Virgin Mary crowned Queen of Heaven—in the big part in the center; and so that becomes a very common theme because many, especially in France, Gothic cathedrals are dedicated to the Virgin. We're going to see that she has a privileged place not just in Notre Dame de Paris but Notre Dame de many other places as well; so we'll see this pattern fairly similarly, for example, in the facade of Notre Dame in Paris.

But on either side of that sculpture are what are called jamb statues. Again, these have been used in Romanesque churches, but these are particularly beautiful and influential. You can probably pick out some of these figures, but I want to look just at the one on the right. It is the figure of Abraham, and you can see there he's with his son Isaac and you can see the angel over his shoulder stopping him from killing Isaac. It's a very, very beautiful piece of sculpture, and this kind of jamb statuary will become common, if not universal, in the great Gothic cathedrals of France. Here are a couple statues on the other side: We have the prophet Simeon holding the Christ child, and we have Saint Peter holding the cross. But the most extraordinary figure in this collection is the figure on the right here, John the Baptist. Look at his legs cross. This in many ways is sort of old and new. It has a lot of that motion that we associate with Romanesque sculpture; remember all that movement we saw in Last Judgments and in capitals. But here it's expressed as a jamb statue; so we're going to have these jamb statues becoming important parts of Gothic cathedrals, but the figures will be a little bit less animated, a little bit more straightforward standing figures and even sometimes—as we'll see especially at Reims and Chartres—interacting with one another. But anyway, we see the beginning of these wonderful Gothic jamb statues at Senlis.

Finally, I want to look at the cathedral of Noyon. It sort of looks like a fortress; this is a strong Gothic building, and a very beautiful one. Unfortunately, all of its sculpture is gone. This is the main entrance, and you can see where all the sculpture was: the jamb statues, the statue over the door, the statue between the two doors, the statue in what are called the archivolts, the arches over; all of it's gone. By the way, this is the cathedral where John Calvin was baptized, he was from Noyon; and these statues were, in fact, destroyed in the wars of religion. But let's go inside: I want to focus right now on the transept, because both transepts—the crossbar of a cross-shaped church—are rounded, and this is very unusual; there are only a couple of these left. They are so beautiful. You can see here, I'm looking into this rounded transept; here is some of the architecture in the upper levels of it, but look at that. This is looking up at this rounded transept; isn't it beautiful? You can see, by the way, the sort of interesting kind of vaulting you have to do if you're vaulting this sort of odd-shaped space. But the way these rows of windows light this up is just really extraordinarily beautiful.

Here is the nave—this is a church that's been much damaged in a lot of ways; and, in fact, it's been revaulted so we're not going to pay any attention to the vaulting—but I want you to look at the elevation here, because we have not three but four levels. We have what look like two different kinds of galleries: We have a big gallery where people could be right above the aisle; and then we have this sort of little in a sense fake gallery—you really couldn't be up there and attend the mass—we call that the "triforium" and we're going to see that eventually in Gothic what's going to happen is the gallery is going to disappear, the triforium is going to become somewhat bigger, and the top windows are also going to become a lot bigger to make up for the space that's lost with the gallery. But this four-level elevation is clearly an experiment to make these buildings taller, and boy does this soar; and we can see it soaring here through these various levels of architecture as we look up along one of those pillars.

I want you to look here another way: Again, the vaulting's been redone; in fact, it was six-part vaulting originally, although there's not really the same kind of dramatic alternation between major and minor arches that there was through Sens Cathedral. But look up here: We look up at the vaulting through all of these four levels and you can also see that there is vaulting inside the gallery, and here we see that gallery and that triforium together really lifting this church up; it's as if you're just squeezing another layer in. Again, this won't last very long, although we'll see it at Laon; but it's another one of those experiments, and clearly height is so important here because this is an experiment in a soaring cathedral.

We've taken a look now at these three big stone cathedrals built within a decade or a decade and a half—or at least begun—after Saint-Denis. Now what we're going to do is move on and take perhaps the two most famous early Gothic cathedrals, Laon and Notre Dame in Paris, and we're going to do a lecture on each of them before we move on to that next piece of development, which will be the cathedral of Chartres.

Notre Dame in Paris
Lecture 8

"Notre Dame" means a lot of things other than a 12th-century Gothic cathedral. We have all kinds of images in our mind from later times. ... But even in the 12th century, when the cathedral was built, it was special.

There are many cathedrals in France dedicated to *Notre Dame*, "Our Lady"—that is, the Virgin Mary. Properly, we should call the cathedral Notre Dame de Paris, just as we should say Notre Dame de Chartres or Notre Dame de Laon or Notre Dame de Reims and so on; but to most people, "Notre Dame" is first and foremost a reference to the magnificent 12th-century Gothic cathedral in the heart of Paris.

Although Paris was not a capital in the modern sense in the 12th century, it was one of the most powerful political and administrative centers in France and became more so over the course of the Middle Ages. At that time Notre Dame shared the Île de la Cité, an island in the middle of the Seine River, with the palace of the king of France. Metaphorically, if not quite literally, Notre Dame was in the shadow of the royal palace, and vice versa; in some ways, the history of France and the history of the cathedral are uniquely entwined. Notre Dame was where medieval composers began to experiment with polyphonic music. While Notre Dame was being built, the Cathedral School of Paris (later called the University of Paris) began to flourish; one even finds scenes of medieval Paris's student life among the sculpture in the cathedral. Intellectually, musically, politically, and architecturally, Notre Dame is a very important place.

Like most cathedrals, Notre Dame has been altered since its completion. Some sculpture and stained glass were removed just before the French Revolution. During the revolution, much of the exterior was damaged. For a brief period, the cathedral was no longer a cathedral; it was dedicated to the Cult of Reason and later to the Cult of the Supreme Being. After the revolution, it became the cathedral of Paris once more, and artisans, including the sculptor Viollet le Duc, worked hard to restore the building, but it was hard to repair the damage.

The construction of Notre Dame began 1163 under the supervision of **Maurice de Sully**, the bishop of Paris. It was built very quickly, over a period of about 40–50 years, and without interruption, thanks to the patronage of the royal family and a wealthy clergy; unusually, the merchants did not contribute much to its construction. This continuous building campaign gave Notre Dame an unusual unity of form. The famous facade, unlike those found on most Gothic cathedrals, is symmetrical. A row of statues representing the kings of the Old Testament runs above the three entrances—all post-Revolution copies, although some of the heads, stored offsite during the revolution, are on display in the Musée de Cluny. Above the central door is, as we now expect, a Last Judgment scene, including le Duc's restoration of the resurrection of the dead and, at the top, rows of angel sculptures that look very different at different times of day. Above the left portal is the Coronation; above the right is Saint Marcel, an early bishop of Paris. The facade includes two towers, which became the Gothic standard, and another tower (again, not original) rises from the crossing of nave and transept.

The east end has a rounded apse with an extraordinarily wide double ambulatory. The 14th-century **rood screen** that separates it from the rest of the choir is decorated with stories of Jesus after the Resurrection. The nave, too, has double aisles. In fact, Notre Dame is the longest and tallest cathedral we have visited so far. The roof is the same type of six-part vaulting we saw at Sens, but the elevation is much, much higher, and unlike at Sens, the pillars supporting the main arches and the transverse arch are identical. This symmetry helps lead the eye to the altar

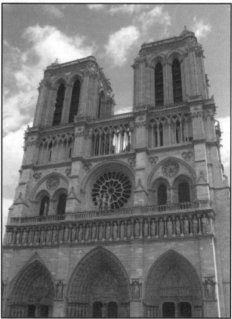

The twin towers of Notre Dame de Paris's facade became the Gothic standard.

without distraction. Above the gallery is a row of **clerestory** windows. These windows are relatively small; such windows grew larger as the style developed. They are also replacements, although a few have been restored so that visitors can see the original arrangement. The transepts were added in the 13ᵗʰ century, and they are quite narrow proportionately. The two rose windows with lancet windows underneath were added in the late 13ᵗʰ century. The center image in the north rose window is the Virgin and Child; that in the south is Christ. This orientation is very common. Above the north transept portal is carved the legend of Theophilus and his deal with the Devil, including the Virgin Mary rescuing his soul from damnation—an inspiring message of hope and salvation for the faithful.

This continuous building campaign gives Notre Dame an unusual unity of form.

Cathedrals should be looked at from many different angles both outside and inside to appreciate them fully. Visitors in Notre Dame in particular should take the time to ascend one of the towers. From there they can view the **flying buttresses**, which were likely invented here, as well as the **gargoyles**. ∎

Important Terms

clerestory: The upper part of the elevation of a church. The size of the windows in the clerestory grew dramatically in the Gothic period.

flying buttress: A buttress built external to a cathedral that supports the stone roof of a Gothic cathedral and allows much of the wall to be made of glass.

gargoyle: A water spout, often in the form of a grotesque, on the roof of a Gothic building. The terms gargoyle and grotesque, however, are not interchangeable.

rood screen: A wall constructed between the lay and clerical sections of a church. Most were removed from Catholic churches after the Council of Trent. The best surviving examples are in England and in the German cathedral of Naumburg.

Maurice de Sully (r. 1160–1196): Bishop of Paris who conceived of and carried out the plan to build the cathedral of Notre Dame in Paris.

Suggested Reading

Erlande-Brandenburg, *Notre-Dame de Paris*.

Frankl, *Gothic Architecture*, chap. 2.1.

Wilson, *The Gothic Cathedral*, chaps. 1–2.

Questions to Consider

1. What do you find to be the most interesting features of Notre Dame in Paris?

2. Compared to other early Gothic cathedrals we have looked at, is Notre Dame in Paris justly famous or only accidentally famous because it is located in Paris?

3. Why is it both a blessing and a curse for Notre Dame to be in the middle of the capital city of France?

Notre Dame in Paris
Lecture 8—Transcript

When we hear the term "Notre Dame," as opposed to "Notre Dame," what we almost automatically think of is the cathedral of Paris, we simply call it "Notre Dame." But as I've already pointed out and we'll see again and again and again, there are many cathedrals in France—in fact, most of the ones we're going to look at in detail—dedicated to Our Lady; that is to say, the Virgin Mary. We really properly should say Notre Dame de Paris, just as we should say Notre Dame de Chartres and Notre Dame de Laon or Notre Dame de Reims or whatever it might be; but nevertheless, it's clearly ingrained in our minds that Notre Dame first and foremost is a reference to Paris.

It's also obvious that "Notre Dame" means a lot of things other than a 12th-century Gothic cathedral. We have all kinds of imagines in our mind from later times. Perhaps the most famous one is from the book and then the great movie "The Hunchback of Notre Dame"; and we have a picture here, a still, from an early version of that movie and that's how we sort of imagine Notre Dame: the hunchback up in the tower with the gargoyles and whatever. That's all fine and dandy and legitimate—after all, *The Hunchback of Notre Dame* is an important novel and an important film—we, however, having said this, are going to ignore all that and we're going to look at Notre Dame in its 12th century context.

But even in the 12th century, when the cathedral was built, it was special; and let me suggest some reasons why: First of all, obviously, Paris is the capital of France. "Capital" is a little bit later term really, but clearly it was a political and administrative center of France and became more so over the course of the Middle Ages; and so it is special in that way. It's marked in being special in that way by the fact that if we look at Notre Dame, it is on an island in the Seine (the Île de la Cité) and one of the things that it shared on the island was the space dedicated to the palace of the King of France. Today, only small parts of that palace survive and a 13th century royal chapel survives, Sainte Chapelle, which we'll look at a little bit later on. obviously, this island in the 21st century looks different than it did in the 12th or 13th; it was dominated by the two great figures, the Bishop of Paris and the King of France, and they lived almost—not quite, but almost—across the street from each other. It's fair to say metaphorically, if not quite literally, that the cathedral of Notre Dame was in the shadow of the royal palace, and vice versa. It's also clear, because of that, that in some ways the history of France and the history of the cathedral of Notre Dame are entwined in a way the political history of France is entwined with almost no other building, except perhaps for the cathedral of Reims, because that's where the kings were crowned.

It's also important to say there's something else special about Paris: At the very time that Notre Dame was being built, it was a time of the flourishing of the Cathedral School of Paris, one of the great intellectual centers of the 12th century. It's the place, for example, where the great philosopher Peter Abelard taught. In fact, by about 1300, parts of that Cathedral School had become kind of quasi-independent of the cathedral, moved over to the left bank of the Seine, and became the University of Paris, the most important university of the Middle Ages; so Paris was an extraordinarily important intellectual center. Thomas Aquinas, for example, was a professor in the 13th century at the University of Paris. It's also worth mentioning that Paris is extraordinarily important in the history of music, because the music of the early Christian centuries was monophonic, everybody sang the same notes at the same time; Gregorian chants. It was really more than anyplace else in the cathedral of Paris that there were experiments with polyphonic music, people singing different notes at the same time; harmonies. So for many things—intellectually, musically, politically, architecturally—Notre Dame is a very important place.

In many ways, it doesn't look a lot like it looked when it was finished at the beginning of the 13th century; of course, that's true to some extent of all cathedrals, but it's more so true of Notre Dame. In the 18th century, some of the sculpture was removed before the French Revolution along with many of the stained glass windows; more light and bigger doors were the results. Then, during the French Revolution, much of the facade and other parts of the cathedral were damaged or destroyed. In fact, for a while the cathedral of Notre Dame was no longer the cathedral of Notre Dame; it was dedicated to the Cult of Reason and later on to a Cult of the Supreme Being. After the revolution, of course, it went back to being the cathedral of Paris but it was hard to fix so many things that had happened.

I want to show you a piece of sculpture from the 13th century on the south transept of Notre Dame to illustrate the fact that we have this continuing relationship of the University of Paris (education) and Notre Dame. We don't quite know exactly what these are, but they're usually assumed to be something like scenes from student life in the Middle Ages. They survived the French Revolution—for one thing, they're not in front—but let me take a look at something that only partially survived the 18th century: This is the main portal; this is the sculpture over the door, and I want you to notice there are three levels in this area we call the "tympanum," this sort of bulgy triangle area, I guess we could call it. The top two parts, if you look, are in one style, the bottom part is in a different style, because in the 19th century after the revolution there is an attempt to restore the sculpture of Notre Dame. Some of it was restored fairly carefully by the architects and artists who worked, some was more recreated and re-imagined; so the bottom third of this piece of sculpture, this tympanum, you can see is in a very different style. It was designed by a 19th-century very important guy in restoring Romanesque and Gothic things after the Enlightenment and the revolution, a guy named Viollet le Duc; but as you can see, it is certainly not in the same style as the cathedral itself.

Here is the famous facade, and unlike most Gothic cathedrals it is symmetrical. In fact, the whole cathedral was built very quickly, probably in a period of 40–50 years—very short—and there was never an interruption in the building because there was so much patronage, in large part from the family of the king, although the clergy of the cathedral were also pretty wealthy. This was so well-patronized that it was built fairly rapidly. For example, when we look at Chartres, we're going to see towers finished several hundred years apart; here we don't have that at Notre Dame, and the facade is justly one of the glories of all Gothic cathedrals. One of the things you will notice is that there are three portals with sculpture, and then just above it running all the way across you can see a row of statues. They are, in fact, statues of kings. No doubt, they are meant to be Old Testament kings; but by the time of the revolution in the late 18th century it was often assumed that they represented the kings of France—who, after all, lived almost across the street, we don't want to forget—and so you can imagine during the revolution all those statues were destroyed; every one we see there is a copy.

A few decades ago when a new building was going in near the cathedral they found some of the statues, or at least they found some of the heads; so these are the original late-12th/early-13th-century heads of the kings. They didn't find all of them and they didn't find the rest of the bodies, but we at least do have some remnants. These are in the Musée de Cluny, which is a couple blocks away from Notre Dame. Here's one of them; they really are quite beautiful even in their damaged state—they've, after all, been underground for almost two centuries—but nevertheless, it again reminds us of how much changing, how much refurbishing, how much restructuring has been done because of the fact that this cathedral means so much, it represents so much. If the cathedral can be stripped of its kings, that's a sign against royalty and against monarchy at the time of the revolution. Some cathedrals in other places were also badly damaged during the revolution; luckily for us, as we'll see, Chartres and at least the facade of Amiens were more or less spared, so we're going to be able to see them in a richer, fuller way than we can look at Notre Dame.

I want to just walk around the building a little bit, looking at the facade and the side. Here we are on the left bank of the Seine, and here, as we've walked further to the east, we can look back on Notre Dame and see its front towers, its beautiful east end—rounded, of course, like most cathedrals are—and that wonderful tall tower at the crossing; it's a narrow tower but nevertheless quite a beautiful tower although it, too, like so many other things here is not original. This building was begun around the year 1163, and it was the work primarily of the Bishop of Paris at that time—his name was Maurice de Sully—an important bishop who supervised this project; again, he had royal support and royal money, and the bishop himself was wealthy. That is to say, the cathedral and its clergy had a lot of land from which they derived income. Most of the cathedrals, as we'll learn later, involved on and off campaigns—you build for 20 years, and then there's no more money—but with the combination of the royalty and the wealth of the church, this continued. In fact, the merchants in Paris didn't contribute really anything to the building, while without the merchants in many cities—we'll see this in Chartres, for example—the cathedrals would have never been built, there would have been no money to build them.

I want to take you inside, and we're not going to walk in as we usually do from the front, but rather I'm going to take you straight to the back, which is what we're looking at here in this particular image because it's an extraordinary ambulatory—remember, that's the pathway around the east end, around where the altar is so you can walk behind the altar—and like Suger's at Saint Denis, it is a double ambulatory, it is very wide. By the way, I have to tell you, one of the most annoying things about the Notre Dame in Paris is the fact that when you go in—and, of course, it's always crowded because it's in Paris—there are so many bright bulbs and chandeliers (I use the term loosely), bunches of lightbulbs together it's hard not to be caught in glares; it's hard to look at something without having to shade an eye or two. But we're going to do the best we can given the possibilities for photographing here. Here we can see something of this very broad ambulatory; here we see it from another angle where we can see that there is this row of columns such as we saw at Saint Denis. By the way, unlike Saint Denis, the nave, too, has double aisles; so the whole building is extraordinarily wide, and we'll see that aisle a little bit later on.

I want to show you this image because we're standing in the ambulatory looking through one of the arches and then looking up into the vault of the choir. It reminds us that as we move around a cathedral we need to move a lot, we need to look at a lot of different angles, because you'll find some extraordinarily beautiful combinations of things: close up and far away; low vaulting, high vaulting; lighting in different times of the day in different ways; sometimes lighting with color because there will be stained glass windows where the light will be shining through and casting color onto the stone. I'm going to say this no doubt many times, but cathedrals need to be visited carefully, looked at in a lot of different angles both outside and inside, and they need to be visited more than once because, of course, the light coming from the outside comes from different places at different times of the day and in different times of the year.

Now let's look at the interior of Notre Dame, again, with all those glaring lights. It's an enormously tall cathedral and it's extraordinary long; longer and taller than any we have seen so far. Again, it was all built in one we call it "building campaign," so there's a kind of unity to the architecture, despite, again, all the changes that have taken place over time. If we look here we can see that double aisle, you can see the row of columns that separates the two aisles; again, an extraordinarily spacious and beautiful building. Here is a vault; you can see it is the same six-part vault that we've seen in other cathedrals, that we've seen in Sens, for example. But you'll notice the way the pillars reach up to support that vault is very different here at Notre Dame than, say, at Sens.

I want to take you back simply to look once again at the nave, and then I want you to look at the elevation. We have here the aisle—and again, it's a double aisle—then we have a gallery, and then as you can see we have an upper part, and there are windows in that upper part called clerestory windows. We're going to see they're going to get bigger over time as cathedrals develop, but we need to recognize this beautiful elevation. Here you can see that gallery, and it's a very big gallery; there are windows inside the gallery and then the clerestory windows up above it. Very often when we're walking around we don't focus on those kinds of architectural details, but it is important to look; and again, you can see with all the angularity of the piers that rise up, of the various arches—you have one arch, then three arches, then you have the window up above—one wants to look at all those proportions, for example.

Here, we take a look at an interesting situation because those clerestory windows, which you see in the far left of this photograph, are not original; in fact, originally the clerestory contained a round window in part of it—you see that in the corner there; we're looking in the transept here—and then up above it was more wall, so it was a lot darker. What happened? They discovered in restoring the church that these clerestory windows had replaced the original arrangement when doing some work, and so they decided to restore a couple of these so that you could see what it would have been like, except for the fact that more light comes in today from the original design than what would have come in the 12th century. Here again you can see it, so that in the left we have a recreation of the original—although, again, that little window would have been wall—and then we see the clerestory windows; so what we have here is partly a restoration of the original and partly a 13th-century fixing, if you will, or repair or remodeling of the cathedral.

Here we look up at the vault, and as you can see again it's that six-part vault. You can see those clerestory windows, those 13th-century windows, going with the 12ᵗʰ-century vault; but it really is quite an impressive structure. What I want you to notice is that we're going to look at the piers that hold all this up, and if you look up from this pier you can see that it goes through a column and then it goes on up and, in fact, the piece that runs straight up and makes the transverse arch divides these vaults; in other words, this is a separation of two six-part vaults. Compare that with this column next to it that goes up to the rib that is in the middle of one of those six-part transverse arch vaults. Remember in Sens you had an alternation of pillars and that double column; here, we have gotten rid of that alternation and all these great columnar piers and pillars are the same. They end up doing different things because there are major and minor ones because you have the six-part vault, but they all look alike. Notice that when we look at the interior how much your eyes were led all the way to the altar because there was nothing sort of alternating, there was nothing breaking that rhythm to lead your eyes that way; so this is a conscious change in what had been built just really a couple decades before at the cathedral of Sens.

The transepts are also not original; the transepts were added in the 13ᵗʰ century, and they're quite narrow transepts, I might add. Because the church is so wide, the transepts when they were built don't stick out very far; and once again, it's a kind of peculiarity of Notre Dame, although it's not unique to Notre Dame. Here, again, we are looking at a corner where we have the nave to the left and then one of the transepts to the right so we can get an idea of how deep that transept is; and the answer is: not very. The transept is also not very wide because it doesn't have any aisles even though, of course, there are two aisles on each side of the nave. Like every cathedral we're going to look at, there are a lot of differences, even in the original plan let alone all the remodeling. There is no cookie cutter cathedral, and even though I think we can make the argument that beginning really with Chartres there's a kind of formula that tends to be more faithfully reproduced in other cathedrals as opposed to Notre Dame and Laon—which we'll look at in the next lecture—and Sens and Senlis and Noyon that we've already looked at in this sort of experimental phase, these are perhaps more different from each other; but nevertheless, there will never be a standard, cookie cutter, here's the plan, here's the prefab Gothic cathedral. That's why it's always worth visiting a lot, and you can never say, "Seen 1"—or seen 10, for that matter—"and you've seen them all."

The windows in the transept are, in fact, a little bit later than the transept themselves. They come from later in the 13th century and they're two beautiful rose windows, and we can see here the pattern of one of them: the large circle with the lancet windows underneath. Each of the two transepts has, in fact, these windows. This is the north rose window and it contains in the center the image of the Virgin and Child, something very common to north rose windows as we will see in other places; and here is the south rose and it contains Christ, because we associate the south transept with the life of Christ and the coming again of Christ because it receives more illumination, being on the south, than does the north porch. We'll see how that works itself out in more detail, especially when we look at Chartres cathedral.

I want to take you back outside, because luckily—and it's still true, I took this picture many years ago but it's still true—you can, if you don't mind standing in line, go to the top of one of the towers of Notre Dame, and it's really worth doing. Remember that flying buttresses, I've suggested, were invented at Notre Dame and for Notre Dame. The earliest ones were in the east—we'll take a look at those in the minute—and then these in the nave were added because the building was built from east to west; so the earliest buttressing was in the east end. All of these buttresses are, again, not original and probably a little bit more elaborate than the original ones. We don't know; we don't have the original ones, or pictures or drawings of them. But nevertheless, we really get a classic view—there's a gargoyle, which is sort of a water spout, after all, on the right side—and we get to look at this beautiful buttressing system. Now we look at the cathedral from the east end, and you can see how big the buttresses are in the east. Again, these are not original; but it almost looks like great oars coming out from the east end of the cathedral. This is a beautifully—and, in fact spectacularly—buttressed church, although the buttresses come from a little bit later period than the building itself.

I want to return to the facade and take a look at some of the sculpture. Again, let me remind you about that row of kings, we saw some of their heads; they are right up above the three portals. We looked at this picture before, this is the tympanum; this is the sculpture over the main door, and it is the Last Judgment. Again, this is an idea that we find in the Romanesque period: We've seen this at Autun, we've seen this at Conques, and we would see it at other Romanesque churches had we toured them more thoroughly. Here we have it again, and we will see it again and again and again; at Amiens, for example. Again, leaving aside the fact that we have two different kinds of sculpture, this is the great Last Judgment; so at the top is Christ the Judge, in the center is the separation of the saved—they go up to our left, which is Christ's right—and the damned, and then down below, that recreated 19th-century part, is the resurrection of the dead. I just sort of cringe a little bit when I see it because it's so the wrong style for the rest of this sculpture, but Viollet le Duc did what he did in the 19th century and nothing's going to change that.

One of the things about this particular Last Judgment is over the arches—what's called the archivolts, over this—are these wonderful and beautiful angels, just these lovely rows of angels. Again, it's wonderful to see them at different times of the day: In the morning, they're in the shade; and in the afternoon, of course, they catch the sun and they catch the sun at different angles at every minute. If you walk by Notre Dame, go off and buy some souvenirs, and come back and walk by Notre Dame again those angels will, in a sense, attract you differently; different parts of the angels and different angels will be lit up because of the angle of the sun. Here, I was glad to have this photograph in sort of bright light so you can get an idea of that shadow and that brightness and imagine—it doesn't exactly dance; the sun doesn't move that fast—but over time, several times during the day to come back you see different things and you observe it differently.

On the left portal we have sculpture dedicated to the Virgin; quite properly, of course, because this is, after all, Notre Dame de Paris. This is the story of the end of the life of the Virgin and her coronation in Heaven. On the right portal—we're not going to look at details because there are a few others things we're going to examine first in our remaining minutes—but the portal on the right is interesting because it is dedicated to a local saint, Saint Marcel, who was an early bishop of Paris. We have, in a sense, a traditional, local patron saint on the right, we have the Virgin Mary on the left, and we have Judgment in the center. Think what that means: We all, the theology of the church would say, need help; and those who are in Heaven are in a position to help us. How's that for a pair of intercessors to not guarantee but to help us to get to the Heaven side of that judgment? One of our own—that is to say, a local bishop—and the Virgin Mary, our patron saint and the grandest of all intercessors because she is, after all, the mother of Jesus.

I also want to show you some other sculpture because in addition to the sculpture on the facade, there's some on the north and south sides in the transept. I want to look at this: It's on the north transept; in fact, next to this would have been where the clergy who were attached to the cathedral lived. On the other side is the river; and so this would perhaps not even always have been visible to everybody. But we see a very beautifully-sculpted portal from the 13th century here; and I want to move in on it and take a look at it, because we have a variety of stories. I'm going to focus on the center part of it because I think it's particular interesting. It's a story of a guy named Theophilus, and according to the legend, Theophilus wanted something very much, and the Devil said, "I'll get it for you, but it'll cost you your soul; you have to hand over your soul to me." So we see Theophilus kneeling there before the Devil and making a deal; a pretty powerful story. At the other end, it turns out it's good news, because Theophilus recognizes what he's done and he calls on the Virgin Mary; and you can see the Virgin Mary there is taking care of the demon. This is a parable story with a happy ending, and it's one of many moral tales that we find in stained glass windows—although not many are left in Notre Dame—in sculpture, in the sermons that were preached in these days because saints were not only intercessors, they were examples; and one of the ways that saints were examples is that many of the saints did some pretty bad things and repented and are saved.

What a good story to see; what happens if you've done something awful in your life and you say, "I'm doomed"? This story tells you even if you made a pact with the Devil you call on the Virgin Mary for help. It's important for us to realize that these stories are perhaps somewhat entertaining to us, but these stories really are powerful in driving home the message of the church, one of which is there is always hope because we have some very powerful intercessors; what we need to do is repent.

I want to show you one more piece of sculpture at Notre Dame and it happens to be back inside the church, because around the ambulatory was built in the 14th century this wonderful screen. In other words, the ambulatory itself is sort of walled off from the central part of the choir where the altar is, and as you walk around the ambulatory you see all these stories; they're painted and colorful today, but they tell in this case the story of Jesus after the Resurrection. The story we see just to the left of center is the story of Jesus having dinner in Emmaus after the Resurrection, a story that's told in Luke; and in the next scene, what we have is Jesus appearing to the Apostles, a story that comes from John. So another kind of sculpture is interior sculpture; most of this kind of sculpture has been destroyed in various kinds of remodeling, but it does happen to survive not from the 12th but from the 14th century in Paris, and I wanted you to see that.

Although Notre Dame is not the best preserved of the buildings, it is not the most authentic cathedral because so many things have happened to it, it is like no other cathedral in its importance to France, again, politically, intellectually, culturally, as well as artistically. This is the great building dedicated to the Virgin Mary in what for every Frenchman and Frenchwoman is the heart of their nation.

Early Gothic Style—Laon
Lecture 9

> If we look at the center [portal], we have ... the Virgin Mary: her death, Assumption, and Coronation. The Virgin Mary has really literally taken center. ... It reminds us, even if it's not followed in other cathedrals, how deeply important and central the Virgin Mary was, especially in the 12th century.

Today, Laon is a small city of no major political or economic import in France, but in the Middle Ages, it was one of the favored homes of the kings of the West Franks. In 1122, there was a violent rebellion by the rising merchant class that led to the murder of the bishop of Laon and some autonomy for the merchant class, so it was an interesting and important place in France when the cathedral was built beginning in the 1150s.

The original design of the cathedral called for seven towers: In addition to the two on the facade and the one on each transept that we see today, each transept was meant to have a second tower, and a central tower was also planned. The cathedral's towers are very tall and angular, topped by statues of oxen, which may be a tribute to the oxen who hauled the stone to build them.

One peculiarity of the cathedral as built is that the apse is flat, not rounded, and it contains a rose window; this is unique among French cathedrals. This was not part of the original design; around 1205, the original rounded apse was dismantled and the flat apse replaced it for unknown reasons, but the design inspiration probably comes from a Cistercian monastery church nearby. At the center of the rose window is a depiction of the Virgin and Child, as we saw at Notre Dame, and the surrounding panels show apostles, kings, and the Elders of the book of Revelation. The long, thin, pointed stained-glass windows below are called **lancet windows**. Moving from right to left, the windows tell the story of Jesus and his early followers, beginning with the Annunciation on the far right and ending with Saint Stephen, the first Christian martyr, on the left. The central lancet window shows a sequence of events from the entry into

Photo courtesy of Dr. William Cook.

The white stone of Laon's six-part vaults make the interior feel light and airy, despite the relatively small clerestory windows.

Jerusalem, through the events of the Passion, up to the appearance of Christ at Emmaus.

The facade has deeply recessed doorways, a rose window, an arch beside each of the the towers, and a fully sculpted portal above each door, along with jamb statues, tympanum, and **archivolt** statues—that is, carvings of little figures over the main tympanum. A good deal of this sculpture is replacement. The left portal shows the Adoration of the Magi, surrounded by an image of the Psychomachia (an allegorical battle between Virtues and Vices) and several prophets—both pagan and Old Testament. The center portal shows the death, Assumption, and Coronation of the Virgin Mary; this preeminence given to Mary may again be a Cistercian influence. The central archivolt is decorated with a Tree of Jesse. The Last Judgment we would expect to see in the center is over the right portal. The most unusual feature of this sculpture is that Jesus is flanked by Mary and Saint John the

Evangelist, who according to medieval belief are the principle intercessors for all humankind.

Finally, on the rounded archivolt above the left-hand portal is a sculpture of the **Seven Liberal Arts**, represented by pagan sages such as Cicero and Aristotle. Perhaps the Christianity being practiced here was not quite as narrow-minded as we often associate with the Middle Ages. On the other side, we also have sculpture above the window there—again, there's no tympanum—and it, too, is interesting because it tells the story of Creation, and you can see God holding various medallions that show the various works of creation. On the corresponding right-hand archivolt, we have the Old Testament Creation story. Overall, the facade is a comprehensive—if scattered—catalog of medieval philosophy.

Laon Cathedral does not have the height of Notre Dame in Paris, but it makes up for it in length: 18 bays (that is, sections between two columns or pillars), plus the transept. It has six-part vaults supported by alternating major and minor columns. The vault above the crossing, which supports the foreshortened crossing tower, is supported by four great pillars; but although incomplete, the crossing tower is tall enough for its own triforium and clerestory windows, mimicking the elevation of the nave.

In contrast to the flat choir, each end of the transept sports a small, rounded, apse-like chapel, added in the 15th or 16th century. The apses contain single ambulatories and walled-off chapels, which make the space feel less open than most apses, a hint to the novice that this was not part of the original design. ■

Important Terms

archivolt: An arch over a tympanum. Archivolts often contain small statues, most commonly of angels.

lancet window: A rectangular window that is pointed at the top—the most common shape for a stained-glass window.

Seven Liberal Arts: The curriculum of the medieval schools: grammar, rhetoric, logic, arithmetic, geometry, music, and astronomy. These are often depicted on Gothic portals along with practitioners both pagan and Christian. The most famous depiction of this theme is found on the facade of Chartres Cathedral (the discussion of which begins in Lecture 10).

Suggested Reading

Bony, *French Gothic Architecture of the 12th and 13th Centuries.*

Frankl, *Gothic Architecture*, chaps. 2.1, 3.1.

Stoddard, *Art and Architecture in Medieval France*, chap. 12.

Wilson, *The Gothic Cathedral*, chap. 1.

Questions to Consider

1. How do the 18 bays and 4 levels of elevation at Laon draw our eyes both horizontally and vertically?

2. What do you think of the unusual (for France) flat east end of Laon cathedral, and how does it make your first look at Laon when you enter different from a cathedral with an apse?

3. What does it tell us that sculpture on the exterior of Laon Cathedral honors learning (the Seven Liberal Arts), Christ and the Virgin, and the oxen who dragged the stone up the hill?

Early Gothic Style—Laon
Lecture 9—Transcript

We're ready for another lecture on Notre Dame; not Notre Dame de Paris, another one of the cathedrals dedicated to the Virgin Mary but in a different space: in what's today still a very small city, the city of Laon in eastern northern France. Laon today may be a small city of no major political or economical import in France, but in the Middle Ages it was an important place. For a while in the 9th and early 10th centuries, in fact, it was one of the favored locations of the descendents of Charlemagne who ruled what we would call "France" today—it was then called the Kingdom of the West Franks—and so although there was no capital because the kings moved around a lot, it was one of the places where the kings stayed often. I mentioned in Lecture 7 that in 1122 there was a violent rebellion by the rising merchant class that led to the murder of the Bishop of Laon and the establishment of some autonomy by the merchants, so it was an interesting and important place in France at the time this cathedral was built beginning in the 1150s.

As we approach it, Laon is a town on a hill and we have this wonderful view of the cathedral; and if you look at it you can see that there are, in fact, four towers. Of course, Notre Dame in Paris, which we just looked at, has two towers in front and a spire toward the back at the crossing, but here we see four towers, and as we come to look at Laon more closely we discover that's only part of the story. Here is the facade of the cathedral of Laon, but as we move around the cathedral we will see that we get this extraordinary view of towers and places where towers were meant to go that, in fact, were never made. Here, for example, as we move around to the south side we see the transept—again, the crossbar of the cathedral—and you can see here there is one tower, but there's also a place for another tower; there was to be a tower on each side of each transept. You add those to the two in the front and you get six; of those six, of course, two are not built. Then, in the middle, you get a crossing tower; not just a spire, but an important tower. So this building was designed to have seven towers, although they were never all completed. We can only imagine what that would have looked like; but certainly as we saw in the initial view, what we have now is literally a beautiful, towering cathedral.

There is one particular peculiarity to this cathedral. I'm going to take you to the back now, and what we see is a rose window in the back; there are buildings right around the back of the cathedral so we can't quite get up to it, but you can see that rose window in the back. We're not used to seeing a rose window in the east end of the cathedral; in fact, this is what it looks like when you walk in: This is the only major cathedral in France that has a flattened-off east end rather than a rounded ambulatory with a rose window and three huge lancet windows. This is not part of the original design; around 1205, the original rounded apse was dismantled and this replaced it, and we don't quite know why. The model, however, for this idea of a flattened east end with windows probably comes from the churches of the Cistercians. Remember, we've seen a couple Cistercian churches and I talked about the fact they had this sort of half-Gothic style; one of the parts of Cistercian architecture was a flattened east end with several chapels on each side of where the altar was, and that seems to be what's at work here. There was a Cistercian monastery not very far from Laon. But we really don't know why this happened, and it really was not imitated later on in other French Gothic cathedrals.

Let's return to the facade of this cathedral, and notice that it has much-recessed doorways; those arches come fairly far out, as you can see. It has a rose window, an arch on either side before we get to the towers, and in each of those three doors we have a fully sculpted portal; so we have three portals: the one in the center, which is the biggest obviously, and one on either side. They have jamb statues, they have tympanum, and they have the archivolt statues; that is to say, carvings of little figures over the main part of the sculpture, over the tympanum. A good deal of this sculpture is replacement; we're going to look, actually, only at the original parts. For example, we're not going to look at the jamb statues—although they're very nice reproductions—we're going to look at what is left from the latter part of the 12th century when this work was done.

We're going to look first at the left portal, and we can see that it contains, again, the tympanum, the archivolts, and the jamb statues. If we look closely, we can see here that what we have is the story of the birth of Jesus and the coming of the Three Kings, the Adoration of the Magi. Here we see the birth of Jesus in detail, very beautifully sculpted, as you can see, as part of the tympanum of this left portal. Then we have around it on either side in the archivolt some very interesting things: First of all, we have what's called the Psychomachia. Based on a work of literature, it's an allegorical battle between Virtues and Vices, and that's one of the themes depicted here. The other is that we have prophets of the coming of Christ. What's particularly interesting is some of the prophets are pagan prophets and some are Old Testament prophets.

Let's take a look at a couple details: Here is one scene from the Psychomachia, and you can see the Virtue trampling on the Vice; this is an elaborate allegory written a half a millennium before this sculpture was done. Here we see one prophetic image: This is the image of the Hebrew children in the fiery furnace from the book of Daniel. We have Old Testament and pagan prophecies, and we have this Psychomachia, a very interesting collection and a very unusual collection in part of small sculptures around the main piece. If we look at the center, we have the story of the end of the earthly life of the Virgin Mary: her death, Assumption, and Coronation. This might strike us as surprising, and it is surprising because we're used to having Last Judgments in the center. Actually there is a Last Judgment at Laon, it's going to be off on the right portal and we'll look at it in a minute; but it's very interesting to note here that the Virgin Mary has really literally taken center. That did not happen at Notre Dame de Paris, it will not happen at Notre Dame de Amiens in the cathedral of Amiens, but it does happen here in Laon. It reminds us, even if it's not followed in other cathedrals, how deeply important and central the Virgin Mary was, especially in the 12th century. By the way, the Cistercian monks—and, again, their building model was used here for the east end— were particularly dedicated to the Virgin Mary. Bernard of Clairvaux wrote great lyrical poetry to and about the Virgin Mary; and, in fact, even to this day every Cistercian monk takes as his first name "Mary." If you meet Brother William at a Cistercian monastery, his name technically is "Mary William"; and so we're reminded here of the strength of the cult of the Virgin Mary. That's going to be important; hold onto that idea, because in many ways the most sacred relic of the Virgin Mary is going to be preserved at Chartres, and we'll see how she's dealt with at the cathedral of Chartres.

At any rate, as I said, we have here these stories; the bottom part is not original so I show you the Coronation of the Virgin Mary here. Then, if we look in the archivolts in the central part of the facade of Amiens, we have what's called the tree of Jesse; we've seen that before in the window at Saint Denis. Jesse has a dream; he's the father of David, and from him springs the line that ultimately results in the Virgin Mary, his descendant, and, of course, Jesus, his descendent. We have here the tree of Jesse as an important theme; and there, in fact, you see Jesse in the center and you see above him King David. You can recognize him as King David because King David is, in fact, playing a harp.

Here we have the right door, and this is where we have the Last Judgment. It is smaller and it is not in the center; again, a very unusual situation for the Last Judgment. It's an unusual sculpture, and I want to look at it for a minute because it's interesting in a lot of ways. We see in the upper part of the tympanum we have Christ there, and then right at his feet—they're almost invisible—is the resurrection of the dead, and then down below in the lowest part is the separation of the saved from the damned. But even if we look just at Jesus here, you'll notice on either side is a much, much smaller figure. They are the two great intercessors for humankind—the Virgin Mary and John the Evangelist—but they're so small that they almost get lost in this scene. What we see is Jesus, this dominant figure at the Last Judgment, but the intercessors for us—the principle intercessors for all humankind— sort of get lost. There are the folks coming out of their tombs. You can see that they're right below the feet of Christ, but if you don't look carefully you'd miss them completely. It's very interesting to see the proportions; they're really odd in this particular piece of sculpture. The sculpture is very beautiful.

By the way, in case you're wondering what Hell might be like, here's still another picture of what happens if you don't behave and if you don't call on the saints to use their power for you, a repentant sinner; here was have some pretty bad scenes of Hell. Then in the archivolts here, we have, as you can see, elaborate sculpture; and what we have, as it turns out, are the elders of the Apocalypse, the 24 elders). But look in the outermost part on the right: Those are the foolish virgins. We see the virgin down below—so it's in the very lower right-hand corner of our picture—she has her lamp, but her lamp is turned upside down because it is, in fact, empty; and, of course, she's on the right side of the sculpture as you would expect, which is Jesus's left and therefore she's on the Hell side. Let me show you a detail from the other side: There is one of the wise virgins exactly opposite her and, of course, she is on Christ's right, our left, and she is in Heaven. We have this wonderful allegory worked into the archivolt. You may recall at Saint Denis, it actually was in a series of statues on either side of the door; here, it's incorporated more intimately into the sculptural program. It's really quite a lovely thing.

I want you to think about this sculptural program; but we're not finished yet, because look at the facade here and you'll see above the left and right doors there are arches. By the way, they are rounded arches, those are not pointed arches, on either side of the rose window and underneath those arches there is no tympanum but there is sculpture in the archivolts. We want to take a look at it even though it's hard to see when you go to Laon unless you have binoculars, which, of course, leads to the question: How did people in the 12th century see it? Here we see the sculpture on the left-hand side and it really is quite interesting; and what we have depicted here is what is called the Seven Liberal Arts, the curriculum of schools in the Middle Ages. It's important because Laon was a serious intellectual center, especially in the first half of the 12th century, before places like Paris—and Chartres, too, in some ways—became more important academically and intellectually.

But here we have depicted the Seven Liberal Arts, and what we'll see here are men sitting at desks and writing and whatever, and what's interesting is most of the men who are represented there as symbolizing the Seven Liberal Arts are pagan; for example, you would have Cicero representing rhetoric, or Aristotle logic. It's interesting to see that collection of people; and remember right below this we saw in the archivolts there were pagan as well as Old Testament prophets of the coming of Christ, something that testifies to the fact that the kind of Christianity that was being practiced here was not quite, we might say, as narrow-minded as we often associate with medieval thought. On the other side, we also have sculpture above the window there—again, there's no tympanum—and it, too, is interesting because it tells the story of Creation, and you can see God holding various medallions that show the various works of creation.

Let's step back for a minute and think about what we have in this sculptural program. To say the least, it is comprehensive: It goes from Creation (upper right) to Judgment (lower right); it includes the Old Testament and the New

Testament; it includes pagans, Jews, and Christians. I guess it's fair to say that even though it's comprehensive, it's sort of scattered; that is to say, we can't sort of say, "Now how do all the pieces fit together intellectually very well looking at the facade of Laon?" But the pieces by and large are there, and they are going to be sort of sorted out and clarified in other sculptural programs in places like Chartres and at Amiens; but be aware that the pieces are already basically in place here in the second half of the 12th century at Laon.

There's one other part of the facade we need to look at, and those are these wonderful towers. Let's stand at the base of one of them. Their angularity strikes us. In certain levels they are basically four-sided, in other levels they are octagonal, and they soar up to the heavens; we can see them here. You notice there are a lot of statues up toward the top, and we want to zoom in on those statues because they're pretty interesting. They are oxen. You might ask: What are oxen doing in a prominent place way up there—stone oxen, by the way, which presumably are pretty heavy, probably heavier than oxen—what are they doing way up there in the top of the towers at the top of the hill in the cathedral of Laon? We think it is a kind of tribute to those oxen, because the stone that built this cathedral, or of which this cathedral was built, came from down below and the oxen brought all that stone up, and they are in a sense memorialized. It's really quite a beautiful and interesting piece and unique, as far as I know, in fact, to the cathedral of Laon.

We took a glimpse in the interior just a few minutes ago just to get a look at the east end because I pointed out that it's unusual, but let's go back inside. This is a quite beautiful cathedral. The stone's a light color, has almost a kind of yellowish quality to it, and both inside and outside there are times when it's so luminous it almost seems to kind of glow, a very gentle glow. I find this one of the most beautiful and moving experiences in all the visits I've made to cathedrals all over Europe and beyond, going into Laon Cathedral. Perhaps also it's in part because instead of seeing more or less more stone at the far end you have these glorious windows to look at as well. It is quite a spectacular sight.

It's 18 bays long, a bay being defined as "a section between two columns or piers." It's 10 bays in the nave and 8 more bays in the choir beyond the transept; so it's 18 bays plus the transept in the middle. It's extraordinarily long; it's not particularly high, but it's extraordinarily long and beautiful and, again, almost glowing. It has, as we've seen in other early Gothic cathedrals, six-part vaults; and if we take a look at the elevation here you can see that there is some difference between one column—these really are columns rather than pillars—and another. One column, as you can see, is straightforward column; the next one down has little columns, little mini-columns, thin columns, attached to it; so there is some alternation here and, in fact, the alternation is very systematic. As we look up, for example, we look into the gallery and the triforium because, like we saw at Noyon, this has four levels of elevation: the aisle, the gallery, the triforium, and the clerestory windows above. But I want you to notice that we have a minor pier on the left; so we have three of these sort of stone "columnettes" rising up. The one on the right is a major one, it's the one that has the big transverse arches that separate the double bays of the six-part vault, and you can see there are five rather than three of these thin, stone, pipe-like columns that go up. It's, again, rhythmical that we go from major to minor to major to minor; it's quite beautiful. Again, we're going to find that eventually this is going to be sort of changed so that every pier is alike and we're also going to move to four-part vaults when we move on into the High Gothic period. But I really love this alternation, and I love these beautiful patterns; and again, you have to imagine different times of the day when the light strikes all these different angles different and, again, with this whitish stone the church sort of glows.

Here we get a look at this alternation as we look down the nave; again, this long, 10-bay-long nave of the cathedral. It has one aisle on each side—not two like we saw at Notre Dame—and now we're looking down that aisle and, of course, you can see that it's the right-hand aisle so you can see the nave over to the left side of this photograph. Again, it, too, is beautiful. In some of the bigger cathedrals we're going to look at some of these aisles and say, "My gosh, they're as big as a lot of churches"; even this one is impressive in its size, and again, Laon is not one of the very high cathedrals.

The crossing tower in Laon is spectacular. Look at this: We see these four great pillars that hold up the center of the building. We have the nave to the left, the choir to the right, and the transepts at the top and bottom; so where they come together you'll notice we have this very high tower—we saw it from the outside—a very unusual vault for a very unusual space, but this tower is so high that, in fact, it has its own triforium and clerestory windows, and it repeats therefore the upper elevations of the entire church, just spewing it up to the sky. I want to show you this from a different angle: Isn't that spectacular to look up there, follow these pillars—I'm standing right underneath the keystone as you can see here—and looking up and seeing how the light comes in through those high clerestory windows? It is a place I like to spend some time when I am, in fact, in Laon, which is as often as I can be.

One of the peculiarities is on the transept, on the east side of each transept, there is a chapel with a rounded apse; we're looking at it from the outside here. What's unusual about this is remember the east end is flat, but the east side of the transept isn't; again, it's a different pattern and it's one of those things that there are people who say, "This is the most beautiful thing I've ever seen," there are people who say, "I like it the way the other cathedrals do it," but once again we see variety, we see experimentation, we see different kinds of beautiful construction using the same basic elements, but here we have a kind of mini-apse that's rounded on either side of the transept even though the ultimate final apse at the east end of the church, as we know, is flat.

This is one of those transepts, and I want to show you that there are windows and, in fact, some of the stained glass windows exist in these transepts. We see that there is a single ambulatory, and one of the things—actually I don't like it every much here at Laon cathedral—you can see that the chapels have been sort of blocked off from people because they have little walls with doors in them, and so the chapels are all blocked off and it's not open space, and I don't like that very much. I'm happy to report, those walls if you will—those entrances to the chapel that are almost always closed—are not original, they were, in fact, put there in the 15th or 16th century during the Renaissance; and, of course, now they're important in and of themselves because they're old and treasured and venerated and traditional, but gosh I wish they hadn't have ever put them there because it does sort of make the single ambulatory seem even smaller and more squeezed in and more closed off than it would be otherwise.

I again want to show you the exterior of the east end, the flat exterior, and there we can see the rose window. We're going to come around, of course, inside and look at that and the lancet windows below it from inside. Here is that rose window, and it really is a beautiful rose window. It has the Blessed Virgin Mary and Child in the center and then in the pieces around it, it has, in fact, a number of figures as you can see: Apostles, Elders (meaning the 24 Elders from the book of Revelation), and Kings (meaning Old Testament kings). It brings together a number of groups that surround Christ: Apostles, his followers; Elders, who accompany him at the Last Judgment; and Kings, who are his ancestors. It's a very nice collection of people, if you will, in this rose window.

This is the left lancet; remember there are three lancets, so we're going from left to right. This particular kind of window with the pointed top, long thin window, is called a "lancet window," at least when it's near the ground; when it's up high it's going to be called a "clerestory window," so we have some vocabulary things here. Anyway, great big tall window, low to the ground we'll call a "lancet window." Again, this is dedicated to a couple interesting people, a couple interesting saints. One of them is Saint Stephen. Saint Stephen is the first Christian martyr. His story is told in Acts of the Apostles, Chapter Seven. You may recall from that story if you've read your Acts of the Apostles recently that Stephen is a vociferous Christian, not afraid to preach, not afraid to challenge his fellow Jews. Ultimately he is executed, he is murdered; and the way he's murdered is by being stoned to death, they throw rocks at him. You can see Stephen kneeling down on the right, you can see the light from Heaven accepting him, and you can see those who are attacking him on the center and on the left. The other figure in this window is somebody we met in stone at Notre Dame, and the very fact we will have met this person in two cathedrals in a row says something about the popularity of the story: This is the story of Theophilus. Remember Theophilus? He's the guy who makes the pact with the Devil. We see that here, and the whole story unfolds; obviously you can unfold it in many more scenes in stained glass than you can in stone, and so this is a more complete version, if you will, of the Theophilus legend. It's a very beautiful window.

The central lancet, which you can see has a different pattern for displaying the stories; it's not just one boxed story after another, but here was have various designs into which the stories are fit. It's appropriate because, remember, in front of this is the principle altar. This is the story of Christ's passion, and it includes, in fact, the story of the Last Supper that, of course, is reenacted on the altar; so it's appropriate that this window tells the story of Christ's passion. This is the lowest part of the window and you can see what it shows is Jesus's entry into Jerusalem. The story actually takes two scenes: On the left is Jesus coming in, and then we have Jerusalem and people greeting him on the right; up above, you can see the Last Supper. In this second, you can see the betrayal of Jesus by Judas; you can see Judas coming up and giving Jesus a kiss. Here we have stories from the time of the Resurrection—of course, the Crucifixion is there, I've moved to the top of the window—but I want you to look at the story in the lower right quadrant. You can see it's a table. It is a dinner—not the Last Supper because this is after the Resurrection—this is the story of Jesus having dinner with the pilgrims at Emmaus, and what's interesting is the way the story is told they don't recognize who Jesus is as they go to dinner together. But in the breaking of the bread they recognize Jesus and then Luke tells us that Jesus disappears. Look at the way Jesus disappears in this scene: You see the men at the table and you see the table. Look right above the center of the table. You see the red? That's Jesus's robe and those are his feet; he is sort of literally flying out of the dinner, and you can see just his feet and the bottom of his red robe. That's the way they depict the biblical story of Jesus disappearing.

Finally, we have the window on the right, which shows the infancy of Jesus. So we have Jesus's infancy here, his passion and resurrection in the center, and then some of the stories that happen after Jesus's time—that is to say, Stephen and Theophilus—and therefore in a sense in our time on the right. But here, for example, we have the Annunciation; this is the first story in the sequence: This is the Virgin Mary and the angel Gabriel is visiting her. This is beautiful early 13th-century stained glass. We're going to see, of course, the most famous stained glass at Chartres and spend a whole lecture on it, but I want you to note: Chartres does not have a monopoly on beautiful stained glass. Here we have the scene of Jesus's presentation in the temple in Jerusalem; so you see on the left are Mary and Joseph and on the right are those preparing to receive Jesus in the temple.

We have now, in the last three lectures, looked at six Gothic buildings starting with Saint Denis, those three cathedrals we looked at in Lecture 7, and then Notre Dame in Paris and Notre Dame in Laon. This wraps up our coverage of the early Gothic cathedrals in France, and now we're ready to move to the most famous and the most complete of all the great Gothic cathedrals: We're going to spend a good deal of time, three lectures, looking at the cathedral of Notre Dame de Chartres.

Chartres—The Building
Lecture 10

> Certainly the cathedral of Notre Dame in Paris is the most famous cathedral in the world, in part, of course, because it's in Paris. But I guess I would say to anybody who is going to Europe once ... to go see one cathedral: Go to Chartres.

Chartres Cathedral—about an hour outside of Paris by train—is by far the best-preserved Gothic cathedral in France. Almost all of its sculpture and stained glass has survived the wars of religion, the French Revolution, and the ravages of nature and time. At Chartres, we get the whole package: an extraordinary building, an unprecedentedly large and complex sculptural program, and a great display of stained glass. Therefore,

© iStockphoto/Thinkstock.

The cathedral of Chartres is the most complete, comprehensive Gothic cathedral in Europe and is also considered the first High Gothic cathedral.

we will spend three lectures on this remarkable structure, starting here with the structure itself.

Chartres was an important pilgrimage city, home to an extraordinarily important relic: the cloak of the Virgin Mary, said to have been brought here from Jerusalem by Charlemagne. Of course, Charlemagne never went to Jerusalem, but this cloak was a gift of Charlemagne's grandson, Charles the Bald, to Chartres, and therefore Chartres became, in a special way, a place of the Virgin. The front of its Romanesque cathedral was destroyed by fire in 1134, and a new facade was added in the 1140s, during the so-called Transitional Gothic period. The rest of the Romanesque building burned down in 1194, but the facade (and the cloak, which was housed in the crypt) survived to become the seed of the Gothic cathedral. With money (including royal funding) and even labor pouring in from all over France, reconstruction began almost immediately on what is now considered to be the first **High Gothic** cathedral.

Besides being a pilgrimage city, Chartres was arguably the most important intellectual center in 12th-century France. Its cathedral school was home to some of the most significant teachers and most advanced thinkers in all of Europe. This is reflected in the cathedral's facade; for example, above the right-hand portal, a tympanum sculpture of the Virgin and Child is surrounded by the Seven Liberal Arts on the archivolt.

One of the most interesting features of Chartres is the buttressing. The nave, the transepts, and the choir are all buttressed—these are the original buttresses, not replacements—and they are not only functional but beautiful. A visitor to Chartres can get the best views of them from the north tower and from a park at the east end of the building. Another noteworthy feature is the amount of glass; this may be best demonstrated in the choir, where the spacious double ambulatory is surrounded with many vivid stained-glass windows. The buttresses allowed the walls to hold enormous windows by taking so much of the weight of the roof. Incidentally, the roof is composed of copper and wood, rather than stone.

Despite all of these windows, entering the cathedral, a visitor's first impression is of darkness; this is partly the result of the age-darkened stone and partially because of the colors of the stained glass. On the floor of the cathedral is a great maze. The traditional explanation for this feature is that this path is a symbolic pilgrimage to Jerusalem; it may also represent the journey of the soul toward God.

We have seen four-level cathedral elevations at Noyon and Laon; here, the gallery level has been eliminated; the elevation shows an aisle, a triforium, and a clerestory. Yet the cathedral of Chartres is taller than these other cathedrals, because the aisle is high and the clerestory is huge. Looking up, we discover four-part vaults, rather than six-part ones; each pillar carries equal weight (yet still alternate slightly in design—a holdover from the earlier style), and the vaults are rectangular. Also unlike some of the earlier ribbed vaults, these vaults have keystones. ∎

The Parts and the Whole

In *Gothic Architecture and Scholasticism* (1951), art historian Erwin Panofsky argued that the theology being developed at Chartres's cathedral school, among others, was comprehensive and straightforward—that is to say, the scholars asked very big questions and structured their arguments very systematically. **Thomas Aquinas**, for example, in attempting to combine all human knowledge into a single book, broke his arguments down into smaller and smaller pieces. In other words, he was trying to relate the parts to the whole—including the ultimate whole of all reality. Panofsky goes on to argue that Gothic architecture and sculpture show this same approach to theology. Does the architecture of Chartres seem to support this argument? Its monumental size, the openness of its structure, and the harmony of its design seem to say yes.

Important Term

High Gothic: The style of Gothic at the end of the 12th and early part of the 13th centuries that begins with the cathedral of Chartres.

Thomas Aquinas, Saint (c. 1224–1274): Dominican friar and theologian and philosopher at the University of Paris. His *Summa Theologiae* is an undisputed masterpiece of scholastic thought.

Suggested Reading

Adams, *Mont-Saint-Michel and Chartres.*

Jantzen, *High Gothic.*

Panofsky, *Gothic Architecture and Scholasticism.*

Questions to Consider

1. What are the features of Chartres that become the 'default' form of Gothic cathedral for the next half century?

2. How does the fact that we have a facade of one era, the rest of the church from a second era, and a tower from a later era affect our experience of Chartres Cathedral?

3. Do you think that Chartres Cathedral is indeed a fitting temple for the Virgin, since that was the goal of its builders?

Chartres—The Building
Lecture 10—Transcript

Certainly the cathedral of Notre Dame in Paris is the most famous cathedral in the world, in part, of course, because it's in Paris. But I guess I would say to anybody who is going to Europe once and is going to go see one cathedral: Go to Chartres. Chartres is so different from Notre Dame in Paris in this respect: I talked about how many times Notre Dame has been added on to, hacked up, fixed, redone, repaired, restored, and so on; Chartres, which is southwest of Paris—about an hour on the train—is the opposite; it's by far the best preserved. Yes, it wasn't quite all built at the same time, although generally built in a relatively short time; and yes there have been some things fixed up from time to time; but not only did Chartres's sculpture escape the destruction of, in France, religious wars, the French Revolution, and acts of nature but so did almost all of its stained glass windows. So when we go to Chartres we get in a way we get nowhere else the whole package: We get an extraordinary building; an unprecedentedly large and complex sculptural program; and the great display of stained glass. We're going to spend three lectures on Chartres cathedral: now looking at the building; in the next lecture looking at the sculpture; and finally a lecture dedicated to the stained glass windows. By the way, if you go to Chartres by public transportation from Paris, the train goes through Versailles on the way to Chartres. Let me urge you—I don't want to say anything about Versailles—but if you do that trip, whether you stop at Versailles or not, keep on going to Chartres and you will have, I think, one of the great experiences of your life, aesthetically and I want to argue intellectually.

Chartres was an important pilgrimage city like so many of the places with great Gothic cathedrals. Again, the cathedral is an urban thing, it's an ecclesiastical statement, but it's also about pilgrimage because Chartres had an extraordinarily important relic and we're looking at here, it is still preserved: It is the cloak of the Virgin Mary. We are told that when Charlemagne went to Jerusalem he brought this cloak back and gave it to the cathedral of Chartres; that's the story in the Middle Ages. There are a couple problems with that story; one is that Charlemagne never went to Jerusalem. But this cloak, however it came into the possession of the French kings, was a gift of Charlemagne's grandson, Charles the Bald, to Chartres; and therefore Chartres became, in a special way, a place of the Virgin. It had an important Romanesque cathedral that was undertaken by a famous bishop of Chartres named Fulbert of Chartres, and in 1134 a fire destroyed the front of the cathedral—not the entire building, but the front—and therefore a new facade was added in the 1140s, and that's what we're looking at here, with some alteration. This is a new facade of the 1140s built onto a Romanesque cathedral that withstood that fire in 1134.

Think about the date: the 1140s. Of course, this was the time that we have the building of the very first Gothic buildings: Saint Denis and the cathedral of Sens. If we were to describe the architecture and sculpture of the facade of Chartres cathedral, with the notable exception of the left or north tower that wasn't completed until the 16th century, if we sort of block out that tower we're looking at essentially a facade that is, we would say, transitional between Romanesque and Gothic; it is being built just as the earliest Gothic structures are being completed. As you can see, it has a large sculptural program and it also has four big stained glass windows: three lancets and a rose window on the facade; of course, we'll look at the sculpture in the lecture that's after this one, and we'll look at the windows—obviously from the inside—in the lecture after that.

In 1194, just about 50 years after the building of the facade, the cathedral burned down except for the facade; Fulbert's old Romanesque cathedral burned down. Immediately there was grief, because the fear was the Cloak of the Virgin had been destroyed in the fire. But when the Cloak of the Virgin was discovered to still be there, it was taken as a sign that the Virgin Mary wants a more splendid temple, if you will, than the one that had been standing. In Chartres itself, and with money and even labor pouring in from all over France, almost immediately they began the rebuilding of all of this cathedral except for the facade. The new facade, as it was in the 1140s, is the old facade of this cathedral; and everything behind the facade was built beginning in 1194. Because of patronage, which included royal patronage, and because of the vigor and fervor of the merchants and others in Chartres, the building was built in a relatively short period of time. We have two different styles: this transitional style in the facade, and then we have the rest of the cathedral that we usually call the initiation of the High Gothic period, taking some of the experiments that had been done in the earlier Gothic cathedrals and selecting elements from some, rejecting other elements, and this building then became an important pattern, not for exact copy but for a basic plan, for a whole set of subsequent cathedrals that include places like Amiens and Reims, which we'll be looking at a little bit later on. We need to be aware simply of the history of this building so we get to watch the evolution in style, especially in sculpture and windows, from the facade to the rest of the cathedral.

As I pointed out, although everything behind the facade is new, one piece of Fulbert's cathedral did survive: the crypt; that is to say, the basement, essentially, of Chartres cathedral. By the way, it's the biggest of all crypts of Gothic cathedrals, and it can be visited, although very few of the people who go there do come and visit it. This was the place where the Cloak was kept, although now it's kept in the main part of the cathedral. We have a Romanesque crypt, a Transitional Gothic facade, and a High Gothic building; it is, again, an extraordinary journey in style simply to walk around.

Chartres was not just a city with a cathedral and a relic; it was arguably in the 12th century—and in the 11th, I might add—the most important intellectual center in France. The Cathedral School—the school attached to the cathedral of Chartres—had some of the most important teachers and had some of the most advanced thinkers of all of Europe in the 12th century. In the cathedral, both on the facade and in the inside of the cathedral, we see evidence of that intellectual heritage at Chartres. For example, we have here in one of the pieces of sculpture—this is the right portal of the facade—if you look at the archivolts (the little arches of statues over the main part of the sculpture), you will discover that they are the seven Liberal Arts, the curriculum of the school. We saw those, although they were hard to see because they were up high, in Laon, and they were detached from any other subject matter; but here you will notice that they surround the story of the incarnation of Christ, and the Virgin and Child at the top of the tympanum, and then surrounded by the seven Liberal Arts. We'll look at that in more detail; but this is one particular reference to the intellectual aspect of what Chartres meant, not only locally but really internationally in the 12th century.

The other is a stained glass window: This is the south porch, the south transept, of Chartres cathedral, and these are the lancet windows below the rose window. We'll not look at the one in the middle right now, but the two on either side you'll notice there are men, and then there are other men sitting on their shoulders. The big men standing on the ground are four Old Testament prophets: Isaiah, Jeremiah, Ezekiel, and Daniel. The four people sitting on their shoulders are the four evangelists: Matthew, Mark, Luke, and John. They're all labeled, by the way, in the glass, so we don't have to guess at this. What does this have to do with anything? This is sort of a weird image. The answer is that one of the great teachers in the school of Chartres, Bernard of Chartres, made the famous statement, "We are dwarves on the shoulders of giants"; we are not as great as those who came before us, but because they came before us we can see farther." That's used here to depict the relationship between the great Old Testament prophets and the evangelists; again, this is a tribute in a real sense to the intellectual heritage of this great cathedral school at Chartres.

This is the diagram of the cathedral; I want to spend just a second with it. Obviously we're looking at it and the west end is on our left, and so we enter between those two towers and you can see it's a single-aisled nave, it's a reasonably short transept, and it's a double ambulatory in the east end with some radiating chapels. We'll come back to this actually again, but I just want you to get an idea of the shape of this building, what it would look like if you'd sort of stand on top and take the roof off.

One of the most interesting things at Chartres is the buttressing. Remember we've seen, looking at Notre Dame, that flying buttresses were invented at Notre Dame, although we don't have any of the original flying buttresses. Chartres is completely buttressed—that is to say, in the nave, the transepts, and in the east end of the church—and these are the original buttresses; and probably building on what they learned at Notre Dame, they are more systematic and consistent than even they were at Notre Dame. We get an extraordinary chance to look at buttressing; and as it turns out, the public is allowed to climb one of the towers—the north tower, the bigger tower—and so we can look at the buttresses from a number of angles. Here we are just about at the level where the buttresses attach to the wall of the nave of the church. You can see how they stick out, and then you can see in those pillars—let's take a look from further up now—you really get an idea of how those pillars hold, or push rather, take some of the weight, from the roof so the walls right below that green roof don't have to absorb all the weight of the stone roof. We really get a sense how buttressing works by looking at these, especially from above.

I also want you to notice that the buttresses are not only functional, they're beautiful. They are not just some sort of ugly structure you have to have, but they've been made to be beautiful; so they enhance the beauty of the church as well as hold the roof up. You can see that by looking through the different layers of buttresses here; and let's get real close and you see the individual pieces are, for example, here, a kind of stylized Corinthian column. They're extraordinarily beautiful and interesting, and they're something to observe not just from an engineering point of view but as part of the aesthetic of the cathedral. We're going to look now in the east end of the church and I'm going to show you some different angles of the buttresses; because, again, one of the things one does in a church like this is walk around and look from every angle—in some cathedrals you can actually walk right under the buttresses (not very many); some, like Chartres, have a beautiful park behind the cathedral so you can really get a look at the east end (and you want to go in the morning because the sun is shining on the east end—and get a real sense of what these are like. Everyplace you stand you get a variety of looks at windows, the building itself, and the extraordinary angularity of these buttresses. Here's still another example as we stand right at the back of the church and look in this case around toward the north transept. Or look here when we stand back a little further: We see the chapels in the lower part and then that wonderful system of buttresses in the upper part.

I also want you to notice if you look here we have great big windows at the top, those clerestory windows; great big windows at the bottom in those chapels; so that even with a big stone roof we have really walls of glass. Perhaps we can see that best here in some of the buttressing of the nave, and you can see between the buttresses we have what look like one level of glass and then another level of glass, and then where the green is, of course, at the top that's the beginning of the roof. The roof is high-pitched and it's made of wood and covered with copper, but nevertheless, we see those buttresses going into the base of the vault, and it's extraordinary to think about the fact that we really do have walls of glass in this particular place.

In each transept, there is a porch that, like the facade, has three doors, all sculpted; in fact, there is more sculpture and more elaboration in the two doors on either side of the transept than there is in the front. Again, when we come back to the sculptural program we'll be looking at the facade sculpture, which is done in that transitional period, and we'll be looking at this, the south porch, and its opposite, the north porch, both of which are done in the very beginning of the 13th century and therefore really are of a somewhat different style, and we'll be able to talk about the evolution of the Gothic style.

What's inside Chartres cathedral? I have to tell you a couple things about this photograph. I've been coming to Chartres for almost 50 years, and when I was there just a couple of months ago I discovered that finally they're cleaning all the stone inside. You can see they've cleaned the top part of the choir. I'm standing in the east end looking west where that rose and the three lancet windows are. Isn't that extraordinary? Because normally—and still one walks in the front because one doesn't see this right away from the front, one sees the dark stone when one walks in—the church seems dark. We're so used to the theology of light that we talked about at Saint Denis that we're surprised to find the church is so dark inside. But, of course, it's dark in part because the stone is darkened, and it's also dark because Chartres has retained its stained glass windows and not had them removed and had clear glass put in, which we find, for example, in places like Amiens and others that we'll look at.

This is in the nave, and you can see it feels sort of dark: The stone looks dark, and there's just not a lot of beams of light shining through because you can see especially in the upper windows but also in the lower window in the aisle there those are all filled full of stained glass. Here I'm standing in the choir and looking up, so the lower part of the stone is very dark, the upper part: Look at it; look how bright it is. Even with all the windows in stained glass as you can see there, there nevertheless is this lightness. By the way, this was taken in the morning so the light is coming directly through the windows we're looking at; again, it's darker in the afternoon because the light is shining on the facade of the cathedral in the afternoon. Here, I just want to show you, again as a way of introducing ourselves, it feels sort of dark as you walk in but look at those lights; and the lights, of course, are not pure light they are all colored light. Again, at any given time of the day, you'll see color patterns on the floor, on the wall opposite a particular window, depending on where the sun is shining. We need to get over the fact that it seems almost disappointingly dark when we walk in and we realize that the reasons are the discoloration of the stone and even more than that, the fact the windows are not clear glass.

On the floor of the cathedral is a great maze. You can see it here, although, of course, there are chairs on it. In other words, it's sort of a puzzle that you can walk around to get to the center; we'll also have one at Amiens that we'll see. But one of the interesting questions is: What's it doing here? Why is there a maze in the middle of the floor of the nave of this cathedral? One traditional answer is: It's a way for people symbolically, when they come to Chartres, to take their own pilgrimage to Jerusalem, because you have to wander and wander and wander and wander. The one in Amiens, there are no chairs on it now and I watched somebody walk the maze and it took a lot of steps and about 10 minutes to get from the outside to the center even though it's not very long as the crow flies (of course, the whole point of a maze is it doesn't go as a crow flies). At any rate, it is a kind of pilgrimage; but I think we also need to consider that the maze is there to do a different kind of pilgrimage. It's not just about "I can't really go to Jerusalem so I'll sort of pretend to, I'll sort of symbolically go on Crusade or on pilgrimage to Jerusalem" but rather it is the journey of the soul to God.

Let's look at the way this building is constructed. Remember we saw in attempt to make the building higher, a cathedral like Noyon or Laon had four levels: It had the aisle, then the gallery, then the triforium, then the clerestory windows. You can see Chartres has only three; the gallery has been eliminated. It probably didn't have much function in a cathedral; not nearly as much as it did in a monastery where it'd be a place for women pilgrims to stay and sleep over night, and so on and so forth. Here we have the aisle, then the triforium gallery, and then these huge clerestory windows. This is a very tall building; this is taller than Laon, this is taller than Noyon, and yet it has three levels rather than four. Why is that? First of all, the aisle is very high and the clerestory is huge. We have these very, very large windows at the top, and it's important to point out that's made possible by this wonderful buttressing system we saw on the outside. There is this huge window space that we can see in the clerestory with two lancet windows and what we call an oculus at the top above them; an eye, if you will.

Here is that triforium; you can see that it's very simple. It's made up of a series of Gothic arches; you can see the pointed arch of the aisle below and just the base of the clerestory windows up above. If we look up, we discover that the vaults are not six-part like we've seen in several of the early cathedrals beginning with Sens, but rather they're four-part so that each pillar carries equal weight; there's not that alteration between major and minor arches. Therefore, one bay—that is to say, the section marked off by two of these great pillars—is rectangular; rather than having a two-bayed square vault, we have a one-bayed rectangular vault. Again, we're looking up into the cleaned vault of the choir of Chartres cathedral, surrounded by those spectacular and large clerestory windows. You can see every one is the same; so we have this series, there's no alternation of any kind, so when we walk in our eyes are drawn to the east, to the altar, where the body of Christ is and beneath which, in the crypt, is the cloak of the Virgin Mary. Our eyes take us where we need to go. You can see also that unlike some of the earlier ribbed vaults, this does have a keystone; so there is a piece fit in—actually several pieces fit in—to make this large keystone, another advance in the building of these Gothic vaults.

I want you to look at the pillars, because remember, every pillar carries the same weight; and yet what we discover is the pillars are slightly different. Let me go back here and show you this one: Some of the columns—the major column part of the pillar—are round and the little columns attached to them are angular, and then the next one is the opposite; and we can see that as we move from this one to this one. You see, this is a squared-off or angular column and then we have the rounded columnettes; the other is just the opposite. There is a little bit of alternation in the way that these are made, even though ultimately in cathedrals that follow Chartres, this minor difference between one and the other will, in fact, disappear. Here, we can take a look at two together. You can see that these two great pillars are just a little bit different, one from the other: one with rounded, with angular little parts; the other angular, with rounded little parts. Again, that's sort of what's left over, if you will, of that old notion of the alternation of one kind and then another because of the old way of vaulting with the two-bay, six-part vault;

kind of an interesting evolution that we see here at Chartres. Usually when you walk into a cathedral like this you're so awed by the general architecture and size and, of course, here by the stained glass windows that one very often doesn't catch those kinds of details. It's worthwhile not doing your half-hour photo shoot in Chartres cathedral but really spending a day and taking a look at those buttresses on the outside from different angles, and so on and so forth.

Let me go back to the diagram, and again we can see that there is one aisle on either side of the nave, and then we're going to take a look now at the other parts of the church—the transept briefly and the east end—as a way of finishing up our tour of Chartres the building. Here we have this double ambulatory, and again, it's spacious and wonderful, and all the windows are again stained glass; so there's a lot of light coming in, so it's pretty light here in the ambulatory. But again, it's colored light; it's hard for the camera to capture that, but it's colored light. You can see the window on the farthest right of this photograph has a lot of color in it; so do all the windows if you stand right in front of them. Here's another way of looking at the ambulatory: This is the most curved part—that is to say, the part that goes around the east end of the primary vaulting—so we're walking actually now; I'm standing almost behind the high altar.

As we look at this building, let me say a couple things about a broader way of understanding it and its achievement, and the achievement of Gothic. In 1951, a famous art historian named Erwin Panofsky wrote a book called *Gothic Architecture and Scholasticism*, and in the book he makes an interesting argument. He talks about the kind of philosophy and theology that was being done at a place like the University of Paris in the 13th century and in development stages at the cathedral school in Laon, the cathedral school in Chartres, and the cathedral school in Paris. He argues there are certain characteristics of that kind of theology: It is comprehensive and inclusive; that is to say, what the scholars tried to do is take very big questions. In fact, Thomas Aquinas, 13th century scholastic theologian and philosopher, ultimately tried to combine all human knowledge and understanding into one book. The fact that he failed to do it shouldn't surprise us; but what an effort and what an idea.

Secondly, he says, the structure of scholastic thought is out front. For example, Thomas Aquinas says, "Here is a question. Now I'm going to break that question down into sub-questions; I'm going to break the sub-question into sub-sub-questions." It doesn't have, if you will, any literary style to speak of; what it does have is clarity so that you have a piece, and then a piece of a piece, and a piece of a piece of a piece, and so on. In every little question that Thomas asks, he says, "Here's my question; here are some answers that might suggest we should say 'yes'; here are some texts that suggest we might say 'no'; let me try to resolve them." The structure, if you will, is not hidden behind a rhetorical scheme, but rather the structure is there to see.

Finally, what Thomas Aquinas and others do, according to Panofsky, is try constantly to relate the parts to the whole: What does this little piece have to do with the bigger question I'm trying to answer? I always try to get students to think about that when they're writing essays, to think about the big question and little questions that they're dealing with; I'm being more medieval with them than they know. Panofsky, in *Gothic Architecture and Scholasticism* argues that we see the same approach to reality, the same approach to things, in Gothic architecture and sculpture. We're going to deal with the sculptural side of that later on when we take an examination of the facade of Amiens cathedral.

But think about Chartres in terms of what I just described as the scholastic method: First of all, God knows it's monumental and complete, especially when we think about the windows and the sculpture that we're going to examine and we had only just little glimpses of so far. Secondly, the structure is open and there to see. Look at the flying buttresses: There's not something covering them up so you don't see the structure, but the structure is there and displayed, and in many ways displayed proudly. It wouldn't be the same building if you couldn't see the structure. And certainly there is a great deal of interplay of whole and parts. Look here: We have these extraordinary soaring upward lines on the inside, but notice below the windows and above the aisle—that is to say, on either side of the triforium—we have these lines, these stone bars if you will, that run horizontally, so that we have a constant interplay between vertical and horizontal. In some ways, people have said—because the kind of book that the Scholastics wrote was called a "summa"—and have said I think quite rightly, Chartres and the other great Gothic cathedrals are summas in stone.

Chartres—The Sculpture
Lecture 11

I watch people, including very good, very learned people, at a place like Chartres ... and it's not that they miss so much because they're careless, lazy, or uninterested—that isn't it at all; they in a sense don't know how to see the stuff because they can't see it as 13th-century people saw it.

Cathedral decoration was meant to be not merely beautiful but also functional. Examining details of Chartres's sculpture, with particular attention to the 12th- and 13th-century context in which it was created, will help us understand how these images functioned in medieval culture to teach, instruct, inspire, and even strike fear. To that end, we look at three sets of sculpture on each of the three porches of Chartres Cathedral.

The facade, constructed in the 1140s, contains three portals with sculpture in the tympana and archivolts, as well as jamb statues. The jamb statues are elongated and columnar, and while they don't all look alike, there are similarities among them—namely, that they seem to be part of the architecture. Scholars believe that the men and women portrayed here are Old Testament kings and queens—thus this door is called the *porte royale.* Above the jamb statues, what appears to be a set of Corinthian capitals is actually a band of narratives of the lives of Mary and Jesus.

The right-hand tympanum shows stories related to the Incarnation of Christ. On the bottom of the double **lintel** we have the Annunciation, Visitation, and Nativity of Christ. On the upper lintel is the Presentation. Above these, in the triangular section, are the Virgin and Child enthroned, flanked by angels. Even the arrangements of the figures are significant; in the Nativity, Jesus's cradle appears above Mary, as on a sacrificial altar, and note how, although this cathedral is dedicated to Mary, Jesus is at the center of all three parts. In the archivolts, the Seven Liberal Arts are represented by symbolic female figures and important male practitioners of each art. The left-hand tympanum depicts Christ's Ascension, so his arrival on earth on the right is balanced by his departure from earth on the left. The gap in between reminds us of the gap in time between his first coming and his promised return. On the left-hand

The central portal of the facade of Chartres Cathedral draws on images from the book of Revelation.

archivolts are the signs of the zodiac and men at seasonal labor—heavenly time and earthly time shown side by side.

Above the central portal, we have Christ's return, the apocalyptic Christ. He is surrounded by four winged creatures from the book of Revelation: the lion, the ox, the human, and the eagle. In the archivolt are the 24 Elders who according to Revelation will surround Christ on his return. On the lintel below, we find the 12 apostles, accompanied by the prophets Enoch and Elijah—two Old Testament figures who were taken up to heaven without having died.

The north and south **porches**, built roughly 75 years later, look very different from the facade. They are deeper and larger, with more sculpture. A cathedral's north porch, because of its association with darkness and shade, is traditionally the Old Testament porch; on Chartres's north porch, we find the days of Creation represented, including an image of God creating Adam very different from the later (and now ubiquitous) Michelangelo version. Theologically, it stands as a reminder that humans are all the children of God. The jamb statues, both here and on the south porch, appear to be independent of the architecture, with greater detail and more natural poses, facing both outward and inward.

The right-hand portal's tympanum, quite unusually, shows the story of Job— the innocent sufferer, a prefiguration of Jesus. Many scholars also think that in the early 13th century, Job represented the church's suffering: from the corruption of wealth and power, from the Albigensian heresy, and from the Muslim conquest of Jerusalem. In the lintel is judgment of Solomon,

Not an inch of display space on Chartres's portals is wasted. Even the door lintels are elaborately sculpted.

prefiguring the Last Judgment. The left-hand portal shows more of the life of Christ. Whereas the facade showed iconic, static images, these versions are more active, theatrical: The figures are interacting, not standing stiffly side by side. This is a new level of realism in medieval sculpture. Making a closer examination of the jamb statues of this portal, one will notice that each figure stands on another, tiny statue; these are called **socles,** and each one tells us something about the person above. The Virgin, for example, stands on the Burning Bush of Exodus 3. The bush flames but it is not consumed; the Virgin is with child but her virginity is not destroyed. We can imagine the socles as being like margin notes in a manuscript.

The central portal is called the Portal of the Virgin, and the images here are all related to Mary. A sculpture between two doors is called a **trumeau**; here we find one of Saint Anne holding the baby Virgin. The jamb statues show a series of Old and New Testament figures leading us to Christ and teaching us where to go from Christ—his successors, Saint Peter and the popes. Note the individuation of the figures; John the Baptist, for example, looks thin and ascetic.

We had the past on the north porch; we find the present and future on the south porch. The right-hand portal is dedicated to the confessor saints—that is, saints who were not martyred. The martyr saints are found on the left-hand side. Above Stephen, the first Christian martyr, stands Christ, the ultimate martyr. In the center portal at last we find the familiar Last Judgment. Christ the Judge is in the trumeau; he stands on a lion and a dragon, a reference to Psalm 91. (In the Middle Ages, sometimes the lion would symbolize pagans, and the dragon, heretics—here perhaps the Albigensians.) The jamb statues show the apostles. The Last Judgment itself differs from previous ones we've seen not only in location but in the appearance of Mary and John as full-sized figures beside Christ. The resurrection of the dead is up on the upper archivolts, with heaven and hell on the lower archivolts to Christ's right and left, respectively.

It's clear that the three porches of Chartres Cathedral form a coordinated program of sculpture, with images that overlap and reinforce each other. It shows the sort of completeness that Panofsky suggested is characteristic of medieval scholastic thought. ∎

lintel: The stone over a door, perpendicular to the posts. In Gothic cathedrals, they are often sculpted, usually continuing the theme of the tympanum above.

socle: A small sculpted base of a jamb statue.

trumeau: A statue between the doors of a major portal of a church, for example, the statue of Christ in the central portal of Amiens Cathedral or a similar one on the central portal of the south porch at Chartres.

Suggested Reading

Adams, *Mont-Saint-Michel and Chartres*.

Jantzen, *High Gothic*.

Katzenellenbogen, *The Sculptural Programs of Chartres Cathedral*.

Mâle, *The Gothic Image*.

Miller, *Chartres Cathedral*.

Questions to Consider

1. Comparing the two different styles of sculpture at Chartres, and in some cases the same figures and stories in both styles, which do you find more beautiful? More moving?

2. What should we conclude from the fact that there are pagan figures on the facade of Chartres Cathedral?

3. How do all three sets of portal sculpture together give us a comprehensive understanding of Christianity and the road to salvation?

Chartres—The Sculpture
Lecture 11—Transcript

This lecture may seem rapid-paced even by my fairly rapid standards, but let me tell you why. We're going to look at three sets of sculpture on each of the three porches of Chartres cathedral: the front done in the 1140s, and the north and south porches done in the early part of the 13th century. There are a lot of statues, but it's not a matter of just getting an impression of what the statues are like, either in style or in content; we really need to examine a lot of details because a quick glance might not even help you identify a story or a person, let alone the context in which that story or person is set. We're going to go not exactly on a merry-go-round, because we're going to stop and look at everything carefully, but I do want to make sure we see enough details, both to understand the themes of the sculpture, and also I hope to sharpen everyone's critical eye in such a way. I watch people, including very good, very learned people, at a place like Chartres—I do some of my watching of people, not just of the statues and the windows in the buildings—and it's not that they miss so much because they're careless, lazy, or uninterested, that isn't it at all; they in a sense don't know how to see the stuff because they can't see it as 13th-century people saw it, and I'm going to try to recreate some of that.

So again, hold on a little bit tighter than usual even—and I know I'm sort of a lickety-split guy—but I think you'll find this will be a useful way of coming to understand how the sculpture works, not just what it looks like, and what it means, which to me is the essential thing. This is never art for art's sake; this is art to teach, to instruct, to inspire, and sometimes even—as we've seen in the Last Judgments—to strike fear.

First, we are going to look at the facade of Chartres cathedral and the sculpture that was done in the 1140s. As we can see, there are three portals here with tympana, with sculpture overhead (the archivolts), and with jamb statues as well. These jamb statues are really quite interesting. You can see they're elongated and columnar, and certainly they don't all look alike; there's a certain kind of individuation in these statues. But as we look at different groups of them, I think you can see that there are a lot of similarities and they seem almost to be part of the architecture; it seems that if you took them away, something might fall down. Not just some meaning is missing, but some part of the building is missing; and we're going to see that it's something that's going to change as we move to the north and south porches. But aren't they beautiful? What we see here are men and women; many have crowns. We've always assumed that they are, in fact, Old Testament kings and therefore ancestors of Jesus. That's almost certainly true; that's why we call this the "Royal Portal" (the "Port-Royal"). We also find that there are women crowned, obviously, therefore, queens—there are important queens, after all, as well as kings in Hebrew history—and we find there are some men who do not have crowns. We assume, although we don't know from any written evidence, that they are Old Testament prophets; so this is an Old Testament portal. These are people that welcome us in the statues to Jesus. Look at some of the beautiful faces and details: Look at the braids of this queen; and here we have this king with his distinguished beard; here we have one of the prophets.

As we move to the statues that are part of the facade over the doors, we're going to look first on the right side, then on the left side, and then we're going to move to the center. We will not always do that, but we will, in fact, do it with all three porches here at Chartres. I want to take a look at the stories here, because this is the story of the Incarnation; this is the nativity of Christ. It begins in the lowest part; the rectangular parts of this are called "lintels." Within this great tympanum there are, in this case, actually two lintels as you can see; so I'm going to be using sometimes that language to distinguish one part of this from another. If you look in the very lower left-hand corner you'll see the Annunciation, the angel Gabriel coming; the Visitation, Mary going to visit Elizabeth. If you look in the center you see in the lowest part the birth of Jesus; up above, the presentation in the Temple; and then straight up above that we have the Virgin Mary holding the baby Jesus. You see, Jesus is the center of things, and even though this is a cathedral dedicated to Mary, Jesus is the center; he's in the middle in all three parts.

Let's take a look: This is a Nativity; as you can see, it's been damaged. But we're used to nativities having a manger or maybe Mary holding Jesus; in some traditions Jesus is actually being washed in a nativity scene. But here we see the Virgin Mary, and above we have this cradle with Jesus lying there. What's going on here; it doesn't seem very moving, it doesn't seem very emotional, it doesn't seem very maternal? That part over the Virgin's "bunk," if you will, looks a lot like an altar; because even here in the Nativity, we are reminded that Jesus is going to be sacrificed. He is the sacrifice for sin. Remember, when you walk inside and look toward the altar, you are looking where the sacrifice occurs again and again whenever the mass is said and the bread and wine are consecrated. So this has, if you will, theological and liturgical meaning; it's not just an odd way of depicting the birth of baby Jesus. This is the presentation in the Temple; and again, notice in the very center, there's an altar. Once again, there's this sense of Jesus being placed on the altar, and it's extraordinarily important for us to understand how this sculpture relates to what the building is and to what goes on inside.

As we look at the whole thing again, we see again in the upper part of the tympanum we have the Madonna and Child; so we see the baby Jesus three times. What's interesting here—and we looked at this briefly in the previous lecture—is what's in the archivolts, because here is where we have represented the seven Liberal Arts, the curriculum, if you will, of the medieval schools: grammar, rhetoric, logic, astronomy, mathematics, geometry, and music. Each one is represented symbolically by a female figure, and then each one is represented by an important practitioner of that art. Some of those practitioners—I mentioned this when we looked at the similar sculpture in Laon—are, in fact, pagans, like Aristotle and so on. Let's take a couple looks: This is the way that Grammar is depicted—grammar is the first of the subjects you study—and so Grammar is represented as a woman with two little boys that she's instructing; and you'll notice one is paying attention, and one is pulling hair. We see children learning and we see children misbehaving, a very human touch in this elaborate scheme of learning and theology.

Here we see a couple of the practitioners, and you'll see how much detail there is: They have lap desks they're working with; you can see their styluses hanging on the wall behind them. It's an extraordinary look at what scholars looked like at Chartres in the 12th century; there's no way historically to know what these ancient figures looked like. Here's another one on the other side where, again, we see his lap desk and his styluses. So in many ways what we have in this particular set of sculptures is Mary represents wisdom as the mother of Jesus, the mother of God (remember, her cloak's inside). She represents the mother of God, she represents wisdom; and then she's surrounded by the human practitioners of wisdom—some of the great ones—and by the categories through which we get wisdom: through grammar, rhetoric, logic, and all the rest. It's a really very beautiful sculptural program.

Let's now move to the left side, and what we have on the left side here is the end of Christ on Earth; we saw the beginning of Christ on Earth, now we have the end of Christ on Earth and what we have is Christ going up into Heaven. We have the Ascension in the top, and we have angels below him, and apostles below that. Notice again the balance: We have the beginning, Christ comes; Christ in physical form goes away. In what ways is Christ still present on Earth? Of course, there are a lot of possible answers to that question; the number one answer is in the Eucharist, which we saw represented with Christ coming: Just as Christ came to us in human form, he comes to us still in the form of bread and wine because his human form has gone away; we see him going up to Heaven. It reminds us that there is this gap in time between Christ coming and Christ coming again as judge; and that's where we live: in that time between the first and second comings of Christ.

What's in the archivolts here? The answer is: The signs of the Zodiac, and the kind of work done in each month of the year. In this one, for example, you can see among others Cancer the crab; and if we look on the other side, you can see the figure in the lower left is pruning the vines, so that there is each month represented by both a Zodiac sign and a labor, because we live in time that's measured by the stars, we live according to this cycle of the months. We'll see this, by the way, again—in some ways even more dramatically—when we look at the sculpture in the cathedral of Amiens; it is a common theme in Gothic sculpture. Now, in the center, we have Christ coming again; this is the apocalyptic Christ. You can see Christ in the center, and he's surrounded by four beasts, four animals, that are described in the book of Revelation: the lion, the ox, the human, and the eagle. We see down below a group of men, we'll come back to them in a minute; and then in the archivolt what we have is the 24 elders, who are also described as surrounding Christ at the time that he comes again. So those animals—they're all winged, by the way, because that's the way they're described in the book of Revelation, and before that in the book of Ezekiel—but there we see the lion; by the way, these four also represented the four evangelists. In this case, the lion represents Mark; the other three evangelists are represented by the other three beasts of the apocalypse.

If you look at the lintel down below, if you count there are 14 people: 12 of them, the 12 in the center, are apostles; the other 2 are 2 Old Testament figures, Enoch and Elijah, who are seen to be Old Testament figures who did not die but went up to Heaven (remember, Elijah goes up in a fiery chariot). The reason they're here is because since they aren't described as having died, they are thought to be coming back to life on Earth as a prelude to Christ coming again; so they become apocalyptic figures as well, so that's another reminder that we need to be prepared because Christ will come again. So on the right Christ has come; on the left, Christ in body has gone to Heaven; and in the center, Christ will come again.

Once again, I want you to stand back because there's even more sculpture here that is hard to see. Look just above the jamb statues and you'll see that there is what looks like Corinthian columns up above all of them with sort of fancy capitals, if you will. But, in fact, they're not Corinthian columns with fancy capitals; it is all a band of narratives that runs all the way across and it tells the story of Mary and Jesus. I'm just going to show you two details. These are things very few people ever bother to notice because they're so taken by the much bigger statues. But look at this, how we have several capitals blended together, and the capital really is, again, not Corinthian, not acanthus leaves, it is the Last Supper. Isn't that a beautiful way of depicting the Last Supper? This is right above those jamb statues. Look here: in the one on our right you can see that this is the kiss of Judas; Judas is reaching out to kiss and therefore betray Jesus. You can see the Last Supper over on the left, and therefore you can see how this works as a narrative. It's really quite extraordinary.

Let's now go to the north and south porches. Before we get to particulars, I want you to just glance for a minute at how different these are going to look. The porches—this happens to be a detail of the north porch—are very much deeper; there's lot more sculpture, and it's bigger, as you can see. The jamb statues are going to appear more independent and not pieces of the architecture; and here we look through a series of portals (this is actually the south porch). We're also going to see greater detail, greater individuation, and more natural poses. Let me give you one example: This is actually the back of a statue at the edge of one of the portals, and it is a saint who is a knight—you can see his shield there—but look at the way his chain mail, his armor, is made with extraordinary detail and verisimilitude.

We're going to be looking now at roughly 70 years, 75 years, after the sculpture we've just seen and we're going to see continuity but we're also going to see a great deal of a new world visually. This is the north porch, and the north porch traditionally is the Old Testament porch, up to the time of the coming of Christ. Why? Because in our hemisphere the north gets less light; it is more shaded. This is actually taken at a particular time in the spring in the afternoon when there is some direct light; but obviously there's much more light on the south porch. By the way, this north/south pattern will be reflected in the windows as well as in the sculpture on the outside; as you can see, three very highly-articulated portals.

You'll notice in the general picture that all the way out to the edge of this porch there are little figures running around each of the arches, and in the center arch here in the north porch I want you to look at some of the details just to give you an idea of what we can find. There, for example, is the beginning of Creation; here we have the separation of land and water. The details show us the days of Creation, and they're really quite beautiful. Look at this one: This is the creation of the fish (you see them in the water down below) and the birds (you see them up above). Then, on the right, we have the creation of the animals; and on the left, it is so beautiful, look at God creating Adam. We're used to the Michelangelo version, and of course this is very different and obviously three centuries before Michelangelo; but I want you to look at God who embodies power and wisdom and love, and this son that he is fashioning. Of course, Adam is his son, and Adam is meant to live in the Garden of Eden; and, of course, Adam rebels and therefore God has to send a part of himself in a real sense. But we are all sons of God; in fact, that's why Jesus came to make us again, because that's what we were originally meant to be. But isn't this a beautiful thing? There are other details like this that really will enlighten us and make us, I think, even inspired, whether we're religious or not, if we just take the time—and perhaps a pair of binoculars—and look at the details.

Let's look at the three porches that we have here in Chartres cathedral. On the north porch: This is the right porch, and you can see it has statues—jamb statues, many of them—some facing out toward us, some inside. The parts that are facing outside were made a few years later and are sort of an addition to the original program and, in fact, we aren't even quite sure who all of them are. But let's now zoom in a little bit, and we have here in the tympanum an unusual story, the story of Job. We don't find it depicted all that often. You can see that literally Job is lying there in his dung heap with his friends and his wife. In fact, let's get real close and you can see there Satan; I mean, look at that: Satan and that poor man Job.

Does Job remind you of anybody? He should; he should remind you of the suffering Jesus, because he is the innocent sufferer. It's a prefiguration, a prelude, to the coming of Jesus. But also many people think that the presence of Job here also represents the fact at this time—that is to say, the early 13th century—the church was also suffering. In some ways it was suffering from corruption and having too much wealth and power, but it was also suffering, from its own perspective in the 13th century, in a couple specific senses: One, there was a major heretical movement in southern France called the Cathars or the Albigensians—in fact, the Albigensian Crusade was probably going on when this sculpture was made—and two, the Holy Land, which had previously been captured during the First Crusade, was back in the hands of Muslims. So probably in some real ways we might be encouraged to think of this figure representing the suffering church as well as the suffering Christ. Then down below in the lintel of this piece of sculpture we have the story of the judgment of Solomon; again, an Old Testament story where the Wisdom of Solomon and him as judge prefigures Christ as judge, and that's an important thing as well. You can see there are jamb statues again—as we step back once more to look at this portal—and let me simply point out they too, are all Old Testament figures. One of them is the Queen of Sheba because, of course, she's associated with Solomon, who's one of the figures in the lintel.

Let's move now to the left side, and what we have on the left side is the incarnation of Christ; in other words, this series of work brings us up to that time. Again, we can see how richly and elaborately decorated it is. I want to look at the jamb statues here, because the stories of the incarnation we have seen several times. Take a look at these jamb statues: What we have is a prophet—and you can see you have me missing a head here—and then we have the Annunciation; so we have Gabriel and the Virgin Mary. Notice what's new here: Those two figures are interacting with one another. They're not standing straight and tall and looking straight out, or simply being iconic figures that symbolize something, there is the Virgin Mary having this conversation with the angel Gabriel that's recorded, of course, in Luke's gospel. It's that very engagement of the figures, which means of course they're slightly turned toward one another, their draperies reflect that; there's a new kind of realism—it's not photographic realism; that's not the intention—but there's a new kind of realism to this as we come to look at these stories that we've seen in Romanesque and we've seen in early Gothic but we're now seeing in a new way. On the opposite side is another pair with another prophet and this pair is the Virgin Mary and Elizabeth—Elizabeth, her cousin, the mother of John the Baptist, and of course Mary goes to visit her; we call this the Visitation—and once again, they are engaged in a kind of commerce, a kind of discussion; a loving relationship that's expressed in stone.

You might have noticed by this time if you're an observant person that down below all these statues there are little bitty statues on which they're standing, and we could do a lecture or two just on them. Those little pieces are called "socles," and each one tells us something about the person above. Look at the Virgin Mary, she's on the far left here, and look at the socle down below. It's not a person, it's the Burning Bush; it's the Burning Bush from Exodus 3 when God appears to Moses in the Burning Bush. The Burning Bush flames but it is not consumed by fire, it doesn't burn and that's seen as a representation of the Virgin Mary: She is with child, but her virginity is not destroyed; she is mother and virgin. Each one of these socles adds a kind of commentary, a kind of marginal commentary, much like in manuscripts of scholastic theology there are marginal comments that are written into these manuscripts, sometimes by several hands in the same manuscript over time.

Now I want us to look at the central porch because it's all about the Virgin Mary; and again, we should not be surprised, this is once again Notre Dame de Chartres. By the way, the figure in the center between the two doors is called a "trumeau"—another one of those terms we have to learn—and this trumeau statue, you look at it and you say, "Ah, Virgin and Child." No, it's actually Saint Anne, the mother of the Virgin, holding the baby Virgin Mary. It is a different image because this is dedicated to the Virgin. Here, I also want to look primarily at the jamb statues because it's a collection of Old Testament people, and then by the time we get all the way to the right a New Testament pair that lead us to Christ and teach us where to go from Christ. So we have here, for example, figures that go all the way back to the book of Genesis; the second one from the left, for example, is Abraham and there you can see he's with his son, Isaac. Notice the man with the column: That's Moses. Moses is not depicted here primarily as a deliverer of the Ten Commandments; he is the one who holds the column on which the bronze serpent sat. Remember we saw that image, which is a prefiguration of Christ, in the window of Saint Denis. Here we see it in stone.

As we move to the other side, we again get these extraordinary figures. The one holding the baby is the prophet Simeon who is in the temple when Mary and Joseph bring Jesus into the temple. Then look at the figure next to the right of John the Baptist. There is an acetic: He is skinny, he holds the Lamb of God, and his cheeks are sunken. It's not just, "Ah, let's make him look like all those other Old Testament prophets; it's a very individuated way of imagining John the Baptist. Notice also it's a much calmer version than the one we saw at Senlis where John the Baptist is standing there with his legs twisted; look at this, this is the gaunt acetic, this is the voice crying in the wilderness. How does that transition us to the church? The guy on the right is Saint Peter, of course the prince of the apostles, but also his successors are the popes, the heads of the Catholic Church.

Now let's move to the south porch, which is going to be the New Testament and the church, and the coming of Christ again porch. In other words, we had the past on the north porch; now we have, in a sense, the present and future on the south porch. You can see here it is, again, lit by a great deal of sunlight; you can also see from the people there how big this is. Let's move first to the right side of the south porch, and what we have is a doorway dedicated to the great confessor saints; that is to say, men who didn't die for the faith, but men who did heroic things. On the lintel we have two of the most heroic of them all: The famous French saint, Saint Martin of Tours. Martin of Tours famously is a solider, sees a beggar, and cuts his cloak in half and gives it to the beggar. That cloak, by the way, was preserved in Tours, which is not all that far from Chartres. On the other side of the lintel here, the lower part of the tympanum, we have a story of Saint Nicholas of Barry. Remember Saint Nicholas came (body-wise) to the West in the 11th century because his body was stolen, and we saw the church of Saint Nicholas in Barry in southern Italy. This is the most famous story of Saint Nicholas. He finds out that there's this man who has three daughters but no dowries for them; he's going to sell them into prostitution or into servitude. You can see on the very far left, young Nicholas comes along and drops three bags of money into the room where they are so that these girls could have dowries and be married. Again, these are the great "good deeds" saints, if you will. The jamb statues on either side are, in fact, statues of other great confessor saints.

Let's move to the left porch: Here we have stories of martyrs. On either side, we have jamb statues of various martyrs, but I want you to look here because what we have in the lower part is the first Christian martyr, a story we've seen in glass in Laon: We have the stoning of Saint Stephen. Here—sort of a pun, I guess—the stoning of Saint Stephen is sculpted in stone, so that the stones they're throwing really are stone. We have here the story, therefore, of the first Christian martyr, and then up above him stands Christ, who is, of course, the martyr that makes all the other martyrdoms worthwhile because martyrdom is imitating the martyrdom of Jesus, if you will; and Acts of the Apostles makes that connection, and so does the designer of the sculpture here at Chartres cathedral make that connection between Stephen the first Christian martyr and the one for whom he is martyred, Christ the great martyr up above.

But I want to focus first and foremost on the center, because again—we're used to seeing this in other cathedrals in different places—we have a Last Judgment, and I want to look at some of the similarities and differences of this porch with other Last Judgments that we've looked at. First of all, here's the great trumo statue; here is Christ the Judge, with his arm raised and carrying the book. You'll notice here, he's standing on something that looks a little bit precarious and peculiar: He's standing on a lion and a dragon. Psalm 91 says, "On the lion and the viper you will tread and trample the young lion and the dragon." This is seen in Christianity as being a prophesy of Christ, who will trample these symbols of violence and evil; and, in fact, in the Middle Ages sometimes these were allegorized to mean the "lion" would be pagans because they sort of roar what they do, while the "viper" would be heretics because they're sort of sneaky. We can imagine somebody seeing this statue, thinking about the Crusades, thinking about those Cathars, those Albigensians, those heretics in southern France; we can read this in a lot of different ways, but what we have here is a great image of Christ and an image taken from the book of Psalms.

On either side, in the jamb statues, we have the 12 apostles. We can recognize them by some of their standard symbols: for example, the one furthest to the right in this picture—and that's nearest to the door, because the door is to our far right—is Saint Peter, and you can see he has his keys, as you would expect. On the other side we have the other apostles that we can recognize, beginning on the far left with Saint Paul. So Paul and Peter, the two great apostles—one to the gentiles, one to the Jews—are paired, and the other apostles are there as well. Here is the Last Judgment itself. You can see Christ in the center, you can see down below the archangel Michael dividing the good from the bad, and we'll take a look at some details of that. There is Christ. Remember at Laon, Mary and John, the intercessors, were tiny? Notice now they're full-size people, so we really grasp who they are as intercessors. Then we have this wonderful image of Michael, the archangel, and you can see the good on one side and those going to Hell on the other side. By the way, there's Hell; it is really once again the Hellmouth that we've seen in earlier Romanesque images, in particular in the monastic church at Conques.

Notice, though, what the artist has done: He's removed the resurrection of the dead to the second level up of the archivolts, and the first level—that is to say, the bottom level, since we're looking at Christ's right side—shows the souls in Heaven, and over here we see the resurrection of the dead on the second level and then we see the souls of those who are being tortured in Hell. I guess we could end with a bad pun and say in this case, the Devil literally is in the details. But at any rate, despite the bad pun, what we have seen here is this extraordinary display of sculpture. I think it's clear there is a good deal of coordination between the themes of the three porches: They overlap; they reinforce one another; they even restate certain things, especially about the Virgin Mary and Christ coming back to Earth. But this is the completeness that I talked about in the last lecture that Erwin Panofsky talks about as a characteristic of scholastic thought; it just seems hardly anything is left out. And if you think that's true of the sculpture, wait until we see the windows.

Chartres—The Windows
Lecture 12

When most people think about Chartres Cathedral, if they know anything about it, they know the windows—and rightfully so, because while we have a few windows at Laon [and] several other Gothic cathedrals … there's nothing like Chartres. It is the mother lode of medieval stained glass for its quantity and for its quality, for its stories, for its color.

There are about 175 windows in Chartres Cathedral; about 150 of them have most or all of their original 12th- and 13th-century glass. The patterns of light in individual windows, as well as the general pattern of light in the cathedral, change from hour to hour and season to season. They are one of the great wonders not just of Chartres, not just of the Gothic, but of the world. In this lecture, we'll focus on the oldest glass, that in the facade; the rose windows and lancets in the north and south transepts; and some of the narrative windows in the aisles and ambulatory.

In the facade, the rose window is set above three lancet windows, of which the middle is larger than the others. The rose window repeats the theme of the tympanum below: the apocalyptic return of Christ. The lancet windows are somewhat narrative and can be "read" from bottom to top. One shows the lineage of David, from Jesse to the Virgin Mary. The center lancet tells the life story of Christ from the Annunciation to his adulthood, some from the Bible and others from later folk legend. To the other side, the lancet shows the Passion, from the Transfiguration to the Resurrection. One interesting feature of this window is a green crucifix; often, in medieval art, Christ's cross was green because it is regarded as the Tree of Life.

The rose window in the north transept has five lancet windows beneath it. The rose window contains the Virgin and Child surrounded by angels, Old Testament kings, and prophets, matching the Old Testament theme of the north porch. At the bottom of the rose on either side, two small windows show the coat of arms of **Blanche of Castile**, the French queen who paid for the window. The lancet windows are among the most interesting and important in terms of learning how to read the cathedral as medieval people would. The center lancet contains Saint Anne (again, as seen outside) and the Virgin Mary. In the side lancets stand four Old Testament figures: Melchizedek, David, Solomon, and Aaron. The smaller figures crouched below them are, respectively, Nebuchadnezzar, Saul, Jeroboam, and Pharaoh. In other words, the good leaders dominate the evil ones, in size, posture, and position.

> "We are dwarfs . . . on the shoulders of giants." We can't understand the New Testament without the Old.

The south transept windows, again, share their theme with the doors beneath. In the center of the rose window is Christ, surrounded by the four apocalyptic beasts the 24 Elders. Mary and Jesus are featured in the center lancet, a reflection of Anne and Mary—the mother and child of the previous generation—on the north side. The four side lancets display the four major prophets of the Old Testament: Isaiah, Jeremiah, Ezekiel, and Daniel. On their shoulders are the Four Evangelists: Matthew, Mark, Luke, and John. This reminds us of the words of Bernard of Chartres, "We are dwarfs . . . on the shoulders of giants." We can't understand the New Testament without the Old, but Matthew, Mark, Luke, and John can see farther than even the greatest of the Old Testament prophets. It's interesting and complex theology, and it's beautiful art.

We now turn to some of the lower lancet windows found throughout the cathedral. Although they are not arranged thematically in the space, that is how we will visit them. First, we look at a 13th-century "redemption window." Although it contains a Crucifixion scene, it has several odd features: Adam is there, catching the blood pouring from Jesus's body. Abraham and Isaac act out their story in the background as Jesus is taken down from the cross. David is seated below on a pelican, a medieval symbol of the life-giving power of sacrificial blood. The scene of Christ's entombment is flanked by images of Sampson battling against imprisonment and death. Once again, in relating the events of the Old Testament to the New, we are shown dwarfs on the shoulders of giants—we are understanding the new only by looking at the old.

Notre Dame de la Belle Verrière

The most famous, and arguably the most beautiful, window at Chartres is a 12th-century window known as Notre Dame de la Belle Verrière—"Our Lady of the Beautiful Window." It is one of the few windows from the old cathedral that the architect of Chartres deemed worthy of the new building. Depicting the Virgin and Child enthroned, along with stories from Christ's early ministry, the vivaciousness and brilliance of the colors, along with the intricacy of the images, make it one of the great works not only of stained glass, but perhaps of Gothic, or even Western, art.

Many other windows are also dedicated to Old Testament stories, and many more to parts of the New Testament, including Jesus's parables. Yet others depict the saints' lives. There is, for example, an entire window dedicated to Saint Nicholas; among its lessons is dedication to church fast days. Saint Placid's window shows his conversion and the famous image that inspired it: the crucifix between the antlers of a stag. Another window shows the martyrdom of Thomas à Becket in Canterbury Cathedral, which took place mere decades before Chartres was constructed.

Still other windows are dedicated to more secular-seeming themes. A zodiac window, like the zodiac sculpture outside, is shown alongside the seasonal lives of ordinary people. One window is dedicated to the legendary exploits of Charlemagne, who, according to tradition, gave the cathedral its prized relic, the Cloak of the Virgin.

A word about the making of these windows: Although the materials—silica and lead—were available in large quantities, the colors could be quite expensive, especially at Chartres, where most of the color is directly in the glass, not painted on as at later cathedrals. Why did the cathedral's designers go to the trouble of making such intricate, beautiful, but expensive windows? They did so mainly because these windows draw people in with their beauty, so they can learn from the stories for the sake of their souls. Although we will see more glass in this course, we've now seen the best. ∎

Blanche of Castile (1188–1252): Wife of King Louis VIII and mother of King Louis IX. She was the donor of the rose window of the north transept of Chartres Cathedral, and her family coat of arms is prominently displayed there.

Suggested Reading

Adams, *Mont-Saint-Michel and Chartres*.

Jantzen, *High Gothic*.

Miller, *Chartres Cathedral*.

Questions to Consider

1. Why are there so many saints and stories in the windows? Shouldn't the art keep us focused on essentials rather than taking us in so many directions?

2. Are these windows biblically accurate? Does it matter?

3. Why are so many of the stories in the windows, even when a window has biblical themes, inventions of a later time rather than an illustration of the Bible?

Chartres—The Windows
Lecture 12—Transcript

We have looked at the spectacular building of Chartres cathedral, and then we examined this extraordinary collection of sculpture on the three portals of Chartres cathedral; if Chartres had nothing else, it would be one of the great buildings of the world. But I think when most people think about Chartres cathedral, if they know anything about it, they know the windows; and rightfully so, because while we have a few windows at Laon—as we've seen—a few windows in several other Gothic cathedrals including some significant collections of original glass, still there's nothing like Chartres. It is the mother lode of medieval stained glass for its quantity and for its quality; for its stories, for its color. There are about 175 windows in Chartres cathedral; about 150 of them have most or all of their original glass. A few have modern stained glass windows, a few have a kind of gray-colored window we call grisaille, which we'll see more of, especially when we get to England. But basically imagine that 150 of the 175 windows have essentially been preserved. It was not easy: During World War II, for example, virtually all of the glass was removed and hidden in the countryside, and Chartres cathedral was a recreation center for German troops; and then afterwards, they put all the glass back in. I can't even imagine the detailed maps, the puzzle, of putting these umpteen thousands of pieces of glass back together. But they are preserved, and they are one of the great wonders not just of Chartres, not just of the Gothic, they are one of the wonders and the miracles of the world.

We're going to look at several different kinds of windows. We're going to look at one group that comes from the 12th century. Remember, the facade of Chartres cathedral was not destroyed in the 1194 fire, and therefore it has windows from the 1140s; so we have some 12th-century glass. We're going to look at in some ways the most special windows in the cathedral: the rose windows with the lancets below of the north and south transepts. We are not going to look at the upper windows around the nave, the transept, and the choir; they almost all contain figures of individual saints. But we are going to look, just taking glances, at the lower windows in the aisles and in the ambulatory because they are all, or almost all, narrative windows, and we're going to look somewhat episodically at some of those.

As I've already mentioned, when we walk into Chartres cathedral we're sometimes surprised by its darkness. Now remember as we look in the choir as it is today, we see that the upper part is clean, the lower part looks like it's a totally different kind of stone. Even with the new lightness that we have here, we can see that all the windows have colored glass in them, and therefore the cathedral comes off as somewhat darker than, say, Amiens where the original windows have largely been destroyed. This window I want you to look at because it reminds us of how the light patterns change. I took this at a particular time of the day when some of the window is in shadow from a piece of the cathedral's architecture and some is getting the direct sunlight; so some stories stand out and some are darker. But, of course, the patterns of light in individual windows like we see here, as well as the general pattern of light in the cathedral, changes all day long and from season to season. Again, at the risk of being incredibly repetitive, go back, go often, go at different times of the day, go at different times of the year; you want to see all of the splendor and the beauty of the interior, as well as the exterior, of Chartres cathedral.

We're standing now in the east end of the church looking back toward the entrance, back toward the west, and we see this wonderful rose window and three lancet windows, the center one being bigger, of course, than the others. Now that we get closer we can look at the colors in the window, and we see the beautiful pattern of this rose window and we can see that the lancets, especially the left and center one, are divided into what look like many very difficult to see from a distance stories; many little figures, if you will. The right one is not really a narrative, and therefore the theme is sort of grander physically in the window and doesn't take quite so much squinting to see. The rose window is, in fact, important because it contains Christ and figures from the book of Revelation, from the Apocalypse. Remember what's in the sculpture over the main door underneath this? We have the Apocalyptic Christ. We just don't have time to do it, alas, but one thing to think about is not just the relationship of one piece of sculpture to another or one window to another but the relationship of the placing of windows and sculpture; how certain things are reinforced whether we are outside or inside. We'll see that on both the north and south transepts as well.

We're going to look at least briefly at some episodes from all three of these lancet windows. Beginning on the right—this is the base, the lowest part of the window—as you can see this is the Tree of Jesse. So we have Jesse, the father of David, sleeping and we see the tree coming up right out of Jesse, and then we have a series of Hebrew kings, obviously not all of them—because David, the son of Jesse, lived 1,000 years before the time of Christ—so we don't have all of the ancestors, if you will, going up, but we have representatives of them. The center lancet, which is the largest as you can see, contains stories beginning with the Nativity of Christ—actually beginning with the Annunciation of Gabriel—and telling the story of the life of Christ through his infancy and into his adulthood.

These are the six lowest panels, and you can begin to read them. You can see that in the left side there is the Annunciation, in the center there is the Visitation—that is to say, Mary and Elizabeth—and then we have the Nativity. In the second scene up above on the left we have the angel coming to the shepherds; we begin a whole continuation of the narrative with the shepherds and the Magi. In fact, the Magi story is extraordinarily elongated, containing many episodes that are not contained in the Bible but developed later on. Here we have some of the upper scenes that show the transition from the infancy to the adulthood to Christ; but I want you to just look at one window in the lower left, the one you can see the best there, and you see there are no people there. The story is that when Mary and Joseph were traveling in Egypt they went by a temple of idols and the idols fell over; and that's what you see there: The idols come "a-tumblin' down," if you will, in that particular scene. Again, not a biblical story; but we need to remember the Bible is often supplemented with other stories. For example, in the north rose window, we're going to see—and we've already seen in statues—Saint Anne, the mother of the Virgin, holding the baby Virgin. Saint Anne's not in the Bible; the parents of Mary are never mentioned. They come from a later source, which we call the Proto-Gospel of James; and although scholars knew it didn't have the same status as the Bible itself, nevertheless, many other books were regarded as having, if you will, genuine, if not information, truths—at least symbolic truths—to tell about the people and events at the time of the Bible, in a sense to supplement the Bible.

If we look on the left lancet, we have the story of Christ's Passion, and it begins—this is the lowest part of it—with the Transfiguration. You can see Christ there appearing between Elijah and Moses with Peter, James, and John sleeping below; and then we have the story of the betrayal of Judas; and up above the Transfiguration you can see the Last Supper; and the narrative goes from there. When we get up a little bit further, of course, we have the Crucifixion and the Resurrection. One of the reasons I wanted to show you this is: Did you know the cross was green? We think of the cross as sort of a dark, and in a sense kind of ugly, wood; but very often in the Middle Ages the cross is depicted as green in windows and in manuscript illuminations (paintings in books). Why? Because it is the Tree of Life; that is to say, we have the opportunity for eternal life because Jesus conquered death on the cross, and therefore, in a kind of interesting juxtaposition, the wood that brought death to Jesus is really the Tree of Life. It's interesting. Sometimes we even find in illuminations in manuscripts the cross is also decorated with flowers to show it's essentially alive, it is life; an interesting detail that we have.

There is one 12th-century piece of stained glass that also survived other than in the west wall of Chartres, and it's now been remounted into a 13th-century window, and we call this Notre Dame de la Belle Verrière, this beautiful window of Our Lady and Jesus. It's regarded by I think almost everybody as one of the greatest of all stained glass windows, in large part because of the vivaciousness and the brilliance of the colors, the reds and the blues. Again, if you saw this 10 minutes earlier or 10 minutes later, the blue might have been a little darker or even a little bit brighter; that's sort of the way windows are, as I've tried to point out. But this is regarded as one of the gems, and it's now been moved, it's actually right where the south transept as it moves into the ambulatory; but it is the other 12th-century piece of glass that survived.

When we go to the north transept, we have, as you can see, an extraordinary rose window with five lancets underneath. Remember that the north side gets less light than the south side and the sculpture outside leads us to the time of Christ and emphasizes Old Testament and the life of the Virgin Mary; so is it true here in the north window of Chartres. This is a detail of the rose window, as you can see; it contains the Virgin and Child surrounded by angels, Old Testament kings, and prophets. You can see some of the kings are in those interestingly scattered squares and their names are there so that we can identify them; so it has the same basic theme in the rose—and, as we'll see, in the lancet—as the exterior of the north porch has. These lancet windows are among the most interesting and important in terms of learning how to read in the way that medieval people could read images and make connections. In the center is Saint Anne with the Virgin Mary; you may recall on the outside of the north porch we have Saint Anne and the Virgin Mary in the trumeau statue that divides the two main doors. Again, there's this relationship between the inside and the outside; they're not copies, but they emphasize, sometimes in different ways, the same kinds of themes.

The two lancets to the left and to the right contain four important Old Testament figures. From left to right they are: a great figure from the book of Genesis, Melchizedek (whom we'll meet again, by the way, in the cathedral of Reims); then David; and then after Anne and the Virgin we have Solomon and Aaron. You'll notice there are small figures below them, and they're very interesting small figures because, of course, the big guys are all Old Testament good guys. They provide positive models; they move us toward Christ. But down below are the other side of the coin: Underneath Melchizedek is the Babylonian king, Nebuchadnezzar, who destroyed Jerusalem in 587 or 586 B.C. Underneath David—it's hard to see—we have David's predecessor Saul, the unsuccessful king of the Hebrews, committing suicide. Underneath Solomon, we have a usurper king who took part of the kingdom away from Solomon's son, and his name is Jeroboam; and again, he's one of the bad guys. He causes a kind of schism—or "state split," if you will—following the death of Solomon, and that northern state goes off in a very bad way. That's where the famous Jezebel is found, for example, later on. Finally, underneath Aaron, who is the brother of Moses, we have Pharaoh; the Pharaoh, of course, whose son was struck dead by God because he would not let the Hebrews go. We have positive and negative models; we know which is which from the way they're depicted, their size, and their positioning: The good guys are standing, if you will, on the bad guys. This window is paid for by the queen of France, Blanche of Castile, wife of Louis XIII and mother of the famous Saint Louis, Louis IX, who ruled from 1226–1270. The little windows at the bottom of the rose on either side are, in fact, part of her coats of arms; so she, in a sense, signed her window as the donor.

Let's now move to the south transept: It gets more light; it is, of course, therefore the New Testament side if you recall from our sculpture. In the center of the rose window is Christ, and around him are the four apocalyptic beasts—we've seen them on the front of Chartres cathedral—and the 24 elders who are always present at the Last Judgment because, as we're reminded, they were there, in a sense, in the book of Revelation to prepare us for the time of judgment. So the window, again, reflects themes actually on both the west facade and on the south porch.

We've already looked very briefly, in a completely different context, two lectures ago, at the lancet windows. We have Mary and Jesus—remember opposite is Anne and Mary, so this is next generation—in the center, and then we have these four big, old guys (although one of those four big, old guys is beardless); they are the four so-called major prophets of the Old Testament: Isaiah, Jeremiah, Ezekiel, and Daniel's always depicted as beardless. On their shoulders are the four evangelists Matthew, Mark, Luke, and John carrying out and translating into a kind of biblical metaphor that phrase of Bernard of Chartres, "We are dwarfs . . . on the shoulders of giants." I want to point out that very often that phrase—if you sort of Google it—you'll find that there are a gazillion different people for whom it is claimed they said that first. Take it from me, it's Bernard of Chartres. So that image here shows us our transition from Old to New Testament; we can't understand the New Testament without the Old, but Matthew, Mark, Luke, and John can see farther than even the greatest of the Old Testament prophets. Again, it's interesting theology and complex theology, and it's beautiful art.

We're going to look now at a series of the lower lancet windows all around Chartres cathedral. They are not in any obvious order; in other words, what we don't say is, "Well, we have to look at this one, and then the one to the right of it continues the story." They don't seem to be organized in that way. We're not going to take a tour around in the sense of going from A to B to C to D; I'm going to move around rather thematically and talk about some of the windows, again, just episodically. The last time I was there I had my binoculars and a very detailed book that led me through all the windows, and I'd been working on the windows for about three hours—and, by the way, having a very good time doing it—and I thought I'd been doing it for a half an hour and I kept thinking, "Why am I hungry?" The answer is: because it was lunchtime. These can really be engrossing; and again, it's the color, but it's not just the color. Why are these windows beautiful? The main reason is because they will attract people to learn from the stories, and their souls are at stake. This is very serious business. We're in a cathedral; we're not in a museum, we're not in an art gallery. We always need to remember these stories are what these windows are all about.

This is a kind of allegorical window; you can see parts of it are missing and also parts of it have been replaced. This isn't a completely 13th-century window, although we know, at least in the parts that have been replaced, what was there before they were damaged or destroyed. We call this a redemption window because, you might be able to see about two-thirds of the way up, there is a Crucifixion; it is about our redemption. But it's not so much the narrative of the Crucifixion—although there are several stories—but it's the fact that every one of those stories is related to Old Testament scenes. Once again, looking at the theme from the south lancets in the transept of Chartres—the dwarfs on the shoulders of giants—we have another version of understanding the new completely only by looking at the old. Here we have the Crucifixion of Christ; and if you look down below there's somebody kneeling and catching the blood that's pouring out of Jesus's body. That is Adam, because it is through Adam that all of us died; it is through Christ's obedience that all of us can live. We have Christ and Adam juxtaposed; and by the way, Saint Paul juxtaposes Christ and Adam in his Letter to the Romans, Chapter 6. This is a kind of visualization and imaginative expansion of an idea that we can trace back to Paul.

Here we have the story of Jesus's deposition—Jesus being taken down from the cross—and on either side is the story of Abraham and Isaac; they're sort of packing up on the left and you can see the altar on the right. But down below the Crucifixion is David—immediately below—and David's sitting with a bird. That seems sort of odd. It turns out to be a pelican, because it was believed in the 13th century that pelicans, when their baby pelicans rebelled, the babies were thrown out of the next and then the mother realized that they would all die. But the mother learned—again, it's a long legend—that the only way to bring those babies back to life was with her own blood; and so the pelican pecks its own breast, the blood goes into the mouths of the baby pelicans, and they are allowed to live. We would say, "That's not very good natural history," and that's true; they didn't know that. But do you see how that resembles the story of Jesus's sacrifice for us? Humans were rebellious and God threw them out of the next (the Garden of Eden) where they all died, and God decided to give them a chance to live and the way to do that was through God's own blood, the blood on the cross. So the pelican is there as a representative of Christ; in fact, a little after 1300 in Dante's *Divine Comedy*, Dante refers to "Christ our pelican," taking note of this legend and expecting his audience to be familiar with it.

Here, toward the bottom, we have Christ being laid in the grave, and on either side we have stories of Sampson: on the left, Sampson carrying off the gates of the city of Gaza—these are stories in the book of Judges; sort of looks like a cross, doesn't it?—and on the right, Sampson is wrestling with and tearing open the mouth of a lion because Christ, in a sense, has to wrestle with death. These stories are seen as prefigurations of the events going on in the middle. We also have a window that tells the story of Creation; I'm just showing you a detail here. By the way, you might notice, every window has different patterns—here, a kind of quatrefoil with a little quatrefoil in the middle and design all around; sometimes they're straight boxes of narrative; sometimes there are diamond-shaped stories—that all the windows are not just different in content, they are different in design. Here you can see the Creation and the various stories involving the Creation—the Fall and the expulsion from the Garden of Eden—in this window.

Here we have a story dedicated to Noah; the whole window is the dedicated to the story of Noah that, of course, is humanity's second chance (and humanity didn't do very well, if you recall). Here are just a couple details in these pieces; again, notice the design. Here we see in various stages the Ark of Noah. It's a very beautiful and interesting window because it shows a lot of nature, because there are animals and there are storms and things; so instead of being so dominated by people, we get looks at obviously a very kind of stylized way of depicting nature. Here's a Joseph story; you can see that Joseph is in the well down below at the bottom of this diamond right above the circle. So there are many windows dedicated to Old Testament stories.

I'm not going to look at them because we're so used now to seeing New Testament stories that I'm going to skip over the New Testament windows, but let me remind you A) there are lots of them; and B) some of them are great expansions of Jesus's Parables; Jesus tells the parable of the Good Samaritan. There's a whole window of the Good Samaritan, but, of course, many of the stories are imagining, filling in, the pieces in between the basic narrative that Jesus gives. There's a prodigal son, there's a Good Samaritan, and there are others as well; so there are windows that are both narratives and windows that are meant to illustrate some of the great Parables of Jesus.

We also have interesting windows of saints' lives. This is one of my favorite stories: This is a story from the infancy of Saint Nicholas; and there's a whole window dedicated to Saint Nicholas, and we know that there is statuary of him outside on the south porch of Chartres, we've already seen it. But at any rate, the story is he was such a good baby—meaning he's going to be such an obedient child—that you see he's there with his mother; and he's to nurse, but it's Friday in this story, and Friday is the day of fasting for the church, and so Nicholas turns away from his mother's breast. Obviously not a historical account of little baby Nicholas, but a lesson for us about the fact that we should fast on the days the church says to fast. This is a story of the conversion of Saint Placid; he was out hunting and he saw the vision of Christ crucified between the antlers of a stag and he is converted. We see that very colorful story depicted here.

This is actually a pretty modern story—that is to say, this had just happened 40 or 50 years before this window was made—this is a window dedicated to Thomas à Becket who was murdered in Canterbury cathedral (see Canterbury cathedral, if you will) in 1170, just 25 years before the new cathedral of Chartres, which includes this window, was begun. There's also a very interesting zodiac window. We've seen signs of the zodiac; we've seen them, for example, on the facade of Chartres cathedral. We will see them again in stone in Amiens. Here they are in glass; you can see, for example, in the month that's labeled with Pisces there, what do you do? You try to stay warm. Look at that guy on the left there sitting by that blazing fire. Isn't that a wonderful way of using the colors of stained glass? Here was have a springtime scene, it's June; we see, therefore, the working with the crops. And here we have winter scene: the slaughtering of the pig on the left and then the banqueting up above it; and you can see the signs of the zodiac as well. In the one below, you can see the work of that month is putting the cork in the barrel of the new wine.

Finally, I want to show you a window about Charlemagne. Remember, Charlemagne gave the Cloak of the Virgin to Chartres; and Charlemagne, obviously, is an important figure in French history, part of its mythology as well as its history. In stories that are close to but not exactly taken from the 11th or 12th century poem *The Song of Roland*, we have some of the great and heroic endeavors of Charlemagne. We see some medieval battle scenes: Here we see Charlemagne—he's labeled "Carolus," simply Latin for "Charles"—we see the banner; here we see the besieging of a city; and here, in a story that is in *The Song of Roland*, we see Charlemagne's trusty vassal Roland trying to break his powerful sword Durendal so the Muslims won't get it. Again, this is mostly legendary; there was no battle in Spain between Christians and Muslims at the time of Charlemagne, but this is part of the legend.

Let me end by simply saying a brief word about how you make stained glass windows. First of all, the main ingredient is silica, and it is easily available, obviously, in great quantities. You heat it until it becomes liquid in molten form, and then you add the color; and the color comes from various metallic oxides: copper for green; cobalt for blue; the red, very expensive gold. Then, when the glass is cooled, it is cut into the requisite shapes and it is fit into the pattern of the windows with lead; so whenever we look at a window we see little thin lines, those are, in fact, pieces of lead that are holding the glass into place. The glass that we saw at Chartres, 12th and 13th century, tends to be rather pure colors. For example, there's relatively little paint on early stained glass: They'll paint in drapery, they'll paint in facial features and so on, but there's not a lot of paint; it's more pure color. In the later stained glass—and we'll see some from Beauvais and Troyes later on—there'll be a lot less pure color and a lot more painting on the glass.

So although we will see more glass, and we've already seen a little bit, we've now seen the best, both in terms of the art but also the complexity and interesting qualities of the stories that the stained glass at Chartres tells. Now, we're going to go east and north to Amiens.

Amiens—The Limits of Height
Lecture 13

> This sounds sort of simple, but this is a rock roof 140 feet (approximately) above the ground, and it seems to be floating. ... We can understand why somebody can walk in and imagine for a minute: This must be something like—or to use Pseudo-Dionysius language, analogous to—entering Heaven.

Amiens Cathedral is, in a word, enormous. In the early 13th century, Amiens was a prosperous dye and cloth manufacturing city and home to an important relic of the Fourth Crusade: the (alleged) head of John the Baptist. Having lost their cathedral to fire in 1217, Amiens's citizens seized the opportunity to build a spectacular replacement and began construction in 1220.

We begin with the flying buttress system which, if anything, is more elaborate than Chartres's. The spires that come off of the buttresses are more elaborate decoratively than they were at Chartres. At the back of the cathedral, we see not one but two rows of enormous windows that make up most of the walls of the choir's chapels. The exterior of the north transept is blocked from view by other buildings, so we will focus on the south. At the south transept we find another view of the beautiful, symmetrical buttresses and some interesting sculpture. In particular, around the top of the rose window are little stone figures, climbing up the left side and tumbling down the right. This represents the Wheel of Fortune—a reminder that all material things are subject to fortune and are impermanent; we need to focus on what is permanent, the spirit.

Below, there is a remarkable trumeau statue (actually, a copy; the original is found inside the cathedral) of the Virgin and Child called La Vierge Dorée, "The Golden Virgin," because her vestments were painted gold. Its beautifully expressive faces and detailed drapery are examples of an emerging style of Gothic sculpture. In the tympanum, we see a procession of the relic of a local saint, a medieval slice of life. On the archivolts are Old Testament figures that are in remarkably good condition and easy to recognize.

Inside, the cathedral soars, and we notice more light in the east end than in the west thanks to a **glazed triforium**—that is, a triforium with windows—in the choir. The vaults are about 140 feet high, the highest of any complete cathedral, and the vault at the crossing of nave and transept is dizzying in its height and complexity. Our eyes are lifted up by the light and by the stone, but at the same time our eyes are cast down by the detail on the floor, where we find a pilgrimage maze, as we did at Chartres. The roof seems to float because of the size of the clerestory windows. These windows have four lancets, two small oculi, and one large **oculus**. In the triforium, we find a carved horizontal design above and below; this feature, called a **stringcourse**, is the only carved, decorative stringcourse in a Gothic cathedral. Each bay is

The remarkable soaring vaults of Amiens Cathedral are 140 feet high.

composed of two arches with two columns in its lower part and a cloverleaf design above. Note that there are very few original stained-glass windows in Amiens; most of them were removed in the 18th century. Although this is a loss, it allows us to focus on the organization, structure, and pattern of the windows themselves.

Approaching the choir, the aisle's arches narrow. We see light coming in at all three elevations, thanks to that glazed triforium, which is an innovation in Gothic design; in fact, the clerestory and the triforium are starting to become parts of one bigger unit. The ambulatory is a large, double one; the chapels surrounding it have, as we noted from outside, enormous windows.

Amiens cathedral, structurally, really takes us to the limits of what Gothic architecture can do. ∎

Important Terms

glazed triforium: A triforium with windows.

oculus: A round window usually placed above a pair of lancet windows.

stringcourse: A decorative horizontal band running around a building.

Suggested Reading

Frankl, *Gothic Architecture*, chap. 3.2.

Jantzen, *High Gothic*.

Panofsky, *Gothic Architecture and Scholasticism*.

Questions to Consider

1. How much did height matter for people in the Middle Ages? How much does it matter for us?

2. How significant is the glazed triforium, the middle level of light that we see in the apse when we enter Amiens Cathedral?

3. Can one experience a foretaste of heaven when standing in Amiens Cathedral?

Amiens—The Limits of Height
Lecture 13—Transcript

You might be thinking to yourself: "The course is now half over, where does Cook go from there? We spent three lectures looking at Chartres cathedral, a place like no other religious edifice in the world; what's he going to do," you might be asking, "or what did the French do," a better question, "that's not a letdown?" I have a two-word answer: Amiens Cathedral. You may recall I mentioned in the very first lecture, that this is not an aesthetic judgment but Amiens is my favorite of all the cathedrals; so to me, we go from highlight to highlight in looking at Amiens. Amiens has virtually no stained glass, so we're going to spend two lectures rather than three on it, one on the building and one on the sculpture of the facade.

As we look at the facade, it was begun in the year 1220, one of the things we're struck by—as I pointed out, because this is the very first picture we saw in Lecture1—it is enormous. There is a person in blue in front of the left portal in this photograph, and that just reminds us how extraordinary this building is. It is awesome and soaring. When I came back recently after I'd not been there for several years, I was also struck by the fact that the front was black when I was young, it was so filthy; and now—at some enormous amount of Euros I can't even imagine—there's a project in the works to clean all of Amiens cathedral, the entire building, and they have completed the facade and the south transept. So it was new to me: some of the details, I hadn't seen before; but more than that, it was the way it was meant to be seen, without industrial pollution and pigeon droppings. It is more beautiful than I remembered it when I first went there at the age of 17.

Amiens is about 100 kilometers (about 60 miles) north of Paris, and it was an important city in the Middle Ages; it's still a reasonably-sized city, about 100,000 people or so. It is the center of a region of France that most of us know by name because of its association with World War I: It is in the heart of Picardy. It was famous in the Middle Ages because it made a certain color dye, and it also was a cloth manufacturing center; so it was a prosperous city. In 1217, the old cathedral burned down, and three years later the cathedral of Amiens was begun. I want to pause just for a second and point out that we've been going primarily in chronological order and the cathedral we're going to do after Amiens is Rennes, and Rennes was actually begun a bit before Amiens. You might ask: Why is Amiens out of order here? Because Rennes was built the normal way—that is to say, it began in the east and built toward the west—so the facade is the last thing done. Unusually, Amiens is built from west to east, so that the facade is oldest (built first) and the choir is the newest part. Because we're going to focus so much time on the facade in the next lecture, I thought it was proper to put it in this sort of odd order because the facade we're looking at comes from the beginning time of the building of this cathedral.

In addition to this simply being a prosperous city that had a chance to build a glorious new cathedral because of the fire of 1217, there was another reason to make this so spectacular: Even though it is dedicated to the Virgin Mary (it is Notre Dame de Amiens), it also has a relic that it got just about a decade before the beginning of the building of this cathedral. As part of the loot from the sack of Constantinople by the Fourth Crusade, the head of John the Baptist—or at least the alleged head of John the Baptist—came to Amiens; and although one can't see it today, it is still preserved in the cathedral in the north transept. But at any rate, having this precious relic was another reason to build a grand building; and so that is what we have: this extraordinary cathedral of Amiens.

I want to begin, in addition simply to looking at the facade to get our orientation, to look as we did at Chartres at the buttressing system that, if anything, is more elaborate than Chartres. This is the east end of Amiens Cathedral. As you can see, part of it, over to the right, is somewhat restricted; but we nevertheless get a good view of the east end of this extraordinary building. As we look, we can see again the angularity of the flying buttresses, and every single place we stand gives us a new view. Here we can see some of those flying buttresses really flying, for example; here we can look up in some of the spires that come off of these flying buttresses, more elaborate decoratively than they were at Chartres; here we get another angle where we can see below some of the buttresses are the chapels that radiate around the east end of the church. As we look straight at the back of the cathedral we see something, although on a bigger scale, that we saw at Chartres: We see in the chapels down below these enormous windows, and then we look up above and we see another row of enormous windows; and since this is the last part built of Amiens Cathedral, we're going to see when we go inside—this will be more obvious—some new developments in the Gothic style that make the east end even more luminous at Amiens than it is at Chartres. Again, we have almost walls of glass as we look at this extraordinary building.

This nice, gleaming, newly-cleaned southern transept we're going to look at. In general, this is a lecture about the building; but since we're going to focus on the facade sculpture in the next lecture, I at least want to take a look quickly at this transept and the sculpture that is here. First of all, notice that because this street runs right into it, we can see the flying buttresses on either side; we can see the symmetry of them, something we lose when we look at the angularity of them around the east end. But here we really see that, and you can see that there is a tympanum—a very large one, I might add—with a trumeau statue, and a very beautiful window in the transept.

The window I want to look at not so much for the glass—we're going to look at it when we go inside and then come back out and glance at what's called the "tracery," the stonework that makes up the shape of the window—but if you look carefully, right around the upper part of the round window you see that there are little stone figures, statues, and the ones on the left are climbing up and the ones on the right are tumbling down. That is the Wheel of Fortune, because the Wheel of Fortune is an image that reminds us of the fact that all material things—that can be money, political power, health, all of those things—are subject to fortune; and, of course, we all know that in our lives: The best-laid plans very often don't lead us where we want to go; healthy people get diseases; and whatever. We just are not in complete control and we need to remember that. It also means that we then need to focus on those things that do last forever, which is not health, not money, not power, but rather, of course, our soul, our spirit, those things that are not of the physical world. So putting the Wheel of Fortune around this window, using the window as the wheel and seeing it turn by seeing the movement clockwise where some go up and some go down, remind us of important things.

This is the tympanum and, of course, you can see it's surrounded by jamb statues; there's a trumeau statue, and a very important trumeau statue. Here we have the Virgin Mary and the Christ child. Look at it: Look at the smile on her face, look at the folds of the vestments. This is later than the facade—again, we built from west to east—and so this is a still-emerging style, a style beyond, in terms of time, the style we saw at Chartres on the north and south porches. The expression, the balance that she has, the way the drapes fold; all of these things quite beautiful, quite extraordinary. The name of the statue—this is actually a copy of it because the original's inside and you can't get very good pictures of it—this is called "The Golden Virgin," "La Vierge Dorée" because, if you look carefully, you'll see (because they've reproduced this in the copy very faithfully) her robe is gold. We have to imagine—we just see a little bit of that color left—how beautiful and stunning that would be, to approach the cathedral, this enormous building, down this street that leads us into the south transept and there is this gleaming Virgin.

I just want to show you a couple of details from the sculpture because it's very beautiful and very realistic. This is the procession of the relic of a local saint of Amiens. You can see his coffin up above and you can see people carrying it, and then the folks down below the coffin are people who are crippled or have other things to ask God to help them with and they're asking this saint, and they're trying to reach up and touch the coffin and actually be in contact, if you will, as close as possible with the relic, the physical remains of the saint. It depicts a piece of medieval life: Pilgrims very often slept all night at the tomb of the saint that they had come to visit, whether that's Saint Francis of Assisi or whether that's one of the saints we've run into in France. Here we have a bishop—a holy bishop, a local saint—celebrating mass, and you'll see the chalice on the altar and you can see the hand of God reaching toward the altar very dramatically, sort of coming out from behind the altar.

I also want you to look at the archivolts because there are some very interesting pieces there. You can see there are many, many figures, mostly—although not all—Old Testament figures; but they're very beautifully and carefully sculpted and easy to read, so I just want to show you a couple as illustrations of what you can find. Here, for example, is Jonah coming out of the mouth of the fish that swallowed Jonah. It's very clear to see there because you can see the body of the fish and Jonah is emerging. Over here, in the upper part, we have one of the Old Testament prophets who is being persecuted—as Old Testament prophets are wont to be—and if you look carefully you can see they're about to saw him in half; you can see that the guys who are standing have a great big saw and they're about to saw him in half. These are very dramatic illustrations of biblical stories, lives of saints, here in the south transept of Amiens.

Let's go inside. As I mentioned in Lecture 1 when I had my students there a couple months ago, you only enter Amiens Cathedral for the first time once in your life; and yet, somehow or other, it never ceases to thrill me, just simply how the church soars. You'll notice there's more light in the east end than the west end because you'll see that not only do we have these big clerestory windows that we're used to, but where we have the triforium there are also windows in it now. That's an innovation that we see in Amiens, and it's going to be developed in other cathedrals. We'll take a look at the choir where that, we call it now a "glazed triforium," is; we're going to take a look at that a little bit later, but I want you to realize why there's more light in the east than in the west.

The vaults here, from the floor to the keystone, are about 140 feet high; and, by the way, this is the highest of all vaults for a complete cathedral. There are some vaults we'll look at later on in Beauvais that are a little bit higher, but only a piece of Beauvais Cathedral was ever built; so what we have here is the highest of all the Gothic cathedrals, and does it soar. Here the photograph is taken from the aisle, and we can look up into the opposite aisle and the triforium and those enormous clerestory windows as we get a picture of the extraordinary soaring quality of this building. Our eyes are, of course, lifted up by the light and by the stone, but at the same time our eyes are cast down because you can see that in the middle of the floor here—you can see this much more clearly than we could at Chartres because there are no chairs here—there is the maze, and one of my students actually walked the maze and even though it's a fairly small space, it took him almost 15 minutes to get to the center; and so again, we have this pilgrimage maze such as we saw in Chartres as well. Again, we just want to look up; we want to look at the vaulting, and we watch it soar. Here we're standing by one of the pillars and looking straight up where we have the high vault on the left and then we have the vault of the aisle on the right, and as you see when you look at that vault on the right, it's pretty high, too; wait until later on when we look at a picture of the aisle and you will see what I mean.

Here, we simply look at the extraordinary roof of this building. Again, this sounds sort of simple, but this is a rock roof 140 feet (approximately) above the ground and it seems to be floating because of the size of the clerestory windows. It's just hanging up there in space; it really is the kind of vault of Heaven. We can understand why somebody can walk in and imagine for a minute: This must be something like—or to use Pseudo-Dionysius language, analogous to—entering Heaven. There is the vault—the same kind of vault we have at Chartres; each bay is the same—and we have these rectangular, ribbed vaults as you can see here; and again, notice how they float because of the windows on either side. And you'll notice here the keystone, and it's a very lovely keystone with a design in it. So we just soar up to look at these vaults of Heaven, if you will. Here's the aisle. If we sort of took away what we can see on either side and I showed you this picture and I said, "How's this for a church," you're likely to say, "Wow, that's a big church." we're standing actually in the transept looking toward the west on one of the side doors; that little window you see at the far end is on one of the side doors. It looks like we're in this enormous church while, in fact, we're in the aisle.

Because of the extraordinariness of these vaults, I want to look up a little bit more; we just need to hang out a little bit more in the nave of Amiens. Once again, here is the basic elevation; and I want to take you up in pieces. You can see that we have these columns with the rounded smaller columns, and then we go to the triforium, then we go to the clerestory; I want to take you up in pieces to look at the beauty of all the stone that lifts us up to Heaven. First of all, here is the capital of the column—this really is a column; we can call it a pillar or a pier but, of course, this really does take the shape of a Corinthian column—and you can see that there are these smaller columns attached to it. This is the first place where there is a horizontal line across what we see as the capital. Then we move on up to the triforium, and you see at the bottom of the triforium is this carved design, again, going horizontally; the term for those horizontal stone pieces—we see one above and below the triforium— whether it's carved or not, it's called a "stringcourse"; again, there's a lot of vocabulary in Gothic. We have this beautiful carved stringcourse—we'll come back at it in more detail in a minute—and we see now how we move up toward the clerestory windows.

Then, as we go further up, we get to the top of those windows. We have another set of columns and then we see the various pieces of the architecture that have been soaring up branch off and become the arches over the windows and become the various arches of the vault; so we followed it all the way up and it just soars. Here's a picture of one of those clerestory windows; again, they are enormous. You can see here, unlike Chartres—remember, Chartres had two lancets and then an oculus—this has four lancets and two little oculi, and then a big oculus; so it's expanded in size, it's expanded in complexity of design. There are very few original stained glass windows in Amiens; most of them were removed in the 18th century. That's, of course, a bad thing; but it does allow us to have more light come into the building and it allows us perhaps to see and pay attention to the patterns because there are no figures or stories in these windows to detract from looking at the organization and structure and pattern of the windows themselves.

I wanted to come back to the triforium because you can see in each bay it's divided into two Gothic arches, and they have columns and a sort of cloverleaf design up above. I want to zoom in on that stringcourse because you can see how beautifully carved it is; this is very high above the ground, this is above that aisle that we looked at. It's extraordinarily beautiful and detailed, and it's the only carved, decorative stringcourse in Gothic cathedrals, so it's unique and beautiful; I mean, it's one of those things without a telephoto lens or a pair of binoculars people pay not much attention to it because you can't see the detail because we're so far when we look up at it. But here, thanks to telephoto lenses, we really get an extraordinary sense of what this is like. Once again, let's put it all together: I'm standing in one aisle looking at the column right in front of me. Looking across the nave, we see the windows in the aisle on the other side and then the triforium and then the clerestory windows. We've had an extraordinary view of this nave; and I've wanted us to move around a lot and look up and look across and look at different angles because it is so wonderful.

Then, we move to the transepts—this is, of course, a cross-shaped church—and this is one of the transepts, this happens to be the south transept. We saw the outside of the transept when we looked at that sculpture. By the way, the north transept has buildings built around it, so you can't get up to it and there's no sculpture on it; so we really know the transepts of Amiens from the one transept, and that's the south. You can see the window now, from the inside, does have glass—it's late medieval glass, but it's not the original glass that was there when the cathedral was built in the 13th century—and the window is of a very complex design. Let's remember now what it looked like outside. There it is; so we can see it from both our approach to the cathedral and the south transept and also from the inside. That's another good thing to do, by the way, when one visits a cathedral. The tendency is to say, "Well, we'll look at the outside then we'll look at the inside," or vice versa; it does a lot of good to do outside and inside, and outside and inside, and look at some of the same things from different angles and different approaches. This is a different experience after you have also seen it from the inside. It really is very important to sort of put on your sneakers and get your water bottle and spend a good deal of time exploring and walking, and whenever possible— and you can do it at Amiens—climbing; in the next lecture, we'll see some photographs taken from the top of one of the towers. These buildings, really if we're going to understand them and see all of the extraordinary details, we just need to move around, and move around, and move around.

I want to remind you what it looks like when we walk in. we're at the west end, we're looking toward the altar, and, of course, we know there is a transept—you don't see it when you stand right in the middle at the back but we know that transept is there—and that means, of course, that there's going to be a place where the transept, and the nave, and the choir cross; there's going to be a crossing ,and the crossing in Amiens, there's just nothing like it. Look up here: Here we have the crossing. The transept is the left to right part, and the nave and the choir are the up and down part, and isn't that extraordinary? You'll notice that the vault itself is different than the vaults of all of the individual bays because you have this coming together, and therefore a more complex vaulting system; but with the lighting coming in from the clerestory windows all around, what a view that is. Again, here's the example of why we need to keep moving: Look at this, and look at that. Here, I'm standing right at the base of one of those pillars and looking up, obviously at a 45 degree angle from where I just was, and it's a different experience. It doesn't' took like you just simply took a couple steps and are looking up again at the same thing. It really is quite an amazingly different view if you move around. It's almost dizzying in its height.

Here is that vault: You can see it's a more complex vault because it's a more complex space, and it's a bigger space; it's a square space rather than a rectangular space. They don't go back to the old six-part vault such as we've seen in the early cathedrals, but rather develop a more complex vaulting system. One of the things we'll see, in part in France but particularly in England in Germany and the Czech Republic, we'll see some of the almost sort of wild experimentation of vault designs; and again, just like we've learned that the rib vault comes from an experiment of dealing with a different-shaped space, so, too, does a lot of the creative vaulting of the later Middle Ages come from experiments such as the one we have here at Amiens.

Here is the choir. You'll notice, by the way, that the aisle has very narrow arches as we approach the area that rounds right behind the altar. But what we need to see is the great innovation here in the choir of Amiens: that glazed triforium. We have these huge windows that are the clerestory, and although they're blocked out largely by the altar—which, by the way, is a baroque altar—you can see that there are also big windows, you can barely see them, in the chapels behind the aisle; but then you have the row of windows in between, now, this glazed triforium. We have light coming in at all three levels, something we have not seen before. Here's a close-up; again, some of these windows are modern recreations, some is original glass, but we don't go to Amiens to look at glass. But look here at how the clerestory and the triforium are starting to become parts of one bigger unit now because they both contain these large, illuminating windows. Here we now look from the ambulatory on one side to the ambulatory on the other side; and so there we see the big windows in the chapel, then the glazed triforium, and then the clerestory windows.

Again, it's always worth stopping to say: The roof is made of rock; the roof is stones. We have some of the weight in these columnar pillars, and we have, of course, some of the weight in the flying buttresses and the buttresses that are extended outside the church that we've looked at. Those two ways of supporting the roof allow us to punch all these holes in the wall so that the wall almost disappears. It's extraordinary.

Here is a picture of part of the glazed triforium at Amiens, and you can see that we not only have the window there but the design—remember this is the last part built of Amiens—is different from the triforium in the nave. Let me remind you what that looked like: Here is the usual triforium that, again, has a wall behind those arches, and this is the somewhat redesigned and glazed triforium at Amiens; so we can really see this new technique, this new idea, this new experience. This is a window from the nave; remember the four parts: the two little oculi and the big oculus. Notice what's happened to the windows of the choir at Amiens: We have now six lancets, they are narrower; and then we have the decoration in the windows above as well. The windows have been redesigned in the clerestory; we now have a new set of windows in the triforium. These comparisons really allow us to see what's going on at Amiens in the choir that's so new and so spectacular.

Finally, I just want to show you here the ambulatory: It is, as you would expect, big and double and light; again, lighter than it would be if the stained glass windows were in it, as we can see. But as we move around behind the altar, there we really get a close-up of the enormity of that first set of windows that are, in fact, in the chapels and in the double ambulatory around Amiens cathedral.

Wow, this is a spectacular building; I find the only building I've ever been in in my life that is as breathtaking when you enter it and enter it over and over and over as Amiens for me is Hagia Sophia in Constantinople. This really takes us pretty much to the limits of what a building can do. Again, there are higher vaults built in Beauvais, but many of them collapsed in 1284 and the cathedral was never finished; so we have some vaults higher than Amiens, but Amiens is the most soaring of all the Gothic cathedrals. Although Notre Dame is in Paris and Chartres is an easy train ride south west, you also want to go north if you're in the northern part of France because you can't really say you've done the Gothic trail unless you've walked into and been awed by the cathedral of Amiens; and we haven't even looked at the facade, the most complex sculptural program of all Gothic sculptural programs. Stay tuned, that's coming up next.

Amiens—The Facade
Lecture 14

The facade of Amiens Cathedral ... will tell us something about the splendor of Gothic, something about the complexity of Gothic, something about the thought of the people who created it, and something about what it's meant to teach.

The facade of Amiens Cathedral may well be the greatest single sculptural display in all of Gothic architecture. Once again, let's try to approach our subject not as 21st-century scholars or vacationers but as the 13th-century people for whom this cathedral was built.

Looking at the facade, we're again reminded of how huge this building is. For example, it is hard to conceive of the size of the statues in the Gallery of Kings above the doors until you consider how tiny a real person is walking on the balcony above them. Below the kings are four buttresses—*not* flying buttresses—and on each buttress there are three very large statues of Old Testament prophets. The kings are, of course, Old Testament kings, specifically the line of David, and the prophets are the 12 minor prophets. So we are led toward Christ by his predecessors.

On closer inspection, the prophets are very individuated, like Nahum with his huge beard and comically long mustache that ties behind his head. On the wall below each prophet are quatrefoils that tell us a little about their lives and visions. Many of them are quite dramatic—the destruction of Jerusalem, Jonah emerging from the whale's mouth—and would have been very familiar to the 13th-century congregation. What's more, they would have been reminders of the doom meted out to sinners, but also of the hope of redemption.

On the right-hand door, we have the past—sculpture that starts with Creation and brings us up to the life of Mary and the birth of Jesus. On the left-hand door, we have the bishops of Amiens—the present. Unsurprisingly, the center door is the future: the Last Judgment.

On the "past" door, the trumeau statue is of the Virgin trampling on a serpent, symbolizing Mary undoing Eve's sin just as Jesus undoes Adam's. To drive home the image, below her are a clothed Adam and Eve being expelled from Paradise. On one side of the door are Solomon and Sheba, Herod, and the Magi. We can identify them in part because of the quatrefoils below, telling their stories. This is a more subtle psychology than we had in Romanesque sculpture; you can't tell on the surface who the bad guy is just by looking—no grotesque face, no demon on the shoulder. The viewer has to be more engaged and perceptive. An interesting detail: In one quatrefoil, Solomon's temple is shown as a Romanesque building; this is how a sculptor of the 1220s chose to depict archaic architecture. On the other side of the door, three

pairs of statues depict the Annunciation, Visitation, and the Presentation (specifically, the meeting with the prophet Simeon). Again, their stories are told on quatrefoils below. Finally, on the tympanum of this door, we find six Old Testament patriarchs, including Moses and Aaron, and the death, Assumption, and Coronation of the Virgin—a reminder that this cathedral's full name is Notre Dame d'Amiens. So this door takes us from Creation to the Incarnation.

The left door, the door of the present, is also a local door, featuring the bishops and saints of Amiens (some of them beheaded and holding their heads in their arms) and the calendar of the year.

© iStockphoto/Thinkstock.

The exquisitely detailed portals at Amiens were designed to be both beautiful and instructive.

The trumeau statue is **Saint Firmin**, a bishop of Amiens; the socle below him shows his martyrdom. On either side of the doors, we have a collection of local saints. The quatrefoils below depict the zodiac in the upper row and the works of the months in the lower, in a scheme similar to what we've seen at Chartres. Not every month is represented by very hard labor; there are times to enjoy the fruits of that labor. These are wonderful because ordinary people can recognize this as the world in which they live; now they live with the saints of Amiens, and they live in this agricultural cycle, not unlike the cycle of Jesus's birth, death, resurrection, and return. In the tympanum, we have six bishops of Amiens at the bottom, balancing those six patriarchs we saw on the right side. Above are scenes of the relics of Saint Firmin being brought into Amiens. Then we have angels in the archivolts; they are the present's messengers from God.

> Ordinary people can recognize this as the world in which they live; now they live with the saints of Amiens.

Finally, we move to the center portal, which is the portal of the Last Judgment. Just inside the doors are the major prophets, two on each side: Isaiah, Jeremiah, Ezekiel, and Daniel. The jamb statues are the 12 apostles. The Last Judgment on the tympanum is surrounded by angels. There are two trumeau statues: Christ above standing on the lion and the dragon, and King David below. Lily of the valley and Rose of Sharon floral images evoke the Davidic monarchy. Then on Jesus's right side we see a tree bearing fruit (the saved), and on his left side we see a tree being cut down (the damned). On either side, we see the fables of Aesop, which were read in the 13th century as good moral guidance. The quatrefoils down below give us the clearest guidance yet: the 12 virtues and 12 vices. Interestingly, all of the virtues are personified as female.

The Last Judgment scene itself, as befitting Amiens, is enormous and complex. At the top we find Christ the Judge, with the intercessors Mary on the left and John on the right, almost as large as Jesus. On either side are angels carrying various symbols of the crucifixion. The good are sent through the gates of heaven, led by a brand-new (at the time the sculpture was made) saint: Francis of Assisi. In the middle is Michael the Archangel weighing souls. The Devil is trying to cheat, and failing. Again, we look up at the archivolt and see the heavenly host of all the angels.

Past, present, and future, the analogy between Gothic architecture and scholastic thought holds true for Gothic sculpture and scholastic thought here at Amiens. It is complex, and it is complete. ■

Name to Know

Firmin, Saint (d. c. 257): Martyred bishop of Amiens. He and other local saints are featured in the left portal of Amiens Cathedral, and the story of the translation of his relics is in the tympanum.

Suggested Reading

Frankl, *Gothic Architecture*, chap. 3.5.

Jantzen, *High Gothic*.

Mâle, *The Gothic Image*.

Questions to Consider

1. How can we say that the portal sculpture is complete?

2. There are 16 prophets represented prominently on the facade of Amiens Cathedral; why are they so prominent?

3. Is the Last Judgment to frighten us, to encourage us, to inspire us, as we prepare to enter the cathedral of Amiens?

Amiens—The Facade
Lecture 14—Transcript

We're going to be looking now at the cathedral of Amiens's facade. To me, this is the greatest single sculptural display in all of Gothic. We looked at a lot of details in three different porches at Chartres cathedral; here—literally, I suppose—we could do all of this sitting in one of the lovely benches near where this photograph is taken from of the facade of Amiens Cathedral, because we're going to focus just on this one set of sculpture. But I think, perhaps, as much as anything we do in the entire course this will tell us something about the splendor of Gothic, something about the complexity of Gothic, something about the thought of the people who created it and something about what it's meant to teach. We're going to approach this as much as possible not as 21st-century scholars or vacationers, we're going to approach it as 13th-century people, whether they are citizens of Amiens, or whether they are coming here on business, or whether they are coming here to see the head and pray before the head of John the Baptist. We're going to try to get inside the head of the 13th century and see what this would mean, what this would say, to the people for whom this was intended.

I know that I've been beating this drum, but it really is a drum worth beating: This is a very big cathedral; and as we look at the facade still again, I want to try to demonstrate that by looking at the row of statues above the doors called the Gallery of Kings and the window that's just above it because here I am standing above the Gallery of the Kings, right in the middle and waving—OK, you don't see me, I'm too small; here I am—and you can get a sense of the size of the window behind me and the kings below me and have an extraordinary sense, again, of the proportions of this building. If we think about the whole facade, we now want to drop down to the three portals; and if you'll look to see as we approach this building, what do we see first? What catches our eye first; what's closest to us? Of course, we have those enormous kings up above, and then you can there are four, we can call them, buttresses—not flying buttresses—that come out, one on either end, and then the two that divide the three doors. On each of them is three statues; three very large statues. It turns out those are Old Testament prophets. Now combine those Old Testament prophets with the kings. The kings are, of course, Old Testament kings and they are the ancestors of Jesus, the line of David. The 12 prophets—3 on each of those non-flying buttresses—are the 12 so-called minor prophets. "Minor" simply means their writings are shorter; it doesn't have anything to do with their importance or the quality of their writings, if you will. But we have the 12 minor prophets and the kings; again, the kings are the ancestors, the prophets are the ones that tell us that Jesus is coming. We first approach all of this sculpture as we are approaching the coming of Christ; and remember, when we go inside, we meet Christ not in stone, not in glass, but in bread and wine at the altar. It's important to see how this is preparing us for what's going to happen inside. That's where the really important stuff happens; and as we approach, we are led toward Christ by both his ancestors (the kings up there in the gallery) and those 12 so-called "minor prophets."

As we come to these doors, we look first at the door on the right because that's going to be the door about the past; that is to say, this is the door that's going to have sculpture that starts with Creation and brings us up to the time of the birth of Jesus and the life of Mary. Then, in the left door, we're going to have the bishops of Amiens and the church in time. So if the right door is past, the left door is present, and you'll not be surprised that the center door is future because it is the Last Judgment; it is the end of time. We talk about the fact that everything's here: We go from Creation as we'll see in a part of the right portal through the church of our own time in the left portal all the way to judgment in the center. Even before we look at the details, as we look at sort of the grand schemes: kings and prophets in two levels, and then past, present, and future. It seems like nothing's going to be left out, and I think we'll have a very strong sense of that.

Before we begin to explore, though, I want one more time, here on the ground, to emphasize size. Here we have the central trumeau statue of the Last Judgment portal and we have this enormous statue of Jesus; a much smaller statue of King David, his ancestor, below—we'll come back and look at these in detail in a minute—and then my intrepid student, Seth, standing beneath that; and so we really get a sense of the size of these statues. Everything in Amiens simply seems to be jumbo-sized, and I think that's clear from this photograph.

I want to look at the prophets, these ones that stick out at us, in a little bit of detail. They're all very different faces, but I think almost everybody's favorite is the prophet Nahum because here we have this enormous statue with this guy with his big beard, but one of his features is he has this long moustache and you can see it stretches around and actually ties behind his head. He's one of the unforgettable figures. Beneath each of these prophets are two quatrefoils, these cloverleaf-shaped pieces with sculpture in them, which tell us about the various prophets. In fact, some of the prophets have two and some of the prophets have four; those that are next to portals have two facing us and then two inside. I just want to look at a couple of these quatrefoils to give us an idea of how dramatic they are. This is a prophet to whom God shows the destruction of Jerusalem; so you see the prophet and God down below, and you see Jerusalem coming to ruins above.

Here, perhaps, is the most famous of all the minor prophets. It's a story we know; it's a story we've seen before; it's a story we've seen, in fact, on the south transept of Amiens: It's the story of Jonah. You can see in the upper quatrefoil Jonah coming out of the mouth of the whale, and below we see another piece of his prophecy: He sits beneath a fig tree and observes the city of Nineveh. These are very dramatic; and obviously people who know their scriptures—or people who can teach folks about these—have the opportunity to have all of these prophetic texts recalled to them. Here's another one where we see the prophecy is in the lower quatrefoil that Jerusalem will be taken over by rats; you see these great, big rats in the city of Jerusalem. These are warnings; they're not only pointing us forward to the time of deliverance, but they're also reminding us of what would be seen in the 13th century as the failures of Israel. There was doom prophesized for the Hebrews for their various sins; it reminds us A) that doom will come to us if we don't behave and we don't believe properly; but also B) that we know there is hope for redemption because we know Christ came to deliver first the Jews and then all humanity, according to Paul and the way he lays out things in his letters.

Let's now go to the right door, and let's take a careful look at this "past" door. On the trumeau, we have the Virgin and she's doing a very interesting thing: She's trampling on a serpent. Of course, it is the very serpent that led Eve into sin, because Mary undoes Eve in the eyes of medieval Catholics just as Adam is undone—or Adam's sin is undone—by Jesus; so it's very interesting to see that serpent. Down below, under the statue, you can see the stories of Creation. We see, for example, in the bottom one the result of sin: Adam and Eve are now clothed; over here we see Creation and the expulsion from the Garden of Eden. Again, we begin with Creation.

Then, on the left side of the door, we have stories from both the Old and the New Testament. The first figures we see are Solomon and Sheba—not the very far left, that's one of the prophets sort of facing partly out—because the story of King Solomon, the son of David, is very important; and then we have four kings on the right side: They are King Herod (bad guy) and the three kings, or Magi (good guys). What's interesting is in the Romanesque Period you'd know which because one of them would have a demon on his back or whatever; but notice this is a different psychological realm because none of them has a gnarled face, none of them is making some ugly gesture, and none of them has a demon sitting on his shoulder. We need to know the stories, we need to read those quatrefoils below that contain the narrative, and what we need to appreciate is in our own lives—we know this; this is a much more subtle psychology, perhaps, than we had before—bad guys look like good guys; it's hard to tell by looking, it's hard to tell by surface. In fact, bad guys in 13th-century Amiens don't have demons sitting on their shoulders so we know; we have to be more perceptive because of the fact that the distinctions between good and evil can sometimes be quite subtle.

Let's look at some of the stories below these two sets of figures. First, Solomon and Sheba: Here we see Solomon sitting on his throne in the upper quatrefoil, and Solomon worshiping in his temple. By the way, notice the temple looks like a Romanesque church because, of course, the sculptor wants to say the old temple has been replaced by the new church, so the temple is depicted in an archaic style by the time this is done in the 1220s. Here we see a story from the three kings: We see the seeing of the star in the upper quatrefoil, and down below we see the kings asleep. Once again, we can read the figures above by looking at the narratives below. The same is true on the other side. We have three pairs here: We have the Annunciation, Mary and Gabriel; then Mary is repeated in the middle pair, it's Mary and Elizabeth, the Visitation; and then in the third we have the presentation in the Temple where Jesus is handed to the prophet Simeon. Again, their stories are told below; some of them are not obvious because some of them are, in fact, Old Testament prefigurations of the events that are going on up above.

Now I want to look at the tympanum above the trumeau statue and see what's up there. Basically, on the lower level we have six Old Testament, we call them, "patriarchs"—we'll see who they are in just a minute—then we have stories of the death, assumption, and coronation of the Virgin; again, not to be surprised, because this is Notre Dame de Amiens. For example, we see Moses, and we recognize Moses because he has the tablets of the Ten Commandments. Notice he has horns. Some of you might know that Michelangelo's Moses, carved in the 16th century, now in Rome, has horns; it's a misreading of a text that talks about light coming from the head of Moses, and so the horned Moses is a common figure. On the other side is his brother Aaron dressed in the garb of the high priest, and in between them sits this box; this is the Ark of the Covenant. We have here all of these Old Testament images: the Ark, Moses, Aaron, the Hebrew priesthood, and so on. Then up above, again, we have the death of the Virgin Mary, she's being put up into her tomb; we have here her being taken up into Heaven; and then being crowned the Queen of Heaven by her son, Jesus. We have gone from Creation; we have looked at Old Testament figures, whether it's Solomon and Sheba or people like Moses and Aaron; we have looked at the coming of Christ, the Annunciation, the Visitation; we have the coming of the Magi, the flight into Egypt, the Presentation in the Temple; all of this collection of stories that get us from the beginning to the time of human redemption through the Incarnation, through the birth of Jesus, and, of course, it comes through Mary. In the archivolts here we have the Tree of Jesse, and therefore another set of the ancestors of Jesus.

Now let's move over to the left door. This door is what I call the door of the present—again, we can see we're greeted by those prophets—because here we're going to focus on the local church in Amiens, this is going to be the local door; and we're also going to focus on the fact that this is the period in which we now live, the time of the church, where, of course, our local version is the bishops of Amiens and the local saints of Amiens and we live in time, we will see here the calendar of the year. The trumeau statue is of a particular bishop of Amiens, Saint Firmin. We see him here: Part of his crosier—that is to say, this crook that a bishop carries—is broken off in his left hand and with his right hand he is blessing. He is a saint and a martyr; and down below, in the sculpture below him on the trumeau, we see—although most of it is badly damaged—we have here the actual execution of Saint Firmin. We're going to see more things in the life of Saint Firmin in a minute.

On either side of the doors, we have a collection of local saints, and we have in the quatrefoils down below an extraordinary depiction of the 12 signs of the zodiac—they're going to be much easier to see here then they were, say, in Chartres when they were in the archivolts—and the works of the months; same thing in the other side. One of the things you will notice is you have saints without heads—or, rather, holding their heads—because these are other martyrs of Amiens that we want to remember. Look at that; isn't that interesting, where we have one of the early martyrs of Amiens, and you can see his body is headless but he's holding his own head because, in a sense, that's his gift; that's his sacrifice; that's his martyrdom; that's his doing for Jesus what Jesus did for him: Jesus died for him, he has accepted the fact that he will die for Jesus. It's a very interesting way, dramatic way, of depicting that.

Let's look at some of the signs of the zodiac, and therefore the works of the months of the year. Here we see a sign of the zodiac, and we can see that in this season of the year we have the harvest of the grapes and the trampling on the grapes—I must confess that when I see this I always think of Lucille Ball trampling on the grapes in that famous scene with her buddy Ethel Mertz—but here we have in the fall season the representation of an agricultural activity that takes place around Amiens. Here we have the sowing of grain. Here we have a winter season, this is Aquarius; and there's not a lot of agricultural activity, but there is some good eating, there's some banqueting. Not every month is represented by very hard labor; there are times to enjoy the fruits of that labor. Here we have another winter scene in Pisces where we have a man who's simply sitting by his fire and trying to stay warm. These are really wonderful because ordinary people—peasants; merchants who travel in the countryside but live in the city—can recognize this as the world in which they live. They live with the saints of Amiens, and they live in this agricultural cycle even if they are urban people because this represents the time we live in, the time of the church that, of course, carries us from the time that Jesus goes up into Heaven, when he ascends into Heaven, and the time that he will come back.

In the tympanum, we have down below six bishops of Amiens, and that's important because they balance those six patriarchs we saw on the right side; they are today's equivalent of the patriarchs. Then we have up above some scenes where the relics of Saint Firmin are being brought into Amiens; you can see the carrying of relics here. Then we have angels—largely, although not entirely—and other folks here in the archivolts. This is time, because angels are messengers from God who come to bring us messages; angels are the ones who bring the message from the eternal God into time, just like Gabriel came from Heaven to announce to the Virgin Mary.

Finally, we move to the center portal, which is the portal of the Last Judgment. Again, we see the minor prophets as we approach. By the way, just inside the doors are the major prophets, two on each side—that is to say, the prophets who wrote long books: Isaiah, Jeremiah, Ezekiel, and Daniel—the main figures of the jambs are the 12 apostles, and then we have the Last Judgment up above with all the angels surrounding it. First of all, again, that trumeau statue with Christ up above (we saw a similar statue in Chartres) standing on the lion and the dragon, like he did at Chartres—there's the lion and the dragon or viper; it's translated differently for us in English, so we have either word, if you will, that describes that originally Hebrew word in Psalm 91— and his ancestor, King David, below. Over here, on one side we have the Lily of the Valley and on the other side we have the Rose of Sharon, two plants that are mentioned in the Old Testament that are related to the Davidic monarchy, the monarchy of King David and his successors. We have these beautiful floral images that reinforce, again, some of the theology. Then on one side we see a tree bearing fruit, and on the other side we see a tree being cut down. One is obviously on our left, the tree bearing fruit, because that's Jesus's right, that's the saved side; this is on our right, Jesus's left. Trees that don't bear fruit—think moral terms here—when we don't bear fruit we'll be the tree that's being cut down.

We actually have on either side also, interestingly enough, fables of Aesop. They were known in the 13th century, and they were also read sometimes as stories that sort of lead us to understand things like the final judgment.

Then we have our wise and foolish virgins that line the doors: There's the wise virgin and there you can see, looking a little bit lascivious with her hips moving and her lamp upside down, is the foolish virgin. Now we have the 12 apostles, 6 on each side, and two Old Testament prophets, two of the four major prophets, on each side; the quatrefoils down below give us the clearest guidance about how we can come to the Judgment without being found wanting because they give us 12 virtues and 12 vices. We know what we should do, and we know what we shouldn't do. So we have the prophets, the apostles, and all of these lessons. Let's take a look.

Here we see some of the apostles: This is Saint Peter; he carries his keys because he receives the keys to the Kingdom of Heaven from Jesus and he carries a cross because Peter, like Jesus, is crucified, although Peter is crucified, you may recall, upside down. Here is the apostle James; he carries a sword because he had his head cut off—that was his way of being martyred—and, of course, we know his body is in Santiago de Compostela, the end of a great pilgrimage route and the site of a great Romanesque church that we've taken a glance at already earlier in the course. Next to them is the apostle John. John is always depicted as young because he's represented that way as the apostle whom Jesus loved in John's gospel, and according to a story not in the Bible he was given a cup of poison, but before he could drink it the poison turned into serpents to warn him; that's why this is his symbol, that's why we know that it's the apostle John.

If we look at some of these quatrefoils, they are extraordinarily interesting. Up above here we have the virtue of courage. All of the virtues are represented by women; this happens to be an armed woman. Down below is cowardice: A knight has dropped his sword and is running away from a rabbit. Here we see another virtue: We have, for example, the virtue up above of obedience and down below the vice of disobedience, because here we have—imagine this on a cathedral—a man dares to argue with his bishop. Here, up above, we have charity, and notice here the woman up above that represents charity is delivering a cloak to a poor beggar, and down below a woman is stocking up everything and storing it in her treasure chest.

Here we have the Last Judgment; and again, because everything at Amiens is so big, this is an enormous and complex piece of sculpture. We're going to work our way through it beginning at the top, but first let's just look straight up and see how all this is surrounded by these choruses and choirs of angels, literally 100 of them; there are a lot of little angels up there in all of these various layers of the archivolt. Here at the top we find Christ the Judge, and the intercessors Mary on the left and John on the right. Remember, like we saw at Chartres, these now are of the same basic proportion—not quite, but almost—as Jesus, they're not lost as little fellows as they were at Laon. On either side of them are angels carrying the various symbols of the crucifixion: the cross, the nails, and the lance here that pierces the side of Christ. Up above, we see another smaller figure of Christ with the swords in his mouth, an image that comes from the book of Revelation and, again, takes us to the time of the Last Judgment.

We have here, of course, a division between the good souls and the bad souls: We see the good ones going off to the left, the bad ones going off to the right. Here we see souls entering the gates of Heaven being greeted by angels. By the way, the person who goes in has on a rope with knots in it; it is Saint Francis of Assisi who was a brand new saint—he was canonized in 1228—when this sculpture was being made, so this is updated; this is not a generic holy person, this is the famous new holy person of our own era, Francis of Assisi. But as Psalm 1 says, "Not so the wicked, not so"; we see them being lined up and sent into a very graphic mouth of Hell. Down below we have the resurrection of the dead: We see the angels sounding the trumpet; "The trumpet shall sound, the dead shall be raised." In the middle is Michael the Archangel weighing souls. The Devil is trying to cheat, but the Devil is not winning because you can't cheat God; even the Devil's power, as great as it is, is limited and cannot affect the Final Judgment. Again, we look up at all of this and see essentially the heavenly host of all the angels.

Past, present, and future; and remember I said when we looked at the building of Chartres Cathedral and I talked about the analogy between Gothic architecture and scholastic thought: Same thing here between scholastic thought and Gothic sculpture. It is complex, it is complete; all, it seems, we need to know has been assembled in a great suma in stone, in this case in carved stone. There is nothing like the complexity and the completeness of the facade of Amiens Cathedral.

Reims—The Royal Cathedral
Lecture 15

Remember we said all the way back in the beginning of the course that an essential part of what a cathedral is ... is a statement of jurisdiction and authority; it is a place of power for the bishop whose cathedra is there. And that's displayed in a really interesting and somewhat unusual way in these windows.

A ll of the cathedrals we have seen so far are important in one way or another—architecturally, decoratively, and so on. But Reims Cathedral is uniquely important to France, because around the year 500, Clovis, the king of the Franks, was baptized here by the bishop of Reims. This makes Reims the birthplace of Christianity in France. Of course, you can tell from these dates that the cathedral we see today is not the original. A fire destroyed the older cathedral in the year 1210; this cathedral was begun the very next year. The facade displays sculpture in a way we haven't quite seen before, and many of the places where we would expect sculpture, we find windows. Where before we have seen the gallery of kings, above the doors but below the rose window, we have a scene of the baptism of Clovis.

It's been estimated that there are between 2,000 and 3,000 statues at Reims, and some of them are quite funny, like a human figure with wings and duck feet. Reims also has many gargoyles, raising the question, why are all these ugly things on a cathedral? Pseudo-Dionysus argued that very often we are helped by distorted forms, because we can recognize their distortion and we can move beyond them to an essence of something.

We have more chances to see more parts of the cathedral from above in Reims than any other cathedral in Europe. From above, you can see that the buttresses have spires on them. Until modern times, people assumed that they were purely decorative; recently, engineers have shown that they actually help and strengthen the buttressing system, although we don't know whether people knew that in the 13th century. We can also visit the space between the top of the vault and the roof at Reims. Remember that from the outside, the roof looks quite sharply pointed, and from inside, arches of the ribbed vaults, although pointed, are not nearly as sharp. In fact, actually, the vaults are fairly flat. What we see here is not the original superstructure; Reims was very badly damaged during World War I, and so the roof's superstructure was essentially destroyed. It was rebuilt not out of wood but out of concrete.

Reims is a big cathedral: about 450 feet, or 130 meters, long. We are used to a dark nave and lighter choir in Gothic cathedrals; in Reims, it's just the opposite. Most of the stained glass in the nave was removed, while much in the choir has remained, so the darker part has more of the original work. The elevation has three levels: aisle, triforium (nonglazed), and clerestory. The vault is a four-part vault, which is more or less the standard by now.

© Photos.com/Thinkstock.

Reims was the site of the crowning of many French monarchs from Clovis to Napoleon.

Often in these cathedrals, there is a wall or screen behind the altar that obstructs the view of the ambulatory, but here it is low; we can see all the way back. The windows above the ambulatory are original, and they're very important. We have apostles at the top, a series of bishops down below, one of whom is labeled the archbishop of Reims, and an image of the cathedral itself. In fact, the bishops are those under Reims's jurisdiction arranged in order of precedence. This window is a statement about authority. One

The Power of Precedent

From 1027 onward, virtually all the kings of France were crowned in Reims Cathedral, but one medieval coronation stands out from this crowd: During the so-called third phase of the Hundred Years' War, in the early 15th century, **Joan of Arc** led **Charles VII** to be crowned at Reims, giving him a new legitimacy that in part turned the tide of the war against the English. So aside from its architectural and spiritual glories, Reims is an important place to French patriots and an important place in the history of France.

20th-century alteration to Reims Cathedral is worth mentioning: The central chapel of the ambulatory hosts a window by **Mark Chagall**.

As we noted earlier, the tympana of the facade doors have been replaced by windows; this gives us more than the usual display of glass when we look from the altar toward the west end. The sides of the doorways, however, are elaborately sculpted. At the bottom are stories from the Old Testament, such as the priest-king Melchizedek giving bread and wine to Abraham. Abraham is anachronistically dressed as a medieval knight; in 13th-century France, no one would have known what an ancient Near Eastern warrior would wear.

The north transept has three asymmetrical doors, the product of more than one building campaign. The hell-bound figures in the Last Judgment sculpture here are unusually calm; interestingly, among the damned we find a king and a bishop, a reminder that authority on earth is not a free pass into heaven. Over one door, we have a piece of locally themed sculpture: the baptism of Clovis combined with the story of Job, perhaps referring to the trials and tribulations of the local church.

Among all the thousands of works of art at Reims, the most important sculptures are the jamb statues in the central portal of the facade. One is a Visitation; its style unlike anything we've seen so far—the drapery and the facial expressions are similar to what we see in ancient Roman statuary. The Annunciation next to it is more in the medieval style, an evolution from

Chartres and Amiens. The highly classicized Visitation statue is an early taste of the art of the Renaissance. ■

Chagall, Marc (1887–1985): Important 20th-century French artist. He designed windows for Reims Cathedral.

Charles VII (r. 1422–1461): King of France. For several years, he was uncrowned and losing ground to the English in the Hundred Years' War. Led by Joan of Arc, he traveled to Reims Cathedral for his coronation.

Joan of Arc (1412–1431): Mystic and charismatic leader of French forces against the English in the Hundred Years' War who was burned at the stake at Rouen for heresy in 1431. Joan led King Charles VII across France to be crowned at Reims Cathedral.

Suggested Reading

Frankl, *Gothic Architecture*, chaps. 3.2, 3.5.

Jantzen, *High Gothic*.

Wilson, *The Gothic Cathedral*, chap. 2.

Questions to Consider

1. Why are the smiling angels so important?

2. How do you respond to the windows where sculpture typically is located on facades, and what do you think of the sculpture of the counterfacade, unique features at Reims?

3. How does standing above the vaults give us a deeper understanding of the construction of a Gothic cathedral?

Reims—The Royal Cathedral
Lecture 15—Transcript

This may sound a little bit like a broken record, but Reims, the subject of this lecture, is a very important cathedral; and, of course, I think it'll be clear that it's important in terms of the building itself: the architecture, the decoration, and so on. But it's also important, in some ways uniquely important, to France. The reason goes all the way back 700 years before this cathedral was built. In around the year 500, the pagan king of the Franks, Clovis, became a Christian, therefore bringing the Franks along with him as Christians, and he was baptized around the year 500 by Bishop Remigius of Reims. That makes Reims a particularly important place, because for the Franks—from whom we obviously get the name "France"—Christianity arrived; it arrived in Reims with that baptism. After 1027, virtually all the kings of France were crowned in Reims; it became the tradition, the practice, the sign of legitimacy for a king to be crowned in the cathedral of Reims by the Archbishop of Reims.

Obviously, many famous kings, many famous coronations; but one stood out above all others and made Reims a particular interest in the later Middle Ages. During the 100 Years' War, the so-called "third phase" in the early 15th century, we know about the great heroic story of Joan of Arc and how she relieved the siege of Orleans. One of the problems that France faced with the English having invaded is the fact that the king, Charles VII, had not been crowned at Reims; and so led by Joan of Arc, Charles VII went to Reims and was crowned there. That gave him a kind of legitimacy, and those events—the relief of the siege of Orleans and the crowning at Reims—are what in many ways turned the tide for the French against the English, and within 20 years the English had essentially been kicked out once and for all from France. That in and of itself, of course, makes it an important place to French patriots and an important place in the history of France.

Having said that, it should be obvious that the cathedral we're going to look at is not the original and it's not the first important cathedral of Reims. There was, as in so many other places, a fire that destroyed the older cathedral in the year 1210, and the very next year the cathedral of Reims that we see before us was begun. It was begun, I pointed out in the lecture on Amiens, before Amiens was built, but we did Amiens first because they were built in different directions. Like most cathedrals, Reims was built from east to west, and therefore when we look at the front of it we're looking at the newest part in some ways; while Amiens was built from west to east and that's why we did Amiens first, because the facade is something that precedes and predates the facade here at Reims.

But at any rate, we want to take a little bit of a look at this cathedral. This is sculpture from the facade that shows the baptism of Clovis; it is in the position where in other cathedrals we have the gallery of kings. Here we have a model of Reims because, as we'll see, the spires are not there now; and this is what Reims looks like today. This was taken very recently, and when you go there, or if you go there, you may discover that some of the scaffolding that we're going to have to look around is down. This cathedral dominates the still rather large city of Reims. As we look first at the facade, I want to emphasize three things about it: First of all, you'll notice that the tympana, the spaces over the doors—of course, we can't see the one on the left because of all the scaffolding—but at any rate, you can see that there's no sculpture there but rather windows, and that's going to obviously have an impact on the way we see the interior of the cathedral a little bit later on; the sculpture of the tympanum has been replaced by windows. Second, I want you to notice that there is sculpture all over the facade of this; not in the tympana but in the archivolts and then in pointed sculptural programs above the door, and then really there's scattered sculpture all over. For example, look at the very far right side: beyond the right door you'll see there is another piece of sculpture, another sculptural program. In many ways, the whole facade displays sculpture in a way we haven't quite seen before. Third, I want you to look over the left and right doors; you can see that the towers have great big open windows in them and you can actually see through those towers and look behind the facade and see the flying buttresses that hold up the nave. Those are interesting and new features of the cathedral of Reims.

We have already seen systematic buttressing—we've seen it at Chartres and we've seen it at Amiens—but I want to take you on a quick tour of the buttressing of Reims, because it's even more systematic; it's even more thorough and more dramatic than those we've seen. We're now standing exactly in the east end; we're looking at the central chapel behind the altar and looking at that buttressing system. In fact, you'll not only see it in this photograph but you'll notice that part of the set for this course, the one over my left shoulder, is also that photograph, and it's kind of stark in black and white; I love the black and white photographs of these Gothic cathedrals. Here we look up through one of the buttresses and see one of literally—I'll talk more about this later—thousands of statues on the exterior of Reims Cathedral. Again, I want to give you an idea of some of the sculptural pieces that decorate it, but also just look from some of the different angles; this is another cathedral you can walk around the east end and really get all sorts of interesting takes on things. Here we're looking at one of the chapels in the ambulatory and looking up toward those spires and again we see the pattern of the buttresses.

We're going to spend some time now upstairs in the cathedral of Reims, because we have more chances to see more parts of the cathedral from above in Reims than any other cathedral that I know of in France or for that matter in Europe. Here we're looking down between two of these great flying buttresses. Here's another angle. You'll notice that these buttresses have spires on the far end of them; that is to say, the end that's away from the building itself. Until modern times, people assumed that they were purely decorative; now some engineers have shown that they actually help and strengthen the buttressing system. We don't know whether people knew that in the 13th century, certainly they didn't know that by any kind of scientific measurement; but it's interesting that what seems to use like a decorative gizmo is, in fact, functional.

I want to take you now in a place that we can go in Reims almost uniquely, and that is between the top of the vault and the roof. Remember that when we look at a cathedral from the outside, the roof looks quite sharply pointed; and yet when we walk in the cathedral, it's clear that the pointed arches of the ribbed vaults are not nearly as sharp as the appearance from the outside. In fact, actually, the vaults, despite the fact they have pointed arches, are fairly flat; and therefore when we look at a cathedral from the outside, we don't see just a covering of the vault, we see an enormous superstructure constructed with this sharply slanted roof. What we're looking at here is standing on top of the vault and under the roof of the building, and at Reims this is open to the public and we can do this. We are looking at the top of the stone roof, but we are underneath what in most cathedrals is the wooden superstructure. I say most cathedrals because Reims was very badly damaged during World War I because Reims was near the front, being in eastern France; and so the superstructure was essentially destroyed and it was rebuilt not out of wood but out of concrete (by the way, largely by American donations). So what we see here is not the original, but it is a concrete copy of the wooden superstructure; and because perhaps it's more stable—not subject to fire and whatever—the public is allowed up for a few hours every day to visit this.

What I'm looking at here is the top of the vault; that's what these ribbed vaults look like from up above, and we're looking down right on the keystone. Now let's go downstairs for a second and look back up. You see that keystone? That's what we just saw from above; we're standing on a walkway that runs right over these vaults. It's an extraordinary experience and gives us another insight into the way these buildings are built. Here you can see some of this more complicated superstructure as I walk from essentially the west end of the nave toward the transept. You can see where that light is coming in; that light is coming in from the crossing tower of Reims Cathedral.

Now we go outside, and we can walk around. There is that steep, pitched roof and there is that crossing tower, more of a spire than a tower. The roofs are often green because they're covered in copper; in some places, especially in the Mediterranean, these roofs are often covered with tile. We look up and see a decorative design that runs along the spine of the roof. Again, from up here, we walk along at the level above the buttresses and just where we begin to get the pitch of the roof and we can see some of the beautiful stonework. These, of course, are all carved stones, and even though they're very far from the ground, they're carved very carefully and skillfully; it's not sloppy up top since nobody could see it from below. Again, I want to give you a series of looks because it's so rare to have the opportunity to be able to meander around much of the exterior up above in Reims Cathedral.

All kinds of sculpted figures: I pointed out there are a lot of sculpted figures on Reims, including all over the facade; but not just all over the facade, all over the building. It's been estimated there are between 2,000 and 3,000 statues, nobody's really counted; and some of them are quite funny. Look at this figure; I want you to look at the feet. This is a human figure with wings and duck feet, as it turns out. You can get a good look there and see the webbed feet. We can look here at a gargoyle; it's really a water spout. We know that there are a lot of these gargoyles on Gothic cathedrals—they are very famous, particularly the ones perhaps that we think of with *The Hunchback of Notre Dame*, that photograph we saw in the Notre Dame lecture—but it's interesting to ponder these a little bit because why are all these ugly things on a cathedral? One of the things we learned from Pseudo-Dionysus—remember him, he's an inspiration to Suger, the creator of Gothic—is that very often we actually are helped by distorted forms, because we can recognize their distortion and we can move beyond them to get to the essence of something; so even distortions are very often helpful to us. Yes, they're a little bit scary, they make good movies, they make souvenirs in small copies; but they probably actually do, in theory, serve some function. Here we have a wild boar nursing its—I guess you call them—"boarlets," piglets if you will; an interesting image. We have lovely faces; we have ugly faces. When we get up top, we get to be up close and personal with an extraordinary variety of sculpture, some of it seemingly playful, some more serious perhaps; maybe even all of it is at least a little bit serious.

When we walk into Reims Cathedral, it's an extraordinary experience. In some ways, the lighting pattern seems reversed from what we're used to; we're used to having a darker nave and a lighter choir. We saw that at Chartres, although that was partly because the choir has been cleaned; we saw it at Amiens because the choir was built later and had the glazed triforium; but here we have more light in the nave than in the choir for the very simple reason that most of the stained glass windows in the nave were removed while much of the stained glass in the choir has remained, so the darker part has more of the original work, if you will, than what we might normally expect.

I want to take a look around now and just look at some of the architectural features. You can see here that there is a three-part elevation: the aisle, the triforium, and the clerestory windows. You can see that the triforium is dark; that is to say, there's a wall behind it, it's not glazed. Nevertheless, with the original windows out, we get a good deal of light. We can look up from one of those pillars and follow it all the way from the base, the ground where this photograph is taken, to the vault; and you can see that as we look from bay to bay standing at a certain angle, in addition to those beautifully decorated capitals we just have all of these verticals. Our eyes are just lifted up; it almost looks like we're looking at rows of sort of organ pipes, if you will, as we're looking at Reims Cathedral. Here we get a view of the elevation straightforwardly; you can see the levels of light, you can look at the triforium. Notice its design is different than ones we've seen: There are arches and they are sharply pointed; they're somewhat different than the triforium arches that we looked at, for example, in Amiens, either in the nave or in the choir. This is the vault; the more or less standard now, we would say, four-part vault. Remember those keystones that we looked at up close from below and above? You can see, taken from the ground level with a wide-angle lens, how far away those keystones are.

I want you to look at the carving on each of the capitals. Obviously they're all a little bit different because they can't be just simply copied; but they're extraordinarily elaborate and beautiful, which means think about how many sculptors had to be involved. Of course, the people who make the most beautiful statues in the world, a beautiful Madonna, you don't need somebody of that skill to make one of these; but this is very hard work and it takes a great deal of skill. Again, there are a lot of these because this is such a big cathedral; in fact, this cathedral is about 450 feet long, about 130 meters long. It's an enormous building, and we have to appreciate how much of this kind of level of craftsmanship is needed inside in addition to those 2,000–3,000 statues that we saw outside. Again, I want to just look around the interior. This is taken from the east end; usually you can't get this photograph from behind the altar because there's a kind of wall behind the altar very often in these cathedrals. Here, however, that wall is low enough; we can look through the candelabra and a metal grill and we can get a look from the back, all the way back in the ambulatory, to the front. Here we see the aisle; and again, isn't this extraordinary? It looks like a large church.

One of the things that strikes us as so different about Reims—and we've already had a hint of this—is now that we turn around and look from east to west, we not only have the rose window with some windows below it but, of course, we have a smaller rose window below that because that is above the tympanum, above the door as you can see here, because the door is, in fact, open and the light is coming in, and there are smaller ones as you look down either aisle. We have this great display of glass as we look to the west. But we also discover, as we get close, that there is sculpture on both sides of the door. You can just barely see some of it here in this photograph; but as it turns out, on the left there is tier after tier after tier of sculpture. This sculpture that we see at the very bottom level happens to be of Old Testament prophets, and then up above we have the story of John the Baptist.

One of the most interesting pieces is on the right side; the lowest piece is an Old Testament story of the man called both priest and king in Genesis, Melchizedek. Melchizedek gives bread and wine to Abraham, and that's what we have depicted here. But look at the figures: There is Melchizedek, beautifully sculpted, and there is Abraham. Abraham is dressed as a medieval knight because Abraham was many things, but one of the things he was is a warrior; and so he's depicted not as anybody could find out or even perhaps imagine warriors would have looked all that time ago, but he looks like a medieval knight. Again, let me show you that entire scene; it's quite interesting for us to look at.

Then we have here the north rose window; and a wonderful window it is because we have the story of Creation in those medallions around the center and then on the far edges of this window we have animals from the story of Creation. It really is quite interesting, and they alternate with angels. The windows in the choir above the ambulatory, as I've pointed out before, are original and they're very important. We have apostles at the top, but down below we have a series of bishops; and the ones right in the center under that large oculus, in the lower part—because the upper parts are apostles—we have two depictions: One is the Bishop of Reims, and he is so labeled; that is to say, it's not a predicative person, it's the Bishop of Reims, the Archbishop of Reims actually. The other one of those windows is the cathedral of Reims itself. I want you to think about what this says. Of course, it says that the bishop—and we'll see he's joined by other bishops in the surrounding lancets—those bishops are apostles; that is part of the theory of apostolic succession.

The Archbishop of Reims was an extraordinarily important French churchman, and because he's an archbishop it means there were several bishops who were under his jurisdiction; just like I mentioned earlier that the Bishop of Paris in some ways was under the jurisdiction of the Archbishop of Sens. The Archbishop of Reims is a big player; and so the rest of these windows, in fact, depict other bishops under the jurisdiction of the Archbishop of Reims. This is a really interesting thing. They're all labeled, and we know from documents that they are arranged in the order in which they would sit at a meeting presided over by the Archbishop of Reims in his cathedral. This is not just bishops; this is not just bishops of specific dioceses; this is a recreation in glass that states the ecclesiastical authority and preeminence of the Archbishop of Reims. It is a statement about authority. Remember we said all the way back in the beginning of the course that an essential part of what a cathedral is: It is a statement of jurisdiction and authority; it is a place of power for the bishop whose cathedra is there; and that's displayed in a really interesting and somewhat unusual way in these windows that we have.

Normally, as you know, I have not mentioned a lot of the more modern furnishings that churches have, although I've said over and over again there's a lot of that. Ok, every rule needs to be broken once: In the central chapel of the ambulatory, there's a 20th-century window that's really quite unusual and beautiful. It's done by the great artist Marc Chagall, and we can see it here and obviously we recognize very different kinds of patterns and designs than we would see in medieval stained glass. I just wanted you to note that, because when you are looking around cathedrals, even though what I want to do is try to present them as much as possible as they were built and as they looked in the 13th century, we should not avoid all those modern pieces that are there for various reasons. As I mentioned, on the exterior, it just seems the whole building—the facade and other parts—is covered with statues. This is an angel; there are—I don't know how many; here's a rough estimate—a gazillion of these. There are a lot of these all the way around the cathedral of Reims and decorating them. Some of the statues, because this is a very big cathedral, are very big. Here's an example of a statue of Goliath—of course, Goliath is a big guy to start with—but this is in the museum in Reims that sits right next to the cathedral, and I just want you to see me standing there with Goliath to get an idea how large some of the statues are on the facade of Reims Cathedral.

This is the north transept, and it's sort of an odd-looking beast because it has three doors and they are asymmetrical. This is obviously the product of more than one building campaign and lacks the kind of unity and pattern of repetition and symmetry that we're used to. Nevertheless, they contain some very interesting sculpture. For example, we have a Last Judgment; and I want to look at it because there are some interesting details. This is the saved, this is the bosom of Abraham; but even though we have a real Hell—that's a real Hell with a real boiling pot—remember in the other images that we've seen, usually the souls going off to Hell have been naked and they've had these extraordinary and excruciating expressions of suffering on their faces; this is more calm. It's not without power; it's not without an element to show us what we should be afraid of; but these guys are going to Hell, they're going to be put into the mouth of Hell, and they look relatively calm. By the way, I want you to notice who they are: There is a king, and there is a bishop. This is a hierarchical society, kings and bishops matter; and remember that they hold office and their office is something that they've received—whether the king or the bishop—from above, but it doesn't mean that if you have one of those high offices you automatically are on the road to Heaven, as we see a bishop and a king heading off to Hell. In the archivolts, we have a group of people we've gotten used to and know by now: the wise and the foolish virgins. In the tympanum, over what used to be a bigger door than it is now, I think, and a more used door than it is now—you can see it's sort of walled up so you can't go in there—we have a piece of sculpture dedicated to the local church here in Reims. We have, as you would expect, the baptism of Clovis; but incorporated into this is the story of Job, the story we saw at Chartres, perhaps suggesting again of the trials and tribulations of suffering of the local church.

Let's go back now and finish up with a look at the sculpture, or at least a little bit of the sculpture, of the facade. Again, there are no tympana; but we're going to look at the sculpture around the two doors that are not covered with scaffolding—and they are the two important ones—the right and the center doors. We're going to look at the jamb statues, because they are of particular importance to us as we finish our visit to Reims Cathedral. By the way, I want you to look at this: Reims Cathedral, the reason we have the scaffolding is they're in a cleaning process; and here's a place where in a previous cleaning campaign the cleaning stopped, and you can see the difference between the dirty statue and the wall behind it on the left and the clean on the right. I made a mention of that with regard to Amiens, but here we can see it dramatically because we have a half-done job, and we can understand what modern pollution, and simply being outside for 800 years, has done to many of these statues.

I want to focus on the right portal and some of the jamb statues there. They are Old Testament figures, ones that we have seen before, for example, on the north porch at Chartres. I just want to look at a few of these statues briefly because they are quite beautiful and, as you can see, they're the new clean ones, and therefore they're almost glistening. Here is Moses. Notice Moses has not one but two things to tell us who he is: He has his column with the serpent on top, something we've gotten used to by now, but he also holds the tablets of the Ten Commandments. We have here the prophet Simeon who holds the baby Jesus; and we have Abraham, that patriarch, looking very old—patriarchs should look old—with his son, Isaac. But the most important sculpture in Reims is the jamb statues in the central portal, and we're going to look at four pieces, two pairs.

This is the Visitation; this is Mary visiting Elizabeth. Look at the style: It's different than anything we've seen. The way the drapery folds, the expressions on the faces; the sculptor of this piece knew and knew very well examples of Ancient Roman sculpture. Look at the folds of the garments here; these are very similar to what we see in a lot of Ancient Roman sculpture. These are really Classicized statues. We have the face here of the Virgin, the face here of Elizabeth, who's old; remember she had been barren for many years. Now compare that with the two statues next to it: This is the figure of the Annunciation; so we have Gabriel and the Virgin Mary. Notice we have a different kind of drapery; look at that compared to what we just saw. This is more in the medieval style; this is more an evolution from Chartres and Amiens to what we have here. So right next to each other we have these two very different styles done within a few years of each other. This is the face of the Virgin; this is the very famous face of the angel. This is the most famous statue at Reims, the smiling angel of Reims; Gabriel's having a ball here, if you will. Look at the two pairs together: The Annunciation in the more traditional medieval style on the left, and the more classically inspired figures of Mary and Elizabeth on the right.

Reims Cathedral, the royal cathedral; one of the most extraordinarily important and interesting buildings in Europe.

Cathedrals—Who Builds? Who Pays? How Long?
Lecture 16

> It's at least interesting to think about God as architect with a compass; we can imagine how this image of God would be generated in a world that produced those wonderful Romanesque and Gothic buildings.

L et's take a break from looking at specific cathedrals and ask some questions about Gothic cathedrals in general: How did these things get built? Who designed them, who built them, who paid for them, how long did it take? What would a work site have looked like? In many ways, we don't know how these buildings were constructed with any certainty, and each cathedral underwent a different construction process. We have as many stories, as many answers to our questions, as there are cathedrals. The evidence we have to work with includes some limited documentary evidence, some manuscript illuminations, and some stained-glass windows.

We have a popular conception of cathedral building: In some moment of crisis, inspiration, or divine revelation, everybody—peasants, clergy, and nobles—dropped whatever else they were doing and built the thing together. Like a lot of popularization, there's a little bit of truth to that; the closest we get to this situation occurred at Chartres after the fire of 1194. When the Virgin's cloak, thought lost, was discovered intact, it was taken as a call from the Virgin to rebuild; thus money and labor came from all over France. Some cathedrals were built quickly; many others were built in fits and starts over a long period; and some were never finished in the Middle Ages.

The moving force behind the construction of most cathedrals was the cathedral chapter—that is, the bishop and his clergy, called the canons of the cathedral. We know about Bishop Suger's involvement in Saint-Denis, for example, and we have the stained-glass window commemorating his work. But we are almost certain that Suger did not design the building; he was the manager, but not the architect. Suger's diaries never mention who the architect or the engineers were. In fact, we have almost no names of these designers; one of the few we have is connected to the repair of Canterbury Cathedral after a fire in 1174. The archbishop hired a man named William of Sens to repair the east end of the church as a monument to the recently martyred Thomas à Becket. It is safe to assume that William of Sens was connected in some way to the design and construction of Sens Cathedral.

We know a little bit more about the architects of the 14th century and later: In Prague Cathedral, busts of **Peter Parler** and the cathedral's other architects are found among the decoration. So as the Gothic period progressed, recognition of the skill and genius of these architects was going up. Also as over time, apparently, the man responsible for overall design and supervision became separated from the workforce, and thereafter his second in command would pass the supervisor's instructions on to the workers. Because this second in command did a lot of talking—that is to say, that was his job—he very often took a name that means "to speak" in French, *parler*. Peter Parler's name suggests that he comes from a line of cathedral builders.

The moving force behind the construction of most cathedrals was the cathedral chapter— that is, the bishop and his clergy.

One unique source of information about Gothic cathedral construction is a set of drawings by the 13th-century artist **Villard de Honnecourt** documenting the construction of the towers at Laon, the nave at Rennes, and more. We don't know that he actually worked on any cathedral, but his drawings show us some of the machinery used in medieval construction.

Let's take a look at the features of a cathedral building site. A lot of different activities would go on simultaneously. Not all workers on the cathedral worked at the cathedral; stonemasons, for example, shaped the stones at the quarry, because it would have been a waste of effort to transport heavier, uncarved stone. Sometimes stone was actually brought by water: There is stone that is part of Canterbury Cathedral, for example, that was brought across the English Channel from Normandy. At the site, the heavy stones were lifted into place via a crane operated by a tread wheel powered by humans. Other work, such as carpentry, would occur on the site itself; remember, wood was not only needed for construction of the cathedral but to build equipment such as scaffolding, tread wheels, tool handles, and so forth.

Other work on a cathedral site included blacksmithing, cart building, and even candle making.

Some late-13th-century records from Autun Cathedral give us information about what sorts of workers were hired, how they were obtained, and what they were paid. We know from documents from Salisbury Cathedral that the most skilled craftsmen were often brought in from the outside, whereas those who "tote that bar, lift that bale" were local farmers hired for the off season. Lodges were built near the cathedral for the masons—not places to live but places to meet, to leave equipment, and probably eventually to share trade secrets. These formed the seed of later secret Masonic societies.

Just as no two cathedrals were built in the same way, no two cathedrals were funded in the same way either. Notre Dame in Paris, for example, was funded primarily by the king, and noble patronage was common. Medieval bishops had a lot of wealth—primarily from renting land, but also from taxes, from selling indulgences, and from pilgrims' donations—so often these projects were church funded. Occasionally, as in Florence and elsewhere in Italy, the cities themselves managed the cathedral project, funded by the guilds. But in most cases, funds came from a variety of sources. Often, images of patrons are found in a cathedral's windows. ■

Names to Know

Parler, Peter (c. 1330–1399): Principal architect of Prague Cathedral and designer of the Charles Bridge across the Vltava River in Prague. His father was a parler, i.e., a kind of head mason and bridge between the architect and the masons. Peter Parler was German and also designed churches in Nürnberg.

Honnecourt, Villard de (c. 1225–c. 1250): French artist and architect whose sketchbook documents the construction of many Gothic cathedrals throughout Europe. The sketchbook is an important source about medieval construction techniques.

Suggested Reading

Erlande-Brandenburg, *The Social and Architectural Dynamics of Construction*, chap. 5.

Gimpel, *The Cathedral Builders*.

Scott, *The Gothic Enterprise*, chaps. 2, 3, 9.

Wilson, *The Gothic Cathedral*, chaps. 1–2.

Questions to Consider

1. Can we imagine how many people and animals and machines were necessary to build a Gothic cathedral?

2. Why was there so much variety in the ways cathedrals were financed?

3. Does it matter to us that most of the design and execution and decoration is the work of anonymous figures? Should it matter?

Cathedrals—Who Builds? Who Pays? How Long?
Lecture 16—Transcript

This marks an interesting break in the course. We have spent the last eight lectures looking at five buildings in a great deal of detail, and the lectures that follow this one—which really means following the period of the great (I suppose we could call them) Classic Gothic cathedrals—we're going to do two things: First, we're going to look at later Gothic in France in the 14th, 15th, and beginning of the 16th century, and we're going to do that by looking at several churches in each lecture. then we're going to do our whirlwind tour of Europe and very briefly beyond Europe looking at Germany, Italy, Spain, and some other places as well—England, of course—but before we take off on a somewhat different mode of operation, we want to stop and ask questions that, by now, I hope all of you are asking: How did these things get built? Who designed them, who built them, who paid for them, how long did it take? Even, perhaps: What would a worksite have looked like?

We have a kind of popular conception of how these cathedrals were built. In some moment of crisis, inspiration, or divine revelation everybody dropped what he, and even she, was doing and peasants, clergy, and nobles all got together and just built the thing. We sort of picture them all working together happily, sharing lunch, maybe even singing a song now and then; I'm obviously parodying a kind of popular idea of how these cathedrals got built. Like a lot of popularization, there's a little bit of truth to that; but let me suggest two problems we need to be aware of: Number one, in many ways we don't know the answers to the questions I posed; or, should I say, we have some glimpses of the answers. Number two, the answers to those questions are different for virtually every cathedral. We have cathedrals paid for by royalty, we have cathedrals paid for largely by merchants, we have cathedrals that were built quickly, we have cathedrals where the money ran out and it took decades and maybe centuries to build it; we have as many stories, as many answers—at least if we had all the evidence we would—as there are cathedrals. A lot of what I'm going to be saying is somewhat generic, although I'm going to try to be as specific as possible and give some illustrations from some documents and, as we'll see, some visual sources that survive.

Let me say a word about most of the visual sources in this lecture. They are primarily, although not entirely, manuscript illuminations; that is to say, pictures painted in books. However, they're not pictures of "how we built our local cathedral." For example, we're going to see one that's an illustration from the Old Testament that depicts the building of the Temple of Solomon. But this will not surprise you if you've been thinking medieval with me now for a while: The Temple of Solomon looks an awful lot like a Gothic cathedral. As we've seen in so many other cases, there's not going to be any attempt in these pictures, very often of biblical stories or stories from the lives of saints, to go back and do the historical research of what the technology or the procedure was then; they will simply use contemporary equipment, contemporary ways of organizing themselves, to illustrate stories that happened a long, long time ago. After all, the Temple of Solomon was built in the 10th century B.C., and we're in the 13th century A.D. They don't know much about what that building looked like; they don't know much about how that building was built. I want you to be aware of what we have to work with: some limited documentary evidence; some manuscript pictures or illuminations; and, in some cases, we will also illustrate things from surviving stained glass windows. We have a variety of sources, written and not written, and we want to keep all that in mind.

Let me start briefly with: Who comes up with the ideas? That is to say, the parameters of the building; who they're going to hire to build the building; what the windows are going to contain; what the sculpture is going to be in the facade. Who decides those sorts of things? Almost certainly the answer to that is the bishop and his clergy. Collectively, the clergy that are at the cathedral with the bishop are called the cathedral chapter, and the individual members are called canons of the cathedral. It is largely, as far as we know— this is a little bit less true in Italy, as we'll see later—but largely true that the clergy make those kinds of decisions. We know, for example—although here we're not talking about a cathedral—in the case of the abbey church at Saint Denis, clearly the moving force was Suger himself, the abbot of Saint Denis.

Of course, sometimes decisions were made slowly, carefully, and rationally about building or making major additions to a cathedral, but at other times the situation is forced. We talked about a fire in Reims, we talked about a fire in Amiens, we talked about two fires at the cathedral of Chartres about 60 years apart. Very often there are urgent necessities because we don't have a cathedral to worship in; we don't have a cathedral that is a symbol and seat of the power of the bishop; we don't have a cathedral that to the world shows us how close we are to God and how dedicated to God we are. Doesn't show others; doesn't show God.

Perhaps the closest story of cathedral building to that early parody or caricature that I gave of everybody sort of rolling up their sleeves and working together happened in the case of Chartres after the fire of 1194. Remember we saw that the relic of the Virgin's cloak was assumed lost in the fire; and when it was discovered that that cloak was indeed preserved, it was seen as a call from the Virgin: "Build me a really nice place. Build me a new cathedral." There were a lot of people in the city, the surrounding countryside, and even from all over France because this was an important relic that a lot of people knew about and had visited. It seems it really was a huge collective effort of money and labor. It may not be they all linked arms and sang at the end of the day, but nevertheless there was a great deal of emotion, of spiritual dedication, of hard work, of people rolling up their sleeves to build this new building that we spent three lectures examining; and even there only examining, in a sense, with a glance here and a glance there.

We know that Suger claims to be the guy who built the abbey church of Saint Denis, and we see him in a stained glass window holding one of his stained glass windows that he commissioned—he didn't make it, after all—and presenting it. But we know also that Suger—or almost certain—didn't design the building; Suger wasn't on the spot every day to say, "Now put that stone over here," "No, no, no I want that statue there," "No, I don't like the face of that Virgin Mary." We don't know who supervised and managed the work and the workforce; we just don't know, because as I mentioned, Suger writes a lot about the building of the abbey church of Saint Denis, including himself going out finding a forest with big enough trees for the wood parts and a quarry with good stone. But he never mentions the day-to-day supervisor, the person that we would call the architect, or the engineers. We just don't know who did it; but it's interesting to think about this.

First of all, here is a manuscript illumination, and what we see is—of course, this isn't a very big church they're building—the building of a church. We see the apse of the church being constructed, and we see his person over on the right—again, this is not a picture of "how we built our cathedral"— but we see somebody over on the right (looking very royal, of course) and supervising. We assume the person who supervised was a little bit more rolled-up with his sleeves than this guy; but nevertheless, somebody had to be the on the scene person, and we know almost nothing about those things. On the other hand, this is a manuscript illumination of the creation of the world. It comes from the 12th century, and isn't it wonderful, because it shows God as an architect with a compass creating the universe. It's at least interesting to think about God as architect with a compass; we can imagine how this image of God would be generated in a world that produced those wonderful Romanesque and Gothic buildings.

As you should not now be surprised, we have almost no names of the people who did the designing. In one case, we do have a name: In 1174, there was a fire at Canterbury Cathedral, and the archbishop and the chapter hired somebody, whose name we know, to rebuild the east end of the church, which was to be built so wonderfully that it would be a fitting monument to hold the relics of the newly-martyred Thomas à Becket. He had been killed in Canterbury Cathedral four years before the fire. We know they hired a man named William of Sens to build this east end of Canterbury Cathedral; we'll come back and look at Canterbury as a building when we look at English Gothic. Notice his name is William of Sens; remember Sens? Sens is the location of the earliest Gothic cathedral. After all, we know only parts of Saint Denis were built, and it was an abbey out in the countryside; but Sens, which we looked at briefly, is the first real Gothic cathedral. It's probably not accidental that they brought somebody; we don't know what William did in Sens, but presumably he had some knowledge or some activity in building this cathedral of Sens.

By the 14th century, we do begin to get some names and even to know a little bit about some architects. In Prague, and we will go to Prague and look at its cathedral later, there actually are busts carved in the cathedral—although they're hard to see with the naked eye; they're way up high and they're small—of the first architect, who didn't get very much work done before he was replaced by this architect: We call him Peter Parler, and I'll talk more about him and his name a little bit later on. But the very fact that we not only have a name but we have an image of him suggests that during the course of the building of these great Gothic cathedrals the reputation, the recognition of skill and genius, of those who designed these buildings is going up; the very fact we have names and, again, this image.

Let's, for a minute, try to imagine that we are on the site of a Gothic cathedral. This is a mockup of what it might look like; this is actually located inside Notre Dame in Paris. But we can see here various kinds of work being done in the construction of this cathedral. We can see in this model people doing various pieces of work; we can see a column almost all the way erected; we can see the base for another column. It's good to use our imagination, and this helps because we have a kind of 3-D image although, again, it's not a photograph of what it would have actually looked like on a worksite. Here's another angle: You see there's a man on top of that column on the right, and you see down below there is this circular wooden thing. It's basically like a wheel that a rat or a mouse runs in but it's powered by humans, and that's used to hoist the stone up; that's where we get some of the power to hoist the stones, by having human power do that in the case of this particular model.

We're back to manuscript illuminations; but look here: We see the building—this turns out to be of a castle rather than a cathedral, but again, that's not the point—we learn something about a medieval building project. We see people with wheelbarrows, people working on stones, and people doing other things; it is a very complicated process because if you think of a cathedral like Notre Dame, Amiens, Chartres, or Reims, all of which were built in relatively short time (a few decades), we have to imagine how many things are going on at the same time. They don't build the building and then somebody says, "Well, let's start the statues"; those are different people, and obviously there are a lot of different activities going on at the same time.

Fortunately, we do have some documentary evidence from the city of Autun. We looked at the largely Romanesque cathedral of Autun in Lecture 5. I pointed out then that, in fact, it had some rebuilding in the Gothic Period, including the huge crossing tower that we saw from a distance when we looked at Autun Cathedral. We have some records from the late 13th century about paying the workforce and hiring the workforce, and so we know some things because of that document from Autun. First of all, not all workers on the cathedral worked at the cathedral. That's especially true with stone. Stone—this is a profound professorial comment—is heavy, and it takes a lot of effort to get stone from one place to another in the quantities that you need to build a cathedral. We're not talking about making a statue or two; we're talking about making thousands of statues along with the building, for example, at Reims Cathedral. So we think that—we know that—a lot of the stone was quarried and then it was cut into the proper shapes at the quarry and then moved to the site, because if you cut the stone after you've moved big chunks then you've carried a lot of weight that doesn't end up in the cathedral and that is a waste of time, it is a waste of money, it is a waste of manpower.

Obviously, stone's the main ingredient; so we can take a look at several illustrations that show us using stone. Here we have a stained glass window at Chartres, and if you look at the center piece and the top piece you will see the carrying of stone and the laying of stone in a big building project. We see people that seem to have impossible loads on their shoulders, so it probably represents the people who are in charge of moving the stone, not the fact that people could lift multiple hundreds of pounds of stone blocks at a time. Here we have another stained glass window from Chartres that shows the building of a tower, and, by the way, notice sitting over on the right side is a statue that's been carved that's going to be ready to go on the cathedral presumably. Here we want to look only at the top half: We again see some cutting of stone, in this case it's done at the site. This may no doubt happen sometimes, especially if the quarry is very close, but it also may represent two different events: the cutting of the stone at the quarry, and then the bringing the stone to the cathedral and putting it into the building.

Here we have a piece of sculpture from the cathedral of Florence that shows a scaffold, a man building a tower and supervising it, and the workers who are actually doing the physical labor. Here was have a mosaic. This comes from Monreale in Sicily that again shows the building of a tower, and notice over on the left we have somebody making mortar. Again, it's more than one job to build a cathedral; it takes more than stone to build a cathedral, as Suger reminds us when he needed a forest as well as needing a quarry. We can see why he needed that forest because we went up in the superstructure, although reconstructed, of Rennes Cathedral, and imagine how much wood would have gone into building that high-pitched roof at Rennes Cathedral, for example, not to mention the wood that's needed for the scaffolding itself and so on. Here again we see a piece of equipment lifting a stone into place; again, these are all various manuscript illuminations that depict, very often, biblical stories. Some of these late medieval manuscript illuminations, the style is more realistic; and so here we really do have a sense of equipment and even some detail of the equipment and some of the complexity of the scaffolding in building in this case a tower, not a cathedral.

I want to show you this image, also a mosaic from Monreale in Sicily. It's actually the building of Noah's Ark, but it reminds us again of the need for woodworkers, for carpenters; and here we see carpenters at work. You can see in the upper right-hand part there is sawing, for example—that's a great big saw that guy has in his hand—because the boat itself, as well as the superstructure on the boat, in this case is being made of wood. In fact, in those documents from Autun we learn about woodcutters; operators of forges because you need a lot of iron; cartwrights because it takes a lot of carters, people moving carts around, to be able to build a cathedral; obviously carpenters; roofers; even candle makers, there are working conditions that are dark and sometimes you work at night; mortar makers; there are enormous numbers of jobs. So supervising the project and the building site was, indeed, highly complex. Sometimes stone, which is so expensive to move, was actually brought by water. There is stone in cathedrals such as Canterbury in England that was actually brought from Normandy by river, across the Channel, to England. We know that much of the stone for the cathedral of Florence was brought on the Arno River to a few miles from Florence and then it was carted from there. We have to appreciate all these sorts of activities in the building of a cathedral.

Let's summarize this part of the lecture by looking at that manuscript I told you we would look at: This is the building of Solomon's Temple; it's an illustration of the Book of Kings in the Old Testament. You see here, of course, it's made to be golden in front—that's why you have the color change there—but you can see there's a Gothic doorway with jamb statues, and you can see people doing various sorts of work on the ground and up above in the building of Solomon's Temple. This is a kind of stylized snapshot, if you will, and perhaps a somewhat idealized stylized snapshot of the building of a Gothic cathedral.

We have to ask, again: Who supervised all this? There must have been some drawings that were made to go on; we don't have any of those drawings. We do have some drawings by a 13th-century architect named Villard de Honnecourt, and he drew pictures of the towers of Laon Cathedral, he drew pictures of the building of the nave of Rennes Cathedral, he drew pictures of various sorts of elements of construction, but we don't know that he actually worked on any cathedral; we don't know that he's responsible for this tower or this part of the nave or the aisle or anything else. But his drawings are, indeed, interesting records. We know that there were things like wooden frames made so that it would make it easier to repeat a pattern or repeat the exact size and shape of cut stone over and over; the shape of a window, the shape of all those little arches in the triforium, wooden models helped to make those more easily replicable, for example.

Apparently, eventually what happened is the man who did the overall design and supervision became separated from the actually workforce, and therefore his number two in command would be the person who takes the instructions from the person in charge and passes them on to the workers; he is the one who is actually out on the site every day carrying out the wishes of, if you will, the grand high poobah sitting somewhere who has designed and has overall supervision powers. Because this second in command did a lot of talking—that is to say, that was his job, to communicate—he very often took the name of the word that means "to speak" in French, "parlay" or *parler*. Remember that we met the architect, the second architect, of Prague Cathedral and his name was Peter Parler, and we know that he came to Prague from Strasbourg, a cathedral we'll look at a little bit later. It is interesting because, in fact, what we want to note is that his name suggests that probably his dad—from whom you take your name—was that second in command guy, and that's a pretty interesting thing for us to note.

At any rate, let me also suggest that we know from documents from Salisbury that the most skilled craftsmen were brought in from the outside (this is not a surprise), and most of the "tote that bar, lift that bale" crowd were locals who were hired seasonally and many of them were also farmers; so they were really busy in the summer because that's the building season and, to a great extent, the farming season as well. We know that eventually lodges were built near the cathedral for the masons, the people who actually put the stone in place; after all, they're sort of the key guys, and there have to be a lot of them once you see the size of these cathedrals. These were not places to live, these were places to meet, these were places to leave equipment, and probably eventually became places where, if you will, their trade secrets were passed on; how they do their work. There are some mason signs; masons sometimes signed individual stones, and some of those still exist within a stone in the walls of a cathedral. But at any rate, later on, especially in England, of course these masonic organizations became kind of secret societies with a great deal of lore to pass on, and it's largely from later versions of the English masons that we get Masonry in the United States.

Ok, who pays for these things? No two cathedrals are built alike; no two cathedrals are funded alike. Notre Dame in Paris, for example, was funded primarily by the king; and we know that sometimes other royals and nobles also funded cathedrals. This is a window in Chartres Cathedral that we have already looked at, and this was paid for by Blanche of Castile who was the Queen of France and the mother of the famous King Louis IX. If you look in the upper part on each side of the rose window, at the bottom of it, you will notice there are designs; those are the coats of arms, or pieces of the coats of arms, of Blanche of Castile. We have another window in Chartres that shows somebody noble; look on the right, you can see that he has his coat of arms there. He is, in fact, paying for the window that tells stories of a saint that are up above. We have royal and noble patronage that we know of.

We need to remember that bishops had a lot of wealth, they owned a lot of land from which they got income, they had some powers to tax—of course, bishops can't tax anyone today, but they had some powers to tax—and it's important to realize, therefore, that much of the money necessary to carry out these projects did, in fact, belong to the church. The church could also offer indulgences; they could offer certain kinds of ways that penalties on earth for sins committed could be taken away by contributing to the building of a church. We have many documents issued by bishops and by the Pope for various indulgences. We also know that sometimes a famous relic would literally be sent out to travel around so that the faithful could come to see it without pilgrimage and, of course, make a donation to the new cathedral where this relic would finally be housed. We know that in Florence and other cities in Italy guilds in the cities actually took over the management of the cathedral project. This is the symbol of the wool guild of Florence, and you will see it in the cathedral because they were in charge, not the bishop, in the cathedral. That's unusual, and really only in Italy.

But we know that in many cases, in most cases if you will, a lot of the work was paid for by groups of people contributing, especially, since these are urban institutions and urban places for the cathedrals, the guilds. This is illustrated by the fact that in many of the stained glass windows of Chartres—we looked at the substance, the content, of them—down at the bottom of many of those windows are pictures of the guild donors. Here we see stained glass window makers; they are offering a stained glass window, and therefore they paid for the particular window that we see here. Or sculptors; you can see the stoneworkers there working on a couple statues, jamb statues it looks like. Or water carriers, a more humble profession; so that we see here various people in the process of doing the work of water carriers. Here we have shoemakers; and by the way, there are several illustrations of shoemakers because there's the making of a shoe and there's the trying on of a shoe. We also have some very good social history in these windows. Here we have the butchers; see that nice cow head and that raw meat sitting on the table. Here we have the farriers; those who are, in this case, making horseshoes and putting the horseshoes on a horse. Here we have a furrier, and he has a beautiful ermine coat there and we see him showing it to a customer in this particular piece of the window. We get these wonderful glimpses of these folks who not as individuals like a noble or a queen but collectively came together to pay for windows and have themselves in some way memorialized and honored in those windows, and very often the windows contain the stories of the patron saints of those guilds.

Even with these sources of funding, it's important to say that while some cathedrals were built quickly, many others were not. Some were built in fits and starts over a long period of time; some were built and then the next building phase a different style comes in, so we have a mixture of styles; some never got finished in the Middle Ages. Prague and Cologne cathedrals, which we'll look at, were both finished in the 19th century; only the choirs were done in the Middle Ages. Again, in every aspect of the building of these cathedrals, there are as many stories—if we just had all the evidence—as there are cathedrals; but at least we can give a kind of overview and look at some examples of how these buildings were built.

Now we're ready to go on our tour of Late Gothic France, followed by our tour around Europe—and again, briefly beyond to the New World—to take a look at still more wonderful Gothic cathedrals.

New Developments in Gothic France
Lecture 17

Bourges is one of the very best of all the Gothic cathedrals. But again, it doesn't seem to be in the line of Chartres, Amiens, Rennes. ... Although there are many things about Bourges that make us recognize it as part of the tradition, equally and especially architecturally, there are things that make Bourges different.

In this lecture, we cease to focus on single structures and start surveying a variety of churches, to reinforce the many directions the Gothic took in the later 13th century. We begin at Bourges, south of Paris. The cathedral of Bourges is one of the very best of all the Gothic cathedrals. From outside, your first impression might be that we're missing something. This is the only huge Gothic cathedral with no transept, and so we get an extraordinary uninterrupted line of buttressing from the facade all the way around the ambulatory. We see several levels of windows and two aisles on either side of the nave. Because Bourges is built into the side of a hill, the crypt—one of the biggest of all the Gothic crypts—is partly visible above ground. In the facade, we have not three but five portals, covered in sculpture. Bourges is unusual in a lot of ways, and yet if we look at the facade sculpture, it looks pretty familiar both in form and content.

Inside Bourges, you can see how high the vaults are. The nave has six-part vaults, a return to an earlier style, whereas the aisles have the newer four-part vaults. We also see one of the most unusual elevations of any Gothic cathedral: There are the expected aisle, triforium, and clerestory windows, but the aisle is extraordinarily high. On closer inspection, we have two sets of elevations, one within the other; aisle and nave each have their own three-part elevation. Finally, we see that the pillars supporting the six-part vaults are essentially alike, rather than alternating as in older structures.

Remember that the glazed triforium was first seen at Saint-Denis, in the nave and transept started around 1231. In this configuration, the triforium and the clerestory can be seen as a unit. In fact, we're going to see that the triforium and the clerestory will merge in the late Gothic. Saint-Denis's transept also

© Photos.com/Thinkstock.

King Louis IX, later Saint Louis, commissioned Sainte-Chapelle to house the relics he brought back from the Crusades.

lacks the horizontal lines seen at Chartres and Amiens. It has stronger verticals, emphasizing loftiness. We will see this also in late Gothic.

The cathedral of Troyes, a city south of Paris, was begun in 1220, but construction was interrupted by storm damage in the late 1220s, and ultimately construction continued into the 1600s. The facade is lopsided, with no right-hand tower, and much of the original sculpture was destroyed in bouts of anti-Catholic fervor. Inside, however, the building is filled with light. It was the first cathedral with a glazed triforium all the way around—nave, transept, and choir. There's almost no stone in the clerestory, just what's needed to hold the glass in. Some of the windows are modern, although next to Chartres, Troyes contains one of the most valuable collections of medieval stained glass in existence.

North of Paris, we find the cathedral of Beauvais, which boasts the highest of all Gothic vaults at about 159 feet. The nave of Beauvais is Carolingian, and the transept was built in the 16th century, so only the choir survives. The choir was finished in 1272, and most of the four-part vaulting collapsed in 1284; those sections were replaced with six-part vaults. Like at Amiens, our second-tallest Gothic cathedral, the windows are huge, and the vaults seem to float. The buttressing is elaborate, allowing all that glass in the windows, and was reinforced in modern times.

Let's look at one more church—a small chapel this time, rather than a cathedral. The chapel of Sainte-Chapelle on the Ile de la Cité in Paris is a close neighbor to Notre Dame and was once part of a royal palace. Today it stands in the middle of the Ministry of Justice complex and thus is a bit hard to find. The chapel was built by King **Louis IX**—that is, Saint Louis. He was an extraordinarily pious man, in many ways epitomizing the ideal of Christian kingship in the Middle Ages. He fed the poor, he promoted scholars, and he died on Crusade. In 1239, Louis bought one of the most precious of all Christian relics from the emperor in Constantinople: the alleged Crown of Thorns, which unfortunately was destroyed during the French Revolution. Sainte-Chapelle was built as its reliquary.

> **Next to Chartres, Troyes contains one of the most valuable collections of medieval stained glass in existence.**

Sainte-Chapelle is essentially a two-story glass box. The lower story is a fairly dark chapel. Upstairs is almost entirely stained glass. The rose window in the west end is probably from the 15th century, but a little more than half the glass in these windows is original, despite the destruction wrought during the revolution. Some windows are about 50 feet high; some contain more than 100 different tales, most from the Old Testament. A few are medieval legends. One scene of Moses and the Burning Bush gives us an unusually good view of the lead **tracery** that holds the glass together. ■

Important Term

tracery: The lead or stone into which the pieces of a stained-glass window are fitted.

Name to Know

Louis IX (r. 1226–1270): King of France who obtained Christ's Crown of Thorns and commissioned Sainte-Chapelle on the Ile de la Cité to hold this prized relic.

Suggested Reading

Frankl, *Gothic Architecture*, chaps. 3.1, 3.4.

Murray, *Beauvais Cathedral*.

Stoddard, *Art and Architecture in Medieval France*, chap. 22.

Wilson, *The Gothic Cathedral*, chap. 3.

Questions to Consider

1. What are some of the features that make Bourges Cathedral an alternative to Chartres?

2. Is the nave of Saint-Denis as important for the development of later Gothic as the choir and narthex were for earlier Gothic?

3. How does the function of Sainte-Chapelle help to determine its unique form?

New Developments in Gothic France
Lecture 17—Transcript

As I mentioned in the previous lecture, we're going to change tactics to some extent; not because I simply want to do different things or have different rhythms to the course, but because the development of Gothic calls for a different rhythm. We have spent a lot of time on just a few of the extraordinarily important High Gothic—again, we might even say Classic Gothic—churches and now what we're going to do is more of a survey, first with Bourges Cathedral, a very interesting place, essentially contemporary with Rennes and Amiens but looking very different; if you will, a different alternative to the Gothic that we've seen developing in Chartres, Amiens, and Rennes. Then we're going to look at some later-13th century developments, and to do that we need to go to several different places to examine those developments. That's our plan for this lecture, and I think you'll find it is a good plan.

We begin in the city of Bourges, south of Paris, an important city; and the cathedral of Bourges is one of the very best of all the Gothic cathedrals. But again, it doesn't seem to be in the line of Chartres, Amiens, Rennes; it's a somewhat different tradition. We can see that from the very beginning just looking at this cathedral from a beautiful garden that's adjacent to it. (If you want to take pretty pictures with flowers in the foreground to your Gothic cathedrals, as you can see, go to Bourges in the summertime.) But here we have the cathedral of Bourges; and you might say to yourself: We're missing something. Of course, what we're missing is a transept. This is the only one of the huge Gothic cathedrals that has no transept; and so we get an extraordinary look at the buttressing because it's not interrupted, in a sense, from the west facade all the way around the ambulatory.

Let's move around a little bit: Look at that row of buttresses; we don't ever have a row quite that long because that row is interrupted by the transept in other Gothic cathedrals. If we look here, straight at the south side of the nave—of course, there really isn't a transept—of Bourges, we see several levels of windows; we see there really are two aisles on either side. We saw that in Notre Dame, but that was not the pattern of Chartres, Amiens, and Rennes; and so this is also a very wide cathedral, and we'll see how that impacts the facade in just a minute. Here is the rear of Bourges Cathedral—you can see, by the way, that it doesn't have towers on both sides of the front; that it's going to be asymmetrical when we get around to the front—but again we see the windows at various levels and these almost oar-like buttresses of Bourges. Here, as we just move around a little bit, we see those levels of windows; and because Bourges is actually built in the side of a hill, that big crypt of Bourges—one of the biggest of all the crypts—is, in fact, partly visible because part of the crypt is above ground because of the fact that the church is built on the side of a hill. We're at the downside of the hill, and to make it all the same height you have to have this aboveground as well as in-ground crypt.

As I said, when we move around to the front what we notice is this is sort of a different place, because it has—count them—five entrances, five front portals, all of which have a good deal of sculpture on them. Not three like at Chartres, Amiens, or Rennes, but five portals wide. There's a door into the nave, there's a door into each of the principal aisles, and there's a door into each of the secondary aisles. Again, Bourges is just different in a lot of ways; and yet if we look at the sculpture in the central portal at Bourges, it looks pretty familiar both in the form—jamb statues, tympanum, archivolts, and whatever—but also in content, because this is (surprise, surprise) the Last Judgment. So although there are many things about Bourges that make us recognize it as part of the tradition, equally and especially architecturally, there are things that make Bourges different. By the way, there are many people, including scholars and art historians, who love Bourges and see the alternative as at least as interesting and beautiful as the standard that is set at Chartres and then passed on to Amiens and Rennes.

Here is the interior: It soars, as you can see, as do other cathedrals. You will immediately see how high the aisles are; and if you glance up at the vaults rather than look toward the altar for a minute you will see that's not the kind of vaults we have at Chartres, Amiens, and Rennes; we are back to the six-part vaults that we saw in places like Laon, for example. Again, we have certain elements that are old—this older kind of vaulting—along with this extraordinarily expansive aisle and the double aisles that give it its wideness. We are used to those vaults from, again, the early period of Gothic, but here they are the choice at Bourges. There are alternatives; Chartres has the alternative of the rectangular, four-part vault. Here, the architects at Bourges show this older, six-part vault. Here we are looking down one of the aisles, and now we're looking across this cathedral; we're not looking down, we're looking across. We're in one aisle, and then we look through that aisle; there's another aisle, then there's the nave, and we look over to the other side. One of the things we can do is see extraordinary ways of vaulting. Here, for example, if you look, on the right we have the vault of the second aisle, then the vault of the first aisle—they're both four-part vaults—and then, just to the far left in this photograph, we see part of the vault of the nave; so we have the six-part vault, four-part vault, four-part vault. Isn't that an extraordinary picture; a way of looking at various sorts of vaulting and three different levels of Gothic vaulting in the same building?

Let's look across and see one of the most unusual but beautiful elements of Bourges Cathedral. Let's look at the elevation: First of all, we have this extraordinarily high aisle; and then we have a triforium, although you can see it's designed somewhat differently than the triforia we've seen other places; and then the clerestory windows. But wait a minute; look within the aisle: Within the aisle, we have the second aisle, a more traditional triforium, and a set of clerestory windows; we have two sets of elevations, one within the other, so that we have windows in the second aisle, windows in what we would call the clerestory of the aisle, and then windows in the clerestory of the nave. We have light coming in three places and we have a total of six levels of elevation, three within three; it is a design unlike any other. Here we look down the principal aisle: It is narrow, but as we've seen by looking at different angles it's extraordinarily high and has its three-part elevation within it. Again, I want you to look from an aisle to an aisle into the nave into an aisle, and then at the very bottom of this photograph we just see the second aisle; so because, thank goodness, we have good telephoto lenses we can see five separate sections across this cathedral: aisle, aisle, nave, aisle, aisle. Again, nothing like it.

Whenever you walk around a cathedral, again, you want to look at a lot of different angles; look at the stone. Remember, this is a six-part vault; but as you can see, each of the pillars is essentially alike (there actually are slight variations). It doesn't have that alternation like at Sens or at Laon; it is virtually the same, pillar to pillar to pillar, and yet we know that the pillar supports differentially because there's the major transverse arch and then there's the middle part of the six-part vault and, of course, they alternate. Now we're looking into the choir, into the apse, of Bourges Cathedral.

Moving from Bourges—which, again, is essentially contemporary with Amiens and Rennes—we want to move forward just a little bit in time. Remember we saw that the choir of Amiens Cathedral had a glazed triforium, and that it allowed in another layer of light. The place that it first developed was not at Amiens, but it was at Saint Denis. Remember that Suger built the front and the back of Saint Denis, but not the middle; the middle in Suger's time remained a rickety Carolingian church. Beginning in 1231, that was replaced, and it was replaced by this new nave—and transept, I might add—and even upper part of the choir; all that comes from beginning in the fourth decade of the 13th century. It is extraordinary because look not only at the glazed triforium, look at the clerestory windows: They are essentially taking up all of the space of the clerestory; look at that. Here we see the choir—again, this is on Suger's ambulatory—but we can see how these windows are so large and filled full of figures. Now, all of the stained glass is modern; none of the stained glass we're going to see here at Saint Denis is original. But there is the glazed triforium, and you see how the triforium and the clerestory together really can be seen as a unit; I've taken this picture especially to see it framed by the pillars and then by the base of the triforium, and if you saw this out of context—which I've tried to make you do here—what you could say is, "Ah, there is a unit of architecture between the lower windows and the upper windows." That's what's going opt happen: Eventually, we're going to see that the triforium and the clerestory are essentially going to merge into one unit; and in some churches later on, the triforium will disappear into just these much elongated and larger windows.

Here we see the transept of Saint Denis; again, the transept as well as the nave, which is on the left, are all new beginning in 1231. Here, another thing we want to notice: Remember how we've seen at Chartres and Amiens—I emphasized this in both—what we really have is verticals and horizontals sort of constantly interplaying with one another. Remember that beautiful stringcourse at Amiens that was carved with leaves? Look here: We stand at the base of this pillar and look up to the vault, and nothing interrupts us; it goes straight up. This has stronger verticals, in a sense uninterrupted by horizontals; and so we always know there's an emphasis on verticality and height in Gothic cathedrals, but here we really see that instead of that very interesting interplay of having our eyes go toward the altar and go up, here the architecture really encourages us to look up. Again, we know that much of Saint Denis, front and back, are the beginning of Gothic; and so Saint Denis is sort of an odd building because it has pieces of very early, beginning Gothic style and then it has the nave and the transepts in this newer style.

Now we're going to go to a cathedral, although it was begun in 1200 there was a huge storm that did great damage to it in the late 1220s and it sort of began again, and this is the cathedral of Troyes, a city south of Paris. By the way, a beautiful city; a city that's way, I think, under-visited by cultural tourists. It has a cathedral; it has other important monuments including other Gothic churches we're going to look at in the following lecture. You can see here from the facade that it's sort of lopsided—or it looks lopsided; it doesn't have a tower on the right side—and you can also see that sculpture's gone; more sculpture that was destroyed in various times of anti-Catholic fervor. But Troyes is a beautiful city with a beautiful cathedral; and it does have a lot of tourists, just not cultural tourists: It's the shopping mall capital of France; it has all the outlet malls that surround this beautiful and lovely city.

Let's go inside: The cathedral of Troyes is the first cathedral that's fully filled with light because of the fact that all around it—nave, transept, and choir—all of it has the glazed triforium. You can see that as we look to the east end because you can see the windows in the chapels around the ambulatory, then you can see the glazed triforium, then you can see the clerestory windows; so this is just full of extraordinary light. Again, we see these windows where there's almost no stone in the clerestory; the stone basically just is to hold the glass in. here we look up from an aisle into these wonderful windows; so again, I always like to look at a lot of different angles so that we can look at this architecture from many different places. Not just walk in, snap a couple shots, walk around to make sure you aren't missing a big thing in the cathedral, and then walk out; I think sometimes when I'm inside a cathedral for two or three hours I will have walked three quarters of a mile without ever leaving the building because I just want to see it from everywhere.

Here's a straighter shot of these windows with the triforium and, in this case, also obviously these big clerestory windows. Here is the choir; look how light it is. By "light" here I don't mean "light" as in "airy," but I mean "light" as opposed to "dark." You can see there are many stained glass windows in place. Some are modern, although there's a lot of medieval stained glass at Troyes; in fact, next to Chartres, it is one of the most valuable collections of stained glass. There are many reasons I would recommend seeing this cathedral and this town, but the glass, as well as the architecture, is one of them. In fact, I'm just going to show you a couple stories here from the glass to remind us we have good 13th-century glass in places other than Chartres. Again, Chartres is numero uno, but in the world of medieval stained glass the places that have, if you will, the second-, third-, or fourth-best collection of stained glass have extraordinary things; and we don't want to fall into that "I'll go see the superstar cathedral and then I will have seen everything." Even if that superstar cathedral is Chartres with its architecture, its sculpture, and its windows, get out; get out and see a variety of buildings if you have a chance to travel to France. Here we have a stained glass window that shows Jesus, Mary, and Joseph in the flight into Egypt. Here we have a story: If you look in the lower circular piece there we have Jesus curing a sick man, and then up above we have Jesus performing an exorcism; so you can see the demon flying out of that possessed person right above that possessed person's head. Again, what we have is an extraordinary variety of stories, Old Testament and New Testament—I just showed you New Testament here—saints' lives, and all the rest; so there's a lot to learn in terms of the beauty of the glass and also in the stories of the glass here at the cathedral of Troyes.

Now we journey north of Paris to Beauvais; in fact, Beauvais is an alternate airport for Paris, although it's about 70 kilometers from Paris. Beauvais has a claim: It has the highest Gothic vaults, period. We're going to enter through the transept. The nave of Beauvais is Carolingian; we saw a picture of it way back when in Lecture 2 when we were talking about the first thousand years of Christian building. The transept, such as we're looking at here, was built in the 16th century; so only the choir survives. It was finished in 1272—the choir was—and in 1284, most of the vaulting collapsed. The vaulting of the choir was rebuilt with some structural changes obviously; and so at about 159 feet, the vaults of Beauvais Cathedral are the highest of any Gothic building. We enter through this really late Gothic, quite elaborate transept, and we begin to walk around the cathedral. There's not much of it because, again, we really only are going to look at the choir; we're not even going to spend any more time in the transept.

But as we get a look toward the choir, as we walk into the transept and begin to look through the columns as the transept meets the choir, we see something extraordinary. Notice we have huge clerestory windows, really in two sections, and then two other levels of light. Look at that; I mean, you know by now I'm an Amiens fan, and when we were looking at Amiens I talked several times about how the cathedral of Amiens just soars. This is basically another 20 feet higher than the vaults of Amiens, and we're looking up in the choir. The very east part—that is to say, the vault right at the east end—that, in fact, is the original vault finished in 1272. The others are replacements; in fact, originally the vault was in four parts, and when they replaced it—again, partly to make it structurally more likely to survive and not fall down again—it was replaced by six-part vaults as you can see; sort of odd-shaped ones, because they're still fairly rectangular rather than more square as the traditional ones were at Bourges and earlier on at places like Laon.

Everywhere you look, I mean, the aisle is something like 70 feet high; and so inside the aisle we look out into the choir of Beauvais and we can stand by one of the pillars and look up, and it's this extraordinary scene. It's another one of those places where I keep having to tell myself, although I perfectly well know this and so do you by now, that roof that seems to be floating in light is made out of rocks; and so one of the questions we're going to have to ask as we go outside Beauvais Cathedral is: What does this buttressing system look like? It looks pretty elaborate, as it turns out. Look at those buttresses, and look at the windows. Again, we see the levels of light and we are aware that these buttresses do an awful lot of the holding up of that roof because the walls are made of glass; what an extraordinary notion.

These buttresses really seem to fly. Now you can see they've been reinforced in modern times by these rods; this is a very delicate building. I don't think you have to worry that it might fall in on you when you walk in, but obviously this is a building that's had some tough times and it perhaps really does stretch the limits of what the technology of Gothic can do. Here we see a buttress with a gargoyle on one piece of it and all these other decorations alongside of it. Beauvais, although it's a short visit because there really is no sculpture there, there's very little stained glass windows that will be of interest to most people, and not a very big space, it's a "wow"; it really is one of those "aha" moments we have, even for those of us who are used to doing Gothic and are used to being in extraordinary, awesome places.

We're going to finish off by looking at a spectacularly interesting, very small church. First of all, it is not a cathedral. We've been pretty much being doing cathedrals and cathedrals alone for a while. Let me suggest that especially in the next lecture we're going to be looking at some Gothic churches that are not cathedrals: We're going to be looking at monasteries and parish churches. When we travel around Europe and leave France finally, we are going to be looking at different kinds of buildings, primarily cathedrals but college chapels, royal chapel, parish churches, and churches that belong to religious orders in cities, in particular when we look at a Franciscan and a Dominican church in Florence. We might want to adjust to the fact that not every Gothic building is a cathedral, even though most of the buildings we've looked at are that. Of course, we also know the first Gothic building—or at least the first Gothic pieces—that is to say, at Saint Denis, we know that Saint Denis is (or was) a Benedictine monastery and not a cathedral.

This is the chapel of Sainte Chapelle, the Holy Chapel. It stands on the Ile de la Cité in Paris, therefore is shares an island with Notre Dame; in fact, it's just a couple blocks away. It's very hard to see today because most of the royal palace, of which this was a part in the Middle Ages, has been destroyed; there is a piece of it left that one can visit as a museum. But what's replaced the royal palace is large government buildings, and, in fact, this is inside the Ministry of Justice building on the Ile de la Cité (or, rather, the complex of buildings that is the Ministry of Justice). Therefore, when you go in, you not only have to buy your ticket, but you also have to go through a metal detector because you're going to be in a place that's important in the French government and has to be protected. So Sainte Chapelle, if you don't know it's there, you're not going to find it; and although it's obviously present in the guidebooks and people who know Paris know it's one of the real gems, it isn't of the size of Notre Dame, but in magnificence, it gets an "A."

The chapel was built by King Louis IX. Louis IX is Saint Louis (San Louis) and he was king from 1226–1270. You may recall that his mother, Blanche of Castile, paid for the window in the north transept of Chartres Cathedral. Louis IX was an extraordinarily pious man; in many ways he comes closest perhaps to epitomizing the ideal of Christian kingships in the Middle Ages. He fed the poor, and sometimes dined with the poor; he promoted scholars, he had dinner from time to time with the professor over on the Left Bank named Thomas Aquinas; he was a holy man, in fact he died on Crusade, he died in the city of Tunis in what's now Tunisia on the way to trying to capture (unsuccessfully, I might add) the Holy Land. In 1239, Louis bought one of the most precious of all Christian relics from the emperor in Constantinople, who was at that time a Latin-speaking emperor—there was a lull in the Greek-speaking emperors between 1204 and 1261 when Latin emperors ruled in Constantinople—from that emperor, Louis IX bought the crown of thorns. I think, today, many people, whether it's the head of Saint John the Baptist, or the cloak of the Virgin Mary, or the crown of thorns, people want to say, "How do you know; is this genuine?" Of course, the quick answer is, "We don't know for sure." By the way, that crown of thorns that he bought in 1239 was destroyed during the French Revolution, so we don't have it anymore to try to do some sort of testing at least to see if we can date it properly.

But at any rate, what do you do with a crown of thorns? The answer is: You build a spectacular reliquary to put it in; and Sainte Chapelle is that reliquary. It is essentially a glass box, and it's in two stories, as you can see when looking at the facade. The lower story is actually a fairly dark chapel and was used for the staff of the palace of the king. We climb a stair and this is what we come into: a room filled with stained glass windows. We're looking at the apse, at the place in front of which there would have been a smaller reliquary containing the crown of thorns. Here we look the other direction; you can see that the walls are just big stained glass windows. The rose window that we look at in the west end of Sainte Chapelle is, in fact, probably 15th century, so it's newer than the windows on the side; and a little more than half the glass in these windows is original despite the fact of the French Revolution that, among other things, took all the relics—there were other relics than just the crown of thorns—out of here.

The windows (some of them) are about 50 feet high; look at that. Some of them contain more than 100 stories; and, as you would expect, not every window has the same pattern. If we take a look at this window we can see it has a different configuration of how the stories are arranged than the window we just looked at. Most of the stories, by the way, are Old Testament stories and some of them really are quite obscure; I sat scratching my head trying to remember my book of Leviticus and Numbers when I was there a few months ago. It's difficult to decode the stories. But we can see some stories here that we can recognize. This is a story that takes place actually in Jerusalem: it is the emperor Heraclius, a 7th-century emperor, bringing the true cross—it was much bigger than that, obviously—back to Jerusalem after he had captured it from the Persians who had captured it from Jerusalem; so it's a famous story about the true cross. Here we have a story of the moving of the Ark of the Covenant, and you can see in this stained glass window Moses because, as we've learned, Moses has horns in medieval iconography. Here we have the vision of Ezekiel; so we see the wheel within a wheel in the right side of this quatrefoil. Here we see David with the very bloody head of Goliath, holding the head by the hair in his left hand.

I want to end with this; again, we're just being very selective in looking at Sainte Chapelle. This is the story of Moses and the Burning Bush—you can see God in the Burning Bush—but the reason I put this in as the last picture for us to look at is because of the angle at which I took this you can see all the leading; you can see all the pieces of lead that hold the glass together. It's called "tracery," and this lead allows us to have all these pictures put into place by these small sections of glass. I wanted you to see that; I talked about it when we looked at the windows of Chartres, but this gives us a good example of how we can see all that leading that's going on there.

We've taken a look now at a series of 13th-century Gothic buildings. Now we're going to move on to the 14th, 15th, and early 16th centuries and see what the last flourishes of Gothic looked like in France.

Late Gothic Churches in France
Lecture 18

> We're used to learning our history in periods—there's the Middle Ages, then there's the Renaissance. … We think of Gothic as a medieval form of architecture, and therefore when the Middle Ages ends so should the Gothic period end. There are a lot of problems with that, because we know that, in fact, history is more continuous than we sometimes imagine when we read the history books.

W e talk about the development of humanism thought in Italy by the middle of the 14th century, and we usually think of the Renaissance, at least in Florence, in high gear by about 1400 or so. Italy moved into a new style of architecture around the 1420s. But we need to remember that while these cultural shifts took hold in Florence, the rest of Europe remained medieval in thought and style for quite a long time. Gothic architecture and art in fact continued in France until the early 16th century.

The late 13th-century style we discussed in the previous lecture is often referred to as the **rayonnant** style; most of the buildings we're looking at now are what we call **flamboyant** Gothic. The word "flamboyant" comes largely from the designs of rose windows. Compare the rose windows of Chartres and Troyes, for example. The stone tracery at Troyes is somewhat more elaborate and decorative. Also at Troyes, we see that the decoration of the central portal archivolts overlaps into the next layer of the architecture; that's going to become more and more characteristic of the flamboyant style. We saw this in the 16th-century transept of Beauvais as well.

The cathedral of Rouen, in northwestern France, is perhaps best known from Monet's paintings of the facade. Most visitors walk around the cathedral on its south side because of the lovely park and beautiful views of the building. Around the north side, there are just some attached buildings, so it may seem an unattractive view, but careful exploration reveals a little street that dead -ends in the north transept, which has some interesting decoration. The Last Judgment over the center portal is somewhat damaged but has some interesting details that illustrate some developments in medieval sculpture. On the side of the saved, the bodies move lyrically; they have independent facial expressions, rather than uniform happiness. We also have low-relief panels in addition to the sort of decoration we have seen elsewhere.

There are several other late Gothic churches in Rouen that are really quite extraordinary, such as the 14th-century monastic church of Saint-Ouen. Although parts of the facade were not finished until the 19th century, we see many flamboyant

© iStockphoto/Thinkstock.

The cathedral of Rouen offers many interesting views besides the facade made famous by Monet.

features: the stonework in the rose window over the entrance; linear, upward-surging spires on the flying buttresses; larger, almost bulging chapels on the east end. Inside, the windows are enormous proportionate to the walls, and the triforium and clerestory almost blend. The pillars have no horizontal lines. The vaults remain simple, four-part ones. A few blocks away is the smaller church of Saint-Maclou, another local saint like Ouen. This church has a very large crossing tower and a facade with five portals, like at Bourges. The figure of Jesus in the Last Judgment portal sculpture is less formally posed than we're used to. The design of the facade points upward, and, unusually, it is slightly curved; there is more opportunity for experimentation when you're dealing with smaller scales.

In Troyes, the small church of Saint-Urbain was begun in the 13th century by Pope Urban IV, a city native. We've talked about how in this later style, everything points upward, but this church has two very powerful horizontals on the front in addition to its very strong verticals. The south porch is elaborate and very odd: From close up, it looks sort of jumbled, but standing back, we see an overhang upheld by buttresses, almost like a free-standing structure. Inside, we have two levels of light; the triforium has become a set of large lancet windows with a division two-thirds of the way down. The nave has no triforium at all.

At Troyes, we see that the decoration of the central portal archivolts overlaps into the next layer of the architecture; that's going to become more and more characteristic of the flamboyant style.

Down the street, we visit the church of Mary Magdalene. On the south side of this church we see big windows in the aisle and a tower on the right side. Except for those big windows, this is a fairly standard 13th-century church: We have an aisle, and a blind triforium, and clerestory windows that don't quite fill the whole space. One of the church's most interesting features is its stained-glass windows, which illustrate the shift from purely colored glass to painted glass.

Finally, we move to the church of Saint-Étienne (that is, Saint Stephen), in Beauvais, across town from the cathedral. The nave is early Gothic, as you can see from the smallish clerestory windows. But the east end is almost blindingly bright because of the late Gothic approach to windows. Notice there is no triforium at all, just huge clerestory windows above the aisle. The stained glass shows an extraordinary expressiveness in the figures; we are in a whole new visual world. ■

Important Terms

flamboyant: The late Gothic style in France, featuring, among other things, tracery in rose windows that is flame-shaped.

rayonnant: French term for the style of Gothic architecture and decoration that developed around the middle of the 13th century.

Suggested Reading

Frankl, *Gothic Architecture*, chaps. 3.9, 3.12, 4.6, 4.7, 4.10, 4.12.

Murray, *Beauvais Cathedral*.

———, *Building Troyes Cathedral*.

Stoddard, *Art and Architecture in Medieval France*, chaps. 26–27.

Wilson, *The Gothic Cathedral*, chap. 3.

Questions to Consider

1. Are the late Gothic churches of France something of a letdown after the age of the building of such massive cathedrals?

2. How do you respond to the decorative qualities and even playfulness of the flamboyant Gothic churches and windows?

3. Did the Gothic style "run out of steam" or somehow become decadent at the end of the Middle Ages in France?

Late Gothic Churches in France
Lecture 18—Transcript

Let me start with a little bit of chronology: We're used to learning our history in periods—there's the Middle Ages, then there's the Renaissance—and very often (and I think somewhat wrongly) we think of the Renaissance as the rejection of the Middle Ages whole cloth. I don't think that's so; but one of the issues is we think of Gothic as a medieval form of architecture, and therefore when the Middle Ages ends so should the Gothic period end. There are a lot of problems with that, because we know that, in fact, history is more continuous than we sometimes imagine when we read the history books. But let's remember a little bit of chronology, and then apply it from Italy—the birthplace of the Renaissance—to France.

We talk about the development of humanism or humanist thought in Italy by the middle of the 14th century, especially associated with the name Petrarch; and we usually think of the Renaissance, at least in Florence, in high gear by about 1400 or so. Let me suggest, however, that it did not have an architectural phase; in other words, we really don't move into a new style of architecture, even in Florence, until the 1420s, and we associate that with the name of Filippo Brunelleschi who, among other things, designed the dome of the cathedral of Florence. But we need to remember that when humanism and a new form of architecture take hold in Florence, that does not mean that Europe becomes a Renaissance place; and, in fact, many forms of medieval thought and style last a lot longer outside Florence—and later on Venice and Rome, and other places in Italy—than they do in the Italian peninsula. So what I want to suggest is that we really need to recognize that Gothic architecture and art continues in France until the early 16th century.

A couple things to remember about that: Again, the Renaissance, as a set of ideas and art forms, arrives later in France than it does in various parts of Italy spreading from Florence. For example, in the early 16th century, King Francis I invited Leonardo da Vinci to come to France, and indeed he did and died there in 1519. But also let's remember that the new Renaissance style of art and architecture from Italy is foreign in France. They'll catch the Italian bug eventually, all of Europe does; but the Gothic style is first and foremost, of course, a French style, born and bred and practiced in France, and so the

Gothic lasts a lot longer—although with many changes and some influences from Italy—in France than it does in other parts of Europe, especially in the Mediterranean. We're going to be looking at some 14th-, 15th-, and even 16th-century Gothic churches and Gothic decorations in this lecture.

In the last lecture, when we talked about the developments in the later 13th century where I especially emphasized the importance of the glazed triforium and the extended light that we have because of that, I did not give that style a name, and I'll confess why: I don't like the term very much. But we do call that style the rayonnant style; that is to say, that style that we associate with Saint Denis (the nave) and the cathedral of Troyes. I do want you to be familiar with that term. Most of what we're going to look at today is, in fact, what we call "flamboyant Gothic"; the latest Gothic style or collection of styles in France. We have, starting with Saint Denis (to review), the beginnings of Gothic, and we talk about the first more or less 50 years as early Gothic (Notre Dame, Laon, and whatever); then we talk about the high Gothic (that's Chartres, Amiens, and Rennes); then we talk about the rayonnant period, which we covered in the last lecture; and finally today we're going to focus on this flamboyant style.

The word "flamboyant" comes largely from the designs of rose windows. You may recall what the rose window with the lancets below it looked like in Chartres Cathedral, for example. I want you to look at this 14th-century transept from the cathedral of Troyes—we looked at Troyes but we did not look at this piece of it—and you can see that the stained glass window pattern is somewhat more elaborate, the tracery (in this case the stone tracery) is more elaborate and decorative than it was in the style of Chartres, for example. Let me also suggest another aspect of the later Gothic style. This is the facade—alas, again, if you recall all the sculpture's been destroyed. Notice what happens, look at the central portal: You can see that there is some decoration above the archivolts and that actually overlaps into the next layer of the architecture, and there's a lot of that interweaving and overlapping; that's going to become more and more characteristic of the flamboyant style. You may recall when we were at Amiens we looked briefly at the transept, which I pointed out was built later—or at least the windows were put in later—and here we really begin to see that flamboyant style, a much more decorated, dynamic motion-filled, almost, set of tracery and glass patterns that we see. So those are some things we can look for and develop: more elaborate tracery of windows, more dramatic patterns, and a lot more decorative style on the exterior including pieces of decoration that don't go from layer to layer to layer like Chartres or Amiens but overlap one another in a more dynamic and perhaps dramatic style.

Let's begin first at the cathedral of Rouen, which is in northwestern France, and this picture itself is important for me to say something about. When you stand in front of the cathedral of Rouen—which many people like to do, in part because of the Monet paintings of the facade of Rouen Cathedral in various times of the day—you discover if you walk along the south side there is a lovely park and you can stand back and take beautiful pictures, and therefore when people walk around the cathedral, that's the direction they go. If you walk around the north side of Rouen Cathedral there are buildings attached to the cathedral, and you sort of say to yourself, "Well, I don't want to walk along there, I won't be able to see the cathedral." But if you do walk along that side—and this is, again, a good reminder about how to explore a cathedral—you discover there is a north porch and that it's accessed by a little and narrow street off the street you're walking along as you're basically out of sight of the cathedral, and if you walk down that little bitty street that dead ends in the north transept as we see here we get some interesting things, some interesting decoration. You can see the window above, and you can also see how the piece of architecture over the portal sculpture again penetrates up into that space that we would normally see reserved for a clear view of the glass.

While we're here, let's stop and look at this sculpture, even though it's somewhat damaged. It's a Last Judgment, as you can see. We have the resurrection of the dead below and the separation of the good guys from the bad guys in the middle and, of course, the upper part, as you can see, is missing. But I want to look at a couple details because I want to say a little bit about some sculptural developments. Here we have the saved, and if you look at them—of course, saved are happy—these are very sweet-looking saved people; that is to say, remember we're used to seeing the saved sort of marching off, looking happy to be sure, to the gate of Heaven. Here we see them sort of embracing and we see the bodies moving more lyrically; we see different kinds of expressions on their faces. This is, again, a development of a later style of Gothic sculpture; some would say a warmer style, a more emotional style. On the other side, things look a lot more like we're used to: boiling pots, devils getting people, and all that sort of thing. I also want to point out that along the doors we have these interesting low-relief panels as an extra part of the decoration; so in addition to the jamb statues, the tympanum, and the archivolts we have another kind of decoration that's been employed here. This is just simply one detail of a centaur to give you an idea of the development of some of this late Gothic style of decoration and sculpture.

We also entered the cathedral of Beauvais through the transept, which was built, I pointed out, in the 16th century. Now that we come back and look at it for a moment, you can see how it fits that definition I've been developing of this later Gothic style, and in particular of the flamboyant style. Look again at the tracery of the rose window, for example, and also notice that once again the decoration above the portal itself overlaps in our vision into the lower part of the glass of the transept of Beauvais Cathedral. Here, as we can focus in on a detail, we really see, first of all, in the very bottom of the picture is that piece of the architecture coming up and then you can see this beautiful, lyrical, dramatic, flaming (flamboyant) style in the tracery of the stained glass window. It's much more elaborate, much more dynamic than the way the rose windows we have seen have been laid out, whether it was at Saint Denis, or Laon, or, in fact, of course, classically at Chartres.

I now want to turn to a church we've not looked at before, although we're going back to the city of Rouen. There are several late Gothic churches in Rouen that are really quite extraordinary, and this is one of them. It was built in the 14th century, and it's named Saint Ouen. It was a monastic church but, in fact, it's longer than the cathedral, and the cathedral is a very long building. First of all, we have the facade with some of the decorative features I've already talked about, although parts of the facade were not finished until the 19th century. Once again, if we look at the tracery, the stonework in the rose window over the entrance, we can again see the elaborate decorative pattern. In the back of the church, I think we see that the chapels and the spires on the flying buttresses are in some ways more linear, more upward-surging, than we've seen before. The chapels on the east end almost bulge out from the east end of the building itself; they are larger in proportion than we're used to. Remember the very subtle chapels we started with, almost sort of scalloped, open chapels at places like Saint Denis; in fact, I pointed out that's one of the innovations of Saint Denis: how the chapels off that double ambulatory were really worked into the design and the spaciousness of the ambulatory. Now you can see these chapels have been made into almost little buildings that have been attached to the east end of the church. They're quite dramatic and they're quite beautiful, but they're quite different than what we've seen. As I said, for the second church of Rouen—that is to say, other than the cathedral—this is an enormously large church, as you can see. It was begun in 1319, although as I pointed out it took a long time to build and, in fact, wasn't finished until the 19th century.

I want to just take you around the interior, because as we glance from different angles—you know that's what I like to do; I like to stand on my two feet, and move around, and look at the design and the patterns of the architecture in the building from many different angles—we'll see the continuing development of the Gothic style. Here, for example, you see we have very large windows even in the aisle, and then you can see we have a glazed triforium and then the clerestory windows really do fill that entire space above the triforium. Looking up here next to one of the pillars, you can notice that there are no intervening horizontal lines, so as we've seen the tendency already in places like Troyes, once again we see the upward thrust of the architecture; the very pieces of stone that make up this building lift up our eyes toward the vault and toward those extraordinary clerestory windows. Looking straight across from aisle to the other, we really see the elevations of light here. Here is a detail of the clerestory plus the triforium and, of course, as we've seen happening beginning with Saint Denis and Troyes, they begin to blend together and we'll see by the end of this lecture the complete blending together of these styles.

Looking straight up, obviously, at the vault; a simple four-part vault, a kind we're used to. Perhaps a little fatter, a little less-narrow rectangle, but nevertheless the same kind of vaulting we've seen. Vaulting is going to get very complicated in some Gothic churches outside of France especially; the French don't, if you will, play as much with the vaulting as say the English or, as we'll see, the Germans or the Czechs do. Here we see the choir—again, the three layers of light—and it has a spectacular crossing. Here we have the four parts coming together: the two transepts, the nave, and the choir. This is a beautiful, soaring building and standing in the ambulatory looking across with the high altar between us and the opposite side of the building; again we get a sense of the lightness of Saint Ouen in Rouen. Our last look, as we look back toward the west end, and we see that rose window with the flamboyant tracery that we looked at when we came in. Like in many churches, some of the light is interrupted by the later installation of an organ; sometimes, by the way, as you're looking at cathedrals this will become downright annoying because it will block out even some of the stained glass in some cases.

Still staying in Rouen, we go just a few blocks away really to the smaller church of Saint Maclou. Saint Maclou's a not-very-important saint in the whole history of the church; obviously it is to Rouen, but not a well-known saint (nor is, of course, the one we just talked about, Saint Ouen). This has a very large crossing tower, even though it is a small church, but it's really the facade that strikes us as a really beautiful expression of an architectural style. Look at this: We have, even in this little church, five portals. We've really only seen that in one cathedral, and that was the cathedral of Bourges, which was this enormous, wide thing. You can see with the person in the photograph here that this is not a very big church, and yet there are five portals; and look at the buttresses, and look at the way the architecture is designed. Here we stand back a little bit—I happened to be there when they were having some sort of neighborhood fair, so I couldn't get a photograph without these little pennants—but nevertheless, you can get an idea of the size of this church and the elaborateness and the intricacy of the design.

Here, again, we're standing closer and looking up and you can see there's sculpture; and I do want to take just a peek at the sculpture. This is, too, a Last Judgment, but I want you to look at the figure of Jesus; it's a very differently designed and executed form of Jesus. It is a little bit less formal than the poses that we're used to; the face of Jesus is perhaps a little bit less stereotyped, we might say, that we know that the face of Jesus that we've gotten used to from places like Chartres and Amiens, this is a little bit different conception of Jesus and notice he's resting his feet on an orb; so there are some differences in the design. This sculpture, like the sculpture we saw earlier on the north porch of Rouen Cathedral, isn't very well preserved and hasn't been cleaned in a long time, as you can also see here. This church was very badly damaged in World War II and still suffers from some of that.

I again want to leave you with some of the architectural design here: all of the things that point us upward here on the outside; we've seen all the things that point us upward in a church like Saint Ouen, here we see how the design of the facade points us upward, everything points up. You'll also notice in this photograph that the facade isn't flat; it's slightly rounded or curved. Again, that's an interesting innovation. We don't find this in any of the large buildings; but, of course, there is a little bit more opportunity for experimentation when you're not dealing in such monumental scale as a cathedral or a church like Saint Ouen. We get some very interesting pictures of, if you will, further developments and experiments in the building and decorating of Gothic churches, and we get very good looks in the city of Rouen where we've seen already three churches: the cathedral, the monastery of Saint Ouen, and this small gem of Saint Maclou.

Now we're going back to a city we've been to before: the city of Troyes. We're going to look at the church of Saint Urbain; again, a fairly small church, as you can see. This was actually begun in the 13th century by Pope Urban IV, who happened to be from Troyes. In fact, this church stands at the place where his father's—who was a middling merchant—shop was, and he obtained the land and he had this church built named for his patron saint; he took the name "Urban" as pope, so this is Saint Urbain. It took a long time to build because, among other things, even when you're Pope you get in legal disputes, and there was a big legal dispute between the builders of this church and the nuns who had owned the land before. We don't need to go into that in any detail, but it is an interesting notion. I've talked about the fact that what we're going to see in this later style is a lot of radical ups, a lot of everything pointing up; but look at this church: There are two very powerful horizontals on the front, the lower one just above the three portals and then a smaller one right between the big window and the small window at the very top. So here we have this interesting interplay of very strong ups, very strong verticals—we can see it in the pinnacles over the arches of the sculpture and we can also see it in those two columns that go up on either side of the main door—and yet it is, in a sense, sort of played out with those powerful horizontals. It's a very interesting design.

I want to show you one other piece of the exterior, quite a wild thing in some ways: This is the south porch of Saint Urbain, and as you can see it is an elaborate and very odd kind of Gothic structure. We're going to look at it from a number of different angles because it's so unusual. Here, in one particular place standing to the right of it, you just say, "I don't know where all those pieces go. It looks sort of complicated to me; I don't get everything that seems to be going one way and another and crossing one another. It looks sort of jumbled." But let's stand back, and what we see is that there is an overhang off the building itself that's upheld by buttresses, so what we see in the very farthest left here is a flying buttress just for this little porch that's been built; sort of an interesting idea. This is the porch; again, it comes out from the building and seems to be almost a free-standing structure. We have these interesting, not quite our regular four-part vaults in two pieces as a kind of porch for the north side of the church of Saint Urbain. It is, indeed, a sort of odd-looking piece and, again, another one of those more flamboyant pieces of late Gothic architecture in France.

If we go inside, we can see that there are two levels of light, which really have combined; notice that, therefore, the triforium—which is the lower part of the windows, of course—really now isn't a triforium in any way that we can recognize it from one of those early Gothic cathedrals; what we really just have is some great big lancet windows that have a major division about two-thirds of the way down. As we take a look here, you can see that in the part on the right—that is to say, I'm standing in the nave of this church— there's no triforium at all; it is the aisle and then the big clerestory windows. We really see that once we get this notion of the triforium being glazed, then there are all kinds of different ways of dealing with it, even to the point that the triforium—here in the nave, anyway—completely disappears; you would never know that the upper window in the upper right of this photograph really evolves from two different architectural pieces: the triforium on the one hand, and the clerestory windows on the other.

Now we're going to go down the street a little way in Troyes. You may recall when we were looking at the cathedral, I pointed out what a lovely city this is; that we have the cathedral, we have the church of Saint Urbain, and now we're going to go to another church, the church of Mary Magdalene— Madeleine, in French—and it, too, is going to be an interesting church that took several hundred years to build, but part of which is in this flamboyant style. Here we see this church—we're looking at the south side of this church—and what we see here is big windows in the aisle and a tower on the right side. But I want you to notice that except for those big windows, this is a fairly standard 13th-century church; and, in fact, if you look in this photograph, you will see that the architecture, although this is not a very big church, is the same kind of architecture that we have been looking at in 13th-century Gothic churches: We have an aisle, and a blind triforium, and then we have clerestory windows that don't quite fill that whole space between the triforium and the arch. We look at that and say, "Ah, that's sort of your standard high Gothic piece"; and indeed it is.

But when we move to the east end of this church—this is another of these little churches that took hundreds of years to build—first of all, we encounter a screen, a decorative stone screen. Let me say a word about them: Almost every church in Europe had decorative stone screens. In other words, what we see as a sort of uninterrupted look from east to west or west to east in a church would have been somewhat interrupted depending on the size of the walls, and we will see this, by the way, in English cathedrals. The reason we'll see it there is because these screens were by and large ordered taken out in the mid-16th century as part of the Catholic response to the Protestant Reformation. A few survive for various reasons—for one thing, this is not completely opaque, you can see through it—but, of course, by that time England was no longer under the jurisdiction of the Roman church, and therefore in England many more of them survived. They have in other parts of Europe, too: There's a very famous one in Naumburg, in the eastern part of Germany, because it was Lutheran by the time the Council of Trent said, "Get rid of those walls that separate the priest from the laity."

One of the most interesting things here in this church is the stained glass windows. This is the window of Creation, and this was done in the early 16th century. We're going to focus in on the middle part of it here. it's interesting because if you look at the scenes we can see in their entirety, the lower scenes there, the ones on the left and the right are the story of Noah, on the left is the building of the Ark, on the right is the flood; the middle ones are the story of Cain and Abel, the sacrifice of Cain and Abel and then Cain murdering Abel; the stories up above are of Abraham and Moses. We can see how different these windows are because they are much more articulated with regard to the details of the sky color, the vestments, and all the other pieces because, as I pointed out when we looked at Chartres windows, we're going to have much more painted glass rather than pure blocks of color with a little bit of paint, and that's very well-illustrated here in this Creation window at Mary Magdalene. Here is another one of the windows there, again from the beginning of the 16th century. You can see the flaming tracery in this lancet window; this is the story of the Tree of Jesse, a scene we've seen many times, for example, in one of the lancet windows in the west wall of Chartres. But how different it looks here, as you can see with all the colors and the drama, and we're going to look later on in just a couple minutes at another early 16th century late Gothic example of a Tree of Jesse window.

But I want to show you two more details here at Mary Magdalene, just again to illustrate styles. Here's a story we've seen many times before: this is God appearing to Moses in the Burning Bush. Here we have the story of Abraham and Isaac; you can see Isaac carrying things that are going to be used to start the fire for the sacrifice. We can see that this almost looks like a landscape that's painted on glass rather than emphasizing the pure color of the glass, one of the standard changes in the development of stained glass windows in the late Middle Ages.

Finally, I want to move to the church of Saint Etienne, Saint Stephen, in Beauvais; again, we've been to Beauvais before to see the cathedral, if you go there walk across to the other side of town and come see this interesting church. First of all, one of the things you will discover is, like the church we just saw, the nave is, in fact, early Gothic. You can see that from the exterior, and the clerestory windows. Notice again they're not very big; they don't take up the whole space of the clerestory. But look what happens when you walk in and look toward the east: You see you're in this lovely Gothic building, and when you look to the east you're almost blinded by light because there's so much more light coming in the late Gothic east end of this church. I really like this particular image because it really shows, we're used to seeing some churches way back at the beginning where we had sort of dark Romanesque churches and then there was Gothic light at the end of that; here we are already in a light Gothic church and we are struck by the extraordinary light that's bursting into this late Gothic edifice. I want to show it to you from the outside. You can see these big windows—we're going to look at a couple of them in a minute—and here we can see the buttressing and, again, the windows that dominate this building. Here we can see those windows. Once again, notice there is no triforium at all, just these huge clerestory windows above the aisle; and if you look—and you'll see this in many Gothic churches, by the way, that have clear glass—very carefully you can actually see some of the buttresses through the windows and, of course, they're what is holding up this building.

But again, I want to end our look at Gothic in France with these early 16th-century windows and just illustrate how far we've come in terms of style, in this case focusing on the stained glass. This is the story of Saint Martin of Tours giving his cloak—or half his cloak, actually—to a beggar. This is a wonderful window of the Tree of Jesse, and we'll do a couple details to show how different it is from the one we examined in some detail at Chartres. There is Jesse sleeping; there is David with his harp; and at the top of the tree, blossoming at the top, is the beautiful Virgin Mary with the Christ child. Isn't that wonderful? Finally, a Last Judgment window; we've seen lots of last judgments, in stone especially. Take a look: There is God in Heaven with the intercessors; there is Michael the archangel weighing souls; and here are two details from Hell. Aren't these expressive? What a different visual world we're in, even though we're in a lancet window of a Gothic church. And I just can't resist leaving you with a demon.

We've come a long way from those Romanesque churches and Saint Denis to where we are here at Saint Etienne in Beauvais. We've watched now, if we count the Romanesque Period, almost 500 years of the development of style of buildings and of decorations. We've done France pretty thoroughly, and now we're ready to go on our trip around the rest—or much of the rest—of Europe, and we'll be starting that in the next lecture when we go across the channel and arrive at Canterbury.

Early Gothic Architecture in England
Lecture 19

> The earliest Gothic piece of a building—which is the choir, the east end, of Canterbury Cathedral—was designed by a Frenchman … [but] Gothic fairly quickly in England becomes an indigenous style, and therefore it's going to take on a lot of its own characteristics, some of which will surprise us.

England seems, in many ways, wedded to the Continent, yet to this day the English are ambivalent about their role in Europe. As Gothic architecture and design crossed the English Channel in the Middle Ages, although the buildings created in this style are recognizably Gothic, we will also find some significant differences from Gothic as it manifested in France and elsewhere in Europe.

First of all, we can more or less arrange the great cathedrals of France chronologically; that's much harder to do in England. Often the cathedrals of England took hundreds of years to build, and by and large they didn't start from scratch. Many English Gothic cathedrals have Romanesque elements and multiple styles of Gothic in the same building. Note that what we have called Romanesque in France and elsewhere is more properly called **Norman** in England—meaning a style that appeared after the Norman Conquest of England in 1066. Traditionally, scholars break English Gothic into three periods: early Gothic or early English (late 12th–13th century), the **decorated style** (14th century), and the **perpendicular style** (15th–early 16th century).

Second, although we believe that the earliest Gothic structure in England, the choir of Canterbury Cathedral, was designed by Frenchman William of Sens, by the early 13th century French architects and engineers had virtually ceased to work at English work sites. In other words, Gothic fairly quickly became an indigenous style in England and took on a lot of its own characteristics. Some common differences include less emphasis on height (as a whole, Gothic cathedrals in England are about two-thirds the height of their counterparts in France); thicker walls (meaning there is little or no external buttressing); and galleries that do not disappear but become an important part of the elevation, whereas the triforium does not take hold. Also, English sculptural programs take on different forms, focusing less on portal decoration and more on spreading out to a greater extent both internally and externally. Unfortunately, because of the Puritan movement in particular, much more cathedral sculpture was destroyed in England than in France during the Reformation. Finally, we will find a lot more historiated capitals in English Gothic churches.

In 1174, a fire destroyed part of Canterbury Cathedral. The new east end, called the Trinity Chapel, was designed by William of Sens not only to replace the original choir but to house the relics of the recently canonized former archbishop of Canterbury, **Saint Thomas à Becket**. Interestingly, Thomas had lived in exile in Sens for a while during his feud with King Henry II. William may have been chosen because Thomas had previously admired his work.

Thomas à Becket's martyrdom made Canterbury a major pilgrimage site.

Looking at a diagram of Canterbury Cathedral, and you can see from the different types of vaulting that the building was constructed in different segments. The more complex nave vaulting, for example, indicates a later period. There are also two transepts, and the stone used to construct the building is of different colors; both of these features will become fairly common in English cathedrals. Some of the darker stone is a form of limestone called **purbeck**. Several interesting original stained-glass windows survive in Canterbury, many of which relate to Thomas à Becket: his martyrdom, his miracles, and his pilgrims.

We turn from Canterbury to the 13th-century Salisbury Cathedral. Begun from scratch in 1220, unlike most English cathedrals, it was finished rapidly, within about 50 years. Seated in an open stretch of lawn, it has two transepts and, most strikingly, an enormous spire—a 14th-century addition—that stands 404 feet high. There are no flying buttresses, and the east end is flat rather than rounded; we will find that the standard in England. The facade once displayed a lot of sculpture, not only over the portals but all over. Inside,

The Importance of Canterbury

In the early Christian period, England was part of the Roman Empire and became largely Christian as the empire did. With the invasion of the Anglo-Saxons, Christianity shrank in numbers and influence. In 597, the pope sent a mission to England led by Saint Augustine of Canterbury (not to be confused with Saint Augustine of Hippo). They landed at Canterbury in the little Anglo-Saxon kingdom of Kent, and Augustine baptized the Kentish king, Ethelbert. Canterbury is thus the birthplace, or at least rebirth place, of Christianity in England, and the archbishop of Canterbury, in both Catholic and Anglican times, has always been the Primate, or first bishop, of England. As if that were not enough to secure Canterbury's importance, in 1170, Archbishop Thomas à Becket was murdered in the cathedral on the orders of King Henry II. Thomas was quickly canonized, and Canterbury became an important pilgrimage site in England, as memorialized in Geoffrey Chaucer's *The Canterbury Tales*.

we see two colors of stone again. The walls are very thick, made of dressed stone on the outside and rubble fill in the middle.

Wells, in southwestern England, is a small town today but once battled with Bath to be the preeminent city in the Diocese of Bath and Wells. The 13th-century Wells Cathedral has an extraordinarily wide facade with about 500 sculpture niches spread all over it, about half of which still display statues of biblical and postbiblical holy people. On the east side, we notice a building attached by a corridor to the flat choir. This is called a **Lady Chapel**. In England, few Gothic cathedrals were dedicated to the Virgin Mary, but most added Lady Chapels in her honor. There is also a chapter house attached to the north side of the building. This was a meeting house for the canons of the cathedral.

Inside, we find beautiful harmony; like Salisbury, this cathedral was built in one push, although in the 14th century two supporting arches and a more complex vault were added beneath the crossing tower to prevent its collapse. The elevation shows a very strong set of horizontal lines, both below and above the triforium—remember, a triforium is unusual for England—so we perhaps are more inclined to look forward (toward the altar) than up as we would be in a French cathedral. The historiated capitals show scenes of peasant life as well as biblical stories. The crossing tower has a later, fancier Gothic vaulting. The Lady Chapel's interior is in a style similar to the flamboyant. The chapter house is octagonal, which required a special umbrella of ribbed vaulting.

Lincoln Cathedral had a history of disasters in the 12th and 13th centuries, and so several parts were rebuilt more than once. It is a very long cathedral with a very wide facade that incorporates some Romanesque elements. Inside, we see different forms of vaulting; some use more ribs than we're used to. (We will see more decorative vaulting in England and the Czech Republic than we ever found in France.) The most interesting vault in all of Lincoln Cathedral is an asymmetrical, almost zigzag vault in the 12th-century Saint Hugh's Chapel, named for the bishop of Lincoln at the time. We don't find a lot of rose windows in English Gothic, but Lincoln's transepts have rose and lancet windows with a good deal of original stained glass. ■

Important Terms

decorated style: An intermediate style of English Gothic architecture and decoration, largely coming from the 14th century and distinguishable from early Gothic and the later perpendicular style.

Lady Chapel: A chapel dedicated to the Virgin Mary, built as a separate but connected part of some English Gothic cathedrals.

Norman: When speaking of architecture, refers to the Romanesque style in England.

perpendicular style: The latest form of Gothic architecture and decoration in England, coming from the 15th and early 16th centuries.

purbeck: A kind of dark English stone resembling marble that is used widely in English Gothic cathedrals.

Name to Know

Thomas à Becket, Saint (r. 1162–1170): Martyred archbishop of Canterbury. Only four years after his martyrdom, Canterbury Cathedral was mostly destroyed and a new Gothic choir was begun, in large part to accommodate the pilgrims coming to his shrine.

Suggested Reading

Draper, *The Formation of English Gothic*.

Frankl, *Gothic Architecture*, chaps. 2.1, 2.8, 3.3, 4.1.

Wilson, *The Gothic Cathedral*, chap. 1.

Questions to Consider

1. How can the Gothic style be so different with England a mere 30 miles from France?

2. What are some of the distinguishing features of English Gothic?

3. How do you respond to cathedrals in England that contain both Romanesque and Gothic parts? Harmony or cacaphony?

Early Gothic Architecture in England
Lecture 19—Transcript

We all know that to get to England from France isn't very hard: one can take a boat; a few people, of course, have swum; one can fly, that used to be actually a very quick way; and, of course, one can drive or take a train through the Chunnel. England seems, in many ways, wedded to the Continent, even though we know just from watching the news that the English are still ambivalent about their role in Europe. We know, for example, they belong to the EU, but they don't have the euro, and even before crises evolved with the euro there seemed to be relatively little interest in giving up the pound sterling for the euro. As we turn to Gothic across the Channel in England, we need to realize that some of the terms are going to change and, although the buildings we're going to look at are recognizably Gothic, there are going to be some differences that we need to be aware of; so a little bit of prep work before we begin.

First of all, we can more or less arrange the great cathedrals of France chronologically—there's this one, and then this one was built a little bit later, then these two were sort of built at the same time—we've done all that. It's much harder to be chronological in England. Certainly we have some starting dates, but so often the cathedrals of England took hundreds of years to build, and although we're going to see two exceptions to this in this lecture with Salisbury and Wells, by and large they didn't start from scratch. How many fires did we have where only a little piece, or the crypt, or nothing was left from the fire? That was common in France. But in England we're going to see many cathedrals that have some Romanesque elements and very different styles of Gothic in the same building; so we need to be aware of the fact that almost every building—again, there are exceptions—is going to have chunks of different styles of Gothic and even some Romanesque.

Let's do a little bit of terminology: We've used the word "Romanesque" consistently in France, but if we go way back to the time when we actually discussed Romanesque in the early lectures I pointed out that the Romanesque style in England is referred to as "Norman"; so I'm going to try to be consistent, or at least give both terms, and talk about "This Norman piece of a building." That means after 1066 and before Gothic; so we want to keep that in mind. We need to remember this because if we look at the cathedral of Durham, for example, a building we examined for its vaults, we know that this monumental style of architecture is important; and therefore when Gothic is to some extent imported into England in the latter part of the 12th century, it's going to blend with Norman architecture, just like Suger used Burgundian architecture and style from Normandy in the building of Saint Denis. There are going to be different combination because the Romanesque or Norman tradition in England is a little bit different than the Romanesque tradition in France.

Another thing to so say is that the earliest Gothic piece of a building—which is the choir, the east end, of Canterbury Cathedral—was designed by a Frenchman as far as we know, but by the early 13th century it seems that French had virtually ceased to work at Gothic worksites. In other words, Gothic fairly quickly in England becomes an indigenous style, and therefore it's going to take on a lot of its own characteristic, some of which will surprise us, some of which will look foreign to us given how much we've focused on the French style. It's clear—again, England isn't very far away from France, after all—that the insularity must have been deliberate; it isn't "Oh, gosh, who'd ever think of hiring a Frenchman to design a building," or, "Gosh, it's so far away," or, "Who would we ever know to hire?" Clearly, those aren't the issues. This insularity I think says something about England and the English character and not about the economics of bringing in a foreigner to help out or to design the building.

Let me suggest some differences that we will notice over and over again: First of all, there is less emphasis on height. We've seen the soaring Amiens and the soaring Beauvais and so on; English Gothic cathedrals by and large don't soar. In fact, as a whole, they're about two-thirds as high in their elevations as typical French Gothic cathedrals. The walls are extraordinarily thick; and therefore we're not going to have until the very end of the Gothic period in England the great light shows that we saw really beginning with the nave of Saint Denis in the 1230s. The result of not so much height and very thick walls means there's little or no external buttressing; flying buttresses are a rarity in England, it's fair to say. We'll also remember that on the Continent in France the standard elevation of a Gothic cathedral was an aisle, a triforium, and the clerestory windows. We know in the early Gothic there was also a

271

big gallery, but that gallery disappeared. The gallery becomes an important part of the elevation of English Gothic and remains so; so we're going to see a lot of galleries rather than triforia in many of these cathedrals.

Although there was a good deal of English Gothic sculpture, it takes somewhat different forms. There are less concentrated designs around portals as a sculptural program and more the spreading out of sculpture into different parts of the church, interior and exterior, as we're going to see. We also need to remember that especially because of the Puritans in the middle of the 17th century most Gothic sculpture in England alas is no more. I showed you the portal of that cathedral of Noyon where you can see where the statues were supposed to be but they weren't there; we see a lot more of that in England than we do in France.

Just one other interesting peculiarity: Remember when we were looking at Romanesque churches—for example the Church of Mary Magdalene at Vézelay—we saw that a lot of the interior decoration involved historiated capitals, capitals with stories or sometimes allegories carved into them, and we haven't seen any of that in France in the Gothic period; that mode of decoration disappears. But, as we'll see in just a few minutes, in the Gothic cathedral of Wells, and in other places too, we do have interesting sculpted historiated capitals in Gothic buildings; so that's another thing that disappears from the French tradition but does not do so, or at least does not do so as early, in the English tradition.

Some terminology: We've talked about—although, again, I mentioned I didn't like all the terminology very much—periods of Gothic in France. We've talked about the Early Gothic, the High Gothic, the rayonnant that we associate with that glazed triforium and whatever, and then the flamboyant period. Traditionally, scholars break English Gothic into three periods, which we call (cleverly enough) Early Gothic or Early English, then the Decorated Style, and then the Perpendicular Style. Basically, let me try to put it chronologically this way: The Early English style is the latter part of the 12th and the 13th centuries (obviously these are approximations), the Decorated Style 14th century, and then the Perpendicular Style—we'll see why that term comes along—in the 15th and early 16th centuries; for like France, England will be building Gothic buildings in the first part of the 16th century.

Gothic begins in a particular place in England, just as it did in France. In France, we say the beginning of Gothic: Saint Denis; in England, the beginning of Gothic: Canterbury. In 1174, there was a fire that destroyed much of Canterbury Cathedral and that becomes the date from which we can date the building of the Gothic parts of Canterbury Cathedral. Before we look at the building, I want to say just a little bit about Canterbury. In the early Christian period, when England was part of the Roman Empire, England became largely Christian as the Roman Empire did. But with the invasion of the pagan Anglo-Saxons, Christianity didn't disappear in England in the fifth and sixth centuries but it certainly was shrunk in its adherence and in its influence; and then a mission sent from Rome in 597, led by Saint Augustine of Canterbury—not to be confused with Saint Augustine, the great theologian from North Africa; we're looking at a modern statue of Saint Augustine of Canterbury that's actually on Canterbury Cathedral—he brought missionaries and they brought about the conversion of England, again, to Christianity. They landed at Canterbury in what was then the little kingdom of Kent and Augustine of Canterbury baptized Ethelbert of Kent as the first Christian Anglo-Saxon king; so Canterbury is the most important ecclesiastical center in England. There are two archbishops in England—of course, they're Anglican rather than Catholic now, but nevertheless there are two—the Archbishop of Canterbury is numero uno, and the Archbishop of York in the north is number two, and we'll look at the cathedral of York in the next lecture. We call the Archbishop of Canterbury the Primate of England, he's the first bishop of England; and so Canterbury Cathedral is an important ecclesiastical center. It's an important place, again, of ecclesiastical power, and traditionally the Archbishop of Canterbury is the most important churchman in England.

If that's not enough to make Canterbury special, in 1170—just before that fire of 1174—the Archbishop of Canterbury, Thomas à Becket, was murdered in the cathedral. Here we have a medieval depiction of that murder in the cathedral. Becket, within three years, became a canonized saint; his relics were, of course, at Canterbury and therefore Canterbury also becomes an important pilgrimage center in England. Remember, Geoffrey Chaucer's *Canterbury Tales* are all about pilgrims going to Canterbury: "The hooly blisful martir for to seke"; "We go to seek the blissful and holy martyr," meaning "We go to the shrine of Thomas à Becket." So when the new east end of the cathedral was designed following the fire of 1174, among other things it was a place for the relics and a place for pilgrims to visit when they came to Canterbury. A lot of stained glass was destroyed in various times of tumult in England, but we do have some windows; we'll look at some more in a minute—and here's a window that shows Bishop Thomas à Becket.

William of Sens was called from the city of Sens in France to design (we assume) the east end of Canterbury Cathedral, which we call Trinity Chapel; so this is the first Gothic piece, the first piece of a Gothic building, in England. It's interesting because, as I mentioned in an earlier lecture, William of Sens is from (after all) Sens, which is where the first complete Gothic cathedral was built; after all, Saint Denis is only pieces, remember, and it's not a cathedral. Furthermore, Becket had been for a while in exile in France because of his sort of running feud with King Henry II of England, and therefore it's interesting that the architect came from a city where Becket had lived in exile. Maybe he came home and said, "They have a heck of a cathedral in Sens; it would be nice to have a place like that." Who knows; but at any rate, William of Sens came and designed this interesting building.

I want to show you a diagram of Canterbury Cathedral, and you can see from the various ways that the vaults are depicted here that the building was built in different segments. The nave, for example, which is on the left side of our diagram, you can see the vaulting is much more complex and comes from a later period. You also see there are a lot of things attached to it, and there are actually two transepts, as you can see. That becomes fairly common in English cathedrals, and I'll talk a little bit more about that later on when we have the opportunity of why you might have two crossbars of the cross, two of these transepts in certain cathedrals.

I want to look right now at the architecture itself, because if you look at it you say, "Aisle, gallery, clerestory windows, vault"; all of this is sort of standard for French Early Gothic. But there is one interesting thing that's going to become traditionally English here, and that is if you look carefully—you can see it perhaps better on the right than on the left, even though the left side has a lot more light in it—you can see that the stone of the building itself is of different colors. The very tops, the abacuses they're called, of the capitals are, for example, of darker stone and some of those columnar, cylindrical pieces of stone that go up and the little arches in the gallery are made of a darker stone called purbeck—it's very often called purbeck marble, although it really is a kind of limestone—but it's highly polished and therefore we have some color contrasts in the actual stone, and this becomes something, as I said, we will see over and over again in English Gothic architecture.

There are some really interesting stained glass windows that survive in Canterbury, and needless to say many of them deal with Thomas à Becket. Here, for example—how's this for a story you want to put up in your church?—this shows King Henry II, who had at least by some ways of telling the story ordered or at least suggested the murder of Becket; here he is doing penance in Canterbury Cathedral. Then we have miracles that Becket performs: in this one, the man on the left has an arrow through his neck and Becket will heal him. In the other one I want to show you, we have somebody coming to the shrine, to the tomb—and, after all, these windows are right around the tomb—for a cure; so the story of Becket and the politics of the murder of Thomas à Becket, and the fact that this is a shrine to come to is all enshrined, if you will, in the cathedral of Canterbury.

Having looked at a piece of one building, we're now going to look at two cathedrals that were built from scratch in the 13th century. Salisbury, which we're looking at now, was begun in 1220 and unlike most English cathedrals finished rather rapidly, within about 50 years. Here, by the way, is the diagram of it; and again, you see there are two transepts. Let's walk around a little bit and look at this building, which in some obvious ways is Gothic, and yet looks quite different than what we've seen in France. Here, as we look at the cathedral of Salisbury, the thing that strikes us is this enormous tower; it, in fact, is the only major addition after the original building program, it was built in the 14th century. It stands 404 feet high; it is an enormously high and, as you can see, beautiful tower. You'll notice we don't see flying buttresses here. As we look at the east end now, you'll see that it is flat rather than rounded; we know that the French style is rounded and the only major exception that we looked at was the cathedral of Laon, but we will find that it will be the standard here in England. The facade is a facade that displays a lot of sculpture, although most of it is not there anymore; and it's not that the sculpture is concentrated in one or two or three portals, for example, but as you can see—and we'll see this even more at a our next cathedral in Wells—there are places all over the facade for sculpture.

As we go inside, this really is a beautiful building. You will immediately notice, by the way, that there are these lighter and darker stones—again, that contrast that we saw in Canterbury is going to become a very important piece of the way that English Gothic cathedrals are built—and we can see it as we look to the elevation; again, we have the aisle, triforium, and the clerestory windows. We might ask, "How do they build a building"—this isn't particularly high, but it's a great big stone building with windows, after all—"without buttressing?" The support is basically inside the walls; the walls here at Salisbury are enormously thick and, in fact, they're three layers wide: You have dressed stone on the inside, dressed stone on the outside, and a lot of rubble fill in the middle. The walls are very thick, and therefore they can support the vault of Salisbury Cathedral. Here we're looking at it from the other direction; that is to say, we're standing behind the altar and now looking to the west and seeing the lancet windows over the door. This is a marvelous, beautiful, and harmonious cathedral; again, except for the big tower on the outside, all built essentially in one campaign. It sits out in a beautiful lawn because they chose a new place to build their cathedral, not just to build a new cathedral, and it's still a beautiful, beautiful place to visit.

This is Wells Cathedral. Wells is in the southwestern part of England, and Wells is a small town today. In fact, there is a diocese that we call the Diocese of Bath and Wells, and those two towns in the diocese fought over which one should have the cathedral; and the definitive statement was made in the early 13th century when the building we see here was begun, Wells Cathedral, and Bath no longer was a cathedral city. We'll see how the "Bathians," if you will, responded to that later on when we look at a beautiful building from almost three centuries later that was built in Bath, the famous Bath Abbey. But this is an extraordinary building and, again, beautifully set. We see it has—and this will not be the only example we have in England—an extraordinarily wide facade, and if you look on that facade there are niches all over it, about 500, for statues. Instead of the sculptural program primarily being stories or tight collections of figures—or in some cases, like in Rennes, even interacting with each other—we have all over the facade this display of biblical and holy people from post-biblical times. This is one example that we have that's survived; about half the statues in Wells survive and as you can see many of them are not in good condition. Again, the religious wars, especially in the 17th century, have not been very good to Gothic cathedrals in Wells, or in England in general.

We're going to take some time walking around this building, from that broad facade, along the nave, and as we come to the back we notice that after we have the flat east end of the cathedral we have a building attached to it that sticks out beyond it; and, in fact, this is going to be one of two structures that stick out from the cathedral of Wells and this will become not universal but fairly standard. This one is what we call a Lady Chapel. Unlike in France, many of the Gothic cathedrals were not dedicated to the Virgin Mary; but obviously there's great devotion in all of Catholic Christendom to the Virgin Mary, and so many cathedrals added special chapels dedicated to Our Lady and therefore called Lady Chapels. As we continue to move around, we see that Lady Chapel as a kind of attachment; it's a kind of corridor, that takes you from the main part of the cathedral into the Lady Chapel. Again, the setting of Wells Cathedral is so beautiful. As we walk around we can enjoy spectacular views of the building from all sorts of angles; we can get close, we can get far away.

We come to another building as we keep circling around; we're now on the north side of Wells Cathedral, and we see this beautiful building attached. This is called a chapterhouse; it is where the chapter—that is to say, the clergy associated with the cathedral plus the bishop; the canons plus the bishop—meets, and we have this separate chapterhouse perhaps in part because it suggests the important status of the clergy; they, in a sense, get their own private space for meetings. We will go inside both the Lady Chapel and the chapterhouse once we enter Wells.

It's a beautiful building inside, largely built in the 13th century, although it took longer to complete than Salisbury; again, Wells and Bath, the diocese, were in small rural areas basically. You can see the beautiful harmony. You obviously see the peculiarity of the interior of Wells, that upside down and that right side up arch in the middle; be patient, we're going to get to that. I want you to look at just a little bit of an angle, because a we look at the elevation of Wells Cathedral we see that there is a very strong set of horizontal lines, both below and above the triforium—it's actually really a triforium here, and that's unusual for England—but notice how those lines go, and so there are very strong horizontals, and we don't have pillars that go through those horizontals; so we are more focused on the altar perhaps and less inclined when we walk in to look up than we would be in a French cathedral. There are, as I said earlier on in this lecture, some capitals in the cathedral of Wells, and some of them are sort of interesting, what seem to be "peasanty" scenes: a guy with apparently a toothache; a guy with a great mustache; somebody with a thorn or a sore foot; here we have peasants doing "peasanty" things, if you will; and here we see Moses with the tablets. It's interesting that this is a carryover in Wells and other cathedrals; again, it does not carry over from the Romanesque to the Gothic period in France, as we have seen.

We have to look at this arch; this extraordinary arch that goes from the bottom up and then from the top down. It is not part of the design of the cathedral; in the early 14th century, these were installed to protect the tower from collapsing; so this is a structural fix, if you will, but what a brilliant and beautiful fix, even though it blocks our vision of the entire length of the cathedral. What a sight. Every time we move in any angle around the crossing tower where these are located, we get these spectacular views. This actually looks up into the crossing tower, which has a later, fancy kind of Gothic vaulting. But look here: We've talked about standing next to the pillars and looking up at crossing towers; this really ups the ante here at Wells. Here's another example of one of the many interesting views and therefore plays of dark and lightness, because we not only have the arches and the inverted arches, we have those round oculi; and so there's so many places that little bits of light peek in, so many places where there is shadow. It's one of the most wonderful, playful pieces of Gothic architecture we have. Talk about making good out of necessity; it seems to me this does it.

This, built a little bit later than the building we've been in, is the attached Lady Chapel; and, as you can see, it's in a later style similar to the French flamboyant style. This is the interesting and important stairway that runs up to the chapterhouse. The chapterhouse is octagonal, and therefore it brings about new vaulting problems and new clever vaulting solutions. Isn't this gorgeous? It's under this umbrella of ribbed vaults in these interesting patterns that the bishop and the chapter at Wells made the decisions for the diocese.

Let's move on finally to the cathedral of Lincoln. Lincoln kept having disasters in the 12th and 13th centuries, and so several parts were rebuilt more than once because of all that; so although Lincoln has a lot of different pieces from different times, most of it comes from the late 12th and the 13th century. The first thing to say: It is a very long cathedral. As we look at it from different angles, we'll see the beautiful towers and also, again, this extraordinarily wide facade, which actually incorporates some Romanesque elements as well as being a great Gothic display place. I mean, this is an enormous facade, in some ways even more dramatically wide than Wells because we contrast those verticals with this very powerful horizontal. As we walk inside, we see different forms of vaulting. If you want to study vaulting in England, you can go to one cathedral sometimes and see different patterns; but here we see an interesting pattern of vaulting in the nave of Lincoln Cathedral. We can look up at it and see how they use more ribs than we're used to seeing; and again, we're going to get a lot of fancy vaulting and decorative vaulting in England and especially in what's now the Czech Republic, much more so than we ever found in France. The French changed a lot of things over time; they did not change the basic vaulting scheme very much. Here we look down an aisle and get a sense that there's a different, simpler kind of vaulting there, one we're more used to, although the vault at the very top of this photograph certainly is unusual because it vaults an unusual space.

The most interesting vault in all of Lincoln Cathedral was done at the end of the 12th century, and we call it Saint Hugh's Chapel because it was built during the time that Saint Hugh of Lincoln was the Bishop of Lincoln. As you can see, there's a kind of asymmetrical, almost zigzaggy kind of vaulting here; that really surprises us. We don't know particularly why this was done—and, of course, we don't know who is responsible for this design—but it is, indeed, an interesting solution to the vaulting problem of the east end of Lincoln Cathedral. Here we're looking at one of the transepts. We don't find a lot of rose windows in English Gothic, but here we see the rose and lancets, and therefore a particular French borrowing here in Lincoln. There is the window itself, it still contains a good deal of glass as you can see; it's very beautiful.

Therefore, as we finish with Lincoln, we're going to finish our first installation of our look at Gothic cathedrals in England. The ones we're going to look at in the next lecture really are, much more than the ones we saw in this lecture, pieces that are put together at different times; then we're going to see that Decorated Style, and then we're going to see that Perpendicular Style in the development of Gothic in England.

Decorated and Perpendicular English Gothic
Lecture 20

One of the things we see in England ... is in the later Gothic style, the vaults get extraordinarily complex. ... A lot of times, this complexity of vaulting has nothing to do with keeping the building up; the vaulting itself becomes part of the decoration. ... This kind of complex vaulting in the choir of Gloucester, it turns out to be one of the, if you will, prophetic constructions.

Gloucester Cathedral is a large cathedral that has many large Norman/Romanesque features; for example, we find huge, round pillars and rounded arches in the nave, yet above those pillars we find early Gothic vaulting—simple four-part vaults unlike the more complex vaults elsewhere in England. This is just one example of how Gloucester will allow us to ask how the various styles do or do not fit together harmoniously in English Gothic architecture.

The east end of Gloucester Cathedral and the Lady Chapel are in a very different style—late Gothic perpendicular. The windows show why the style is called perpendicular; they have a lot of perpendicular lines, creating rectangular spaces rather than the dancing shapes of the French flamboyant style. The vault is one of the more complex ones we have seen, but this complexity, here and for the most part elsewhere, has nothing to do with keeping the building up; it is purely decorative. In fact, some of the earliest of this fanciful vaulting is in the cloister of Gloucester.

The elaborate late-Gothic fan vaulting of the cloisters at Gloucester Cathedral.

© Photos.com/Thinkstock.

York Cathedral, often called York Minster, is one of the most important churches in England, second only to Canterbury in ecclesiastical rank. The building was begun around 1220 and took 250 years to build. At more than 500 feet, or 130 meters, long, it is the second-largest cathedral north of the Alps, second only to Cologne. Many smaller buildings are attached to the cathedral. The facade has a huge window—although it is not a rose window like we're used to in France—and does not have huge doors with sculptures. The transepts were built first, and their vaulting is made out of wood; in fact, one of the transept roofs caught fire in 1984 and was destroyed. One of the transept windows (unfortunately, not with original glass) was built to celebrate the marriage of the heirs of York and Lancaster after the War of the Roses. The opposite transept has five tall, thin lancet windows called the Five Sisters filled with a gray glass called **grisaille**.

The nave was built in the 14th century in the intermediate decorated style. The vault—painted to look like stone but still made of wood—shows increasing complexity of design, and the windows are somewhat larger than we had in earlier English Gothic cathedrals. In the top of the large facade window, there is some French-style flaming tracery. The choir, built much later, is flat and contains the largest Gothic window anywhere in the world. The original rood screen survived the Reformation; it is covered in statues of the kings of England from William the Conqueror, whose reign began in 1066, to King Henry IV, who reigned in the 15th century. The crossing tower has a particularly beautiful and decorative vault.

There are many peculiar things about Ely Cathedral, found northwest of London; first of all, the facade is asymmetrical and doesn't have a huge main portal. The nave is Norman and has a wooden roof. The elevation is also Romanesque, with rounded arches, a big gallery, and so on. The transepts are also Norman; but what we find in the east end qualifies Ely as one of the greatest of all Gothic cathedrals. First, the spectacular 14th-century crossing tower in the decorated style is octagonal, with the star-shaped vaulting in wood. The Lady Chapel is the largest in England, with complex late Gothic vaulting and huge windows as well. I mentioned earlier that galleries continued to be part of the elevation of Gothic cathedrals in England until very late, and we can see that here.

The largest Gothic church in London is Westminster Abbey, next door to the Houses of Parliament. When construction began in the 1250s, Westminster was not part of London but a city onto itself, the royal city, and this is in many ways a royal abbey. In 1066, King Edward the Confessor was buried in the previous abbey church, and later that year William the Conqueror was crowned here, as all his successors have been to this day. It is a large cathedral, because it serves many ceremonial purposes and thus hosts large crowds.

The 13th-century choir has a round end in the French style, and the vaulting is also familiar from French cathedrals. In fact, stepping outside, we find that Westminster Abbey has flying buttresses—highly unusual in England. Of course, much of the original decoration has been destroyed, as we note from all the plain glass. There were once frescoes in Westminster Abbey, which we associate with Italy but were painted by English artists, some of whom actually did work later in Assisi. The cathedral's nave was built in the

On Gloucester's exterior, one can see a blend of Gothic and Romanesque.

15th century. Although obviously there are stylistic differences, there seems to have been some real attempt to provide continuity of design.

Westminster Abbey's Lady Chapel is often called the Henry VII Chapel. It was added at the beginning of the 16th century and is perpendicular in style. Inside, it is beautiful and highly decorated, with many windows and **fan vaulting**. The bosses are stalactite-like stone carvings that hang from these vaults—a particular English contribution to the Gothic. The tomb of Henry VII and his wife Elizabeth, interestingly, was carved by a Florentine sculptor named Torrigiani in a Renaissance style.

We turn now to Bath Abbey. Recall that the cities of Bath and Wells were once competitors for power within their diocese; Bath was the clear loser, with a dilapidated ex-cathedral, but around 1500, Bath Abbey was built to replace it. Its facade is dominated by a huge window surrounded by a sculpture of angels climbing up and down Jacob's Ladder. Around the back, we find flying buttresses, and in the interior, a great deal of light from the huge windows and fan vaulting on a larger scale than at Westminster.

Finally, we look at the King's College Chapel at Cambridge. This, the greatest of all of the chapels at Cambridge, was sponsored by the early Tudors. This is the largest fan vaulting of all the churches in England, a beautiful place to conclude our tour of England's cathedrals. ■

Important Terms

fan vault: A type of English late Gothic vaulting where the ribs form fanlike shapes.

grisaille: A type of stained-glass window containing shades of gray rather than bright colors and narratives.

Suggested Reading

Frankl, *Gothic Architecture*, p. 180–1, 187–194, 251.

Wilson, *The Gothic Cathedral*, chap. 3.

1. How does the flamboyant style of late Gothic in France compare to the late Gothic (perpendicular) style in England?

2. Looking at the Gothic architecture of England, how insular is it (i.e., how is it a style that developed in a place separated from France, the birthplace of Gothic)?

3. How did vaulting change from the time in which the ribs functioned to allow for the building of large and stable churches to the time of the fan vaults of England?

Decorated and Perpendicular English Gothic
Lecture 20—Transcript

We have some ground to cover in this lecture. In our second look at English Gothic, we're going to examine no fewer than three cathedrals, two abbeys, and two chapels; so we're going to be taking brief looks. I would emphasize that just as I kept pointing out in France, it's good to slow down and look all around, it seems like I'm violating my own rule; and I am to some extent. But the reason is, obviously, we cannot do the other parts of Europe with the same kind of thoroughness that we did France without having a 100-lecture course. What I hope is, whether it's simply observing and listening to this lecture and the previous one and the ones on the other parts of Europe, or if you're traveling, hopefully the care and the time we spent in France—three lectures on Chartres; two lectures on Amiens; individual lectures on several churches—you have learned something about how you go about seeing a cathedral. We may zip through Gloucester Cathedral fairly quickly, but if you're in Gloucester you don't need to; you want to take the same care, the same walking around the outside and the inside, the same looking up and looking at the different angles and checking out the decorations and so on that I did with you in those French cathedrals.

Gloucester Cathedral is one of those that I talked about in the previous lecture that you name a style, it's at Gloucester. It's a large cathedral, as you can see from the image we have in front of us, and it's a cathedral that has large parts still in the Romanesque style, starting with an interesting Romanesque crypt. But as we enter Gloucester Cathedral, we take a look at the nave; and if you are now keying in on various parts you say, "Stylistically, these don't seem to us to go together." Those huge, round pillars and rounded arches that we look at say, "This is a Romanesque building"; and, indeed, this is a Norman—that is to say, English Romanesque—nave, but the vaulting was put on later. We have Gothic vaulting; fairly early Gothic vaulting. Notice that although there are some simple four-part vaults in England, generally speaking vaulting is a bit more complex in England, and we see that here at Gloucester. We have a Romanesque set of walls, but we have a Gothic vault; and that makes Gloucester an interesting place to see how the architects built in a different style on an existing style. Sometimes these experiments, I think, are quite successful, where those juxtapositions really are interesting and beautiful and challenging; other times, I must confess—not here, but in other places—I keep saying, "This just doesn't go with that." Obviously that's a personal opinion; but it is interesting to notice, because we do this more in England than really any other place, how the various pieces do or do not fit together in some sort of harmonious completeness.

The east end of Gloucester Cathedral and the Lady Chapel are in a very different style; they are in the Late Gothic Perpendicular style. Here, if we look at the windows, we can see why it's called "Perpendicular," because you can see that a characteristic of these windows is you have a lot of lines perpendicular to one another, creating rectangular spaces primarily rather than sort of dancing all around in that kind of French flamboyant style where the tracery goes everywhere; so we get an idea of why this is called "Perpendicular." One of the things we see in England—and we will see this in Germany and the Czech Republic—is in the later Gothic style, the vaults get extraordinarily complex; so here is the vault of the Lady Chapel at Gloucester, quite beautiful. But let me point out that a lot of times this complexity of vaulting has nothing to do with keeping the building up; that the vaulting itself becomes part of the decoration. In fact, some of the earliest of this fanciful vaulting is in Gloucester; not here, but in the cloister of Gloucester. We take a look down part of the cloister of Gloucester Cathedral and you can see this fanciful vaulting, and as you look at it you say, "Do all those ribs, circles, and patterns have anything to do with keeping the building from falling down?" The answer is "no"; we can really see here that vaulting becomes decorative, and so we have some experiments like this in the low cloister of Gloucester Cathedral, just as we saw earlier on in France that sometimes innovations begin in small places and then expand to big places. You get this kind of complex vaulting in the choir of Gloucester; it turns out to be one of the, if you will, prophetic constructions because then this idea of the possibilities of decorative vaulting will grow to the main parts of churches, whether it's the Lady Chapel later on in Gloucester that we just saw or whether it's going to be some of the works we see at the end of this lecture.

We now turn to one of the most important churches in England, and this is York Cathedral, very often called York Minster. We hear that word "minster," and we need to appreciate the fact that unlike in France, many of the cathedrals of England were also monasteries—that's true of Canterbury, for example, and many other places—and it has to do with the way England received Christianity from Augustine of Canterbury and those other missionaries who came in the sixth and seventh centuries and evangelized, or re-evangelized, England; that England was not a place as urbanized as Italy or France or Spain and therefore many of the cathedrals are combination monastery/cathedrals, so we very often call this York Minster. York is in the north of England, and along with Canterbury it's one of the two Archiepiscopal seats; so there's an Archbishop of York along with an Archbishop of Canterbury. York was a very important Roman city in the times of the Roman Empire; in fact, Constantine, the emperor who brought Christianity to the Roman Empire—or at least sort of brought it out of the closet in the Roman Empire—was, in fact, first proclaimed emperor by his own troops when he was stationed in York.

This building was begun around 1220. We see the facade here with this huge window; not a rose window that we're used to in France, although in terms of the twin towers on the front it has a kind of French appearance to it. You can see it does not have huge doors with sculptures; so again, we see patterns of difference and similarity. This building took 250 years to build and it was built in stages; and, in fact, although it was begun in the 13th century, it did not get consecrated—it did not have sort of the completion ceremony, if you will—until 1472. It's more than 500 feet long, about 130 meters; there's only one longer cathedral north of the Alps, and that's the cathedral of Cologne, which we will look at in a future lecture, in fact. But because it took 250 years to build, obviously there are many different kinds of Gothic style at York Minster.

This is a diagram of the cathedral just so we get a sense of its extraordinary length, and you can see there are various pieces attached either directly to the building or indirectly so that these cathedrals don't have quite as clean a plan, if you will, to them as most of the Gothic cathedrals in France; we've already seen evidence of that going all the way back to our first look at Gothic at Canterbury. This is the exterior of one of the transepts, and interestingly enough—the transepts were built first—the vaulting is made out of wood; so we have some stone tracery, but that's wood and, in fact, one of the transept roofs caught fire in 1984 and was destroyed. Fire isn't just a medieval danger for cathedrals; it's a modern danger for cathedrals, especially ones that have a lot of wood like this.

There's an interesting window—this is replacement glass—in the transept of York Cathedral because it was built after the War of the Roses—that is to say, the battle between the houses of York and Lancaster—and when the war ended in 1485 with a marriage that led to the establishment of the Tudor dynasty with Henry VII, this window was built to celebrate or to memorialize the fact that now England is at peace and the War of the Roses is over. In the other transept, there's a very beautiful window—as you can see, it's gray glass; it's called "grisaille"—but these five very tall, thin lancet windows, which are called "The Five Sisters," are in fact a remarkably beautiful thing; it reminds us that the windows, to be beautiful and to illuminate the church, do not have to be filled full of narratives and bright colors. This is a window that I like a great deal; I think it's really a wonderful addition even though it doesn't add color to York Cathedral.

The nave—and now we're looking back toward the west with that large window—was built in the 14th century, and this is a style we call the Decorated Style. If we look at the vault, you can see there's an increasing complexity, and you can see the windows are somewhat larger than we had in the earlier Gothic cathedrals in England. What's interesting about the vault here is it looks like stone but it, too, is wood. Unlike the vault of the transept, it's painted to look like stone; so here again an innovation. Even in a wealthy, powerful see—that is to say, diocese—like York, we have here a roof in wood; it's obviously a lot easier to construct in wood than it is in stone. In York, the nave, as we focus in on that great big window that's in the west side, notice the tracery at the top: We do have some of that flaming tracery at the top. If you looked at the bottom two-thirds of that window, you'd say, "Well, a sort of bland design"; but the top part really is very beautiful, and not really characteristic of a lot of English Gothic windows. You can see in the top part what this tracery looks like; it almost looks like a kind of heart shape in the center, but this is very similar to some of the flamboyant tracery that we saw, in fact, in France.

The choir, which was built much later, and you see that in the east end it is flat—very typical of Gothic cathedrals in England—and you can see this enormous window in the east end; in fact, it is the largest Gothic window anywhere. It is extraordinary in this setting of this cathedral; remember, when you walk in the front door—that is to say, the west end of York Cathedral—that is more than 500 feet, more than 130 meters, away from you.

I want you to notice something important that I've talked about, and we've even gotten one glimpse of, but I want to focus on for a minute. You can see here that there is a screen; a kind of wall in the middle of this church. You can get a very good view of it here. These screens were built to separate—remember, this was a monastery as well as a cathedral—the clerical part of the church from the lay part of the church. Cathedrals in France, Italy, and other places have these, too; but as I mentioned in an earlier lecture when looking at a small one in France, these were torn out of Catholic churches by and large in the 16th century as part of the reform of the Catholic Church in light of the Reformation. But in England, many of them have survived; and we see that here and we can look at it. It's a beautiful screen, and as you can see it has many statues. We might think, "Aha, who are all these saints?" These are, in fact, kings of England, and they begin with William the Conqueror in 1066, and they go up to the time that the screen was built with King Henry IV who reigned in the 15th century. Here we see a detail of just some of those interesting statues of English kings.

Finally, I just want to glimpse into the crossing tower of York because I think it's particularly beautiful and has an interesting vaulted pattern. But let me tell you as a preview of coming attractions: You ain't seen nothing yet when it comes to crossing towers, because we're going to move to see the most spectacular of all the crossing towers in the cathedral of Ely. Ely's not far from Cambridge; that is to say, it's north and east of London. One of the things you'll notice here is the cathedral, unlike most French cathedrals, is sort of on the edge of town; and therefore as you walk around it, you not only get beautiful, unobstructed views but you get cows. We really are sort of on the edge of the city here at Ely Cathedral. An unusual and interesting facade; it doesn't have the symmetry we're sometimes used to and it doesn't have a huge portal, and so it's sort of an odd way to enter this cathedral. But then again, there are a lot of peculiar things about Ely.

As we enter, and I'm standing outside the door now looking in, you can see even here that the roof of the nave is made of wood—not wood made to look like stone but wood—because the nave is Norman and you can see the wood as the covering of this extraordinary nave. If we look at the elevation, you'll see all the characteristics that we know are Romanesque: the rounded arches, the big gallery, and so on and so forth. In fact, the nave and the transepts are Norman; and yet, we still say that Ely is one of the greatest of all the Gothic cathedrals. The east end obviously is going to be Gothic, but this is the crossing tower. This was built in the 14th century; we would call this the Decorated Style. But look at this: You can see the wooden roofs on either side; but look up into this extraordinary wooden structure and let's focus in just on the more central part. Isn't that gorgeous; that this really is sort of the big prize of all the great crossing towers? We've seen many—we've seen them in Laon, and we've seen them in other places as well—but this one is really unique; this octagonal tower with the star-shaped vaulting in wood. It really is, I think, one of the beautiful Gothic moments. The Lady Chapel, which as you can see in this photograph from the east end of the church sits over to our right-hand side here, is the largest Lady Chapel in England; and you can see what a beautiful chapel it is. It is extraordinarily lovely inside with complex vaulting and, as we would expect from the Late Gothic period—because this is added after the rest of the building was built—really quite spectacularly large windows as well.

I want now to finish up by looking at the choir, because as we look at it from an angle we can see that, first of all, the gallery really has survived. I mentioned in an earlier lecture that we're going to see galleries continuing to be part of the elevation of Gothic cathedrals in England until very late, and we can see that here; we can look up into the gallery and see the windows in the gallery. Here we see that Ely has a flat east end—again, typical of English Gothic cathedrals—with lots of lancet windows. Ely really is, to me, a trip: We get to look at wonderful Romanesque; we get to look at beautiful Decorated Gothic Style; we get to look at the Perpendicular Style in the Lady Chapel; and we get to look at that crossing tower.

We now move to a church that no doubt many of you have visited: the largest Gothic church in London, Westminster Abbey. It's important to say it was not in the city of London technically, it was outside London, just as Saint Denis, the great monastery near Paris, was outside Paris; and, of course, we know that this is in many ways a royal abbey and we want to look at part of the building of this extraordinary work. It was begun in the 1250s, replacing an older abbey under the sponsorship of King Henry III who had a long reign, from the time he was a child in 1216 all the way until 1272. One reason this abbey took on a unique importance is because in 1066, the beloved and saintly—in fact, he is a saint—King Edward the Confessor was buried in Westminster Abbey; and later on that year when William the Conqueror conquered England and established the Normans—the dukes of Normandy—as kings of England, he chose to be crowned on Christmas Day 1066 at Westminster Abbey to show the continuity with the beloved Edward the Confessor after some fairly ugly battles to get the throne. At any rate, therefore, this is the coronation church as we know. I'm old enough to remember sitting in awe as a little boy watching the coronation of Queen Elizabeth II on black and white television at some absurd hour of the day because of the time difference when I was growing up in Indiana; and so Westminster Abbey's one of those places we simply know, and we know that it's an important place.

We are now standing looking to the west; we'll come back and look at the nave later because the nave was built only in the 15th century, but I want to have you see the expanse of this. It's a very big building because there needs to be space for all the ceremonial purposes that this building was built for. If we look at the choir, which is the part that was built during the reign of Henry III, we'll notice that there's something unusual: It does not have a flat end, it has a rounded end; and so this is very much French influence. We see in the vaulting, we sort of say, "Gosh, I recognize that kind of vaulting, that looks like the choir of a French church"; and, in fact, if we go outside and look here at the transept we'll see that Westminster Abbey has flying buttresses, something I pointed out is somewhat unusual in Gothic churches in England.

One of the things we sometimes fail to remember is how much decoration has been destroyed. Of course, we know when we see the plain glass that stained glass windows have been destroyed, and we know that Westminster Abbey in this choir had stained glass windows with, among other things, coats of arms, because again remember this is a royal abbey because of the coronation of the kings there. But also there were frescoes in Westminster Abbey. We associate frescoes primarily with Italy, but, in fact, we know that there were important fresco artists in England in the 13th century, and some of them actually came to do work in Assisi in Italy in the church that contains the body of Saint Francis of Assisi, a church we're going to visit, by the way, in the next lecture. This is actually not from the choir of the church but another part of Westminster Abbey, but I just use it to show that there have been some discoveries of frescoes and it reminds us that when we look at the decorations we have to try to remember some paintings, some windows and obviously if we had those things it would be a very different experience, just like walking into Chartres is very different than walking into a cathedral that has no stained glass windows, or walking into a church that has elaborately carved portals is a different experience than walking into a church that either doesn't have them or they've been destroyed or removed over time. It's a good lesson for us here at Westminster Abbey.

This is the nave of Westminster Abbey; it was built in the 15th century. Although obviously there are stylistic differences—nobody sat down and said, "We have to try to build this as if we were living in the 13th century when the choir was made"; that isn't the way things worked—nevertheless, there's good reason in looking at all of the abbey together to suggest that there was some real attempt to provide a kind of continuity; it's not just, "Now we're going to build a new half of this building and we're going to make it look like we want to make it look like no matter what," there's some real sense of trying to bring continuity. I think one experiences that in Westminster Abbey; when you walk in you don't say, "Boy, the pieces don't seem to fit," even though part is 13th century and part is 15th century.

One of the most interesting pieces of Westminster Abbey is the Lady Chapel. We don't tend to call it that, but that's what it is; we tend to call it the Henry VII Chapel. It was added at the beginning of the 16th century; Henry VII, again, was the first Tudor monarch. He reigned from 1485, the end of the War of the Roses, to 1509 when he died and was succeeded by his son, Henry VIII (we don't need to go into him here, obviously). This is the exterior of the Henry VII Chapel, and again you can see one of the reasons we call this architecture Perpendicular: just look at all the lines of the Lady Chapel, or the Henry VII Chapel, here at Westminster Abbey. When we walk in—luckily they have lots of nice banners up for us—we can see this is a beautiful and highly decorated building. We can see how many windows there are, and even if we can't quite grasp from a distance what kind of vaulting there is, what strikes us is there's something spectacular about this roof. If we look straight up, we have what's called fan vaulting. This is a kind of vaulting that developed in England at the end of the 15th and the beginning of the 16th centuries, and it's really unique to England. There are other kinds of quite elaborate vaulting that we will take a look at, especially in the Czech Republic and in Germany, but nevertheless fan vaulting is a particularly English kind of Late Gothic vaulting.

Remember when I showed you the cloister at Gloucester? If we go back and look at that, we will see that not just looking at the top of those vaults, but if we look at where those vaults come from we can see that there are a number of vaults that just fan out from each of the pillars along the way, and they're really quite beautiful. That isn't a fully developed idea of fan vaulting; this is a fully developed idea of fan vaulting. One of the things is in addition to all that myriad of vaulting—again, very little of which has to do with holding up the roof—there are these stone almost, we might say, stalactites coming down from the roof. We call them "bosses," and these beautiful stone bosses hang in some ways from these fan vaults. The overall effect is stunning and spectacular. In fact, let's look into this roof and focus on a detail: You can see the designs, and coats of arms, and you can see this extraordinary pattern of the vault, and then you can see the boss coming down. This is an ornate— I'm going to use a word that's inappropriate but I think you'll get what I mean—almost a kind of Baroque Gothic, if you will (to put two different things together). It is so ornate, so decorative, almost so outrageous; but isn't it beautiful? It is a particular English contribution to Gothic.

Let's move on, after we stop and look at the tomb of Henry VII and his wife. This is our final glance at this chapel. What's interesting is even though we have all this extraordinary Gothic vaulting and perpendicular windows, the tomb was actually carved by a Florentine in the Renaissance style, his name is Torrigiani; and so it's sort of an interesting juxtaposition.

Here we have Bath Abbey. Remember Bath was the loser in the "Who gets the cathedral, Bath or Wells?" They had a kind of dilapidated, if you will, ex-cathedral; and about 1500, there is a new abbey, Bath Abbey, built on the site of that dilapidated cathedral. You can see from this aerial shot it really is, as we would expect, in the shape of a cross. It has a lovely facade that's dominated by a huge window, and if you look on either side of the window you can see there's some sculpture. It actually is Jacob's ladder, which shows angels climbing up and angels coming down, very much like the way the story of Jacob's ladder is described in the book of Genesis. As we walk around to the back, again, we just see that he walls seem to be removed; and, in fact, there are flying buttresses here at Bath Abbey. Here's the interior: light and, again, fan vaulting, on a bigger scale than we had, in fact, at the Henry VII or Lady Chapel at Westminster Abbey. If we just look straight up, we have these wonderful walls of glass, these beautiful pillars soaring up, and then, of course, we have the vault literally fanning out from each of the pillars and filling the space of the roof.

Finally, we're going to go to Cambridge in England and take a look at the King's College Chapel. Those of you who are familiar with Oxford and Cambridge know that students live in colleges to be part of the university, and the colleges have many of their own things: dining halls, living quarters, tutors, libraries, and all the rest, including chapels. This is the greatest of all of the chapels at Cambridge, King's College Chapel, which was really sponsored by the early Tudors. It was begun before the Tudor dynasty took the throne, but it was really the sponsorship of Henry VII and Henry VIII that led to the building of King's College Chapel. Here we look inside: This is the largest fan-vaulted of all the churches in England that have this kind of vaulting, and as we look up, again, we get this sense of this glorious expression of beauty that we have.

Let me tell you one of my favorite things to do: Some of you may know that in the Oxford colleges and Cambridge colleges, some of the colleges maintain boys' and adults' choirs, and the most famous of all of them is the King's College Choir. You may see their CDs, listen to them being played on radio or whatever during the Christmas season; but one of the great things to do is to go to King's College Chapel, surrounded by this glorious piece of architecture, and listen to that choir sing sacred music. It doesn't get any better than that.

I'd love to stay longer in England, but we have to go back to the Continent. We're going to pass through France, and our next stop will be Gothic Germany.

Gothic Churches in the Holy Roman Empire
Lecture 21

The Romanesque style is what precedes the Gothic in the Holy Roman Empire, but … Gothic is going to be imported from France, and that's going to mean some major and significant changes in the idea of the shape and design of a church in the Holy Roman Empire.

The area comprising modern Germany, Austria, Switzerland, and the Czech Republic was called the Holy Roman Empire in the Middle Ages. Because this is a big region for one lecture, we have to pick and choose our subjects carefully. We're going to look at the most famous Gothic cathedrals of this region: Strasbourg (part of eastern France today), Cologne, and Prague, then two special churches—one in Germany and one in the Czech Republic—that demonstrate some of the special tendencies of Gothic development in the Holy Roman Empire.

Strasbourg's old cathedral, like so many early churches, was destroyed by fire in the late 12th century. The new church was built around the surviving north transept; that transept and the east end, where new construction began, are Romanesque. Around 1225, a new team came in to complete the building, and that team came from Chartres. Therefore, Strasbourg has a much more French-like nave. But Strasbourg is not a copy of Chartres Cathedral, despite some similarities. Built out of a local, reddish stone, it has a glazed triforium, large clerestory windows, and much higher pillar capitals than at Chartres. The facade has three beautiful sculptured portals, a rose window, and the familiar pattern of tympanum, jamb statues, trumeau statues, and archivolts—all the pieces of a classical French design. But moving closer, we discover on the tympanum the whole Passion cycle: the Last Supper in the lower left; you can see the Crucifixion in the middle of the second level; and the ascension of Jesus into heaven at the top—a longer narrative than we are used to seeing in similar French cathedral settings.

Two of the most beautiful and interesting statues from Strasbourg are in a nearby museum. These are images of two allegorical figures, Synagoga ("synagogue") and Ecclesia ("the church"). Synagoga is blindfolded, carries a broken spear, and has a book in the left hand, all images of defeat. Ecclesia wears a crown and holds a chalice and a cross; it stands erect in a victorious pose. The images are of course problematic, with obvious anti-Semitic implications, but tell us about medieval attitudes toward the relationship between Judaism and Christianity.

The cathedral of Cologne, the largest Gothic cathedral north of the Alps, was started in 1248; it was finished in 1880. In the Middle Ages, only the choir was built. Therefore, we're looking at a mostly modern cathedral, although the builders tried to be faithful to the medieval design. The medieval east end is very high, with a vault height second only to Beauvais. The nave was constructed to match this height. With its glazed triforium and tall, steeply pointed clerestory windows, it may remind us of Amiens. The entire cathedral has regular buttressing, both the medieval and modern parts; the decorative parts of the towers plus these buttresses give the cathedral enormous vertical presence. The facade is the largest of all Gothic facades as well. As you

© iStockphoto/Thinkstock.

Prague Cathedral is the glorious centerpiece of Holy Roman Emperor Charles IV's 14th-century palace complex.

can imagine, Cologne Cathedral had the sponsorship of the Holy Roman Emperor. It is also home to what are believed to be the mortal remains of the Three Kings, so the cathedral was a site of pilgrimage.

The skyline of Prague is dominated by the castle that is now the presidential residence. Inside that palace complex rises the cathedral of Prague, which dates from the middle of the 14th century—although like Cologne, the nave and facade are much newer, completed in the 20th century. It was commissioned by **Emperor Charles IV**, both to glorify his new capital and to house the relics of his holy predecessor, Good King (or Saint) Wenceslas. Only the east end is medieval, and the first architect only completed the ambulatory, around 1350. The second architect we've already met: Peter Parler; this really is his choir. It contains huge clerestory windows and a glazed triforium. These windows are all modern, but they give us an idea of what the originals looked like. Looking at the elevation, we notice a beautiful rhythmic movement to the different bays and an interesting meeting of the verticals and the horizontals. The 14th-century chapel that contains the shrine of Saint Wenceslas retains its original decorations.

> **The cathedral of Prague ... was commissioned by Emperor Charles IV, both to glorify his new capital and to house the relics of his holy predecessor.**

The cathedral has a wonderful buttressing system, but in some ways the most important part of the exterior is the north porch, for two reasons. First, above the portal arches and below the window is a mosaic, a very unusual kind of decoration. It is a Last Judgment with the emperor and empress shown kneeling below Jesus. Second, the vaulting contains something extraordinary and new: The ribs don't always stay in contact with stone; we sometimes call these **flying ribs**, and they may be an invention of Peter Parler.

Now let's look at two special churches, starting with the Church of the Virgin—the Frauenkirche—in Nürnberg, Germany. It's a small church, not a cathedral. It is rectangular, with no transept. There are many niches on the outside for sculpture, although that's virtually all gone now. But it's the inside that's so interesting: The two aisles are the same height as the principal nave, and therefore all the vaulting is of the same height. This opens up the building so that we have a sense of its being much wider. We call this a **hall church**, a style that influences places as far away as Spain and the New World.

Finally, we turn to the cathedral of Kutna Hora, east of Prague. Kutna Hora, in the late Middle Ages, was an extraordinarily prosperous silver mining and coin minting town. Its cathedral was built in the late 14th century by the son of Peter Parler, but the choir was only raised at the end of the 15th century. In the early 16th-century nave, the ribs no longer have much structural importance but have a complex decorative scheme—perhaps the regional equivalent of fan vaulting in England. Even the keystone is highly decorative. The gallery vaulting reminds us of Peter Parler's in the north porch of Prague Cathedral, going every which way and including flying ribs. Because the church has no transept, we can look at the line of flying buttresses that goes all the way down either side. In the 16th century, three tent-like structures were added, so that the building resembles a sailing ship, with the flying buttresses being the oars. Overall, Kutna Hora is an extreme expression of the late Gothic exuberant Czech style. ■

Important Terms

flying rib: A type of rib first found in Prague Cathedral where some of the ribs are not part of vaults but extend unattached from one place to another.

hall church: A church with aisles as high or almost as high as the principal aisle of the nave. This form of Gothic architecture developed toward the end of the Gothic era in Germany.

Name to Know

Charles IV (r. 1346–1378): King of Bohemia and Holy Roman Emperor. Charles established Prague as his capital and commissioned the building of Prague Cathedral.

Suggested Reading

Frankl, *Gothic Architecture*, chaps. 3.8, 3.10, 3.12, 4.4.

Nussbaum, *German Gothic Church Architecture*.

Questions to Consider

1. What Gothic elements are unique to Germany and Bohemia?

2. How can we think about German Gothic as a combination of an inherited Romanesque tradition plus French influence, especially in places such as Strasbourg, Cologne, and Prague?

3. How can the Gothic church Kutna Hora be considered Gothic, given how different it looks both inside and outside from other Gothic structures?

Gothic Churches in the Holy Roman Empire
Lecture 21—Transcript

Now that we've returned from England to the Continent, we're going to do a kind of clockwise movement around France. We're going to begin in the east in what today we largely call Germany but more properly in the Middle Ages we'll call a Holy Roman Empire; then we're going to go south of France to Italy; and finally west to the Iberian Peninsula; and ultimately, at least for a brief moment, to the New World as well.

Having said that, let me point out that as I suggested already, "Germany" is a kind of misnomer, because the Holy Roman Empire consisted of more than Germany in several ways in the Middle Ages. The area we're going to look at in this lecture includes parts of what's now western France, as well as including Germany, Austria, Switzerland, and the Czech Republic, and even those borders aren't exact. One obvious thing to say is this is way too big an area for one lecture, and therefore we're going to be very specialized and highlight certain things. First of all, we're going to look at the most famous of the Gothic cathedrals in that region that we call the Holy Roman Empire, beginning in Strasbourg—which is in eastern France today—and then Cologne, and then Prague, the capital of the modern Czech Republic. Then, toward the end of the lecture, we're going to look at two special churches, if you will, one in Germany and one in the Czech Republic, and they're going to demonstrate some of the special tendencies if Gothic development in the Holy Roman Empire. That is our plan for this lecture.

Let me suggest that before we can begin to look at the Gothic in the Holy Roman Empire, it's worth briefly reminding ourselves a little bit of the fact that the Romanesque style in the Holy Roman Empire, although a localized set of styles really, looked quite different than what we were used to in France. We can remember that by looking at one particular Romanesque church we glanced at briefly when we were doing our look around Europe at Romanesque styles. This is the Benedictine monastery of Maria Laach, and I want to look at it from two angles just to remind you of how different the Romanesque looks here than it does in the areas where we concentrated in France. We're looking at it, obviously, from the side in this photograph, but if you look to the right we are looking at the front; and so the front has a rounded apse as well as, as you can see, three towers. When we look at the back, we discover there are three more towers, and also a rounded east end; so both the east and the west ends are rounded, and we have towers of different sorts going everywhere. This is obviously going to be something we need to remember because A) the Romanesque style is what precedes the Gothic in the Holy Roman Empire; but B) Gothic is going to be imported from France, and that's going to mean some major and significant changes in the idea of the shape and design of a church in the Holy Roman Empire.

We turn first to the cathedral of Strasbourg. Again, today, Strasbourg is part of France. There was—this is going to sound like a story you've heard a lot in the past—a fire that destroyed the old cathedral in 1176, and therefore a new cathedral was begun from the east and the oldest part that survives today is the north transept; and, in fact, those parts of the church are Romanesque. In other words, even in the fourth quarter of the 12th century in this area, they were still building in the Romanesque style, although Saint Denis was underway in the late 1130s in France and we know that entire Gothic cathedrals in the style that came out of Saint Denis were being constructed in France before the fire of 1176 at Strasbourg. However, what happens in Strasbourg is around 1225, a new team comes in to complete the building, which is, of course, most of it after all, and that team came from Chartres; and therefore we have a much more French-like Gothic cathedral as the nave of the cathedral of Strasbourg. As you can see in this image how it dominates the city of Strasbourg today, one tower doesn't get built; so again, like some of the French cathedrals we've seen it has a kind of lopsided look to it. But it's a wonderful and beautiful cathedral; you want to spend at least a little bit of time here.

As I said, in some ways, Chartres is the model for the nave of the cathedral of Strasbourg, but this is not a copy of Chartres Cathedral. You look at this and you say, "Yeah, there are a lot of things that remind me of Chartres, the four-part vault, and the triforium, and the clerestory windows, and so on," but I wouldn't confuse being in Chartres when I walked into the cathedral of Strasbourg. We know that despite these influences, because we've seen in them in France and in England as well, we don't have any building that simply copies in the modern sense any other building. For example, if we looked here, we can see that there is a glazed triforium (different than Chartres), large clerestory windows, and if we look at the pillars we can see that the capital of the pillar really is much higher than at Chartres so at many ways the verticals are more emphasized here than at Chartres Cathedral that was, after all, begun about 30 years before Strasbourg's nave was completed.

We find that one of the most interesting aspects of the cathedral of Strasbourg is the extraordinary facade, and you can see that it has three beautiful sculptured portals; it's very hard to see because of the fact that there really is no plaza or square in front of the church, and therefore when you get there with your camera it drives you crazy, you can't get back far enough to take a picture of it unlike virtually all the Gothic cathedrals we've seen in France, for example. Here, as much as we can have a telephoto lens without too much distortion, we see the facade with the rose window and the sculptural program that, again, is very elaborate and very beautiful. As we move toward the central door, you certainly recognize the pattern here with the tympanum, the jamb statues, the trumeau statue, and the archivolts; all the pieces are there of a classical French design.

But as we move closer and take a look at the tympanum, what we discover is that this is, I believe, the longest narrative cycle of the life or part of the life of Jesus as we see in any Gothic cathedral, because normally—as we've see in places like Chartres and Amiens, where we've looked at the sculptural program in quite a bit of detail—there's a very small number of scenes that's actually depicted in the tympanum. Here, though, we have the whole Passion cycle: You can see the Last Supper in the lower left-hand side, for example; you can see the Crucifixion in the middle of the second level; and by the time you get to the top level, you have the ascension of Jesus into Heaven. We really have this elaborate narrative, beautifully sculpted in wonderful detail, at Strasbourg; again, a longer narrative than we are used to seeing in similar kinds of French cathedral settings.

Two of the most beautiful and interesting statues, I think, are no longer on the facade, they now have copies; but they are these two statues that are in a museum nearby in Strasbourg where one can, obviously, go visit them. These are images of two allegorical figures, one called Synagoga (meaning, of course, "synagogue") and one called Ecclesia (that is to say, "the church"). This is not the first time these images have appeared; for example, they appear at Notre Dame in Paris. Later on, they appear at the crucifixion in somewhat different form in the pulpit by Nicola Pisano that we will see in the cathedral of Siena. But at any rate, I want you to notice these two beautiful statues. The Synagoga, you can see, is blind with a blindfold on, has a broken spear, has a book in the left hand; that the synagogue, if you will, is defeated at the crucifixion. That's the image. This is a troublesome image today in many ways because there are certain anti-Semitic elements to it, obviously. But here we see the synagogue being defeated and you can see the church triumphant because you can see Ecclesia with a crown and a chalice and a cross standing erect and obviously in a kind of victorious pose; so this is an allegorical way of talking about what the crucifixion, what Jesus's sacrificial death on the cross, means. It means the defeat of something and the creation of something else, the church.

These statues decorated the facade of the cathedral of Strasbourg; and again, the copies are still there. As we look at various details of these statues, we can really see how extraordinarily beautiful the statues are, while at the same time the subject matter I think is somewhat discomforting, and should be discomforting it seems to be me because we can't avoid the fact that there was a good deal of anti-Semitism in the church in the Middle Ages and beyond. Here we have an interesting illustration of that, although again, ironically perhaps, it's an illustration of something we regard as ugly in terms of its idea and yet the illustration itself is very beautiful works of art; and that's something we have to sort of wrestle with and try to get our head around.

There's one more thing I want to say about Strasbourg, and that is it's made out of a local stone that is reddish in color and therefore the church, both inside and outside, has a kind of reddish quality to it and I leave it to your imagination what the sun at different angles and at different times of the day does to that reddish stone. But it's a very beautiful building and even though, again, our first thought is it's lopsided and it's squeezed in among a lot of buildings and we don't have a sense of its spaciousness from up close because we can't really get a good look at it up close, it is one of the wonderful Gothic cathedrals that we need to consider.

The cathedral of Cologne was done in 1248; it was finished in 1880. That's a long time. In the Middle Ages, only the choir, the east end, was built; the nave was built in the 19th century and finished only toward the end of the 19th century. Therefore, we're looking at a cathedral where much of it is to us new, although I think quite faithful to the parts that do exist from the Middle Ages. Here we can see it from the front, and it is an enormous building; in fact, it is the largest Gothic cathedral north of the Alps. Here we see it across the river, of course, from the east end and you can see the two beautiful towers in the front, you can see it is cruciform in shape as we would expect, and you can see how it just towers in this large modern city of Cologne.

Let's look at the east end for a minute, because that's the part that was begun in 1248. It is high. The vaults of the choir of the cathedral of Cologne are higher than any other vaults except for Beauvais, and they're just a little bit lower than the vaults of Beauvais. Given the fact that in the 19th century the nave was built at the same height, what that means is this is the highest of all Gothic cathedrals although most of it is not medieval; that is to say, the vaults are higher than Amiens, which is the highest of all the cathedrals that were finished in the Middle Ages. But you can see the enormity of this: You can see how high the aisle is; you can see the glazed triforium; the very steeply pointed clerestory windows; this is quite an extraordinary building. In many ways, the east end reminds us a good deal of Amiens with the glazed triforium and the very high aisle that we see there.

If we stand back in the modern nave and look at the entire cathedral, again, its enormity strikes us. It is quite a soaring edifice into the triforium and then the clerestory windows, and, of course, we see the vaults; the standard four-part vault that we have from this period of Gothic design. If we look straight up at the vault, again, it gives us that kind of almost dizzying sense that we really got when we were standing in Amiens Cathedral a few lectures ago. The entire cathedral has regular buttressing, both the medieval part and the modern part, and we get a sense of that as we look from above; sort of ignore the railroad station and focus on the cathedral there. As we look at the cathedral from more or less ground level from the outside, one of the things that strikes us is the whole building just soars; that is to say, the decorative parts of the towers, for example, plus the buttresses themselves give us this enormous vertical sense, perhaps more than any of the cathedrals we've seen in France.

The facade is the largest of all Gothic facades and, in fact, it's one of several records that Cologne Cathedral has. In addition to having the largest facade, as I said, if you count the 19th century parts then it is the highest vaulted of all Gothic cathedrals, and it is the largest Gothic cathedral north of the Alps. This was a place, as you can imagine, that had the sponsorship of the emperor, where the Holy Roman Emperor would worship; but it was also, like so many other cathedrals we've seen, an important place for relics. The special relic of Cologne is the shrine of the Three Kings; that is to say, this was believed to contain the mortal remains of the Three Kings, or Magi, the ones who journeyed to visit Jesus in Bethlehem. As you can imagine, because, of course, they're famous for their pilgrimage, there were many pilgrims who came to venerate and worship in the presence of the mortal remains of the three Kings.

Let us now go into the Czech Republic and look at the cathedral of Prague. Anybody who has been to Prague knows that the city is dominated by the castle that is still, by the way, the residence of the president of the Czech Republic; but as we look across we see that inside all that palace complex rises the cathedral of Prague, which dates from the middle of the 14th century although like Cologne, the nave and facade were not done until the 19th century and, in fact, were only completed in the 20th century. But what an extraordinary location: not right in downtown Prague like so many cathedrals are right in the center of cities but rather surrounded by the palace of then the emperor now, again, the president. Only the east end was completed in the Middle Ages and the first architect really only completed the ambulatory; that is to say, the part nearest us in this photograph, the part that goes around the choir with the side chapel. It was completed around 1350 because the emperor at the time was the Emperor Charles IV, and Charles IV decided to make Prague his capital. In doing so, he established the first university in the Holy Roman Empire and, since he was also king of Bohemia, this was his residence and he decided to glorify and beautify this city. He had the pope elevate the bishopric to an archbishopric to make it a more important ecclesiastical center and built a suitable place that was not just the cathedral of Prague but, as we'll see in a minute, also a place with great relics: the relics of his holy predecessor, Good King, or Saint, Wenceslas.

The second architect who was brought in completed the east end. We've already run into him; we've talked about him when we talked about how the cathedrals got built. His name is Peter Parler, and he came from an experienced family in building Gothic cathedrals; and this really is, therefore, his choir although it is his predecessor's ambulatory. We saw that his bust is located—it's very small, by the way—in the choir; you can barely see it from ground level, but he is recorded there as the most important of the architects of this great cathedral. Again, the nave was built in the 19th and early 20th centuries—but I just have to tell you for a minute, I've tried not to do this very much, but there are some fairly interesting windows in the modern part; I just want to show you one detail here to remind you of the fact that stained glass windows in modern time are still executed but they're obviously in a very different style, such as we saw the Marc Chagall window when we were in the cathedral of Reims.

You can see in Peter Parler's choir, or the east end of the church, that again we have the huge clerestory windows and we have the triforium that's glazed. These windows are all modern, by the way—there is essentially no medieval stained glass left in the cathedral of Prague—but it gives us an idea of the colorfulness of so many of these churches before their windows were destroyed or removed. If we look at the elevation here in the choir of the cathedral of Prague, I want you to notice first of all there is some beautiful rhythmic movement to the different bays of this cathedral, and second I want you to notice how interestingly there is the meeting of the verticals and the horizontals, because you can see there are horizontal lines that are interrupted by the verticals and verticals that are interrupted by the horizontals. It's a wonderful play on that tension between what draws our eyes up and down from nave to east end and what draws our eyes upward to the vault and ultimately upward to Heaven. I mentioned that this was the place where there were important relics, and the relics are of—as our old Christmas carol goes—Good King Wenceslas. This is looking into the beautifully decorated—and it has its original deocrations—14th-century chapel that contains the shrine of Saint King Wenceslas.

As you would expect, I think, we have a wonderful buttressing system for this cathedral, and we see it here by looking at the east end; but in some ways the most important part of the exterior is the south porch, for two reasons:

We're going to look underneath those three arches there and look at the porch; we're also going to notice that right above the three arches that we see and below the window there is a mosaic, a very unusual kind of decoration. There are two things that draw us to the south porch of the cathedral of Prague that we want to look at for a minute. First of all, if we look at the vaulting of the south porch we see something extraordinary; something new: Some of these ribs don't always stay in contact with stone; that is to say, they actually have space all around them. We actually sometimes call them "flying ribs"; we've talked about flying buttresses, these are flying ribs. We can see them from a couple different angles. This seems to be something that Peter Parler developed, and as we're going to see in a couple minutes when we turn to the cathedral of Kutna Hora, also in the Czech Republic, we're going to see how some of this sort of extravagant vaulting that we see here turns into some unique versions of Gothic vaulting that develop in the Czech Republic and in parts of what's now Germany as well.

The mosaic is interesting. It's important to remember that Charles IV, as Holy Roman Emperor, went to Rome for his coronation and would have seen many mosaics in Italy including in Rome itself; and so he brought artists from Italy, primarily from Venice, to put a mosaic on the south porch, which was the principle entrance of the cathedral, remember, until the nave was built in the 19th century. It is a mosaic of the Last Judgment, with Christ the judge in the center and the emperor and empress kneeling down below; and then we have very traditional iconography of the Last Judgment. We can see it here a little bit more closely; see the emperor and the empress right around the middle arch there. Here we see the resurrection of the dead, "the trumpets shall sound, the dead shall be raised"; we've seen this a lot in stone, now we see it in a mosaic. It seems like an odd way of decorating a Gothic church to us although it's important to remember there was also a mosaic on the first Gothic building, Saint Denis; again, Suger had been to Rome. Here we see on the other side—I wanted to give you a detail—the damned being dragged off and the angel there keeping them from coming over to the Heaven side; this is another one of those reminders: Hell is a pretty nasty place, and Hell is forever.

I want now to take a look at two special churches and special kinds of churches; certain developments that take place in the Holy Roman Empire.

This is the Church of the Virgin—the Frauenkirche, it's called—in the city of Nuremburg; of course, Nuremburg is a city we all know for the trials that took place there after World War II. But this beautiful little church, which sits in a lovely *platz*—or plaza or piazza, if you will—is an interesting kind of Gothic building. It's relatively small; it's not a cathedral; you can see that it does not have a transept, it's rectangular; there are many niches on the outside for sculpture, although that's virtually all gone now; but it's the inside that's so interesting, because the two aisles are the same height as the principle nave, and therefore all the vaulting is of the same height and that just opens up the building so that we have a sense of it being much wider. Of course, we know cathedrals are wide, but they have either one or two aisles on either side of the nave that are different heights. Here, everything's the same height; we call this a "hall church," and we're going to see that the hall church style influences places as far away as Spain and the New World in the Late Gothic Period. This is a good example; and it may have been designed by Peter Parler, the same person who designed the cathedral of Prague, or at least much of the cathedral of Prague. This particular kind of church, the hall church, was even imitated in the latter part of the 15th century with rounded arches in the city of Pienza, Italy because the pope, Pius II, when commissioning that cathedral in his hometown had experienced working in Germany and liked the openness of the hall church and transferred that style, with some changes, to Italy. Again, it's a very interesting and successful form of Late Gothic.

Finally, I want to turn to the cathedral of Kutna Hora, a bit to the east of Prague. Kutna Hora, in the late Middle Ages, was an extraordinarily prosperous silver mining town, and a place where money was minted for the Holy Roman Empire. A cathedral was begun because the city was raised to the level of a bishopric in the late 14th century, actually by the son of Peter Parler, but not much was done for about a century; and at the end of the 15th century, the choir—the east end of the church—was raised. If we look at this particular image, we can see extraordinary kinds of vaulting: We have a four-part vault at the very bottom; then we have this more complex vault in the ambulatory; and then if we look up into the ceiling of the church, the principle vault, you can see it's sort of quite wild. Look at the extraordinary pattern of the ribs in the vault of the cathedral of Kutna Hora. Here we look at it surrounded by these huge clerestory windows; and, by the way, those are coats of arms of various guilds and various noble families. It just reminds us of some things we've seen before—that is to say, the triforium, and the clerestory, and we have the pillars that zoom straight up to the vault—but again, what a vault.

But even this will seem conservative compared to what was built at the beginning of the 16th century when the cathedral was completed. This is the vault of the nave, which was done last; and as you can see, the ribs no longer have much structural importance, but what a decorative scheme this is. This is perhaps the equivalent in the Holy Roman Empire of fan vaulting that we've seen in England. But look at this beautiful flower petaling here, and notice that even though we have pillars, it's hard to note where the bays are; that this has become one big design that's been created here. Everything here is extraordinarily decorative; it sort of can't get more decorative than this, along with that fan vaulting that we saw in England. Here I wanted you to look up with one of the pillars all the way into the vault, and as we stand at an angle we see there's an aisle over to the far right of this photograph, but look at the beautiful gallery up above. If we look at the gallery in some detail, we discover that the vaulting there reminds us of what we saw of Peter Parler's in the north porch of Prague Cathedral, going every which way, some are connected and some are not connected to the roof itself. We have this extraordinary display of virtuosity here, as well as on the principle vaults. I couldn't resist showing you an image that reminds us that from the inside we can see what holds this all up on the outside; this clear window allows us to see the flying buttress outside.

The facade was only completed in the 19th century, and ultimately is not very interesting. But this church has no transept, and therefore we really can look at the line of flying buttresses that goes all the way down either side and then, of course, around the east end. In the 16th century, when they put the roof on the church, they built these three tent-like structures so that the building, to me, looked like a great big ship with the sails and the flying buttresses being the oars. This is one expression, one extreme expression, of the Late Gothic and the exuberant style that we find here in the Czech Republic and also in Germany, different parts of the Holy Roman Empire. We've come a long way from what we saw originally when we looked at Saint Denis, Laon, Notre Dame, Amiens, and Chartres. They were stately and powerful, but sometimes even a little bit somber, certainly solemn. It's hard to find anything solemn or somber either in the inside or the outside of the cathedral of Kutna Hora. It's worth a day trip from Prague.

Now that we've gone east out of France, we're going to cross the Alps and head to Italy.

Gothic Churches in Italy
Lecture 22

There are people who say the Italians never got Gothic. They never really understood it, and although they used elements of the Gothic style in the building of their large buildings, it's such a different product than what we see in France or England or Germany that it's just hard to know even whether the term applies.

Almost nobody goes to Italy to see Gothic cathedrals. Italian Gothic is not even a very comfortable term to say. Why is this? The Italian Romanesque style is more closely related to the forms of classical antiquity than the Romanesque in France and England, for obvious reasons, as Italy was the center of the western part of the empire and home to more classical structures and ruins than elsewhere in Europe. We may recognize some elements of the Gothic in Italian buildings, but Italian Gothic buildings have little in the way of external buttressing. Big windows by and large never appealed to the Italians, who instead told stories through **fresco** painting. The Gothic period was also shorter in Italy than in other places in Europe. It got a late start, and it ended sooner because of the burgeoning Renaissance. By the 1420s, Italians were building big churches like Santo Spirito in Florence, designed by **Filippo Brunelleschi**. It has a dome and a flat, wooden, decorated roof; this becomes a style of the Renaissance that then spreads from Florence to Rome and throughout the Italian peninsula.

We need to look at some examples of Italy's Gothic architecture and decoration to see how it differs from the rest of Europe. A beautiful place to begin is the 13th-century cathedral of Siena. Where we expect a crossing tower, we find a dome where the small transept meets the nave and choir, and the bell tower is set aside as it is traditionally in Italian churches. The sculpture on the facade dates from the 13th to the 20th century. The mosaics at the top, for example, are quite late. However, the facade has a rose window, although the glass is modern; the glass in the rose window at the east end is original. Inside, we see many differences. The floor is inlaid with stories. The arches are round, although there are ribbed vaults. The whole interior structure is striped with black and white marble, matching the colors of the city's flag. Toward the altar, we find more pointed arches.

The most important piece of decoration at Siena is the beautiful Gothic pulpit created in the 1260s by **Nicola Pisano**, "Nick the Pisan," out of a single piece of marble. The panels and the figures at the bottom are among some of the most exquisite Gothic sculpture but are distinct in style from French Gothic sculpture. The figures are quite three-dimensional, fluid, and detailed. The Last Judgment here is both different and familiar; the heaven side is orderly while the hell side is chaotic, but rather than the lap of Abraham, the saved stand simply in rows, looking up at Christ. And of course its location—the altar, not a portal—is different.

Giovanni Pisano, Nicola's son, created two unusual figures that once decorated the facade but are now found in the cathedral's museum. One is of Aristotle, whose presence suggests the Italians were more comfortable with their classical, pagan roots than other Europeans were. The other is of Miriam, sister of Moses. At eye level, she seems distorted, but in fact the sculptor corrected for the fact that she would stand high on the facade, indicating an almost Renaissance-like grasp of proportion.

In terms of floor space, Florence Cathedral is the largest Gothic cathedral anywhere.

Oriveto Cathedral is regarded by many as the prettiest Gothic cathedral in Italy. Perched on a lovely Umbrian hill, Oriveto was once a summer papal residence. The town's original church was replaced with this cathedral to house the relic of a 13th-century miracle. The interior of Oriveto is lackluster in some ways. It's the facade that's special. Most interesting are the four large panels of sculpture beside the doors, created in 1320 by a Sienese sculptor. These are very different from the tympana and jamb statues we are used to. The left panel tells stories about Creation; the next panel, Old Testament prefigurations of Christ; the third panel is the life of Christ; and the fourth panel, on the far right, is the Last Judgment. The sculptures are in high relief and the figures exquisitely detailed and naturalistic.

The Duomo, Florence's cathedral, is the largest Gothic cathedral in the world.

Let's return to the Basilica of San Francesco in Assisi, a monastic church and burial site of Saint Francis. There are a few flying buttresses, possibly added after construction. The facade has a wonderful rose window, a wheel within a wheel within a wheel, perhaps a reference to Ezekiel's vision. The interior is more noticeably Gothic, with lancet windows, four-part vaults, and pointed arches. The windows are stained glass of German and French manufacture, arguably the best stained glass in Italy. The decorative scheme inside is painting, doing the narrative work that windows did in France. The lower part of the nave contains 28 stories from the life of Saint Francis. Traditionally we ascribe these paintings to **Giotto**, although they are likely the work of many artists. There is a kind of budding naturalism about the painting, like that which we saw in the statues of Aristotle and Miriam.

In terms of floor space, Florence Cathedral is the largest Gothic cathedral anywhere. It was begun in 1296; the dome was added in the early 15th century based on an earlier plan. The bell tower is exterior and may have been designed by Giotto. The baptistery is Romanesque. The cathedral has radiating chapels, and we see a familiar maze on the nave floor, as well as pointed arches, four-part vaults, and a rounded choir. It has a very high aisle and small oculi instead of clerestory windows. Other important Gothic churches in Florence include Santa Maria Novella and the church of Santa Croce.

The most obviously Gothic cathedral in Italy is the cathedral of Milan. Started in the 1390s by French architects, it took a long time to construct and has been constantly remodeled over the centuries. The pillars are big with very extended capitals, but many horizontal design elements intervene in the vertical flow. The facade is a mixture of Renaissance and Gothic elements. The elaborate flying buttresses were added in the 19th century to make the cathedral look somewhat more Gothic. ∎

Names to Know

Brunelleschi, Filippo (1377–1446): Florentine architect who won a competition to construct the enormous dome at the crossing of the cathedral of Florence, giving a Renaissance crown to the largest Gothic cathedral in Italy.

Giotto (c. 1267–1337): Early Renaissance painter traditionally held to be the creator of the 28 frescos of the life and miracles of Saint Francis of Assisi on the walls of the Basilica of San Francesco in Assisi; most scholars today think that at most he was one artist who worked on that fresco cycle.

Pisano, Giovanni (c. 1250–c. 1315): Sculptor who carved the large statues on the facade of the cathedral of Siena; son of Nicola Pisano.

Pisano, Nicola (c. 1220–c. 1284): Sculptor originally from southern Italy who settled in Pisa, hence his name. He sculpted the pulpit for the cathedral of Siena.

Suggested Reading

Frankl, *Gothic Architecture*, chaps. 3.7, 3.13, 4.6, 4.13.

Wilson, *The Gothic Cathedral*, chap. 3.

Questions to Consider

1. With the exception of Milan Cathedral, are there any recognizable Gothic buildings in Italy?

2. Although appearing to be so different from French Gothic facades, how does the facade of Orvieto Cathedral resemble in content and plan facades such as that of Amiens Cathedral?

3. Why did the French Gothic style not catch on in Italy the way it did in England and Germany?

Gothic Churches in Italy
Lecture 22—Transcript

Nobody goes to Italy—or almost nobody goes to Italy—to see Gothic buildings, Gothic cathedrals. They certainly go to see churches, whether it's some of the great Renaissance buildings or Baroque buildings in Venice, Florence, Rome, Naples, and other cities. But Italian Gothic is not a term or even very comfortable saying, and if it doesn't sound like something we say or our guidebooks say, art historians, too, wonder about Italian Gothic. We have less trouble defining some of the decoration of Italian churches as Gothic; we talk about Gothic sculpture in Italy, and that makes a lot of sense; but there are people who say the Italians never got Gothic. They never really understood it, and although they used elements of the Gothic style in the building of their large buildings, it's such a different product than what we see in France or England or Germany that it's just hard to know even whether the term applies. But we are going to use it; and we are going to look at some buildings from the 13th and the 14th centuries primarily.

The most obviously Gothic building in Italy is the cathedral of Milan, which was not begun until the end of the 14th century and was designed by French architects. Even there, I think we will see as its building continues during what we call the Renaissance, it's a pretty peculiar Gothic church if we take France, and secondarily England, as our standards. Let's talk about why just for a while. Gothic comes from across the Alps if you are in Italy, and the medieval style—the Romanesque style— in Italian architecture is really more closely related to the forms of classical antiquity that we find in France and England. Obviously there are Roman ruins in France and England, and the western part of Germany, and Spain, and so on and so forth; but there is a lot more of that antiquity today, and then in Italy, because after all, Italy was the center of the Roman Empire. So Gothic was foreign and Classic was closer and more indigenous, if you will.

We're going to see in Italian buildings some obviously recognizable elements of the Gothic. If we look at, for example, the Basilica of Saint Francis in Assisi that was begun in 1228, we will notice among other things it has a big rose window over a Gothic portal. Even though that doesn't look much like a French or an English church, it looks like it's recognizably Gothic. But essentially this building, and other Gothic buildings, have little in the way of external buttressing and we will see in a cathedral like that of Bologna— this is the cathedral of Saint Pretonius or San Petronio in Bologna—one of the biggest churches in the world, by the way—it has Gothic vaults, we see that it has a huge aisle and then windows above, although not the standard clerestory windows and there's no triforium; nevertheless, this is recognizably Gothic. But big windows by and large never appealed to the Italians, because obviously there was this French theology that we traced back to Suger, Saint Denis, and Pseudo-Dionysus about light that didn't seem to be as important in Italy. Of course, we know that the windows—and we saw this at Chartres in particular—are places to tell stories, to tell narratives, to educate. Now there are stained glass windows in Italy—although most of them are made by Germans, French, and even English—but what the Italians liked to do was paint their walls in a kind of painting that we call fresco in wet plaster. The desire for big windows simply wasn't there, because the predominant narrative form of art was the fresco and not the stained glass window.

Another thing to say about Italy is its Gothic period is shorter than in other places in Europe. First of all, it got sort of a late start; after all, we know that France—or at least the northern part of France—is transitioning to Gothic in the middle of the 12th century. We know that Gothic begins in England in 1174 after the fire at Canterbury. But Gothic is slower coming to Italy, and it ends more quickly because, of course, Italy is the home of the Renaissance. By the 1420s, Italians are building big churches that look like this: This is the church of Santo Spirito in Florence; it comes from the first half of the 15th century and it's designed by Filippo Brunelleschi, who also designed the dome of the cathedral as we'll see in a few minutes. If we look at this, we notice it has a flat, wooden, decorated roof and we say, "Gosh, this seems to be a throwback to some of the earliest Christian churches, those basilicas that we saw in the very first lecture," basilicas like Santa Sabina and Santa Maria Maggiore in Rome; after all, Rome's just down the road a piece. So this is a very, some would say, anti-Gothic, but it's certainly a non-Gothic building; and this becomes a style of the Renaissance that then spreads from Florence to Rome and to other places as well, mostly in northern Italy and down to Rome but later on throughout the Italian peninsula. We need to appreciate, in addition to the other issues, that the Gothic Period is contracted in Italy.

However, having said that, certainly there are Gothic buildings—whether it's the basilica in Assisi or the cathedral of Milan—in Italy and, as we will see in a few minutes when we look at Florence, the largest Gothic cathedral; not the highest, but the largest in terms of floor space. The largest Gothic cathedral is, in fact, the cathedral of Florence; so we need to look at some examples of Gothic architecture and decoration—the decoration will be, again, very different from what we've seen—in Italy, and a beautiful place to begin is with the cathedral of Siena. This was begun early in the 13th century, and one of the first things to notice is that where we're used to having crossing towers (we saw them especially in England) or spires like we see at Notre Dame in Paris or Amiens, we have a dome at the crossing where the transept—it's hard to see the transept in this aerial photograph because of the fact there are buildings surrounding it, but there is; not very much of one, but there's some expansion there—and we have this crossing that is not a tower but a dome, and, of course, the bell tower is set aside as it is traditionally in Italian buildings; again, we learned that early on when we looked at, for example, the cathedral of Pisa early in the course.

This is the facade of the cathedral of Siena. We have works on the facade from the 13th century, we have works on the facade from the 20th century, and most periods in between; the mosaics, for example, at the top are really quite late. But as you can see, it's a highly decorated Gothic style with a rose window; although the glass in this rose window is fairly modern, the glass in the rose window at the east end is, in fact, beautiful, precious 13th-century stained glass. As we walk in, the first thing we say is, "Boy, this doesn't look like a lot of cathedrals I've been in"; and by now, at least with me, we've been in a lot of cathedrals. We're first of all struck by the floor: All of the Siena Cathedral floor is inlaid figures and stories, and we can just get a glimpse of some of those as we look down the nave. We'll notice there are rounded arches; there are, of course, ribbed vaults, but many of the arches are, in fact, rounded. This just doesn't look much like a Gothic cathedral that we've seen. When we stand on the ground and look at it, where we can see the floor better, we notice that the columns and, in fact, all of the interior structure is striped black and white. Both of those marbles come from not too far from Siena and Siena's colors—that is to say, the representational colors of its flag of its city—are black and white; so this is a civic display as well as an ecclesiastical display, I think it's fair to say.

As we move toward the altar, we can, by the way, see more pointed arches and we see columns that remind us of the sorts of columns that we've seen as we've looked at various Gothic cathedrals, especially in France. But I want you to focus on what's in the middle of this photograph, because this is the great decoration of the cathedral. There's a lot of sculpture on the outside, and we're actually going to glimpse at a couple statues in a minute; but the most important piece of decoration here is this beautiful Gothic pulpit done in the 1260s by an artist originally from the south of Italy but later on from Pisa named Nicola Pisano; "Nick the Pisan," if you will. The panels and the figures below are among some of the most exquisite Gothic sculpture. We're going to focus in on three of the panels, because I think we'll see the style is quite distinct from the Gothic sculpture of France. If we want to compare, the facade of Amiens was probably done in the 1220s; this is less than 40 years later and, of course, it's in a different genre, much smaller and whatever. But look at the style.

We can see here the Crucifixion in one of those scenes. Look how three-dimensional those figures are; look at the fold of the draperies, the movement of the draperies, the bending of the knees through the draperies. This is very high relief sculpture with extraordinary detail; and, by the way, this is all carved out of one piece of marble, these aren't carved separately and set in. It's, again, one of the great masterpieces of medieval art; of any kind of art of any period of the Middle Ages. But this is certainly something that's quite different than what we have seen in terms of style—obviously not content, but style—in France. The last two panels show us the Last Judgment, and you can see here between the sections of this on the very far left sits Christ; you can see the cross underneath him. Here, we are looking at Hell. We've seen lots of Last Judgments, in tympana and sometimes expanding into the archivolts; for example, the way we saw it at Chartres in the south porch and Amiens. But look at the movement of these figures: Satan is in the lower right-hand corner, look at that ugly mask-like face that he's wearing; and we have this total chaos of Hell depicted quite differently than we had it depicted in the tympana and archivolts in France. On the other side is Heaven. We're used to seeing Heaven as the bosom or the lap of Abraham. We saw it in the Romanesque in Conques; we've seen it in the Gothic in several places. But here, as you can see, what we have with the resurrection of the dead at the very bottom is row after row after row of the saved looking up at Christ.

Notice that one side is chaotic and one side is orderly. Again, that principle is not new; we saw that in the Romanesque Last Judgment at Conques. But here, the way it is laid out, the design of it and the actual carrying out of the pattern makes it a very different experience. Also, we're not looking at it on the facade of this church; we're looking at it as we hear the Bible read and the sermon preached because, after all, this is on a pulpit in the cathedral of Siena.

I want to show you two statues from the outside; two of the many, many statues. A whole series was done around 1295 by Nicola Pisano's—the author of the pulpit—son, named Giovanni Pisano, who probably assisted his father on the pulpit. There are figures from the Old Testament and figures from pagan antiquity that decorate the facade. They've been taken off now because of pollution and problems, and they're in the museum of the cathedral in Siena. But this is a statue, again around 1295, of Aristotle; in fact, Plato and Aristotle are on the facade, perhaps suggesting that in Italy—although we've seen pagan figures represented in Laon and Chartres—perhaps in Italy they're a little more comfortable with Classical antiquity; because after all, again, if you're in Siena you're not very far from Rome, which is, at least in Western Europe, the center of Classical antiquity. Here we have Aristotle, and here we have a figure here called Mary or Miriam; she's the sister of Moses. She looks sort of odd to us as we look at her straight ahead, but we need to remember that she is up high on the facade of the cathedral, and therefore if you stand below and look up she does not look distorted; in other words, the artist has made a correction for where it is. That's very different than that gallery of kings we saw at Notre Dame in Paris, or at Amiens, or the baptism of Clovis and Reims, because all those figures are sort of standing straight with very little movement. Here, the artist has made different kinds of calculations and decisions, and obviously stylistically this is quite removed from those much more formal figures that we saw in France.

Let me remind you one last thing about the cathedral of Siena; it's a story I told you in Lecture 7: The Sienese decided to expand their cathedral so that it would rival Florence's, because Florence was building a great big new cathedral. As we look at an aerial shot we can see the new facade that never got completed and the top right part, and you can see how the church that actually exists was going to become the transept of this new, enormous cathedral and the works were interrupted by the Black Death and never resumed, although those ruins are left.

We're going to move now to what many people would regard as the prettiest Gothic cathedral in Italy; of course, it doesn't hurt if the cathedral happens to be on top of a beautiful hill in a gorgeous hill town named Orvieto in the region of Italy known as Umbria. This cathedral was built as a special place. It was a summer papal residence, the city of Orvieto, so there's a lot of patronage; but a miracle took place in the 13th century near Orvieto. A priest who doubted that the bread and wine were actually the body and blood of Christ was saying mass one day, broke the host, and it bled onto a cloth. That cloth was brought to Orvieto, and this is the chapel where that's preserved. The whole reason for tearing down their sort of rickety cathedral was to build a shrine that among other things proclaimed the doctrine of transubstantiation: that the bread and wine when consecrated actually become the body and blood of Christ. That relic is kept here; this chapel—which you can see is decorated with frescoes, a typically Italian way of telling stories— is, in fact, the north transept of Orvieto Cathedral.

The interior, I must say, is kind of lackluster in some ways. Notice, by the way, that Orvieto, unlike Siena, still has a wooden roof. 13th century Gothic church, you can see the lancet window in the east end, but it has a wooden roof. But it's the facade in Orvieto that's special. Again, it has mosaics that were done in different times, you can see there's a rose window; but I want to concentrate on the sides of the door, at the lowest level, because on each side of each door, for a total of four sections, there are large panels of sculpture. Not tympana with jamb statues; a very different way of telling stories and laying out a complex theological scheme on the portal. We're going to read them from left to right: The left piece, which we're going to look at in some detail, tells stories about Creation; the next piece: Old Testament prefigurations of Christ; the third piece—we're moving from left to right, so we're now on the right side of the center door—is the life of Christ; and the fourth piece, on the far right, is the Last Judgment. We're going to look at some of the details. The sculpture was done in the 1320s, probably by a sculptor from Siena. Siena had become the leader in sculpture because the Pisans had come in and done so much sculpture there that they set up a school, had a lot of assistants, and then some of those folks became independent artists as well.

Here is the story of Creation. It goes from the bottom to the top and, as you can see, contains a number of narratives. We're going to focus in on perhaps the most dramatic of all the stories: This is the temptation in the Garden of Eden; there's the tree, there's the serpent, there's Eve, and there's Adam. This is not very much like anything we have seen; it's very high relief, the bodies are quite naturalistic, the tree is quite extraordinary. Even that wonderful serpent; look at that, now there is a serpent, if you will. I also want you to notice that sometimes you'll read about, "In the Renaissance they started making nude statues again; they wouldn't have done that in the funny old Middle Ages"; those people are pretty nude, and they're not leaving out any body parts, it's worth pointing out. This is an extraordinary rendering of a sculptural program very similar in principle to what we saw sort of scattered at Laon and clear at Amiens: You start with Creation, you end with Judgment; it has scope.

Here is a detail from the stories of the life of Jesus: This is the adoration of the Magi; you can see one of the kings pointing to the star right about the Christ child's head. This is the Last Judgment; and instead of arranging it so much good guys on one side, bad guys on the other side, the good guys are up toward the top and Hell is down toward the bottom. We'll take a look at one detail: You can see that all these, again, very realistic bodies have the kind of rope or chain around them, very similar to what we saw at Amiens or Chartres or other places; but you can see the overall effect of the way this is presented and the style. We have a lot of similarity in content, but a lot of difference in form; that tells us something about the nature of Italian Gothic.

We actually began our lecture with a look at this from a different angle: This is the Basilica of San Francesco in Assisi. You can see Assisi is also a hill town, and the buildings below the church are part of what's called the *sacro convento*, the sacred convent, where the Franciscans, the friars minor, lived. Here we approach the basilica, which has the body of Saint Francis. You can see a couple flying buttresses there; I am actually not sure whether they were added later, but I don't think they're important to the architecture of the church. Again, we have very little external buttressing in Italy. We have on the facade a wonderful rose window, and you can see it really is a wheel within a wheel within a wheel reflecting perhaps on that vision of Ezekiel who sees a wheel within a wheel; we saw that depicted, if you recall, in one of those quatrefoils in Amiens.

The interior is more noticeably Gothic. We can see lancet windows—I was going to say in the east end, but actually the basilica in Assisi is rotated 180 degrees, so we're at the back of the church but we're actually looking west rather than east—we see the four-part vault, we see the pointed arches; we see lancet windows on either side. In some ways, it's sort of a good Gothic church. Certainly it's timid in the amount of light; there really is no clerestory, there really is no gallery or triforium; but nevertheless, you look at this and you say, "Yep, I'm in a Gothic church."

Looking back toward the front we can see that rose window, and the light of those lancet windows gives us a very good view of that four-part vault. One of the things you notice is the vaults themselves are painted; everything in the basilica of Assisi is painted. It is literally covered with paintings: the vault; all the walls. The windows are stained glass, almost all German and French, but they're very beautiful; in fact, many people would say they're the best stained glass windows in Italy. I would certainly say that. But the decorative scheme inside is painting; and, in fact, the level around the lower part of the nave of this church contains 28 stories from the life of Saint Francis. Traditionally we ascribe these paintings to Giotto, a famous Florentine painter. I'm convinced—this is actually an area in which I've done a lot of research—that these were painted around 1291 and Giotto might have had a hand in the design, he might have had a hand in the execution, but certainly it's the work of several artists and there's no good documentary evidence that Giotto was in charge; for one thing, he would have been quite a young man at that time, although God knows it's hard to find painters that are better and probably more precocious than Giotto.

I just want to show you two of them to say something of the style. Remember, if we're looking at saint's lives in French Gothic cathedrals, we're looking at glass; we're looking at a story of Saint Nicholas, or Saint Martin, or whoever it might be. Here we see Saint Francis actually kneeling on a mountain, as you can see. This is a miraculous thing; he actually asked God to bring water out of the rock, and you can see the peasants in the lower right-hand side drinking that water. But there's a kind of budding naturalism about the painting. This is virtually contemporary with those two external statues I showed you of Aristotle and Miriam from the facade of the cathedral of Siena; so what we're looking at is the development of a more naturalistic style both in stone and in painting. Perhaps this is the most famous of all the paintings in Assisi: This is the painting of Saint Francis preaching to the birds, with the trees, with Francis himself, with the birds including the bird in flight. These are very, very beautiful ways of telling the same kinds of stories that are being told in windows in France. You may recall there's a statue of Francis on the exterior of Amiens Cathedral; he's the one who's going into Heaven first. Francis is a saint who has transcended his "Italianness" and is a well-respected and well-loved saint throughout Western Christendom, but we get to know him in very different ways in Assisi than we do in Northern Europe.

The cathedral of Florence, one of the most famous buildings and one of the biggest churches in the world, is a Gothic building. It was begun in 1296, and the dome was only added in the early 15th century. There was a plan for a dome a long time before that; after all, you recall the older cathedral of Siena has a little dome at its crossing. Notice also that the bell tower is exterior; we think it was designed by Giotto in the third or fourth decade of the 14th century. The baptistery—the little building on the far left where people are baptized—is, in fact, a Romanesque building, a pre-Gothic building, and you can see much smaller. We see it has radiating chapels; again, very similar to things we've seen in Gothic cathedrals in France. We look around inside we see there's a maze on the floor, we see pointed arches, we see four-part vaults, we see the rounded apse with windows; this is recognizably a Gothic church. Very often, because ewe associate the dome of Brunelleschi with the Renaissance, we say, "This must be a Renaissance cathedral"; but this is a Gothic building with a fabulous dome, and I think it's worthwhile noting that when we're there. Here we're standing a little bit to the side so we can see it has a very high aisle, and then not really clerestory windows but in that area there are oculi, and you can see they're relatively small. I wanted you to get a sense that we can see the Gothic vaulting; we can see this is recognizably Gothic; but again it's a very different form of Gothic.

There are other important churches that visitors see in Florence; they go to see the Renaissance and, in fact, the three biggest churches in Florence are Gothic: the cathedral; this one of Santa Maria Novella, which was the house of the Dominican order in Siena. Part of the facade was done in the 13th century; it was not completed until the 15th century, but there's a kind of harmony about it. This is very recognizably Gothic: It has the Gothic vaults, it has the pointed arches. It has, in fact, a flat east end with windows and frescoes all around it, I might add; again there are stained glass windows here but it's the frescoes that tell the most important stories in the apse of the church.

This is the Franciscan church in Florence, the Church of Santa Croce, the Church of the Holy Cross. You can see the Gothic windows, you can see the chapels on the aisles; so all of these things we recognize as Gothic features. Here's the interior, again recognizable in many ways as Gothic. It has a wooden roof. This was not built, at least as we see it today, until the 14th century; and yet here, this huge Gothic church—like the cathedral of Orvieto, which is a little bit earlier than this—has a wooden roof; it reminds us, again, that that aesthetic of Gothic is quite different in Italy than it is anywhere else in Europe.

The most "Gothicy"—I don't think that's a word—church or cathedral in Italy is the cathedral of Milan. It wasn't begun until the 1390s and it was done by French architects, and it took a long time to build and it's been constantly remodeled: in the Renaissance Period, some in the interior in the Baroque Period, and a lot of innovations were done to the outside—as we'll see in a minute—in the 19th century. But it is certainly a remarkable building with extraordinary decorations. It's sort of hard to ignore the floor of the cathedral; but we do see that although it looks very different—the pillars are very big with very, very extended capitals; in fact, they really come from a later period, they really are Renaissance by the time we get to this part of the building of Milan Cathedral—but you can see the vaults, but you can also see how odd these columns are as they soar up to the top with lots of things that intervene both in color and in horizontal design to chop them up into pieces. We look here to the side: It's a very wide, it's an enormous building, and an important one: Milan was an important center—in fact, it was the capital of the Roman Empire in the 4th and 5th centuries—and Saint

Augustine, the great theologian (not Augustine of Canterbury, but Saint Augustine; sometimes we call him Augustine of Hippo) was baptized in the cathedral of Milan, a former building on this spot, by Bishop Ambrose, now Saint Ambrose, one of the great theologians of the church himself.

Here we can look up to those columns; we can see the windows at different levels; and again, we can recognize elements that are Gothic—whether it's the vaults, whether it's a kind of stylized elevation, whether it's the pointed lancet windows—but still we say, "This is a little bit different than anything we've seen." Again, the outside: Most of the doors and windows were, in fact, added in the Renaissance style; so the facade itself is a mixture of Renaissance and Gothic styles. As we look around, we see these highly elaborated flying buttresses, a kind of maze of flying buttresses, with all kinds of gizmos and curlicues; almost all of which, by the way, were added in the 19th century to sort of make it more Gothic as they imagined the essence of Gothic in the 19th century. I just leave you with this last picture from Milan Cathedral. By the way, at Milan Cathedral you have the possibility of going up and walking on the roof; not walking between the vault and the roof like at Reims but actually walking on the roof and, in a sense, weaving in and out among this extraordinary vertical set of spirals that is, again, representative of a particular kind of French Gothic in Italy from the very late Gothic Period.

Gothic Styles in Iberia and the New World
Lecture 23

Spain is a unique mixture of pieces of its history—something, of course, we could also say about England or any other part of Europe—but we need to recognize the Roman and Muslim, as well as the Christian, French, and German influence on these particular buildings.

S panish medieval history is dominated by one fact: In the year 711, Arab Muslims crossed the Mediterranean from Africa and conquered most of the Iberian Peninsula and ruled there in whole or in part until 1492. Spanish medieval history is, to a great extent, dominated by the slow process of Christians regaining that land. That means there weren't many Christians, or Christian buildings, in Iberia during the Middle Ages. Although Christians were given freedom to worship, they didn't have the political and economic clout to build grand buildings. When the **Reconquista**—this attempt to reconquer Iberia—gained momentum around the 11th century, monks from Cluny in Burgundy began to establish monasteries in what is now northern Spain, building a number of monastic Romanesque churches. The most important of these is Santiago de Compostela, the great pilgrimage church that held the body of the apostle Saint James.

The first Gothic cathedral in Spain was begun in 1221 in the northern city of Burgos. Although most of it was completed quickly, the western end was not finished until the 15th century, and that stretch of time will be apparent in the variety of decoration. The facade in many ways shows late medieval French developments, such as the rose window, but the spires are open like the ones we found in the Holy Roman Empire; in fact, we think they were designed by a German. So we have a mix of national influences as well. From the side, we see there are a lot of structures attached to the main cathedral—archways, extending corridors, and all sorts of things—we see that in most Gothic cathedrals in Spain. For some people, it's a kind of distraction; for others, this complexity is one of the attractions of Spanish Gothic. The structure has an organic, living quality.

The cathedral of Toledo was begun around 1226–1227, but even before the Muslim conquest, the archbishop of Toledo was the most important bishop in Spain. The first thing we notice is the very wide exterior. Inside, we see a lot of elements that we're used to in French cathedrals. But as we look closer, we notice, for example, there's no triforium in the nave. The double aisles, combined, are wider than the nave. The width is caused by the architects' need to cover the foundations of a nearly square mosque that earlier stood on the site. The choir has a double ambulatory (again, for width) and does have a triforium, where the window shape shows a hint of Muslim influence, perhaps carried forward from the earlier building.

We don't have as much sculpture in Spanish Gothic cathedrals as we do in France, but some of the best is found on the facade portals at Leon. Leon also has beautiful stained-glass windows—the most extensive, many would say, of all the Gothic cathedrals of Spain. The cathedral of Valencia has a Baroque facade, so we skip that and look at the north porch, with its rose window and sculpted portal. The colonnade of rounded arches surrounding the apse calls to mind Roman architecture and reminds us how Romanized the peninsula was under the empire. The stunning octagonal lantern tower with two rows of windows was added during a 15th-century expansion and is perhaps the building's architectural highlight.

© iStockphoto/Thinkstock.

Spanish Gothic architecture testifies to Spain's Moorish past in both its decoration and its structure; this, the Giralda bell tower in Sevilla, for example, was once a mosque's minaret.

In the 15th and 16th centuries, we see some new features in Spanish architecture. The cathedral of Seville, the largest of all Spanish Gothic cathedrals, has a bell tower that was once the minaret of the mosque that stood here before; the rest of the structure was more or less started from scratch. Inside, there are lots of different styles of vaulting, but the German hall church is a strong influence, with aisles almost as high as the nave. Another new feature is **plateresque** decoration, a term derived from silversmithing that refers to the intricacy of the design. The whole facade becomes sort of a sculptural program. Examples include the church of San Pablo in Valladolid and the church of Saint Esteban in Salamanca. The plateresque is neither Gothic nor anti-Gothic—really it is more like Gothic in the process of being transformed.

> **The plateresque is neither Gothic nor anti-Gothic—really it is more like Gothic in the process of being transformed.**

In the same year that the Muslims were pushed to the very tip of the Iberian Peninsula, Christopher Columbus set sail for the New World. Part of Spain's mission in colonizing the New World was the conversion of the native people. Franciscans, Dominicans, and Augustinians were in the New World before the end of the 15th century; by 1511, three dioceses were defined in the New World. A diocese has a bishop, and a bishop has a cathedral; so the cathedral of Santo Domingo was begun in the Dominican Republic in 1511. Finished in the 1540s, it is small but decidedly Gothic in style: pointed arches, clerestory windows, a hall church form, and across each vault a central rib that draws the eye toward the east end.

Sometimes, we need to look at a church and ask, "Is this Gothic or not?" The cathedral of Guadalajara in Mexico has two front towers, but rounded arches; rib vaults, but door pediments. This building wasn't begun until the 1570s, and in some ways it would be hard to call it Gothic at all; on the other hand, it isn't obviously anti-Gothic. Early in this course, we saw how it could be difficult to distinguish the Romanesque from the Gothic. Here again, a structure reminds us that we often encounter not sharp breaks but transitions. We often see a Gothic influence beyond any period we could comfortably call Gothic. So this raises another question: did

Gothic really ever end; or, in some ways, are Gothic ideas and elements of style still alive? ■

Important Terms

plateresque: Spanish architectural style of the late 15th and 16th centuries distinguished by an intricacy of design and ornamentation suggestive of silver plate; *plata* means "silver" in Spanish.

Reconquista: The Christian movement in Spain to reconquer territories lost to Muslim rulers from the time of the Arab conquest of Iberia in 711 until 1492.

Suggested Reading

Frankl, *Gothic Architecture*, chaps. 3.7, 4.11.

Wilson, *The Gothic Cathedral*, chap. 3.

Questions to Consider

1. How does Spain's unique history lead to the unique Gothic structures built there?

2. How can we explain why the Gothic style lingered in Spain far into the 16th century?

3. What does the presence of Gothic architecture in the New World tell us about methods of evangelization that were employed by the Spanish clergy?

Gothic Styles in Iberia and the New World
Lecture 23—Transcript

We're now going to spend a lecture on the Iberian Peninsula and in the New World. Before we begin to look at some of the buildings we're going to examine, it's important to say that Spanish medieval history is dominated by one fact: In the year 711, Arabs crossed the Mediterranean from Africa and conquered most of the Iberian Peninsula—not quite all of it, but most of the Iberian Peninsula—that, of course, had previously been Christian since the fourth century when the Roman Empire became Christian. The Arabs remained as rulers of at least part of Iberia until 1492. If you will, what that means is that Columbus sailing the ocean blue was news number two of the year in 1492; number one was, "We finally kicked out the Arabs after they'd been here for almost 800 years." Therefore, Spanish medieval history is, to a great extent, dominated by the slow and not inexorable process of Christians regaining land in the Iberian Peninsula and driving the Muslims further and further south, until at the end they held on only to Grenada.

There are several important things to say with regard to Christians and Christian buildings during this time. First of all, there weren't a lot of them, especially in the early Middle Ages, because most of the Peninsula was under Muslim rule, and although Christians were allowed to worship in churches they obviously didn't build grand buildings. When the Reconquista— this attempt to reconquer, which involves a lot of foreigners and not just people from Iberia—began to gain momentum and become more and more successful, especially in the 11th century, it was the monks from Cluny in Burgundy that helped to sponsor in some ways the Reconquista, and therefore established monasteries associated with Cluny and built in the Cluniac style once areas were secured for Christians; so there are, especially in the northern part of Spain, a number of important Romanesque churches, primarily monastic churches. The most important Romanesque church in Spain—one I've mentioned several times and we've looked at once and will look again now—is in the very northwest corner of Spain, Santiago de Compostela, which was, among other things, the great pilgrimage church because it held the body of one of the apostles, Saint James, the first of the apostles to be martyred according to the Acts of the Apostles. That is the primary Romanesque heritage of Spain.

The earliest Gothic cathedral in Spain was begun in the year 1221 and, not surprisingly, is built in the northern part of Spain in the city of Burgos. But before we turn to it, let me say this oddity about Spanish Christian building: The most famous of all cathedrals in Spain is not Gothic, it's not Romanesque in its origin, it wasn't even Christian; probably the most famous of cathedral in Spain today is the cathedral of Cordoba in the south, and it was built beginning in the late eighth century as a mosque. It's an extraordinary building, transformed into a cathedral late in the Middle Ages, and remaining today the cathedral of Cordoba. To make things a little bit more interesting and complicated, the mosque was built on the site of an earlier Christian church—again, remember, before Spain became largely Muslim it was Christian—and so this is a Christian holy spot that became a Muslim holy spot that became a Christian holy spot again, and it's a wonderful and interesting building and one deserving our attention. But, since we're studying the Gothic, we're going to look first at the cathedral of Burgos, as I said, in northern Spain.

It was begun in 1221 in the French style and was completed rather quickly, although the very western part was not done until the 15th century. If we look at the inside, we see rather simple vaulting, but we also see something we're going to notice in Spanish cathedrals as we did in English cathedrals: Almost all of these buildings are going to have pieces from different eras. We don't have really any Gothic cathedrals in Spain built in a short period of time in one style like, let's say, Notre Dame in Paris, or Chartres, or whatever with only minor additions later on; and so even as we look inside the oldest of the Gothic cathedrals we see all sorts of decorations and additions to the vaulting and so on of different eras here at Burgos. We simply want to be aware of the fact that we can't study Spanish Gothic architecture as purely and say, "Let's look at a building from this period, let's look at another building from this period" because all of them, it seems, have pieces from very different periods. We need to be aware of that, similar to what I said about most, although not all, English Gothic cathedrals.

The facade of Burgos is impressive and interesting, because in many ways it represents developments that took place late in the Middle Ages in France with the rose window and some of the decoration, especially in the upper part (not so much right around the doors). But the spires are open and they remind us of spires of cathedrals in the Holy Roman Empire, such as the one in Strasbourg or the two in Cologne that we looked at; and, in fact, we think they were designed by a German. We have a Spanish cathedral where we see French elements and German elements, and we'll continue to see that kind of mixture in other buildings that we look at.

While we're here at Burgos, let me say one other thing about this building that also is true of many other cathedrals in Spain. As we look at Burgos from the side, we say, "Boy, there are a lot of things attached to this"; archways, extending corridors, and all sorts of things. That's exactly right, and we see that in most Gothic cathedrals in Spain. How many times did we see in France that you can look straight down with a diagram, with one of our animations, with an aerial photograph and see the church is nice and neatly built in the shape of a cross? But if we look at the designs of many of the Gothic cathedrals in Spain, there's an attachment here, an attachment there; it very often is asymmetrical. Again, we have a more complex and layered kind of building in Spain. For some people who view it, it's a kind of distraction; you have a little bit here and a little bit there, and this doesn't balance this. For others, this is one of the attractions of looking at Gothic cathedrals in Spain; that we get a sampling of a variety of styles. We see the building growing; it has a kind of organic, living quality to it because they tacked this on, then they needed this, then they needed to bury somebody over here, and whatever. I don't want to suggest that one is better than the other, but rather simply that some people are more attracted, if you will, to the purity of some of the French cathedrals, other more to what almost seems like a kind of serendipitous design in the finished product that we have today of these Gothic cathedrals such as Burgos.

A few years after Burgos came the cathedral of Toledo, and Toledo is an important place for Spain. First of all, this cathedral was begun 1226–1227; but even before the Muslim conquest, the Archbishop of Toledo was the most important bishop in Spain. He was what we would call the "primate," sort of equivalent to the Archbishop of Canterbury, for example, in England or the Archbishop of Rennes in France; this was a special place that was important for more than simply the diocese where this building was located. When Toledo was recaptured at the end of the 11th century by the Christians, there was the attempt to elevate this diocese once again to its primacy, and in the 13th century the Pope confirmed that the Archbishop of Toledo is, in fact, the chief prelate in Spain; and so this cathedral was built.

The first thing we notice when we look at the exterior of it is it's very wide; and hold on to that thought because I want to talk about that in a minute. As we look inside, I think we see a lot of elements that we're used to in French cathedrals and that is right; we see a lot of this French influence in the pillars, in the vaulting. I think if we took out sort of that middle part, that screen and decoration, I could probably pretty easily convince you and many other people that this could be very well somewhere in the Ile de France. As we look at it in more detail, we notice, for example, there's no triforium here; so we have the aisle and then we have the clerestory windows. We do have the simple four-part vault that we've seen for the first time really at Chartres; so this is a cathedral influenced by but not a copy of French cathedrals.

It is extraordinarily wide. You can see that it's double-aisled; and, in fact, if you add the aisles together, the aisles are much wider on either side than the principal nave itself. There's an important reason for this, and this will happen in more than one instance in Spain: This is built on the spot where the principal mosque was. We saw that in Cordoba, mosque replaced church; here, church replaces mosque. Winners get to build the big ecclesiastical buildings, if you will. Mosques are of a different shape than churches: They are closer to being square; they aren't, but they're closer to being square. They're not so sharply rectangular as most Christian churches; and so to cover all of the old mosque, it was necessary to make the church very wide, and we really have a sense of that here in the cathedral of Toledo. As we glance through this church, we get a sense—with the ambulatory; you can see there's the double ambulatory here, just as there was a double aisle—as we look from one side to the other, sort of catty-cornered across this church, just how wide it is. I want to focus now on the triforium in this part of the church; there wasn't one, if you recall, in another part of the church we've looked at, but here in the choir there is.

You can see that the arches of the triforium are quite different than anything we've seen; in fact, if you have some experience traveling in any Muslim country, you might say, "Gosh, that sort of looks Muslim to me." It is, indeed, an influence. Although on the one hand, of course, Christians and Muslims are fighting, they also, in many different ways—not just architecturally— learn from and borrow from one another. Here, we think that not only is this in general a Muslim influence in the way the triforium is designed, but it might be—it is at least conceivable—that this kind of arching was, in fact, part of the earlier mosque that was replaced by this building; a kind of transition, if you will, from one building to another. In general, when looking at cathedrals in Spain, one wants to look for ways in which one sees elements of Muslim-style architecture incorporated into these Christian buildings built after the Reconquista.

I want to just turn for a minute or two to the cathedral of Leon—an, as you can see, again, extraordinarily large and beautiful cathedral—and the architecture is not what's principally important here, although it's a very beautiful building; it is the fact that it has, as you can see here looking at the facade, a good deal of sculpture. You can see there are three portals, and there is sculpture in each portal; you can see the flying buttresses and the rose window as well, but the sculpture is important. We don't have as much sculpture in Spain as we have especially in France; and, of course, we had a lot in England that's been lost. But here we have some beautiful portals, and you can just take a look at one of those portals and recognize, again, all the elements from a typical French sculptural program: a tympanum with narrative stories, little figures in the archivolts, and the jamb statues. Some of the best of the Gothic sculpture in Spain is in the cathedral of Leon. Similarly, as we see looking up into the elevation of this cathedral, we want to notice that there are beautiful stained glass windows. We see it from this angle, and also from this angle, that Leon has the most extensive and many would say the best collection of stained glass of all the Gothic cathedrals of Spain; and so it's an important place to come and visit because the two most important decorative elements of Gothic building, windows and sculpture, Leon is an important place to study and it's a cathedral worth a visit.

When we look at the cathedral of Valencia, we don't start with the facade because the facade was redone during the Baroque Period; but rather, we're looking at the north porch and you can see a rose window, and you can see a sculpted portal. It is in this older part not the remodeled part that we can look at some of the work of the Gothic Period. An interesting feature of Valencia Cathedral is this piece of architecture that surrounds the apse. It really is quite extraordinary and unique, and very beautiful I think. If you think about what does that remind me of, it might very well—and I think should—remind you of Roman architecture; and it's important to remember that Spain, or at least much of Spain, came under Roman domination about 200 B.C., so that Spain, other than Italy, was probably the most thoroughly Romanized part of Europe, and this is probably a way that we see Roman influence in the architecture of this Gothic cathedral. This in some ways seems to kind of pay tribute to the Roman heritage just as we saw, perhaps more grudgingly, in the triforium in Toledo that we have here the sort of citation of Muslim architecture. It's really interesting to see some of these unique features because, again, Spain is a unique mixture of pieces of its history—something, of course, we could also say about England or any other part of Europe—but we need to recognize the Roman and Muslim, as well as the Christian, French, and German influence on these particular buildings that we see.

This is the interior of the cathedral of Valencia, and when it was expanded in the 15th century, a lantern tower was added. Here's what it looks like from the outside; but look at it from the inside. This is one of the most beautiful pieces of Gothic architecture that we have in Spain. It's octagonal, as you can see; it has the two rows of windows; and it really is a lantern tower, it really does light the cathedral. This 15th century addition to a 13th century cathedral is perhaps the architectural highlight of this lovely building.

When we get to the 15th and 16th centuries in Spain, we see some new features. We're going to see one of those new features in the cathedral of Seville in the south, which was built in the 15th century, because remember by and large the further south you go, the longer it remained under Muslim control. Then the second of these new features, we're going to see from a couple cities in the north: Salamanca and Valladolid. This is the cathedral of Seville. It is the largest of all Spanish Gothic cathedrals. Again, you can see something that I talked about when we looked at Burgos: There are a lot of things that have been added on; a lot of what look to use like irregular pieces. It's an enormous building from the 15th century. This is its bell tower. It is its bell tower, but although it's remodeled, it was the minaret of the mosque that stood here before; and so, once again, we have a piece of leftover Muslim architecture. The cathedral was more or less restarted from scratch, but they left the tower and where once, no doubt, there was the Muslim call to prayer, later on there are the church bells in that same tower. Again, in some ways, that is the story of Spanish history: going from Christian to Muslim to Christian, as I've suggested.

As we look around inside the cathedral of Seville, it's an extraordinarily complex building; and as you can see from any photograph inside that there are lots of different styles of vaulting and so on. But one of the things that influence this building is that German hall church, such as the Frauenkirche we saw in Nuremberg, because once again we have the aisles about the same height as the principal nave of the church. We're going to see not only does that influence Seville, but it's going to influence the earliest Gothic buildings in the New World. Once again, we see French elements, we see German elements, we see Muslim elements, we see Roman elements in the Gothic cathedrals of Spain because they all are part of the history of Spain. So one development that I want to suggest happens in the 15th century, again, is this influence of the German hall churches. Another is a new kind of decoration that we call the "plateresque"; it actually comes from a word having to do with hammered silver because of the intricacy of the design. You can see here what happens is the whole facade becomes sort of a sculptural program.

This is the church of San Pablo in Valladolid; this is the church of Saint Esteban in Salamanca. Those are, by the way, the two great university towns of Spain. What we see here are old elements and new, because—we'll notice here, for example, there are rounded arches—by the time this is built, 15th or early 16th century, already in Italy the Renaissance is underway and we have new kinds of buildings being built in Italy, and they come to influence Spanish architecture, but they don't replace the Gothic style, they kind of meld into it; so that in the 16th century we have a kind of mixture of Gothic and Renaissance elements. I might add, because of political connections between Spain and Flanders, part of modern Belgium, we also have a lot of influence of the style that comes from what we call the Northern Renaissance in Spain. This plateresque style is not Gothic exactly; it's not anti-Gothic, like some of the architecture and decoration in Italy is; it's kind of Gothic-plus, or Gothic in the process of being transformed. It's important to see that because this is what's underway, these stylistic changes are what are underway, in 1492.

Now let's turn to the second news story of 1492: Columbus sails the ocean blue and lands in the New World. Needless to say, following Columbus very closely were the Catholic Church's orders to build churches and convert people. Franciscans, Dominicans, and Augustinians were in the New World before the end of the 15th century, and they began to preach and to build very humble buildings. But by 1511, less than 20 years after Columbus's first voyage to America, three dioceses were defined in the new world, and in the next half-century many more. A diocese has a bishop, and a bishop has a cathedral; so with the establishment of dioceses comes the building of cathedrals; and the oldest cathedral in the New World today was, in fact, begun in 1511 and finished in the 1540s: the cathedral of Santo Domingo in the Dominican Republic; certainly a building of modest size. But when we think about Gothic architecture—it's a medieval style of architecture—we assume that the style is confined to Europe. But look inside: What we have is obviously and clearly a Gothic cathedral; a small one, a humble one— this is the boonies, after all, in 1511—but nevertheless, this is clearly and dramatically a Gothic cathedral: pointed arches; and, we see here, we have no triforium but we have small clerestory windows. Interestingly enough, this also takes the form of a hall church; that is to say, the aisle and the nave are about the same elevation. We saw that in the cathedral of Seville from the 15th century; we see it here in Santo Domingo at the beginning of the 16th century.

I want you to notice the vaults, because you see running parallel to the windows—that is to say, from our left to right—is a set of ribs that connect all the individual ribs so that we have bay by bay by bay, but they're connected by this line that runs from east to west; and therefore, we have something that helps to cast our eyes, as we walk into the church, toward the east end as well as those elevating columns and arches that have us look up. This is an interesting way of sort of reconciling the verticals and the horizontals here in the cathedral of Santo Domingo.

There were a number of Gothic churches built in the New World; very few of them survive. Like in Europe, a lot of them were remodeled; but also many were destroyed, including many by natural disasters. But, for example, if we go to Quito, Ecuador, although we see that although this cathedral has many non-Gothic elements, you'll notice that as we look toward the altar there, we look through a pointed arch; that there are still Gothic elements left in the modern cathedral of Quito, today. In fact, there are other churches in Quito as well that have some elements of the Gothic in them.

One of the most interesting churches to ask, "Is this Gothic or not?" is the cathedral of Guadalajara in Mexico. As we look at it, you sort of say, "Well, it has two front towers and so on, and that sort of reminds us of Gothic cathedrals"; on the other hand, it has rounded arches and elements of Classical design—you have pediments for the doors, and so on—it doesn't look very Gothic; or does it? Look inside: Again, it's a hall church in type; it has rounded arches; so in some ways it doesn't seem to fit much of the definition of Gothic. But it has these huge pillars that are sort of cloverleaf shaped, very similar to things we saw in France, and you'll see that it has rib vaults; now the vaults are rounded rather than pointed, but it has rib vaults. This building wasn't begun until the 1570s, and in some ways it would be hard to call this Gothic at all; on the other hand, it isn't something obviously not or anti- Gothic.

Here's what this reminds us of, and this is perhaps more true in the New World than anyplace in Europe: Remember at the beginning of course we saw it was sort of hard to know when something Romanesque anymore but was Gothic. We saw rounded arches in the cathedral of Laon, for example, and in the cathedral of Sens; we associate pointed arches with Gothic, so is this really a Gothic building if it has rounded arches? You can say the same thing about the 13th-century cathedral of Siena in Italy. It's hard to know and just have a simple label and say, "Romanesque, Gothic." Here, it's hard to have labels that say, "Gothic, Baroque," which is the style that succeeds the Gothic in Spain, and certain other places as well. Here is one of those places that remind us that it isn't always sharp breaks, but rather it is transitions; and is this a Gothic building? Probably not. Is it a building with clear Gothic elements and Gothic influences? It certainly is.

One perhaps could even say that for the cathedral of Mexico City, designed at the end of the 16th century. Clearly, again, in many elements this is not a Gothic church. But look at the vaults (ignore the dome for a minute): Indeed, they're of the different design than what we've seen in Gothic churches, but they still use ribs as a decorative feature to be sure here. But, of course, we saw ribs being a decorative feature, for example, at Kutna Hora or, for that matter, in King's College Chapel in Cambridge or at Bath Abbey; so the idea that vaulting has become decorative doesn't disqualify it from being Gothic. Again, we're seeing the Gothic influence beyond the period that we usually associate with Gothic.

It's a long way from Saint Denis or Notre Dame in Paris to Guadalajara, let alone Mexico City, not just in miles but in the style of its cathedrals. But it does remind us that for several centuries, beginning in the 12th in the Ile de France, the Gothic style was the dominant form of Christian architecture in Europe. That leads us to this question: If Gothic seems sort of to have ended here in Mexico City or Guadalajara, did it really ever end; or, in some ways, are Gothic ideas and elements of style still alive? Does Gothic make it as a modern (to us) form of architecture, and if so with what changes and transformations? We end here at the end of the 16th century; in the next and final lecture, we'll be looking into the 21st century.

Gothic Architecture in Today's World
Lecture 24

It is the National Cathedral, and one would therefore expect it to have American things, just like you find statues of Joan of Arc or stained-glass windows of Charlemagne in French cathedrals, or a shrine of Thomas à Becket at Canterbury. ... It embraces American ideas, images, and icons. ... Whatever we think of a sort of combination of patriotism and Christianity, certainly it is something that is medieval in its origin.

So what happened to the Gothic between, say, the 15th and 16th centuries and the present? The Italians were the first to reject the Gothic style; in the 15th century Florentine church of Santo Sprito, we see something more like an early Christian basilica, a return to classical architecture that parallels the Renaissance return to classical thought. Presumably, the architects were searching for an earlier and therefore more pure form of Christian design. In Spain, on the other hand, where Gothic got such a late start, the style lingered long enough to be carried to Spain's New World colonies. In northern Europe, which was more heavily affected by the Protestant Reformation, worshipers turned against religious iconography, and many remarkable works of Christian art were damaged or destroyed. The 18th-century Enlightenment took the idea of the light of reason to new extremes and replaced ancient stained glass with modern clear glass in many Gothic churches, and some buildings were deconsecrated and turned over to cults of reason.

In the 19th century, the Romantic movement reversed this trend and embraced the Gothic. The Middle Ages, the thinking went, was a time of nobility, courage, beauty, and chivalry that were lost in the era of urban industrialization. The so-called Neo-Gothic or Gothic Revival style began in England but quickly spread to the United States and eventually all over the world. Look carefully and you will find many 19th-century buildings that are fanciful re-creations of the Gothic style, from the Houses of Parliament (completed in 1860) to the Basilica del Voto Nacional in Quito, Ecuador (consecrated in 1988). Many Neo-Gothic cathedrals have distinct local touches, like the North Cathedral of Beijing's dragon-like flourishes and the Darth Vader grotesque at Washington DC's National Cathedral. The National Cathedral and two other U.S. churches—St. John the Divine and St. Patrick's, both in New York City, will help us grasp the breadth of the Neo-Gothic style.

St. Patrick's Cathedral is the seat of the Catholic archbishop of New York, located in midtown Manhattan near Rockefeller Center. Built in the mid-19th century, it is largely based on English Gothic churches, but it is not a pure copy. For example, like English cathedrals, it has a Lady Chapel and a gallery rather than a triforium, and the vaulting is in the English decorated style. Yet it has a rounded apse like a French cathedral, and the apse has a triforium. These are two very distinctive styles side by side, but both are very traditional.

St. John the Divine is the Episcopal cathedral of New York and, at almost 600 feet long, the largest Gothic church in the United States. It was begun as a Romanesque church, with rounded arches and, originally, a dome. But in 1911, a Neo-Gothic enthusiast named **Ralph Adams Cram** took over the construction. While you'll still see some Romanesque elements in the interior, like rounded arches in the apse, this building also features a wide

Washington National Cathedral, despite its medieval looks, was only completed in 1990.

Gothic facade with five portals, as at Bourges. St. John the Devine also features a gallery and clerestory windows, and the pillars run from the floor to the vault without interruption, soaring like a French High Gothic church. So we are reminded here of the different developments in medieval cathedral architecture in Europe.

Washington National Cathedral—the seat of the Episcopal bishop of Washington, who is Primate of the U.S. Episcopal church—is in some ways the nation's church, the stage for important public events such as state funerals and the National Day of Prayer and Remembrance service on September 14, 2001; such events are very much in keeping with one original purpose of a cathedral. Its facade reminds us of York's, yet like St. Patrick's, it has a rounded east end and flying buttresses in the French style. It has a gallery rather than a triforium and a decorated style vault but a rose window and a high elevation. But most significantly, it has a lot of modern and particularly American features: not only the Darth Vader grotesque, but monuments to American heroes and achievements, like a window celebrating the first moon landing (complete with a fragment of moon rock). It is as much an American building as a Christian one.

> **There are smaller Neo-Gothic buildings all over the United States … and Neo-Gothic is not limited to ecclesiastical buildings; just look at the Brooklyn Bridge.**

There are smaller Neo-Gothic buildings all over the United States; some more notable ones include St. Ann's parish church in Buffalo, New York; the Episcopal cathedral of Indianapolis, Indiana; Loreto Chapel in Santa Fe, New Mexico; and the Episcopal cathedral of San Francisco. And Neo-Gothic is not limited to ecclesiastical buildings; just look at the Brooklyn Bridge. The Gothic today is part of our vernacular architectural language.

It's been reasonably estimated that more stone was quarried during that Gothic era than in any other comparable period in human history, even the era of pyramid building in Egypt. The Gothic churches still standing in Europe today number in the thousands, so for 800 years, Gothic has been a central part of the landscape of virtually all European cities. Adding the Neo-Gothic churches found in every corner of the earth, from East Asia to South Asia to Africa to Latin America, one of the things we realize is if you said to somebody, "Imagine a church," more than likely, the image in their mind is of a Gothic church. These buildings are not only beautiful and powerful; for many Christians, they're the most authentic expression of their faith. ■

Name to Know

Cram, Ralph Adams (1863–1942): American Neo-Gothic architect who took over the building of the Episcopal cathedral of St John the Divine in New York, which was initially to be built in the Romanesque style, and designed the great Gothic building that stands today.

Suggested Reading

Frankl, *Gothic Architecture*, chap. 4.14.

Kendig, *The Washington National Cathedral*.

Stanton, *The Gothic Revival and American Church Architecture*.

Questions to Consider

1. Was there any time after the 12th century in which Gothic architecture was completely shunned and rejected in Europe?

2. To what extent do nostalgia for the European homeland and a simpler past contribute to the building of Gothic churches in modern America?

3. Are the Gothic cathedrals in the United States fantasies of the past, or is Gothic still a form of architecture that is creative and that inspires modern Christians?

Gothic Architecture in Today's World
Lecture 24—Transcript

In this, the final lecture, we're really going to talk about two things: First of all, what happened to Gothic? We got a little bit of a look at that in the last lecture when we saw churches that sort of were and weren't Gothic at the same time; certainly on the surface, except in the most general form of shape, didn't look much like what we've been calling Gothic cathedrals. So what happened to the Gothic from say the 15th and 16th centuries to the present? but second, we're going to talk about an extraordinary revival of Gothic that began in the 19th century and one could argue is still with us today, and even though it may be a Gothic revival and we may refer to that architecture as Neo-Gothic, as we'll see from several examples from all over the world, at least in appearance it's about as Gothic as it gets. There may be modern ways to support things, there may be different building materials, but nevertheless it's clear that for many people Gothic still is the preferred style of ecclesiastical architecture and also in many ways even a style that's preferred for some kinds of secular architecture.

The first place to in some real way reject Gothic was Italy, a place that I've argued in many ways never quite accepted it, never quite got it, never quite saw all the implications of the Gothic style. We can see this in the first part of the 15th century if we take a look at two Florentine churches: one, a church that was built in the 13th century in the Gothic style, a church we looked at before, the Dominican monastery or house in Florence, Santa Maria Novella. It may not have quite all the elements or even all the pizzazz, if you will, of a French Gothic church, but it clearly as we look at it is a Gothic church. We can compare this to the Augustinian house in Florence built in the second quarter of the 15th century and designed by Filippo Brunelleschi. As we look at Santo Spirito here, whatever else we want to say about it, we can say pretty clearly this isn't Gothic. In fact, it looks a lot more like an early Roman Christian basilica—remember that basilica of Santa Sabina we looked at in the very first lecture; it looks a lot more like that: flat roof, rounded arches, as you can see—so that in some ways what happens during the period we call the Renaissance is a return to Classical forms. That means early Christian forms as well as pagan, Roman, and Greek forms; and clearly this is a statement that says, "We are in some way putting aside or rejecting Gothic and we are going back to an earlier"—and presumably something they believed to be more beautiful and more pure—"form of Christian architecture."

In fact, it's interesting that in the city of Rome—which, if you've ever been there, you know is a city of many, many, many churches—there is one, count them one, Gothic church. It's the church of Santa Maria Sopra Minerva, which literally means "Saint Mary over Minerva," and it's a Dominican church in Rome and it sits essentially next to, on the left side of, the Roman Pantheon. Although many people visit this church today, they don't visit it for its architecture. It's pretty nice, but this is not the great Gothic church even of Italy. You visit it because there's a Michelangelo statue, there's the tomb of Saint Catherine of Siena, there's some wonderful frescoes by the 16th century painter Filippino Lippi. When in many ways the most important of all churches in Rome got rebuilt because the old one was literally falling down—that is to say, the old Saint Peter's gave way to the new Saint Peter's—it's in a style radically different than we've been looking at; this is a style that begins as a kind of Renaissance building and ends up, because it takes so long to build, as a building with many baroque features. Clearly, we see the end of Gothic earliest in Italy; again, a place that in some ways, it can be argued, never got Gothic in the first place. In Spain, on the other hand, we saw that Gothic in some ways sort of melded together with the Renaissance style, which after all developed late in Spain because of Spain's particular history; and that therefore in some way this combined Gothic and Renaissance architecture sort of continued into the late 16th century as we saw in places like the cathedral of Guadalajara.

Let's turn now to what happened in the northern part of Europe, north of the Alps. Of course, in the 16th century came the Protestant Reformation, which affected a good chunk of northern Europe; and that doesn't include the places only that are currently Protestant or predominately Protestant like much of Germany but also it included areas like France where there were the so-called "Wars of Religion." In a lot of places in northern Europe—in Germany, in France, in England; although England's going to be something of a special case as we'll see in a minute—not so much was Gothic architecture destroyed, but Gothic decoration was; a lot of sculpture was destroyed, a lot of stained glass, a lot of interior decoration was removed during the Wars of

Religion. We saw, for example, in the cathedral of Noyon in France places for all those statues and nary a statue. As I said, England is something of an exception because in the 16th century, when England left the authority of the Roman church, most of the decoration remained. Monasteries were suppressed, so a lot of monastic churches that were primarily Romanesque were destroyed or severely damaged; and certain Catholic cult places, like the shrine of Thomas à Becket, were destroyed. But nevertheless, it was only in the 17th century with the rise and victory of the Puritans that a lot of Gothic decoration was destroyed there as it had been on the Continent.

The enemies of Gothic were not just the Italian Renaissance thinkers or people with sledgehammers and axes during the Wars of Religion, but in the 18th century, especially in France, we've talked about the growth of the Enlightenment, a kind of new world view that developed. Although, again, the Gothic cathedrals remained, and they remained Catholic churches, many of them were radically remodeled: Get rid of the stained glass windows in many cases—this happened in Amiens—so that more light could come in, a light that no doubt not only represented divine light but also represented the light of pure reason. Doorways were changed, and sculpture was pushed aside because it wasn't very important. Many altars and other furnishings were destroyed to allow for grander things; we saw, for example, baroque altars in places like the cathedral of Amiens. But, of course, for Gothic things could get worse, because at the end of the 18th century came the French Revolution. Down went so much of the sculpture. Remember we talked about that whole row of statues of kings on the facade of Notre Dame, as well as much of the other sculpture, simply being destroyed. In fact, Notre Dame in Paris and other cathedrals were deconsecrated and made into temples of divine reason, and so on and so forth.

But there are some exceptions where although there were certain kinds of destruction, there was also a certain kind of preservation. This is a 12th century, maybe early 13th century, Gothic monastery actually in the town of Kutna Hora in the Czech Republic. Being Cistercian, it is simple and it was a Gothic building. In the 18th century, it was remodeled. They left the outside; the outside, you look at it, pure Gothic. But on the inside, they changed the vaults, they put in a new centerpiece at the crossing with frescoes, and in the aisle they took out the arches completely and put in a series of domes.

It sort of reminds us here about both preservation and sometimes quite radical change.

The 19th century was in some ways taken with Gothic architecture and art. The Romantic Movement in the 19th century embraced the Gothic. The Middle Ages was a time when men were gentlemen and women were ladies; there were none of those grimy factories or those horrible tenements (or at least that's what was imagined with regard to the latter part); and so the Middle Ages became somewhat romanticized, and people wished to recreate something of the values, and the chivalry, and the loveliness, and the elegance of the Middle Ages. There are novels that we call Gothic novels; but what better way to do that than to build Gothic buildings? So in the 19th century beginning really in England, spreading to the United States and all over the world, there was the beginning of the building of large, new churches—some cathedrals, some not—in the Gothic style; and, I might add, many secular buildings in the Gothic style. Picture the Thames in London: The Houses of Parliament and Big Ben? Neo-Gothic. Look carefully and you will see that those are modern buildings, 19th-century buildings, but they are, in fact, recreations—sometimes fanciful recreations, I might add—of a Gothic style. We already talked about the fact that in France in the 19th century, many buildings that had been damaged, sculpture that had been removed, were replaced, sometimes very accurately with modern copies; sometimes rather fancifully, as we saw in the main portal of the cathedral of Notre Dame where the lintel was really in a different style than the upper part of the tympanum.

But what's interesting about this Neo-Gothic style is, again, it was a worldwide style now because, of course, of the communications and the shrinking of the world; the world didn't begin to shrink, after all, let's remember, in the 20th century but in previous centuries it also shrank. Let's do a little survey around the world and see what we see. Set against the mountains; look at this beautiful Gothic building. We might say, "Oh, gee, maybe that's in Austria or some such place"; it's in Quito, Ecuador and it's a church called the Voto Nacional, built at the end of the 19th and into the 20th century. It's an enormous modern Gothic building and in the inside, again, if you look real carefully, if you stood inside there, you'd see some features that would make you say, "I don't think this was built in the 13th or 14th centuries," but at least when you look at a photograph the first thing you say is, "I'm inside a medieval cathedral," and here you are in Ecuador.

Look at this cathedral: It has these two wonderful towers, and you say, "Well, you know, it doesn't quite look like Chartres or Notre Dame in Paris, but gosh, there is a clearly Gothic building." Look at the building on the right; this is, in fact, what's called the Northern Cathedral of Beijing, in China, and you see the Chinese architecture on either side of this building. In fact, in the interior, it really is like a German hall church with the aisles having the same elevation as the principal nave. But as we'll see in many situations, there are local touches, not just in the adjacent buildings but look at that gargoyle; that gargoyle looks less like something that came from Notre Dame and more like something that came from the Forbidden City, which, by the way, is within walking distance of the North Cathedral of Beijing. There are always some local touches when Gothic spreads around the world. This beautiful little church is called the Ned. Geref. Kerk. It's a Dutch name, and it's in the town of Bredasdorp, and Bredasdorp is in South Africa. Once again, we see what looks like, in a sense, a sort of gleaming English parish church or Dutch parish church of the Gothic style but it happens to be in South Africa. Look at the interior here—in a sense sort of put aside the color, perhaps—but look at the architecture: This is a church called Our Lady of Lourdes; but it's not in Lourdes in France, it's in Tamil Nadu in India. The Gothic really is a worldwide style in the 19th and 20th centuries.

Let's, however, now turn to the United States a little bit, where I want to focus principally on three great Gothic cathedrals, one Catholic and two Episcopal: Saint Patrick's in New York; Saint John the Divine, the Episcopal cathedral of New York; and the so-called National Cathedral, which is the Episcopal cathedral in Washington. Let's look at these three great buildings as examples, as really fine examples, of Neo-Gothic architecture. Saint Patrick's, which is located in midtown Manhattan sort of across from Rockefeller Center, which I'm sure many of you know, was begun in 1858 and finished in 1878, although it was added to several times after that. It's largely influenced by the English style of Gothic, but there are other elements to it; it's not a pure copy of any English or even the English style.

If we looked inside, for example, we can't see it in a photograph taking in the west end of the church but there is a Lady Chapel; again, a very English thing, although that was added a little bit after it was finished in 1878. You can see that, as we find in so many English churches, there is a gallery rather than a triforium, and the vaulting of Saint Patrick is in the English Decorated Style, that middle style of English Gothic that we looked at. Those are elements of the English style; and as you would expect, English style predominates in most Neo-Gothic in the United States because, obviously, we have our culture that comes primarily from England. We also see in the aisles here fan vaults; a sort of odd kind of fan vaults. They don't look exactly like those that we saw at Bath Abbey, King's College, or the Henry VII Chapel in London, but nevertheless you can see there are fan vaults that are used as the vaulting technique for the aisles of Saint Patrick. Yet as we look at the apse of Saint Patrick, what do we see? It's rounded, which we know is French—very few English cathedrals have rounded apses—and you'll also see here, there's not a gallery, but rather a triforium. There are some elements of the French style, which is after all the original Gothic, as well as elements of the English style in the great cathedral of Saint Patrick.

Let's turn for a minute to Saint John the Divine. This is the Episcopal cathedral of New York, and it's the largest Gothic church in the United States. It's almost 600 feet long. Think about that: It's an enormously large building; more than one and a half football fields. It was begun as a Romanesque church. Here we see some of the early building; don't pay any attention to the temporary part in the middle there because obviously the nave is going to come out toward us, but you'll see the rounded arch and, in fact, originally there was a dome. But in 1911, a Neo-Gothic enthusiast named Ralph Adams Cram took over and made this into a Gothic cathedral. You'll still see some Romanesque elements on the inside: For example, if you look at the apse of the church you'll see that there are rounded arches; so there are still elements of the Romanesque. It's interesting; just like we find in a lot of English cathedrals, elements of Romanesque and Gothic together, much more so than in France, so we see it here at Saint John the Divine as well.

It has an enormously wide facade with five portals, although they're not all quite the same size, as you can see. But remember we have seen a French cathedral that was five portals wide, and that was the cathedral of Bourges;

and so we do see certain kinds of influence from individual cathedrals as well as more generic borrowing from a variety of Gothic buildings. If we look inside, we discover that there is a gallery along with the clerestory windows; again, borrowing that from England. You will also see that the pillars run from the floor to the vault without any interruption, and we can see that. This is a building that soars; remember, that kind of style with no interruption, with no horizontals to interrupt the verticals, we see beginning in France in the 1230s with the building of the nave of Saint Denis and then later on the cathedral of Troyes and so on. Once again, this doesn't borrow from the earliest form of Gothic in Europe, but rather from a developed style that first develops in France.

Let's turn now to the National Cathedral in Washington. Obviously, we've seen on television many events that have taken place here, primarily funerals; and one U.S. president is buried here, Woodrow Wilson. In many ways, how medieval is that? These were not parish churches, these big cathedrals, they were ceremonial places; they were places for extraordinarily important events; they were places where, almost literally in many cases, all the citizens of the city could pack in the cathedral. To see those kinds of events going on in this cathedral—we usually see them on C-SPAN or the evening news rather than in person—is, in many ways, very much in keeping with the original purpose, or at least an original purpose, of a cathedral. By the way, the Episcopal Church is governed in the United States by a series of bishops and a presiding bishop. This is the seat of the Bishop of Washington, but it's also the seat of the presiding bishop of the Episcopal Church in the United States. It has a beautiful English-like facade that seems to be pretty close to the facade of the cathedral of York, which we looked at it seems a long time ago. It also, despite much English influence, has a rounded east end; and if we look at it with its particular flying buttresses that, to me, standing looking at the image with you, looks very French. Again, a combination of English and French elements; we expect the English to be there, but the French also, after all, were the inventors of Gothic.

If we go into the interior of the National Cathedral, we discover several interesting things: It has a gallery rather than a triforium; it has vaulting in, again, the Decorated English style; it has a rose window. We can look up the pillar all the way to the vault, and we can look at the elevation; it reminds us very much of one of those English Gothic cathedrals with a big gallery, again something that disappears pretty early in the French tradition, beginning at Chartres, in 1194. What's interested about this particular building, it seems to me, is that it has a lot of particularly American features; after all, it is the National Cathedral and one would therefore expect it to have American things, just like you find statues of Joan of Arc or stained glass windows of Charlemagne in French cathedrals, or a shrine of Thomas à Becket at Canterbury. We have a window, for example, that's dedicated to Robert E. Lee, and we see various stages of his career just as we've seen stages in the career of Charlemagne, a saint, a king, or whoever it might be. Here we see him at West Point; here we see him during the Civil War at one of the battles of the Civil War. There's also a window that celebrates not only space, but celebrates man's landing on the moon; and, in fact, in this window is embedded a little piece of moon rock that was brought back by the astronauts. There are many interesting things in the National Cathedral that remind us it is a Christian building; it's an American Christian building.

It has a lot of other modern elements to it: For example, one of the gargoyles shows us not some beastie looking down at us but a different kind of beastie, Darth Vader. By the way, we should not be surprised at that. We were not surprised perhaps to see the Chinese dragon on the North Cathedral in Beijing; and, in fact, had we looked at the sculpture of the church of Saint John the Divine in New York, we would have found the skyline of New York City as part of the sculpture. Again, it embraces American things; it embraces American ideas, images, and icons; and therefore, I think, in that way, too, for better or for worse, whatever we think of a sort of combination of patriotism and Christianity, certainly it is something that is medieval in its origin. It was not invented in churches like this.

These are grand buildings; I mean, the cathedral of Saint John the Divine is about as big as any Gothic cathedral; and obviously Saint Patrick's and the National Cathedral are enormous buildings. But there are Gothic buildings all around us; sometimes we notice them, sometimes we don't. The other day when I was in Washington, I was driving from near Howard University over to the National Cathedral, and since I was in a Gothic-y mood, I counted Gothic churches I went by, and I counted four. That's not atypical; not just of the east coast, by the way, but of all the United States. Let's do a little runaround. Here we have, for example: Look at this lovely Gothic building. By the way, notice the rounded transept like some early French cathedrals such as Noyon. This is Saint Ann's; it's a parish church, not a cathedral. It's in Buffalo, New York. Here, I think we have an interesting image because this church happens to be right downtown in Indianapolis. This is the Episcopal cathedral of Indianapolis, Indiana; this is Christ Church Cathedral with its soaring spire in some ways dwarfed by the large skyscrapers around it; and yet for most people who live in Indianapolis, the most recognizable building on the very center circle of Indianapolis called Monument Circle.

This chapel, which was built in Santa Fe, New Mexico, is called the Loreto Chapel, and it is modeled after Saint Chapelle in Paris. Obviously it's not nearly that grand—it doesn't have, you can see there, nearly as big of windows as Saint Chapelle, which we looked at, which were so extraordinary in their size with 100 different stories in one window—but nevertheless, this is a kind of smaller and more modest version of Saint Chapelle, clearly the direct inspiration for this building. This is the Episcopal cathedral of San Francisco. This is Grace Cathedral, again, a wonderful Gothic church, and inside there's even a maze on the floor reminding us, again, of Chartres or Amiens with the great mazes that we saw there. As I mentioned with regard to England, where the Parliament building is Gothic so that Gothic is not limited to ecclesiastical buildings, the next time you're in New York and you're going from Manhattan to Brooklyn, look at the Brooklyn Bridge. Ah yes, it really is a Gothic bridge. It reminds us of the pervasiveness of his style; again, not limited to ecclesiastical structures but even in many ways entering into vernacular architectural language.

In what we call the Gothic Era, from the 12th really to the 15th or 16th centuries depending where you are, there is an unprecedented amount of building. It's been reasonably estimated that more stone was quarried during that Gothic Era than in any other comparable period in human history including the time of the building of the pyramids in Egypt. Today, nobody can tell you how many Gothic churches still stand in Europe because, of course in part, so many of them are part Gothic and part something else; but the number is in the thousands, we just don't know the exact number. Obviously, for 800 years, Gothic has been a central part of the landscape of virtually all European cities. Furthermore, we need to add to that thousands of Neo-

Gothic churches; as we've seen, literally in every corner of the earth, from East Asia to South Asia to Africa to Latin America. When we do that, one of the things we realize is if you said to somebody, "Imagine a church," don't you think that the great majority of people would imagine something, whether they even could label it or not, that is Gothic; imagine something that looked a little bit like Westminster Abbey and Notre Dame in Paris?

It's not just that these buildings are powerful; they're beautiful, and for many Christians they're the most authentic expression of their faith. They express in the very shape of the building usually the cross of Christ; they focus, at least for Catholics, on the altar where the body and blood of Christ are present in the consecration; they are extraordinary expressions of how many people understand Christianity. I think it's fair to say that ultimately, of all the different styles of church-building, Gothic has been the most successful and the most enduring. I came to believe that when, as a 17 year old, I approached the cathedral of Amiens and I went inside. I was awed then, I was moved then, and when I was there a couple months ago I was awed and I was moved. I've changed my mind about a lot of things since I was 17; I've not changed my mind about the extraordinary beauty and the articulate expression that is the Gothic cathedral.

Cathedral Vocabulary

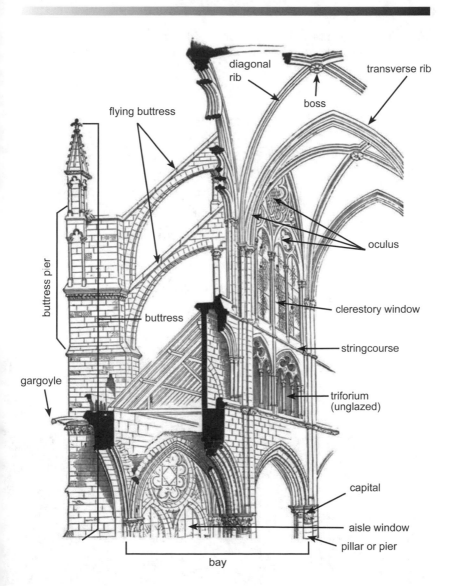

diagonal rib

transverse rib

boss

flying buttress

oculus

buttress pier

clerestory window

buttress

stringcourse

gargoyle

triforium (unglazed)

capital

aisle window

pillar or pier

bay

Timeline

Note: The terms early, High, and late Gothic are properly only used for French buildings, but it is the most convenient way to divide the medieval period for Europe as a whole, so we have used it here. See the Glossary and lecture guides for names that refer to specific periods in other regions.

The Early Christian Period

c. 100 ....Episcopal hierarchy begins to take hold in the Christian community.

312–337 ....Reign of Constantine; conversion of the Roman Empire to Christianity.

476 ....Fall of the Roman Empire in the West.

711 ....Islamic conquest of Spain and Portugal.

The Carolingian and Romanesque Periods

800 ....Coronation of Charlemagne.

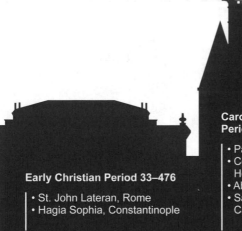

Early Christian Period 33–476

- St. John Lateran, Rome
- Hagia Sophia, Constantinople

Carolingian and Romanesque Periods 800–1140

- Palatine Chapel, Aachen, Germany
- Corvey Abbey *Westwerk*, Höxter, Germany
- Abbaye aux Hommes, Caen, France
- Santiago de Compostela Cathedral, Spain

The Early Gothic Period

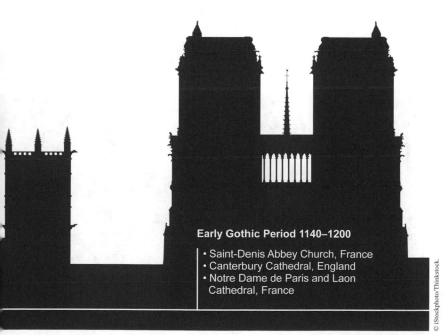

Early Gothic Period 1140–1200

- Saint-Denis Abbey Church, France
- Canterbury Cathedral, England
- Notre Dame de Paris and Laon
  Cathedral, France

© iStockphoto/Thinkstock.

The High Gothic Period

1209...Franciscan order founded.

1209–1229...Albigensian Crusade.

1215...Dominican order founded.

1239...Louis IX brings the Crown
of Thorns to France.

The Late Gothic Period

1265–1274...Thomas Aquinas writes the
Summa Theologiae.

after 1300 ....Dante writes *The Divine Comedy*.

1431...Joan of Arc is burned at the stake for heresy.

1453...The fall of Constantinople to the Ottomans.

1492...Reconquista of Spain is completed.

1496...Santo Domingo, the first
permanent European settlement
in the Americas, is founded.

Late Gothic Period 1250–1600

- Sainte-Chapelle, Paris, France
- Milan Cathedral, Italy
- Lady Chapel, Westminster Abbey, London, England
- Santo Domingo Cathedral, Dominican Republic

High Gothic Period 1200–1250

- Chartres, Amiens, and Reims Cathedrals, France
- Siena Cathedral, Italy
- Salisbury Cathedral, England

The Neo-Gothic Period

Neo-Gothic Period 1730–present

- Basilica del Voto Nacional in Quito, Ecuador
- St. Patrick's Cathedral, New York
- Washington National Cathedral, Washington DC
- North Cathedral, Beijing, China

© iStockphoto/Thinkstock.

The Basic Gothic Floor Plan

This cruciform floor plan is based on the cathedral of Chartres, but its basic features and east-west orientation are found in the majority of Gothic churches in France and beyond. For further explanation of the key architectural terms, see the Cathedral Vocabulary section and the Glossary.

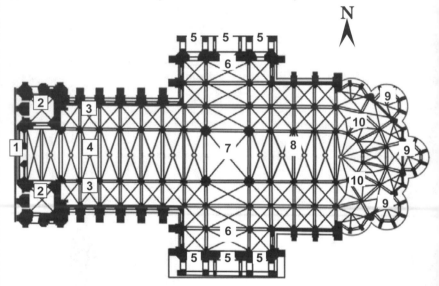

1 Facade
2 Facade towers
3 Aisles
4 Nave
5 Portals
6 Transepts
7 Crossing tower
8 Choir (apse)
9 Radiating chapels
10 Ambulatory

Cathedrals and Churches of Note

The following list contains the most significant religious structures for the study of Gothic and related forms of architecture, many of which are shown and/or discussed in this course.

France

Abbaye aux Hommes: Late Romanesque church in Caen, Normandy with several features that anticipate Gothic architecture, most importantly, the first buttressing cathedral scheme. It is the burial place of William the Conqueror; his wife, Matilda, is buried in the nearby Abbaye aux Dames.

Amiens Cathedral (a.k.a. **Notre Dame d'Amiens**): Early 13th-century Gothic cathedral in the Picardy region; remarkable for its size (particularly its height) and openness.

Autun Cathedral (a.k.a. **Saint-Lazare d'Autun**): Early 12th-century Romanesque cathedral in the Burgundy region; notable for its sculpture by Gislebertus and for its being one of the few remaining Romanesque cathedrals in France.

Basilique Saint-Andoche, Saulieu: A Romanesque church with beautiful historiated capitals depicting biblical stories.

Beauvais Cathedral (a.k.a. **Saint-Pierre de Beauvais**): Unfinished Gothic cathedral in northern France with the highest vaulting ever constructed, about 159 feet high.

Bourges Cathedral (a.k.a. **Saint-Étienne de Bourges**): Early Gothic cathedral in central France with several unusual features; it lacks a transept, has a five-portal facade, and has the largest crypt found in any Gothic church.

Chartres Cathedral (a.k.a. **Notre Dame de Chartres**): The most comprehensive of all Gothic cathedrals, considered the first example of High Gothic. The facade is Romanesque, constructed in the 1140s; the rest of the building began construction in 1194. It is perhaps best known for its extensive original stained-glass windows.

Cluny Abbey: Church of a Benedictine monastery founded in Burgundy in 910. It was once the largest of all Romanesque churches, although only a small part of it survives today.

Laon Cathedral (a.k.a. **Notre Dame de Laon**): One of the first truly Gothic cathedrals, built in the Picardy region in the mid-12th century.

Mont Saint-Michel Abbey: A monastery church on an island just off the coast of Normandy. It has a Romanesque nave and a Gothic choir.

Morienval Abbey: Small Romanesque church in eastern France that has some of the earliest ribbed vaults in France.

Neuilly en Donjon Church: A small Romanesque church in Burgundy.

Notre Dame de Paris: Arguably the most famous Gothic structure in the world, located on the Île de la Cité in Paris. Constructed relatively quickly in the late 12th century, it has a remarkable unity of form. Although much of the exterior stone work was damaged during the French Revolution, some of the original sculpture and stained glass was hidden offsite and later restored.

Noyon Cathedral (a.k.a. **Notre Dame de Noyon**): Early Gothic cathedral in northern France with several unusual features, including a rounded facade and a four-level elevation.

Paray-le-Monial Church (a.k.a. **Sacré-Coeur Church**): Romanesque church in eastern France; it is a smaller version of the mostly destroyed abbey church at Cluny.

Pontigny Abbey: Romanesque Cistercian monastery church in Burgundy that is a good example of the Half-Gothic style employed by the Cistercian architects.

Reims Cathedral (a.k.a. **Notre Dame de Reims**): One of the most important Gothic cathedrals, located in eastern France. This was the cathedral where French kings from Clovis onward were crowned. Its most significant feature is the astounding amount of statuary—numbering in the thousands of pieces.

Rouen Cathedral (a.k.a. **Notre Dame de Rouen**): Large cathedral in Normandy whose architecture spans the early, High, and late Gothic periods. It is probably best known from Claude Monet's paintings of its facade.

Saint-Denis Abbey: This Benedictine abbey church outside Paris, built in the early 12th century on the ruins of its Carolingian predecessor, is indisputably the birthplace of Gothic architecture. The lower choir and narthex, however, are the only surviving parts of the original Gothic construction.

Saint-Étienne de Beauvais: An important late Gothic church in Beauvais.

Saint-Germain des Prés: The largest Romanesque church in Paris, found on the Left Bank; it has often been remodeled but retains many Romanesque features.

Saint-Maclou, Rouen: A flamboyant Gothic church in Rouen, Normandy.

Saint-Martin-des-Champs: A small but important Romanesque church in Paris.

Saint-Martin du Canigou: An early Romanesque church in the Pyrenees, near the French-Spanish border, built just after the year 1000.

Saint-Ouen, Rouen: A large and important 14th-century Gothic church in Rouen, Normandy.

Saint-Philibert, Tournus: A Romanesque church in Burgundy with an unusual early experiment in vaulting.

Saint-Remi, Reims: An important early Gothic abbey in Reims.

Saint-Sernin, Toulouse: A large brick Romanesque church in southern France.

Saint-Trophime, Arles: A Romanesque church in southern France with an important tympanum.

Saint-Urbain, Troyes: A small but beautiful late Gothic church originally commissioned by Pope Clement IV.

Sainte-Chapelle, Paris: High Gothic Chapel commissioned by King Louis IX (later Saint Louis) to house the Crown of Thorns; it lies on the Île de la Cité in Paris, a close neighbor to Notre Dame, and contains many original stained-glass windows.

Sainte-Foi, Conques: An important Romanesque abbey and pilgrimage church in central France that foreshadows many elements of Gothic decoration.

Sainte-Marie-Madelaine, Troyes: A late Gothic church in Troyes containing important stained-glass windows.

Sens Cathedral (a.k.a. **Cathedral of St. Étienne**): The first Gothic cathedral in the world (Saint-Denis, although built earlier, was an abbey church). William of Sens, who designed the choir of Canterbury Cathedral in England, is believed to have been one of the architects here.

Strasbourg Cathedral (a.k.a. **Notre Dame de Strasbourg**): A part-Romanesque, part-Gothic church built around a Romanesque north transept that survived a fire in the late 12th century. Although now part of France, during the Middle Ages Strasbourg was part of the Holy Roman Empire.

Vézelay Abbey (a.k.a. **Basilique Sainte-Marie-Madeleine)**: Arguably the most beautifully decorated Romanesque church in France, with historiated capitals, a lovely narthex, sculpture by Gislebertus, and early examples of groin vaulting.

Vignory Church: An early Romanesque church in northeastern France.

England

Bath Abbey: An important fan-vaulted Gothic church built to rival Wells Cathedral.

Canterbury Cathedral: The earliest true Gothic cathedral in England, begun after a fire in 1174. The choir's principal architect was William of Sens, who may have worked on Sens Cathedral in France. This is the seat of the archbishop of Canterbury, the Primate of the Anglican Church.

Chapel of Kings College, Cambridge: A collegiate chapel built in the perpendicular style with fan vaulting.

Durham Cathedral: A Romanesque cathedral whose principal nave contains the earliest-known ribbed vaulting.

Ely Cathedral: A cathedral with both Romanesque and Gothic parts.

Gloucester Cathedral: A Gothic cathedral significant for the different kinds of ribbed vaulting developed here.

Lincoln Cathedral: One of England's most elaborate Gothic cathedrals. Its east end, called St. Hugh's Choir, is known for its asymmetrical vaulting.

Salisbury Cathedral: The first completed Gothic cathedral in Britain.

Wells: An impressive Gothic cathedral with beautiful harmony of style and one of the few triforia found in English churches.

Westminster Abbey: Benedictine abbey that is now in the heart of London (although Westminster was its own city in the Middle Ages). Built in the Gothic style and having features not normally found in English cathedrals, such as flying buttresses, it is the coronation place of English monarchs since William the Conqueror and the burial place of many of them as well.

York Minster: The usual designation of York Cathedral. The word 'minster' refers to the fact that it was both a cathedral and an abbey.

Aachen Cathedral: A Gothic cathedral incorporating parts of an earlier Carolingian structure, where Charlemagne was crowned Holy Roman Emperor on Christmas Day, 800. Otto I was also crowned emperor here in 936, as were most of his successors for the next 500 years.

Cologne Cathedral (a.k.a. **High Cathedral Church of Saints Peter and Mary**): The largest Gothic cathedral in Germany.

Corvey Abbey: The facade of this Benedictine monastic church in Höxter is a rare surviving example of Carolingian architecture.

Mainz Cathedral (a.k.a. **St. Martin's Cathedral**): Romanesque cathedral with many unusual features and several Gothic additions.

Maria Laach Abbey: A Romanesque Benedictine abbey.

Quedlinburg Cathedral: A fine Romanesque church in the heart of one of the best-preserved medieval towns in existence.

Speyer Cathedral (a.k.a. **Imperial Cathedral Basilica of the Assumption and St. Stephen**): A splendid Romanesque cathedral, one of the largest in existence, housing the tombs of many German kings and emperors.

St. Cyriacus Church: One of the best-preserved Romanesque churches in Germany, found in the town of Gernrode.

St. Michael's Church: An early Romanesque (specifically, Ottonian) church in Hildesheim.

St. Mary's Cathedral: While technically a Romanesque structure, this cathedral in Hildesheim was rebuilt from the ground up in the 1950s after a World War II air raid demolished it.

Worms Cathedral (a.k.a. **Cathedral of St. Peter**): A major Romanesque cathedral.

Czech Republic

Kutna Hora Cathedral (a.k.a. **Saint Barbara Church**): An unusual late Gothic cathedral.

Our Lady of Sedlec: A Cistercian abbey just outside Kutna Hora, originally built in the Cistercian Half-Gothic style and rebuilt in the 18th century in a unique style that is part Gothic and part 18th century.

Prague Cathedral: A large Gothic cathedral surrounded by the palace complex that was once home to the kings of Bohemia. The cathedral was commissioned by Emperor Charles IV to house the relics of Saint Wenceslas; it now contains the tombs of many kings and emperors.

Italy

Basilica of St Francis of Assisi: Begun in 1228, this double church has a Gothic upper level with frescoes and stained glass from the 13th century.

Church of San Vitale: A Byzantine Christian church in Ravenna that was Charlemagne's model for his Palatine Chapel in Aachen.

Florence Cathedral (a.k.a. **Basilica di Santa Maria del Fiore**): The largest Gothic cathedral in Italy, crowned by the great Renaissance dome by Filippo Brunelleschi.

Lucca Cathedral (a.k.a. **Cathedral of St. Martin**): A cathedral located in a city with (among European cities) one of the highest numbers of surviving Romanesque churches.

Milan Cathedral: The fourth-largest church in the world and perhaps the most famous Gothic cathedral in Italy, it took five centuries to complete.

Orvieto Cathedral: A late Gothic cathedral remarkable for its elaborately sculpted facade.

St. John Lateran: The cathedral of Rome, originally constructed in the 4th century.

San Miniato al Monte: The most important Romanesque church in Florence, perched on a hill overlooking the city.

San Nicola, Bari: A Romanesque church in southern Italy built to house the relics of Saint Nicholas.

Santa Croce, Florence: A large, timber-roofed Gothic church of the Franciscan order.

Santa Maria Maggiore: A large 5th-century church in Rome dedicated to the Virgin Mary.

Santa Maria Novella, Florence: A large vaulted Gothic church of the Dominican order.

Santa Maria sopra Minerva: The only Gothic church in Rome, it belongs to the Dominican order and was built on the ruins of a pagan temple—thus its name, "sopra Minerva" (meaning "over Minerva").

Siena Cathedral: A Gothic cathedral notable for its unusual dome.

Spain

Burgos Cathedral: A large 13th-century Gothic cathedral in northern Spain showing strong French influences.

Leon Cathedral: A Gothic cathedral in northern Spain constructed on the site of a Roman bathhouse and early medieval palace.

Santiago de Compostela: The most important pilgrimage church in Europe, located northwestern Spain. It is primarily a Romanesque building.

Seville Cathedral: A massive Gothic cathedral (the largest in the world) that was built in the wake of the Reconquista and houses the remains of Christopher Columbus.

Toledo Cathedral: A 13th-century Gothic cathedral, the seat of the most powerful archbishop of Spain.

Valencia Cathedral (a.k.a. **Cathedral of Santa Maria de Valencia**): A Gothic cathedral built after the Reconquista on the site of a mosque. Its design shows significant Arabic influence; arguably, its most remarkable feature is its octagonal lantern tower.

The New World

Guadalajara Cathedral: One of the last Gothic cathedrals, built in Mexico and completed in 1618. It was damaged by earthquakes several times over its history and is still in danger of collapse at present.

St. John the Divine: The Episcopal cathedral of New York, built largely in the Gothic style (although with some Romanesque elements) in the 20th century.

St. Patrick's Cathedral: Neo-Gothic Catholic Cathedral of New York built in the second half of the 19th century.

Santo Domingo Cathedral (a.k.a. **Cathedral of Santa María la Menor**): A Gothic cathedral in the Dominican Republic that is the oldest church in the New World.

Washington National Cathedral (a.k.a. **Cathedral Church of Saint Peter and Saint Paul**): An Episcopal cathedral built in the 20th century in the Gothic style, located in Washington DC and home to many state funerals and prayer services.

Near East and the former Byzantine Empire

Hagia Sophia (a.k.a. **Sancta Sophia**): The 6th-century cathedral of Constantinople (Istanbul) and arguably the most magnificent cathedral ever built. It is now a museum, having been a mosque for almost 500 years after the Ottoman capture of the city in 1453.

Glossary

abacus: The flat top of a capital. In many Gothic cathedrals, the ribs of the vault spring from the abaci of the pillars in the nave and choir.

aisle: Either all of the parallel sections of the nave of a church or the sections of the nave on either side of the principal, central part. In this course, we use the latter definition.

ambulatory: The rounded aisle or aisles surrounding the choir of a cathedral.

apostolic succession: The belief that bishops inherit the authority that Christ gave to the apostles.

apse: The rounded east end of a cathedral or other church. *See also* **choir**.

apsidal chapels: Chapels that open into the apse of a church. *See also* **radiating chapels**.

archbishop: The bishop of a large diocese with some supervisory authority over the area's other bishops. Such relationships are made clear in windows of the clerestory of Reims Cathedral.

archivolt: The arches over a tympanum. They often contain small statues, most commonly of angels.

Assumption of the Virgin: The belief that the body of the Virgin Mary was taken into heaven from her tomb.

barrel vault: Sometimes called a tunnel vault, a rounded stone roof; the earliest form of stone roofing for a church.

basilica: A rectangular building with aisles and an apse. The basilica was originally a Roman building used for various secular functions such as law courts. Most Christian churches are in shape an adaptation of the basilica, and the term is sometimes used to describe such Christian churches.

bay: One section of the nave, transept, or choir of a Romanesque or Gothic church. Sets of pillars mark a bay.

Benedictines: Generally, monks who live under the Benedictine Rule. However, there are different groups of Benedictines, such as the Cluniacs, and different orders, such as the Cistercians.

bishop: The chief ecclesiastical official of a diocese, believed to have the authority in his diocese that Christ gave to his apostles. *See* **apostolic succession**.

boss: A rounded projection of stone or wood, often decorative, found at the intersection of ribs in Gothic vaulting.

Burgundy: A region (in the Middle Ages, a duchy) to the south and east of Paris. It contains numerous Romanesque churches, including Autun, Vézelay, and Cluny.

buttress: A stone construction designed to support the vaulting of a church. The most famous type of buttress is the flying buttress, but others are hidden in the aisles and galleries of churches.

Byzantine Empire: More properly the Eastern Roman Empire, with its capital in Constantinople. It remained a political entity until its conquest by the Ottoman Turks in 1453.

capital: The decorative top of a column. Some capitals contain leaves or other decorative motifs, while others, known as historiated capitals, contain narratives or allegories.

Carolingian period: The period of European history dominated by Charlemagne and his successors. Though different scholars use somewhat different dates for this period, we will use the years, at least for France, between 768 (accession of Charlemagne as king of the Franks) to 987 (the deposition of the last of Charlemagne's descendents).

cathedra: The seat or chair of a bishop in a cathedral.

cathedral: The bishop's church in a diocese, containing his cathedra.

cathedral canons: Clergy who were assigned to work in the cathedral.

cathedral chapter: The cathedral canons collectively.

chapter house: A room in a monastery or cathedral where the monks or the cathedral chapter would meet.

choir: The part of a church east of the transept and containing the altar. *See also* **apse**.

Cistercians: A reformed order of Benedictine monks founded in 1098 at Citeaux, France. The architecture of the order spread throughout Europe and is an important transition between Romanesque and Gothic (sometimes called Half-Gothic).

clerestory: The upper part of the elevation of a church. The size of the windows in the clerestory grew dramatically in the Gothic period.

commune: A sworn association of important men in a city who sought and often succeeded in winning some independence from nobles and their local bishop.

Coronation of the Virgin: Christ crowning the Virgin as Queen of Heaven. This story is often depicted in Gothic sculpture and windows.

Council of Trent: Ecumenical Council of the Catholic Church which met from 1545 to 1563. Some of Trent's decrees led to a rearrangement of Catholic churches, which in turn led to the destruction of many internal features of Gothic cathedrals.

counterfacade: The inside of the west facade of a Gothic cathedral. Many Gothic counterfacades are pierced with rose windows. Uniquely, the counterfacade of Reims Cathedral contains much important sculpture.

crossing: The place in a cathedral where the nave, choir, and transept come together.

crossing tower: A tower over the crossing.

cruciform basilica: A rectangular, aisled church with a transept, giving the church the shape of the cross. Most Gothic cathedrals are cruciform basilicas.

crypt: The basement of a church, often where relics were displayed. The largest Gothic crypts are in the cathedrals of Chartres and Bourges.

decorated style: An intermediate style of English Gothic architecture and decoration, largely coming from the 14th century and distinguishable from early Gothic and the later perpendicular style.

diocese: A territory, usually a city and surrounding countryside, under the ecclesiastical jurisdiction of a bishop.

double ambulatory: A double semicircular aisle in the choir of a church.

double church: Two churches of basically the same size and ground plan, one on top of the other. The most important double church is the Basilica of San Francesco in Assisi.

"dwarfs on the shoulders of giants": A phrase coined by Bernard of Chartres (but often misattributed in the modern era). The idea of men sitting on the shoulders of giants, that they may not be as large as the giants but that they can see farther, is the source of windows at Chartres Cathedral with the evangelists sitting on the shoulders of the major prophets.

early Gothic: Specifically, the beginning of the Gothic style in England, also sometimes used for French Gothic from the building of Saint-Denis to the building of Chartres Cathedral.

Ecclesia and Synagoga: Latin for "church" and "synagogue"; allegorical figures that can be found in stained-glass windows and more famously on the facades of Notre Dame in Paris and the cathedral of Strasbourg, representing the relationship between Christianity and Judaism.

elevation: The various parts of the interior wall of a Gothic cathedral. Beginning with Chartres Cathedral, there were usually three parts to an elevation, although there were four parts o the elevations of many earlier Gothic cathedrals in France.

Enlightenment: The period of intellectual and cultural history—roughly the 18th century, especially in France—when traditional forms of Christianity, especially Catholicism, were rejected. During this period, many Gothic cathedrals were altered, espccially by having most of the stained glass removed.

facade: The front, virtually always the west end, of a church.

fan vault: A type of English late Gothic vaulting where the ribs form fanlike shapes.

flamboyant Gothic: The late Gothic style in France, featuring, among other things, tracery in rose windows that is flame-shaped.

flying buttress: Buttress built external to a Gothic cathedral that support the stone roofs and allow much of the walls to be made of glass.

flying rib: A type of rib first found in Prague Cathedral where some of the ribs are not part of vaults but extend unattached from one place to another.

Four Beasts of the Apocalypse: The man, lion, ox, and eagle. These beasts, originally mentioned in the prophet Ezekiel, are presented in the book of Revelation and were commonly thought of as representing the Four Evangelists, respectively Matthew, Mark, Luke, and John.

gallery: A space above the aisles of a church created for people not welcome in the main church, such as women, unshriven sinners, and pilgrims. In

France during the Gothic period, the gallery evolved into a blind gallery that was an architectural device called the triforium. The gallery lasted much longer in English Gothic cathedrals.

gallery of kings: A row of large statues of Old Testament kings high up on French Gothic facades. Most of these were destroyed during the French Revolution.

gargoyle: A water spout, often in the form of a grotesque, on the roof of a Gothic building. The terms gargoyle and grotesque, however, are not interchangeable. *See* **grotesque**.

glazed triforium: A triforium with windows.

Gothic Architecture and Scholasticism: A classic study of the relationship of architecture and theology; the work of Erwin Panofsky.

grisaille window: A stained-glass window in gray rather than containing bright colors and narratives.

groin vault: A vault created where two barrel vaults meet at right angles. These vaults were easier to build than barrel vaults because small areas could be vaulted independently of one another. The groin vault was an important step in the developing technology of roofing a large stone church.

grotesque: A sculpture of a fantastical humorous or frightening figure, often a hybrid of human and animal forms. Although many gargoyles are grotesques, not all grotesques are gargoyles. *See also* **gargoyle**.

guild: An organization of a particular group of professionals in a city, e.g. bankers or vintners. In some cities, most famously Chartres, guilds sponsored stained-glass windows in Gothic cathedrals.

Half-Gothic: An intermediate style of church architecture developed by the Cistercian order that bridged the Romanesque and Gothic styles.

hall church: A church with aisles as high or almost as high as the principal aisle of the nave. This form of Gothic architecture developed toward the end of the Gothic era in Germany.

High Gothic: The style of Gothic at the end of the 12th and early part of the 13th centuries that begins with the cathedral of Chartres.

historiated capital: The top of a column decorated with sculpted figures, as opposed to those capitals derived from the Doric, Ionic, and Corinthian capitals of antiquity.

Holy Roman Empire: A political entity consisting, during the Gothic period, primarily of modern Germany, Switzerland, Austria, and Bohemia (now part of the Czech Republic).

iconography: The system of symbols used in medieval sculpture and stained glass; for example, keys as a symbol of Saint Peter or a sword indicating Saint Paul.

Île de France: The area around Paris that was directly under royal control in the 12th century. The Île de France is the birthplace of Gothic architecture, beginning with the abbey of Saint-Denis.

Île de la Cité: Island in the Seine River in Paris, on which the cathedral of Notre Dame is built.

jamb statues: Tall statues arranged in rows on either side of a door of a cathedral.

keystone: The highest stone in a ribbed vault where the ribs cross.

la Vierge Dorée: Literally, "the Virgin golded"; a famous stone statue on the south porch of Amiens Cathedral that was partly gilded.

labors of the months: A type of decoration found on several Gothic cathedrals, consisting of each sign of the Zodiac accompanied by an illustration of the agricultural labor done at that time of year.

labyrinth: A mazelike design on the floor of some Gothic cathedrals, most notably Chartres, which people could navigate from the outer edge to the center. Scholars believe people did this walk as a symbolic pilgrimage.

Lady Chapel: A chapel dedicated to the Virgin Mary, built as a separate but connected part of some English Gothic cathedrals.

lancet window: A rectangular window pointed at the top. This is the most common shape for a stained-glass window.

lantern: A crossing tower that is elevated beyond the rest of the vaulting. English cathedrals (Ely, for example) are known for spectacular lanterns.

Last Judgment: The end of time when the dead rise from their tombs to face judgment and assignment either to heaven or hell. The Last Judgment is often presented in portal sculpture in Gothic cathedrals; for example, over the central door of the facade of the cathedral of Amiens.

lintel: The stone over a door, perpendicular to the posts. In Gothic cathedrals, they are often sculpted, usually continuing the theme of the tympanum above.

major prophets: The authors of the four longest prophetic books of the Old Testament: Isaiah, Jeremiah, Ezekiel, and Daniel.

masons: The men who laid the stones of the cathedrals. They often had lodges and protected some of the secrets of their craft. There is a great deal of mythology associated with medieval masons.

mendicant orders: City-based religious orders that emerged in the 13th century, most importantly the Franciscans, Dominicans, Augustinians, and Carmelites. They built many large Gothic churches, especially in Italy.

Merovingian: The first dynasty of Frankish kings, beginning with Clovis circa 500 and lasting until the middle of the 8th century.

minor prophets: Twelve Old Testament authors distinguished from the major prophets only by the length of their writings. They include Amos, Hosea, and Jonah.

mosaic: A picture made of small cubes of glass and stone. Abbot Suger had a mosaic placed on the facade of Saint-Denis, and there is a large Italian mosaic on the south porch of Prague Cathedral.

Musée de Cluny, Paris: A museum in the former Roman baths of Paris. It is the most important medieval museum in Paris and contains heads from the gallery of kings from Notre Dame.

mystic mill: An allegory of Moses putting grain into a mill and Paul receiving the flour, suggesting a way to think about the relationship between the Old and New Testaments. This is the subject of one of the windows of the abbey church of Saint-Denis.

narthex: The entrance area of a church between the facade and the nave. Eventually, the narthex was reduced or disappeared completely in Gothic cathedrals.

nave: The long western part of a church with a principal aisle and usually one, but sometimes two, aisles on either side.

Neo-Platonism: A school of philosophical thought that developed in late antiquity and was Christianized by an author known as Pseudo-Dionysius. Abbot Suger used principles of Neo-Platonism in the design of Saint-Denis.

Norman: When speaking of architecture, refers to the Romanesque style in England.

Normandy: An area of northwestern France where some of the most important Romanesque churches were built, especially in the city of Caen.

Notre Dame: French for Our Lady, referring to the Virgin Mary. Many Gothic cathedrals are dedicated to Notre Dame, although the cathedral of Paris is often referred to only as Notre Dame.

Notre Dame de la Belle Verrière: A 12th-century stained-glass window of the Virgin and Child in Chartres Cathedral.

oculus: A round window usually placed above a pair of lancet windows.

Oriflamme: A banner believed to have been carried by the armies of Charlemagne. It was one of the great treasures of Saint-Denis.

perpendicular style: The last form of Gothic architecture and decoration in England.

pier: A vertical structural stone support; also called a pillar.

pillar: A massive column-like stone supports for cathedrals.

plateresque: A Spanish architectural style of the late 15th and 16th centuries distinguished by an intricacy of design and ornamentation suggestive of silver plate; *plata* means "silver" in Spanish.

pointed arch: Although used in some Romanesque construction, often considered one of the signature elements of the Gothic style.

Port Royal, Chartres: French term used to indicate collectively the three portals of the facade of Chartres Cathedral. The jamb statues are mostly of Old Testament kings.

prefiguration: A story in the Old Testament that points forward to an event in the New Testament; for example, Jonah coming out of the mouth of the fish pointing toward Christ's Resurrection.

purbeck: A kind of dark English stone resembling marble that is used widely in English Gothic cathedrals.

radiating chapels: Chapels around the apse of a church that open into the ambulatory.

rayonnant: French term for the style of Gothic architecture and decoration that developed around the middle of the 13th century.

Reconquista: The movement lasting until 1492 in Spain for Christians to reconquer territories lost there from the time of the Arab conquest of Iberia in 711.

relic: A bone of or an object associated with a saint. Most relics were kept in elaborately designed containers called reliquaries.

reliquary: An often beautifully decorated container for relics.

Rhineland: The valley of the Rhine River in western Germany where many fine Romanesque churches survive.

ribbed vaults: A section of the roof of a church made by building a skeleton or two or more ribs and later filling in the spaces between with stone and/ or rubble.

Romanesque: A term used for a wide variety of styles of architecture of the 11th and 12th centuries, when many large stone buildings were constructed. The English Romanesque style is known as Norman.

rood screen: A wall constructed between the lay and clerical sections of a church. Most were removed from Catholic churches after the Council of Trent. The best surviving examples are in England and in the German cathedral of Naumburg.

rose window: A round window in a facade or transept with sainted glass in various patterns containing figures and designs.

scholasticism: A form of philosophy and theology that developed and flourished in the 12th and 13th centuries, especially in Paris. The most famous scholastic philosopher and theologian is Thomas Aquinas.

screen: *See* **rood screen**.

Second Vatican Council: Ecumenical Council of the Catholic Church that met from 1962 to 1965. The decrees on the liturgy led to massive rearrangements in all Catholic churches.

Seven Liberal Arts: The curriculum of the medieval schools: grammar, rhetoric, logic, arithmetic, geometry, music, and astronomy. These are often depicted on Gothic portals along with practitioners both pagan and Christian. The most famous depiction of this theme is found on the facade of Chartres Cathedral.

sextpartite vault: A type of vault spanning two bays and containing three ribs. This type of vaulting is characteristic of early French Gothic cathedrals and was superseded by four-part vaults beginning with Chartres Cathedral at the end of the 12th century.

shaft: Usually cylindrical, small-circumferenced stone pieces, attached to Gothic pillars or springing from abaci of columns, that morphed into the ribs of the vaults.

socle: A small sculpted base of a jamb statue.

Song of Roland: French epic poem about Charlemagne defeating Muslims in Spain. Stories from the *Song of Roland* and other poems about Charlemagne are incorporated into a window of Chartres Cathedral.

stained glass: Colored glass assembled in windows primarily to represent biblical stories, saints, and events from the lives of saints.

stringcourse: A decorative horizontal band running around a building.

summa: A comprehensive work of scholastic theology or philosophy.

tracery: The lead or stone into which the pieces of a stained-glass window are fitted.

transept: The wings of a basilica, usually about two-thirds of the way from west to east, that make the building in the shape of a cross.

transitional Gothic: A phrase indicating Gothic architecture or sculpture that still has Romanesque elements, for example the facade and facade sculpture of Chartres Cathedral.

Transubstantiation: The Catholic doctrine, defined in 1215, that at the consecration of the Mass, the substance of the bread and wine is changed into the body and blood of Christ.

transverse arch: An arch of the vault that runs perpendicular to the nave that divides one bay from another.

Tree of Jesse: An image of the lineage of Mary and Christ. Jesse, the father of David, sleeps, and a tree springs from him, bearing Old Testament kings and Mary and Jesus as its fruit. This is a common theme in Gothic sculpture and stained glass.

triforium: A false gallery that is part of the elevation of Gothic cathedrals. By about 1250, the triforia of Gothic churches in France were glazed (i.e., they contained windows).

trumeau statue: A statue between the doors of a major portal of a church; for example, a statue of Christ in the central portal of Amiens Cathedral or a similar one on the central portal of the south porch at Chartres.

Tuscany: Region of north-central Italy that contains the cities of Florence, Siena, Lucca, and Pisa.

tympanum: The space, usually with sculpture, immediately under an arched door of a Gothic cathedral. Sometimes the program of the tympanum sculpture is continued in the lintel below.

Westwerk: A feature of Carolingian architecture that influenced both the Romanesque and Gothic styles.

Biographical Notes

Bernard of Clairvaux (1090–1153): Abbot of the Cistercian monastery of Clairvaux. He was, along with Abbot Suger of Saint-Denis, the most important churchman in Europe. He is largely responsible for the rapid expansion of his order, which had its own distinctive form of architecture that is sometimes called Cistercian Half-Gothic. Throughout western Europe, the Cistercian form of church was duplicated with some local variations.

Blanche of Castile (1188–1252): Wife of King Louis VIII and mother of King Louis IX of France. She was the donor of the rose window of the north transept of Chartres Cathedral, and her family coat of arms is prominently displayed there.

Brunelleschi, Filippo (1377–1446): Florentine architect who won a competition to construct the enormous dome at the crossing of the cathedral of Florence, giving a Renaissance crown to the largest Gothic cathedral in Italy.

Chagall, Marc (1887–1985): A 20th-century French artist who designed windows for Reims Cathedral.

Charlemagne (r. 768–814): King of the Franks and from 800 (Holy) Roman Emperor. There was a cultural revival under Charlemagne, which included building large churches. His chapel in Aachen, still standing, was modeled on the 6th-century church of San Vitale in Ravenna.

Charles IV (r. 1346–1378): King of Bohemia and Holy Roman Emperor. Charles established Prague as his capital and commissioned the building of Prague Cathedral.

Charles VII (r. 1422–1461): King of France. For several years, he was uncrowned and losing ground to the English in the Hundred Years' War. Led

386

by Joan of Arc, he traveled to Reims Cathedral for his coronation, which turned the tide of the war in favor of the French.

Clovis (c. 466–511.): King of the Franks who converted himself and his people to Christianity; he was baptized by Saint Remigius (Remi) in Reims.

Constantine (r. 312–337): Roman Emperor who converted to Christianity and legalized it throughout the empire. He provided a palace for the bishop of Rome and commissioned the first large churches to be built in Rome, including the cathedral of St. John Lateran and St. Peter's in the Vatican.

Cram, Ralph Adams (1863–1942): American Neo-Gothic architect. He took over the building of the Episcopal cathedral of St. John the Divine in New York, which was initially to be built in the Romanesque style, and designed the great Gothic building that stands today.

Denis, Saint (dates unknown): This name may refers to Dionysius the Areopagite, who was converted to Christianity in Athens by Saint Paul, or the martyred bishop of Paris (c. 250) who was buried in the abbey of Saint-Denis, north of Paris. By the 12th century, these two men were merged into one legendary figure who was also believed to be the author of books we today attribute to the anonymous Pseudo-Dionysius.

Edward the Confessor (r. 1042–1066): The last Anglo-Saxon king of England. He chose to be buried at a Benedictine monastery, Westminster Abbey, which later became the place of coronation of English monarchs. In the middle of the 13th century, it was rebuilt in the Gothic style.

El Cid (a.k.a. **Rodrigo Diaz de Vivar**; c. 1040–1099): Famous Spanish hero of the Reconquista. He is buried in the cathedral of Burgos.

Eleanor of Aquitaine (c. 1122–1204): Queen of France (1137–1152) and England (1154–1189) as wife of Louis VII and Henry II, respectively. When she and Louis departed on the Second Crusade in 1147, Abbot Suger of Saint-Denis was named regent.

Firmin, Saint (d. c. 257): Martyred bishop of Amiens. He and other local saints are featured in the left portal of Amiens Cathedral, and the story of the translation of his relics is in the tympanum.

Fulbert of Chartres (r. 1006–1028): Bishop of Chartres and teacher in the cathedral school there. Fulbert was responsible for the construction of the Romanesque cathedral that was destroyed by fire in 1194.

Giotto (c. 1267–1337): Early Renaissance painter traditionally held to be the creator of the 28 frescos of the life and miracles of Saint Francis of Assisi on the walls of the Basilica of San Francesco in Assisi; most scholars today think that at most he was one artist who worked on that fresco cycle.

Giselbertus (fl. c. 1120–1135): Sculptor of the Romanesque style in Burgundy. He probably worked at the church in Vézelay but is best known as the sculptor who signed the tympanum of the Last Judgment on the facade of the cathedral of Autun.

Guibert de Nogent (c. 1055–1124): Benedictine abbot whose memoirs contain the story of the establishment of the commune at Laon in 1122, which included the murder of the bishop.

Henry III (r. 1216–1272): King of England for most of the 13th century. He commissioned the rebuilding of Westminster Abbey in the Gothic style.

Henry VII (r. 1485–1509): First Tudor king of England. He commissioned the Lady Chapel of Westminster Abbey, usually referred to as the Henry VII Chapel. Henry is buried there.

Honnecourt, Villard de (c. 1225–c. 1250): French artist and architect whose sketchbook documents the construction of many Gothic cathedrals throughout Europe. The sketchbook is an important source about medieval construction techniques.

Hugh of Lincoln (1135/1140–1200): Carthusian monk and Bishop of Lincoln. After an earthquake in 1185, Hugh made plans for the rebuilding of the cathedral of Lincoln in the Gothic style. The choir, called St Hugh's Choir, has unusual asymmetrical vaulting.

Isidore of Seville (c. 550–636): Bishop of Seville and author of what essentially became the encyclopedia of the Middle Ages, the *Etymologies*. It was the source for a great deal of medieval lore, including a catalogue of the peoples at the end of the earth, who are depicted in the narthex sculpture of the Romanesque Abbey of Vezelay.

Joan of Arc (1412–1431): Mystic and charismatic leader of French forces against the English in the Hundred Years' War who was burned at the stake at Rouen for heresy in 1431. Joan led King Charles VII across France to be crowned at Reims Cathedral.

John Scot Erigena (a.k.a. **John Scotus Eriugena**; c. 816–867): Irish scholar who lived mostly at the court of the King of the Franks. He knew Greek and translated and wrote a commentary on the works of Pseudo-Dionysius. These works had an enormous influence on Abbot Suger, the builder of the first Gothic church.

Leo III (795–816): Pope who crowned Charlemagne as (Holy) Roman Emperor at St Peter's in Rome on Christmas Day, 800.

Louis VI (r. 1108–1137): King of France who worked hard to rein in nobles and gain greater power, especially around Paris. One of his chief advisors was Suger, Abbot of Saint-Denis, who wrote a biography of Louis.

Louis VII (r. 1137–1180): King of France who grew up largely at Saint-Denis, where he came under the influence of Abbot Suger. When Louis and his wife departed for the Second Crusade, he named Suger regent of France. Louis VII was king when the construction of Notre Dame in Paris was begun in 1163.

Louis IX (r. 1226–1270): King of France who obtained Christ's Crown of Thorns and commissioned Sainte-Chapelle on the Île de la Cité to hold this prized relic.

Martin of Tours, Saint (316–397): A soldier, monk, and bishop of Tours. Episodes from his life are commonly found in Gothic sculpture and stained glass, for example on the south porch of Chartres Cathedral.

Matthew of Arras (c. 1290–1352): First architect of Prague Cathedral. Matthew was summoned to Prague from Avignon by the Emperor Charles IV. His bust in Prague Cathedral is probably the first image we have of a Gothic architect.

Maximos the Confessor, Saint (c. 580–662): Byzantine theologian whose *Mystagogy* probably influenced Abbot Suger of Saint-Denis.

Maurice de Sully (r. 1160–1196): Bishop of Paris who conceived of and carried out the plan to build the cathedral of Notre Dame in Paris.

Nicholas, Saint (270–346): Famous early Christian bishop of Myra in modern Turkey. Nicholas was a highly venerated saint in both East and West, in the latter especially after his body was brought to Bari, Italy, in 1087. The church of San Nicola in Bari is an important Romanesque building. Stories from the life of Nicholas are often found in Gothic sculpture and stained glass. He appears in both media in the cathedral of Chartres.

Otto I (r. 936–973): Holy Roman Emperor. During the reigns of Otto, his son, and his grandson, a cultural revival occurred in Germany, sometimes rather exaggeratedly called the Ottonian Renaissance. The cathedral of Hildesheim is an important Ottonian/Romanesque building.

Panofsky, Erwin (1892–1968): German art historian. He is the author of the classic *Gothic Architecture and Scholasticism*, which brilliantly develops the analogy between the architecture and theology of the 13th century.

Parler, Peter (c. 1330–1399): Principal architect of Prague Cathedral. His father was a parler, i.e., a kind of head mason and bridge between the architect and the masons. He came from Germany and also designed churches in Nürnberg as well as the Charles Bridge across the Vltava River in Prague.

Pisano, Giovanni (c. 1250–c. 1315): Sculptor who carved the large statues on the facade of the cathedral of Siena; son of Nicola Pisano.

Pisano, Nicola (c.1220–ca.1284): Sculptor originally from southern Italy who settled in Pisa—hence his name. Nicola Pisano sculpted the pulpit for the cathedral of Siena.

Pseudo-Dionysius (fl. 5th–6th centuries): A mysterious and anonymous Neo-Platonic theologian whose *Mystical Theology* and *Celestial Hierarchy*, originally written in Greek, were translated into Latin in the 9th century. These works were vital in shaping Abbot Suger's conception for rebuilding the abbey of Saint-Denis, in part because it was believed Saint-Denis was the author of these works.

Suger (r. 1122–1151): Abbot of Saint-Denis and the man generally believed to have created the first Gothic structures, the narthex and choir of the abbey of Saint-Denis.

Theophilus, Saint (dates unknown): Mostly legendary saint. Tradition tells that he made a pact with the devil to become a bishop. Later, he begged the Virgin Mary for forgiveness and received it. The legend of Theophilus is found in stained-glass windows in Laon and Chartres cathedrals.

Thomas à Becket, Saint (r. 1162–1170): Martyred archbishop of Canterbury. Only four years after his martyrdom, Canterbury Cathedral was largely destroyed in a fire and a new Gothic choir was begun, in large part to accommodate the pilgrims coming to his shrine.

Thomas Aquinas, Saint (c. 1224–1274): Dominican friar, theologian, and philosopher at the University of Paris. Thomas's *Summa Theologiae* is the undisputed masterpiece of scholastic thought.

William I, the Conqueror (r. 1066–1087): Duke of Normandy and, from 1066, king of England. William's conquest of England brought much closer connections between France, especially Normandy, and England. William and his wife, Matilda of Flanders, are buried in Romanesque abbeys in Caen, Normandy.

William of Sens (fl. late 12th century): Architect of the choir of Canterbury Cathedral. In 1174, William came from Sens in France to undertake the reconstruction of the choir of Canterbury in the Gothic style.

Bibliography

Adams, Henry. *Mont-Saint-Michel and Chartres.* Whitefish, MT: Kessinger Publishing, 2010. A philosophical and poetic study of the medieval worldview as expressed through the two great cathedrals. Written by the author of the celebrated autobiography.

Bony, Jean. *French Gothic Architecture of the 12ᵗʰ and 13ᵗʰ Centuries.* Berkeley: University of California Press, 1983. Traces the development of the Gothic style in France, focusing on the advancement in stone construction and the new approaches to space and light.

Cook, William, and Ronald Herzman. *The Medieval World View*, 2ⁿᵈ ed. New York: Oxford University Press, 2004. A short but detailed introductory survey of medieval society, philosophy, art, and literature. Includes extensive illustrations and a thorough bibliography.

Courtenay, Lynn. *The Engineering of Medieval Cathedrals.* Burlington, VT: Ashgate, 1997. An advanced text on the science behind the construction of the medieval cathedrals.

Crosby, Sumner. *The Royal Abbey of Saint-Denis.* New Haven: Yale University Press, 1987. A hardcover collection of plans and drawings of Saint-Denis at the time of Abbot Suger.

Draper, Peter. *The Formation of English Gothic: Architecture and Identity, 1150–1250.* New Haven, CT: Yale University Press, 2007. Winner of the 2009 Alice Davis Hitchcock Medallion, awarded by the Society of Architectural Historians of Great Britain. A detailed account of the formation of English Gothic from its roots in continental architecture to its development as a unique style.

Duby. Georges. *The Age of the Cathedrals: Art and Society 980–1420.* Chicago: University of Chicago Press, 1981. A fascinating look at the development of medieval Europe and the society that created the cathedrals and other medieval art. Told in vivid narrative style by a master historian.

Erlande-Brandenburg, Alain. *Notre-Dame de Paris.* New York City: Abradale Press, 1999. Covers every aspect of this well-known and well-loved cathedral, including stunning photos.

————. *The Social and Architectural Dynamics of Construction.* Cambridge: Cambridge University Press, 1994. While short on illustrations, this book looks at the cathedral from a different point of view, studying it as the center of the medieval city and therefore medieval life.

Fitchen, John. *The Construction of Gothic Cathedrals: A Study of Medieval Vault Erection.* Chicago: University of Chicago Press, 1961. Fitchen does an excellent job of explaining the technical aspects of building the Gothic cathedrals. He uses clues from manuscript illuminations, medieval art, and the buildings themselves to reconstruct the engineering processes and building methods.

Frankl, Paul. *Gothic Architecture.* Rev. ed. by Paul Crossly. New Haven, CT: Yale University Press, 2001. A detailed study of the development of the Gothic style across Europe. Particularly useful for its analysis of Gothic architecture in the Holy Roman Empire, Italy, and Spain. Includes beautiful photographs and illustrations.

Gimpel, Jean. *The Cathedral Builders.* New York: Evergreen, 1984. An interesting look at the personalities and politics involved in designing and building the cathedrals. Contains detailed illustrations.

Jantzen, Hans. *High Gothic: The Classic Cathedrals of Chartres, Reims, and Amiens.* London: Minerva, 1984. An engaging scholarly examination of the apex of Gothic architecture in the early 13th century.

Katzenellenbogen, Adolf. *The Sculptural Programs of Chartres Cathedral.* New York: W. W. Norton, 1964. Contains detailed descriptions of each of the sculptures in Chartres.

Kendig, Robert E. *The Washington National Cathedral: This Bible in Stone*. McLean, VA: EPM Publications, 1995. The story of the National Cathedral through the eyes and words of many of those most closely associated with it, from Cathedral Dean to Master Carver and Master Mason to choirmaster.

Krautheimer, Richard. *Early Christian and Byzantine Architecture*, 4th ed. New Haven, CT: Yale University Press, 1984. A thoroughly researched and well illustrated reference covering the history and development of Christian architecture over a broad geographic area and a lesser-known but still vitally important historic period.

Mâle, Emile. *The Gothic Image: Religious Art in France of the Thirteenth Century*. Boulder, CO: Westview Press, 1973. A good analysis of medieval symbolism, with particular attention paid to the influence of Eastern images on French iconography.

Miller, Malcolm. *Chartres Cathedral*, 2nd rev. ed. New York: Riverside Book, 1997. Miller focuses on the stained glass of Chartres, providing valuable insight into medieval iconography. Beautiful photography throughout.

Murray, Stephen. *Beauvais Cathedral: Architecture of Transcendence*. Princeton, NJ: Princeton University Press, 1989. A detailed textbook on the construction of Beauvais Cathedral from the viewpoint of an art historian.

————. *Building Troyes Cathedral: The Late Gothic Campaigns*. Bloomington: Indiana University Press, 1987. A scholarly study of the planning and construction of the cathedral at Troyes.

Nussbaum, Norbert. *German Gothic Church Architecture*. New Haven, CT: Yale University Press, 2000. A heavily illustrated examination of German Gothic, a subject too often overlooked by historians. Offers many useful appendices, including a glossary and a chronology.

Panofsky, Erwin. *Gothic Architecture and Scholasticism*. Latrobe, PA: Archabbey Publications, 2005. Now out of print, but an excellent piece of scholarship and a thought-provoking read if one can find a copy.

Panofsky, Erwin, and Gerda Panofsky-Soergel, eds. *Abbot Suger on the Abbey Church of St.-Denis and Its Art Treasures*, 2nd ed. Princeton, NJ: Princeton University Press, 1979. The complete collection of Abbot Suger's writing on Saint-Denis, along with commentary, illustrations, and an extensive bibliography.

Schütz, Bernhard. *Great Cathedrals*. New York: Harry N. Abrams, 2002. A beautiful book, richly illustrated with hundreds of photos showcasing many of the structures discussed in this course.

Scott, Robert A. *The Gothic Enterprise*. Berkeley: University of California Press, 2006. Readable and informative, this text does a marvelous job of tying the development of Gothic architecture to medieval religious, intellectual, and technological development.

Stanton, P. B. *The Gothic Revival and American Church Architecture*. Baltimore, MD: Johns Hopkins University Press, 1968. An engrossing account of the influence of the British Gothic Revival on American architecture in the mid-19th century. Abundant illustrations.

Stephenson, David. *Heavenly Vaults: From Romanesque to Gothic in European Architecture*. New York: Princeton Architectural Press, 2009. A photographer as well as an author, Stephenson provides breathtaking color photographs of cathedral vaults, as well as interesting commentary on their construction.

Stierlin, Henri, and Xavier Barral I. Altet. *The Romanesque: Towns, Cathedrals and Monasteries*. Cologne, Germany: Taschen, 2001. A broad-ranging resource beginning with religious and secular architecture of the late 10th century—the pre-Romanesque period that connects the Carolinigan to the Romanesque—and ending with a view to the evolution to the Gothic style.

Stoddard, Whitney S. *Art and Architecture in Medieval France*. New York: Harper and Row, 1972. Although not the most current of our resources, this book still includes useful information, starting with a thorough study of Romanesque France, continuing through the early and High Gothic periods, and concluding with the late Gothic, including the rayonnant and flamboyant styles in French art and architecture.

Von Simson, Otto Georg. *The Gothic Cathedral*. Princeton, NJ: Princeton University Press, 1988. An examination of the Gothic cathedral through the lens of the 12th century religious experience. Contains a good explanation of Abbot Suger's theology of light.

Wilson, Christopher. *The Gothic Cathedral*. New York: Thames & Hudson, 1990. An accessible text focusing on the challenges that architects faced in turning the Gothic vision into reality and the remarkable achievements that were made as a result of these challenges.

Websites

Information about many of the structures discussed in this course can be found on the Internet. Some have their own websites. The following are among the best:

http://www.notredamedeparis.fr/-English-
http://www.saintpatrickscathedral.org/homepage/home.html

Many are covered through websites of universities or international organizations (UNESCO):

http://www.learn.columbia.edu/Mcahweb/Amiens.html
http://whc.unesco.org/en/list

Still others are showcased in their country's tourism websites:

http://www.czech.cz/en/66649-kutna-hora-the-cathedral-of-st-barbara-and-the-cathedral-of-the-assumption-of-our-lady-in-sedlec

Notes

Notes

Notes